THE VIENNA COFFEEHOUSE WITS 1890–1938

Gustav aus Caffee Griensteidl

THE VIENNA COFFEEHOUSE WITS 1890–1938

Translated, Edited, and

With an Introduction

By

Harold B. Segel

Purdue University Press
West Lafayette, Indiana

97   96   95   94   93   5   4   3   2   1

Library of Congress Cataloging-in-Publication Data
The Vienna coffeehouse wits, 1890–1938 / translated, edited, and
with an introduction by Harold B. Segel.
        p.   cm.
        Includes bibliographical references and index.
        ISBN 1-55753-033-5 (alk. paper).
        1. Austrian prose literature—20th century—Translations
into English. 2. Austrian prose literature—Austria—Vienna—
Translations into English. 3. Austrian wit and humor—Austria—
Vienna—Translations into English. 4. Vienna (Austria)—Literary collections. 5. Vienna (Austria)—Humor. I. Segel, Harold B.,
date.
PT3826.P7 V53 1993
838'.9120809'943613—dc20   92–24804
                                                     CIP

Design by Anita Noble

Printed in the United States of America

To the memory of those
who never made it back . . .

CONTENTS

EDMUND WENGRAF

ACKNOWLEDGMENTS

I wish to express my gratitude to the following publishers and/or individuals for permission to translate from the German sources listed or for information concerning rights:

Verlag C. H. Beck: Egon Friedell, "Die österreichische Seele," "Das Kabarett," "Geschichte der 'Fledermaus,'" *Das Friedell-Lesebuch.* Copyright © 1988 by C. H. Beck'sche Verlagsbuchhandlung (Oscar Beck), Munich.

Deutscher Taschenbuch Verlag: Egon Friedell, "Die 'Theaterstadt' Wien," "Kabarett Fledermaus," "Haresu," "Wie ich zu Haresu kam," "Als ich Regisseur war," "Was ist eine Tournee?" *Wozu das Theater? Essays. Satiren. Humoresken.* Copyright © 1969 by Deutscher Taschenbuch Verlag, Munich.

Kösel Verlag: Karl Kraus, *Die demolirte Literatur.* Copyright © 1972 by Anabas-Verlag Günter Kämpf KG, Giessen.

Verlag Kremayr & Scheriau: Anton Kuh, "Zeitgeist im Literaturcafé," "Melange = Milch+Kaffee," "Wien ohne Zeitung," "Die furchtbaren Witzerzähler," "Die zweite von rechts," "Der Bohemien," "Die Verhaftung Adolf Loos," *Zeitgeist im Literatur-Café,* zweite, verbesserte Auflage. Copyright © 1983 by Löcker Verlag, Vienna-Munich.

Langen-Müller: Friedrich Torberg, from "Traktat über das Wiener Kaffeehaus," *Die Tante Jolesch oder der Untergang des Abendlandes in Anekdoten,* vierte Auflage. Copyright © 1975 by Langen Müller Verlag in der F. A. Herbig Verlagsbuchhandlung GmbH, Munich.

Helga Malmberg, from *Widerhall des Herzens: Ein Peter Altenberg-Buch.* Copyright © 1961 by Albert Langen-Georg Müller Verlag GmbH, Munich.

Löcker Verlag: Egon Friedell, "Der Panamahut," *Abschaffung des Genies: Essays von 1904 bis 1918.* Copyright © 1985 by Diogenes Verlag AG, Zurich. Egon Friedell, "Praktische Lebenskunst," *Selbstanzeige: Essays ab 1918.* Copyright © 1983 by Löcker Verlag, Vienna.

Anton Kuh, "Erlebnisse eines Monokels," "'Central' und 'Herrenhof,'" "Der Hund als Stammgast," "Tagebuch eines Hotelgastes," "Lenin und Demel," "Der Affe Zarathustras (Karl Kraus)," "Unfug des Kabaretts," "Von der Welt des Variété," "Physiognomik. Aussprüche," *Metaphysik und Würstel: Feuilletons. Essays und Publizistik.* Copyright © 1987 by Diogenes Verlag AG, Zurich.

Philipp Reclam Jun. Verlag GmbH, for the information on the status of the rights to works by Edmund Wengraf.

Rowohlt Verlag: Alfred Polgar, selections from *Kleine Schriften*. Volume 1: *Musterung;* Volume 2: *Kreislauf;* Volume 3: *Irrlicht;* Volume 4: *Literatur.* Copyright © 1982, 1983, 1984 by Rowohlt Verlag, Reibek bei Hamburg.

S. Fischer Verlag: Franz Werfel, from *Barbara oder die Frömmigkeit* © 1929 Alma Mahler-Werfel.

Thanks also to the S. Fischer Verlag for the information that Peter Altenberg's works are no longer under copyright in the United States.

Prof. Dr. Gotthart Wünberg (Deutsches Seminar der Universität Tübingen): Hermann Bahr, from "Die Überwindung des Naturalismus," "Rothe Bäume," *Zur Überwindung des Naturalismus: Theoretische Schriften 1887–1904.* Copyright © 1968 by W. Kohlhammer Verlag GmbH, Stuttgart.

Dr. Veit Wyler of Zurich, the sole heir of the Salten estate: Felix Salten, "Peter Altenberg," "Die Wiener Strasse," "Nachtvergnügen," *Das österreichische Antlitz: Essays.* Copyright © 1910 by S. Fischer Verlag, Berlin.

My translation of excerpts from Stefan Grossmann, *Ich war begeistert: Eine Lebensgeschichte* is based on the edition published in 1979 by Scriptor Verlag, Königstein/Ts.

Frau Annemarie Kotab (Kufstein, Austria) is the proprietor of Friedell's literary estate. Her cooperation is gratefully acknowledged in advance.

Gratitude is also hereby expressed for permission to quote from the following sources:

The Conscience of Words by Elias Canetti, English translation copyright © 1979 by The Continuum Publishing Corporation. Reprinted by permission of The Continuum Publishing Company.

The Spider's Web and Zipper and His Father by Joseph Roth, English translation copyright © 1987 by John Hoare. Original English edition published 1988 by Chatto & Windus Limited. Reprinted by permission of Verlag Kiepenheuer & Witsch, Cologne, and Random House UK Limited.

For permission to print the pictorial material appearing in the book, many thanks are due to the Historisches Museum der Stadt Wien, whose cooperation was most generous, and to the Bildarchiv der österreichischen Nationalbibliothek in Vienna, whose knowledgeable staff once again made every effort to be as helpful to me as possible. The appropriate credits are as follows:

1. Gustav the Waiter, Café Griensteidl. Frontispiece. Drawing 1897. Courtesy Historisches Museum der Stadt Wien.

2. Hermann Bahr, 1909. Courtesy Bildarchiv der österreichischen Nationalbibliothek.

3. Karl Kraus, 1908. Courtesy Bildarchiv der österreichischen Nationalbibliothek.

4. Peter Altenberg. Courtesy Bildarchiv der österreichischen National-bibliothek.

5. Felix Salten. Courtesy Bildarchiv der österreichischen Nationalbib-liothek.

6. Egon Friedell in Oriental Costume. Courtesy Bildarchiv der öster-reichischen Nationalbibliothek.

7. Alfred Polgar. Courtesy Bildarchiv der österreichischen Nationalbib-liothek.

8. Anton Kuh. Courtesy Bildarchiv der österreichischen Nationalbib-liothek.

9. Typical Vienna coffeehouse, Burggasse, about 1910. Courtesy Bild-archiv der österreichischen Nationalbibliothek.

I should also like to express my personal thanks to various members of Purdue University Press for their time and effort throughout the project: to Anita Noble, for her fine work on design; to Carolyn McGrew, for bringing this book to the attention of the reading public; and to David Sanders, for his careful reading of the first set of proofs and his helpful suggestions. My greatest single debt of gratitude, which I am happy to have the opportunity to acknowledge publicly, is to Margaret Hunt, my editor at Purdue University Press. Her enthusiasm for the project from the beginning, her splendidly informed guidance as a trained Germanist, and her good cheer and wit, made work on the book a particularly pleasant experience.

INTRODUCTION: THE VIENNA COFFEEHOUSE IN SOCIETY AND CULTURE

You have troubles of one sort or another — — —

to the COFFEEHOUSE!

She can't come to you for some reason no matter how plausible — — —

to the COFFEEHOUSE!

You have holes in your shoes — — —

the COFFEEHOUSE!

You have a salary of 400 crowns and spend 500 — — —

THE COFFEEHOUSE!

You are frugal and permit yourself nothing — — —

THE COFFEEHOUSE!

You find no woman who suits you — — —

THE COFFEEHOUSE!

You are SPIRITUALLY on the threshold of suicide — — —

THE COFFEEHOUSE!

You hate and disdain people and yet cannot do without them — — —

THE COFFEEHOUSE!

Nobody extends you any more credit anywhere — — —

THE COFFEEHOUSE!

—PETER ALTENBERG,
"Coffeehouse"

1

But the coffeehouse was still the best place to keep up with everything new. In order to understand this, it must be said that the Viennese coffeehouse is a particular institution which is not comparable to any other in the world. As a matter of fact, it is a sort of democratic club to which admission costs the small price of a cup of coffee. Upon payment of this mite, every guest can sit for hours on end, discuss, write, play cards, receive his mail, and, above all, can go through an unlimited number of newspapers and magazines. In the better-class Viennese coffeehouse all the Viennese newspapers were available, and not the Viennese alone, but also those of the entire German Reich, the French and the English, the Italian and the American papers, and in addition all of the important literary and art magazines of the world . . .

And so we knew everything that took place in the world at first hand, we learned about every book that was published, and every production no matter where it occurred; and we compared the notices in every newspaper. Perhaps nothing has contributed to the intellectual mobility and the international orientation of the Austrian as as much as that he could keep abreast of all world events in the coffeehouse, and at the same time discuss them in the circle of his friends.

—Stefan Zweig,
The World of Yesterday

What is a coffeehouse man of letters?

A person who has the time to contemplate in the coffeehouse what others on the outside do not experience.

—Anton Kuh,
Physiognomics: Observations

The mystique of the Vienna coffeehouse is extraordinary. The literature on it is formidable.[1] Even now when it no longer plays the role it once did in the cultural life of the great city, it continues to inspire lore and legend. The challenge to capture its essence is irresistible. One of its most astute observers, Milan Dubrovic, recalls it this way in his book of Vienna coffeehouse reminiscences:

> Were one to define it sociologically, it was a milieu of smooth transitions, of existential mixed forms and relativizing individualities, hence a particularly suitable forum for free speech, impulsive discussion, and the systematic cultivation of lateral communication between divergent groups and clans.

This atmosphere also attracted debate-inclined personalities of the literary, scientific, and artistic establishments
insofar as they were prepared to surrender a piece of their
exclusivity. . . .

. . . It has been too little pointed out that alongside the
writers and artists who already had names, there was also a broad
stratum of intellectuals who constituted the real public of the
coffeehouse. They were people of all stages of life, belonging
to different professional groups, who stood out from the norm
of the average citizen by virtue of a considerably stronger interest in and passionate sympathy for the processes of and developments in literature, the arts, and learning, and had the need
to express themselves on such matters, to debate them, and to
collect the advice and opinion of clever people. There arose this
way a pleasant state of fellowship, security, and community of
the likeminded, and a camaraderie with free, independent-
thinking people who, like oneself, were seekers in search of new
understanding, of the sense of human existence.[2]

The Austrian attachment to tradition and monuments, the nostalgia
for the past, also embraces the Vienna coffeehouse. The first great literary
coffeehouse of the fin de siècle, the Café Griensteidl—whose razing in
1897 served as the occasion for the satirist Karl Kraus's literary demolition
of the "Young Vienna" group of modernist writers who encamped there—
once again occupies a prominent corner on the Michaelerplatz just across
from what used to be the official residence of the Habsburg emperors.
A short walk down the Herrengasse leads to the restored Café Central, to
which the literati and others migrated following the demise of the
Griensteidl. As you enter the splendid and spacious coffeehouse, almost
immediately to the right, your eye is drawn to a life-sized figure of a baldish
walrus-mustachioed man seated at the archetypical small marble-topped
coffeehouse table. The restoration of the Central honors not only another
legendary turn-of-the-century coffeehouse but also its most legendary
patron, Peter Altenberg, the best-known Viennese bohemian of the period
and a master of the literary miniature.

The special place of the coffeehouse in Viennese society and culture
has little to do with antiquity or uniqueness in any absolute sense. The
capital of the Habsburg Empire was not the first European city to domes-
ticate the Turkish *kahvehane,* nor has Vienna been by any stretch of the
imagination the only European city in which writers, artists, and intellectuals developed a fondness for congregating in coffeehouses. Paris and
Berlin would justifiably protest especially the latter claim. But acknowledging the ubiquity of the coffeehouse in Europe and its appeal to the creative

and mentally restless ever in need of places of converse need not detract from or obscure the perceived specialness of the Viennese institution.

Once the Viennese acquired the taste for coffee in the late seventeenth century, in circumstances to be described shortly, their passion for the dark beverage proved boundless and has persisted to the present day. That Vienna may arguably boast more coffeehouses—real coffeehouses as opposed to espresso bars and pastry shops—than other European capitals may be less significant than the fact that it is the only one in which tourist and resident alike can find a printed guide to the city's present-day coffeehouses with thumbnail sketches of their history (of those that have any worth mentioning).[3] Monuments, after all, come in many forms. The deep attachment of the Viennese to their coffeehouses and their traditions shows up in other ways as well. The careful, patently affectionate restoration of the Café Griensteidl and the Café Central, the superb maintenance of the Café Sperl, speak volumes. The literature on the Viennese coffeehouse fills volumes and has no parallel elsewhere in Europe. Nor do the variations of coffee blending and their terminology.

Coffeehouses have served as hangouts for artists and intellectuals throughout Europe wherever they existed. The image of a writer toiling away at a manuscript for hours on end hunched over a little marble-topped table, seemingly oblivious to anything else in the world, is a familiar one. As familiar as that of a group of coffeehouse regulars heatedly discussing a literary work or a painting or a theatrical review or an idea.

But a peculiar concatenation of circumstances lends an irrefutable specialness, perhaps even uniqueness, to the place in literature of the Vienna coffeehouse. The modernist movement, which heralded an Austrian literary coming-of-age, arose in fin-de-siècle Vienna within the context of the coffeehouse.[4] Or, to put it differently, Austrian literary modernism and the Vienna coffeehouse form an inseparable entity. That is precisely why Karl Kraus's deflation of a trend toward which he evinced little sympathy took as its point of departure the announced demolition of the coffeehouse acknowledged as the campsite of the principal exponents of that trend.

The symbiosis of coffeehouse and literati at the turn of the century was hardly exceptional in and of itself; it was, with only a few exceptions, a universal European phenomenon. The proponents of antitraditionalist modernity—the forerunners of the early twentieth-century avant-garde—were at first a self-alienating and alienated species for whom the coffeehouse was an alternative to more staid, formal, and ultimately inhospitable meeting places. The "artistic" cabarets that dot the landscape of fin-de-siècle Europe, beginning with the Chat Noir in Paris in 1881, represented a parallel development. But nowhere else to the degree that it occurred in Vienna did the coffeehouse become so much a part of the literary fabric of the time. In part, this was assured by its prominence in Viennese social life. More important, as the venue of Austrian literary modernism, it not only became the setting and subject of much writing, it also nurtured a type of writing compatible with its own special ambiance.

Social and economic conditions also played a part in the shaping of the Vienna coffeehouse mystique. The chronic inadequacies of Vienna's housing greatly enhanced the appeal of the coffeehouse as an alternate habitation, a public place where artists and intellectuals and their camp followers could comfortably (and cheaply) congregate. But the coffee-house was not just a refuge for the cramped. Well-fed and well-housed professional and business people of the period disposed of considerable leisure time—extraordinary by today's standards—that permitted those so inclined to frequent a favorite coffeehouse for several hours a day. For many, the coffeehouse was an extension of the office and indeed a more relaxed and convivial place for conducting one's affairs or for enjoying the vicarious pleasure of observing others conducting theirs. There was also the possibility of rubbing shoulders with the community of the creative and becoming a part of their world as well. In some instances, the pro-fessional and business people were themselves an integral part of that community.

Then, too, there was the Jewish element. Vienna's large assimilated Jewish population had attained unprecedented cultural prominence by the turn of the century. This is nowhere more apparent than in literature, in the broad sense of the term. The writers of the loose circle convention-ally referred to as "Jung Wien" (Young Vienna) were mostly of Jewish origins, as was their main antagonist, Karl Kraus. Journalism in fin-de-siècle Vienna was largely in Jewish hands. As Robert S. Wistrich writes in his commanding study *The Jews of Vienna in the Age of Franz Joseph:* "The most powerful organs of liberal middle-class opinion in the monarchy—above all the *Neue Freie Presse* (*New Free Press*)—were owned, edited, and largely written by Viennese Jews."[5] This strong Jewish presence in the Viennese literary culture of the period left its own distinct imprint on the coffee-house. And in this respect as well, the Vienna coffeehouse of the period 1890–1938 distinguished itself from its counterparts elsewhere on the Continent.

The purpose of this book is not merely to add more pages to the sizeable body of literature on the Vienna coffeehouse. It is not intended as a collection of literary testimonials and reminiscences. It seeks rather to demonstrate, by way of copious example, that not only did the Vienna coffeehouse of its great age, 1890–1938, inspire an impressive body of writings, but in a more creative sense, that it gave rise to and accommodated a type of literature peculiar both to the world of the coffeehouse and to fin-de-siècle Vienna. That literature comprises a variety of short prose forms, including the impressionistic literary sketch, or miniature, at which Peter Altenberg excelled, the acerbic satires of Karl Kraus, the pithy review and mini-essay for which Alfred Polgar has long been admired, and the feuilleton—that archetypical Viennese literary genre—so handsomely represented by, among others, Felix Salten, whom we know best in English as the author of the much-loved children's tale *Bambi*. If this *Kurzprosa* (short prose) and literary *Kleinkunst* (art of small forms) did not have their true origins in the coffeehouse, they represent, nevertheless, a type of writing to which the milieu of the coffeehouse gave rise and with which it became intimately identified. Its enthusiasts, with hardly an exception, were denizens of the literary coffeehouses—men who lived and breathed the atmosphere of the coffeehouse, who drew inspiration from it. They were authentic coffeehouse wits who thrived on the dynamics and dialectics of café dialogue and transformed it into a literary art. Although well known and widely admired in their own culture, where literary smallness, in the sense of *Kleinkunst*, is not perceived as a liability or failing, they have nevertheless been long overshadowed by such fellow writers as Hofmannsthal, Schnitzler, Musil, and others who made their literary careers in the established major genres of literature—novel, lyric poem, and play.

The turn-of-the-century European cabaret, when cabaret as we understand it first arose, engendered and played host to a variegated "art of small forms." So, too, in the argument of this book, did the Vienna coffeehouse of the period 1890–1938 stimulate and domicile a literary *Kleinkunst* of its own, the literature of writers who made their home in this environment and art and fairly can be dubbed the "Vienna coffeehouse wits." But before this literature is invited to make its own introductions, let us first cross the threshold of the Vienna coffeehouse itself.

THE INTRODUCTION AND POPULARIZATION OF COFFEE IN VIENNA

Legends have a way of simplifying things, and so it is with the history of the Vienna coffeehouse. The year was 1683, in the month of August, and the Habsburg capital was enduring a heavy Turkish siege. The possible loss of the city placed all of European Christendom in danger. The stakes were high. But the courage of the defenders of the beleaguered city, led by Count Ernst Rüdiger von Starhemberg, and the timely arrival of an army commanded by the Polish King Jan III Sobieski turned the tide. The enemy was repulsed on 12 September 1683, and Vienna could in happier circumstances savor the strong dark beverage known as coffee, whose limited acquaintance it had made not long before.

The legendary history of the Vienna coffeehouse locates its origins in the immediate aftermath of the siege of 1683. The hero of the tale is an intrepid adventurer-interpreter of uncertain origins named Georg Franz Koltschitzky (in German spelling). Some believe that he was an ethnic Pole, others that he was a South Slav, Ukrainian, or Armenian. Nor is there any more certainty over his religion, whether Roman Catholic or Orthodox. Be that as it may, Koltschitzky entered Austrian history by successfully passing through the Turkish lines, in disguise, in mid-August 1683 to deliver messages about conditions in Vienna to Charles V, Duke of Lorraine, who was heading up a relief army prepared to come to the city's rescue. It was not the first time that Koltschitzky had penetrated the Turkish camp on spying missions. When the siege was finally lifted, the city fathers sought to reward Koltschitzky and asked him what he wanted. His demand was modest: just sacks of coffee beans left behind by the hastily departing Turks. The wish was granted. Koltschitzky got the beans and a house to boot. It was in that house in the Domgasse, quite near St. Stephen's Square, that he brewed and sold coffee.[6] At first, the Viennese resisted wholesale consumption of the brew because of its bitterness, but when Koltschitzky discovered by chance that the addition of sugar made the taste more palatable, trade became brisk. Further refinements in the form of filtering and adding milk (the beginnings of "Wiener mélange") assured the success of the new beverage.

Although there is too little information with which to reconstruct Koltschitzky's life, it does appear that some twenty years before he is credited with fathering the first coffeehouse in Vienna in the fateful year 1683, he participated in Austrian diplomatic missions to Constantinople. He served both as a courier and interpreter and he is believed to have had a good knowledge of the Turks and their language acquired through earlier travel and possible imprisonment among the Ottomans. In his book on the siege of Vienna, John Stoye describes him in these terms:

> This person, named Koltschitzki [sic], either had a flare for publicity or had fame thrust upon him by the pamphleteers of the period. By the end of the war he became easily the most famous of the messengers in the story of the siege, which makes it very difficult to distinguish between fact and fiction in the account given of his adventures between 13th and 17th August, 1683.[7]

Notwithstanding the ever-present threat of war, peace negotiations in the two decades preceding the siege of 1683 created a favorable climate for an expansion of Austrian-Turkish trade. Toward that end, an imposing Turkish delegation, headed by the "Grand Ambassador" Kara Mehmed Pasha, arrived in Vienna on 8 June 1665 and took up residence in the Leopoldstadt section of the city. It was to remain there until it left under full and colorful sail in March 1666. Before long, Kara Mehmed Pasha was receiving Austrian guests in the sumptuously decorated audience room of Vienna's new "Turkish quarter." Coffee, sherbet (another eastern import), and various Turkish confections were served. So, under these impressive auspices, Vienna made its acquaintance with the beverage that was to become an obsession as well as an institution. And alas—though legend assigns him that honor as well—it was not Koltschitzky who deserves recognition as the first coffeemaker in Vienna but Kara Mehmed Pasha's two Turkish brewers, or *kahveci,* Mehmed and Ibrahim.

If Koltschitzky's adventures during and after the siege of Vienna were the stuff of legend, his historical role in the establishment of the first coffeehouse in Vienna has at long last been stripped of the legendary, undoubtedly with some regret among the many who have savored its romantic flavor. In an exhaustive study of the introduction of coffee in Vienna, the Austrian scholar Karl Teply convincingly demonstrates that credit for the founding of the first coffeehouses in Vienna belongs not at all to Koltschitzky but to two Armenians, Johannes Diodato and Isaak de Luca, as they were then known.[8] Around the time Koltschitzky appeared in Vienna, a very active Armenian colony had already sprung up there. It was peopled mostly by tradesmen who had fanned out in their search for new markets from the two principal centers of Armenian settlement in eastern and southeastern Europe, Belgrade and Lwów (the main city of that region of old Poland known as Galicia, Lviv in Ukrainian—it now belongs to Ukraine—and Lemberg in German). Most of the Armenians in Vienna probably came from Lwów, as it was called at the time, and had largely been assimilated into Polish culture.

Diodato, whose original name was probably Ovanes Diodato, Diodat, or Theodat, was born in Istanbul in 1640, the son of a businessman and jeweler who traveled extensively throughout Europe and eventually settled in Vienna's thriving Armenian community. Aided greatly by his Turkish connections as well as by the Catholicism inherited from his father's earlier acceptance of the Roman Church, he became an outstanding trader. Once the taste for coffee had been acquired by the Austrians and the drink became fashionable, Diodato applied for and was granted the sole privilege of preparing and offering for sale the "Oriental drink" in Vienna for a period of twenty years. The date was 17 January 1685. Diodato died in his adopted city in 1725 at the ripe old age of eighty-five. Before the expiration of his monopoly, Diodato was away from Vienna for several years, during which time his business interests in the city became neglected. Enter his fellow Armenian, Isaak de Luca, whose real name was Sahak Lucasian or Lucas. He had arrived in Vienna in early 1697 and received his municipal citizenship on 23 March that year. We know next to nothing of his origins except for the fact that he came from Erevan. Two months after becoming a citizen of Vienna, he and the daughter of an imperial notary were married in Saint Stephen's Cathedral. Needless to say, his father-in-law's position opened a few doors for him in the right places. An astute businessman, de Luca was quick to recognize the sizeable market for coffee among the Viennese and that Diodato's monopoly, which was inadequate for the needs of the time, was soon to expire. And so he, too, petitioned for a new coffee-trade privilege. Emperor Leopold I acquiesced, and on 10 September 1697 de Luca won his privilege. An imperial edict of 16 July 1700 further empowered de Luca along with three other Armenians and/or baptized Turks (Joseph Devich, Andre Beüm, and Philipp Rudolf Perg) to open public coffeehouses in different parts of the city. By the time of de Luca's death in 1729, there were already at least eleven concessionaires in Vienna. Coffee had done what the Turks failed to do in 1683. Vienna's capitulation was now complete and irreversible.

In "Traktat über das Wiener Kaffeehaus" ("Treatise on the Vienna Coffeehouse"), written in 1959, Friedrich Torberg (real name: Friedrich Kantor-Berg, 1908–79), a popular storyteller and chronicler of Viennese life, describes Vienna as "the city of functioning legends."[9] He then goes on to characterize the Vienna coffeehouse as "by far the most complicated of these legends." Torberg's attempt to grasp the essence of the complication is as enlightening as it is amusing and well worth quoting at length. He starts off with a straightforward affirmative proposition: "A guest sits in the coffeehouse and drinks coffee." The proposition seems to lack nothing in clarity, but as Torberg observes:

> In truth, it lacks everything. It seems to state something, but it signifies nothing. No single conception that it operates with is unequivocal. On the contrary, a series of further questions at once suggests itself. We shall now set forth the three most important:
>
> 1. Who is the guest?
> 2. In what type of coffeehouse is he sitting?
> 3. What kind of coffee is he drinking?
>
> The last question is the easiest to answer and for the layman the easiest to understand. It will also seem obvious to the layman

that in London, for example, you can't go to the Cunard Line and to the question "What would you like?" answer simply: "A ship." By the same token, you can't go into a Vienna coffeehouse and simply order "a coffee." You have to express yourself more precisely. The reason is that the number of types, ways of preparation, colors, and sizes from which you can choose has no boundaries or has them only at a nebulous distance. Whoever doesn't want to risk getting lost would do well to memorize at least a few ground rules. Otherwise he might be tempted to regard the order "nut-brown," which the waiter has just transmitted to the kitchen in nonchalant abbreviation, merely as the color description of the coffee ordered, while what is being referred to primarily is the size of the cup in which it is served. The order would definitely not have been for "a cup of nut-brown" but for "a nut-cup of brown." In clever but poetic code "a nut-cup" indicates the smallest of the three sizes used. The middle one is called "piccolo" and must not be confused with the apprentice server of the same name, who holds the lowest rank in the waiter hierarchy and is, so to speak, the nut-cup among waiters. The largest size is called the "tea-cup," which if it actually contains tea is not referred to as "tea-cup" but as "a cup of tea" "Tasse" [the standard German term for "cup"] is used in Vienna in the meaning of "saucer."

As concerns the different ways of preparing coffee, nowadays you often have to specify "normal" if you don't want to automatically receive something made according to the espresso method. Many establishments simply have no other kind, especially the smaller ones that can't afford two different machines and prefer the more profitable espresso maker. The espresso itself can be prepared "short" or "stretched," according to the amount of water used. As "short," it usually takes the place of the "Turkish" coffee, which is boiled and served in a little copper pot and in the old days was admired for its strong flavor. The "café filtre" native to France never caught on in Austria. And it goes without saying that in the places known as "espressos," no "normal" coffee is sold.

But it was precisely this "normal" coffee, prepared in the "Viennese" or "Karlsbad" way, that established the fame of the Vienna coffeehouse and guaranteed the multiplicity of possible combinations. It is to it that we owe the "mélange" and the "Capuchin," the "brown" and the "cup of gold"—designations whose very names often reveal the proportion in which coffee and milk are mixed. In the "mélange," the ratios are approximately the same; the "cup of gold" has a distinct preponderance of milk; the "brown" has exactly the same distinct preponderance of coffee, while the "Capuchin" is weighted still more heavily on the side of coffee. The knowledge of these combinations is indispensable for a middling professional position. In addition, and needing no explanation, are the "black" or "mocha," the "one-horse carriage" (a "black" in a glass with a great deal of whipped cream), the "Mazagran" (a mocha cooled with a cube of ice and mixed with rum), and an almost incalculable number of variations of the above-mentioned primary colors according to the inclination and fussiness of the guest and usually indicated by a "lighter" or "darker" tacked on to the order.

A perfectionist among the former waiters of the Café Herrenhof always used to carry with him a paint color scale with twenty numbered shades of brown and had the successful ambition of serving his guests coffee in the exact shading desired. Orders and complaints were then handled only by number: "A fourteen with cream, please!" or "Hermann, what's going on? I ordered an eight and you're bringing me a twelve!"

But there were items that didn't transcend their narrower origins and made no claim to any general acceptance. There was, for example, the "Sperber-Turk," a double strong "Turkish" boiled with a cube of sugar, which the Viennese lawyer Hugo Sperber liked to take in the Café Herrenhof before exhausting trials. Or the "splashed Neumann," the invention of another regular customer named Neumann, in which the whipped cream was not placed on the already prepared coffee but at the bottom of the still-empty cup and then "splashed" with hot coffee. The knowledge of all these nuances and fine points, however, can no longer be demanded of the ordinary coffeehouse visitor, since even the ordinary coffeehouse waiter today commands a considerably less than thorough knowledge and himself isn't conversant with all the different species in common use.

The Coffeehouse *Stammgast*: A Profile

No discussion of the Vienna literary coffeehouse in its prime can ignore the Jewish aspect of it, as previously suggested. The coffeehouses in general were obviously open to the public at large, and the only ones that had a distinctly Jewish character were located in a primarily Jewish district, such as the Leopoldstadt. But by the same token there is no escaping the fact that the ones that can lay claim to any cultural significance derived much of their vigor from their Jewish patrons.

What particularly distinguishes the Vienna literary coffeehouse in its heyday, that is from the 1890s and the emergence of Austrian literary modernism to Hitler's annexation (Anschluss) of the country in 1938, from coffeehouses elsewhere in Europe was its heavily Jewish character. While making such a claim, which is in fact widely acknowledged, it must be emphasized that the Jewishness I refer to has nothing to do with a people's beliefs or customs. The Jews who were prominent in late nine-teenth- and twentieth-century Viennese cultural life had at best a tenuous relationship with Judaism. A number had converted to Christianity. A few, like Karl Kraus and Otto Weininger (1880–1903), the author of the highly idiosyncratic *Geschlecht und Charakter* (*Sex and Character,* 1903) and a suicide at the age of twenty-three, could serve as prime examples of the complex phenomenon of Jewish self-hate. All spoke German as their first language and regarded themselves both as Austrians and as products of Germanic culture. But if they imported no special Jewish awareness to the coffee-house, no Jewish self-consciousness, they did carry with them the gregari-ousness, intellectual curiosity, argumentativeness, and appetite for explor-ing the resources of language characteristic of the Jewish liberal bourgeois intelligentsia of the period. Like the cabaret, the fin-de-siècle literary coffeehouse was a miniature stage, but in the Viennese context some of its leading players were artists and intellectuals of Jewish background to whom verbal and mental showmanship could be aphrodisiacal.

Before 1938 the Jewish population of Vienna numbered about a quarter of a million people.[10] We know what became of most of them after the German annexation. Besides their numerical prominence, there was hardly a sphere of Viennese cultural and intellectual life in which Jews were not highly visible. If nineteenth-century Austrian political liberalism cre-ated conditions favorable to such large-scale assimilation, it ultimately be-came the logical scapegoat for those who resented Jewish ubiquitousness in Austrian and especially Viennese society once the poison of virulent anti-Semitism spread throughout the Habsburg Empire at the turn of the century.

The Jews who became the most loyal supporters of the coffeehouses, their regular patrons or *Stammgäste,* were by and large professional and business people: physicians, attorneys, journalists, critics, schoolteachers, factory owners, tradespeople. Of the arts, the only one in which the Jews were truly prominent was literature. Jewish painters, actors, theater direc-tors, and architects were far fewer. The two best-known architects of Aus-trian modernism, for example, Adolf Loos and Otto Wagner, were not

Jews. Neither were such prominent artists as Gustav Klimt, Oskar Kokoschka, or Egon Schiele. Because the Habsburg Empire was anything but a democracy, Jews still had no access to certain careers unless first formally "purified" through de facto mandatory conversion. This was indeed true for state service, the higher ranks of the privileged and pampered officer corps, and most university posts. For all the prominence of Jews in Austrian intellectual life, few professorships were open to them without prior Christianization.

Taken as a whole, then, the pre-Anschluss Viennese intelligentsia was predominantly bourgeois and heavily Jewish. The coffeehouse was a natural magnet for them. Apart from the gregarious impulses of the intelligentsia—the desire to share ideas, to discuss them, argue them, refine them—practical considerations also enhanced the appeal of the coffeehouse as a common gathering place. What lent the archetypical Vienna coffeehouse much of its mystique was its unhurriedness, its reputation as a place where one could spend virtually as much time as one wanted and consume as little as one wanted. The extent to which the regular patrons frequented their favorite establishments reflected the amount of free time they had at their disposal. Some of the coffeehouse denizens—writers such as Egon Friedell, Hugo von Hofmannsthal, Karl Kraus, and Arthur Schnitzler, just to mention a few—were financially well off, mostly because of inherited means, and did not have to pursue regular employment. Besides coming from a comfortable family, Schnitzler had a successful medical practice that also guaranteed him financial independence as well as time to devote to literary and related pursuits. Others, such as Felix Salten, Alfred Polgar, and Edmund Wengraf, had journalistic careers that permitted them and even encouraged the time spent in coffeehouses. Or to view the matter somewhat differently, they wrote nominally under the umbrella of journalism but specialized mainly in feuilletons and reviews—which meant that they were not ordinary work-a-day journalists in a contemporary sense—or they extended their careers into essay and fiction writing, which was cultivated by and large on a free-lance basis. This was certainly the case with Salten, Friedell, Polgar, and Kuh. Some of them—Hermann Bahr, Arthur Schnitzler, Hugo von Hofmannsthal, Franz Werfel, Joseph Roth, Robert Musil—wrote and published a great deal of fiction and drama and lived the largely uncircumscribed lives of creative artists, which meant that, to varying degrees, they commanded the leisure to devote to coffeehouse society. Although he came from a well-to-do merchant family, Altenberg soon alienated his family and lived as a bohemian by choice. He never held any regular employment not just because he frowned on such a life but because as a youth he received a patent to bohemianism when a doctor had precluded the possibility of his working on grounds of his neurotic condition. As the most prominent, indeed legendary, bohemian of turn-of-the-century Vienna, it was only natural for him to become the archetypical coffeehouse man of letters.

The occupations, or lack of them, of the coffeehouse habitués offer only partial explanation for the leisurely atmosphere of the establishments and the time people spent in them. The age itself was different. Mass communications were not what they are today, and very often the coffeehouse was one of the best places to get together with people and find out what was going on both locally and in the world. Not everyone had or could afford a telephone—once that instrument had become part of the culture—and so relied on an accommodating coffeehouse waiter to take calls. The coffeehouse was also a convenient place for the transmission of handwritten messages. Since Vienna suffered from a persistent shortage of good housing and apartments were often cramped and cold, especially in the economic turmoil following the First World War, the lure of the coffeehouse as a kind of home away from home was irresistible. They were usually warm enough, well lit, and spacious, with the possibility of as much or as little privacy as one wanted. If the tables were generally on the small side and topped with marble slabs, they were adequate for writing and if located in a less-trafficked corner could serve as a little study to compensate for the lack of one in a private residence. The broad array of newspapers available provided plenty of reading material while the game rooms with their billiard and card tables offered another type of diversion.

In light of its attractions, from the Viennese point of view, it was only natural that the coffeehouse itself would become a part of the modern Austrian literary tradition. Indeed it did, so much so, in fact, that there is almost an excess of material from which to draw colorful descriptions. Yet few works rival Joseph Roth's novella *Zipper und sein Vater* (*Zipper and His Father*, 1928) in the keenness with which the coffeehouse's place in the Viennese consciousness is portrayed:

> After Arnold starting working at the Finance Ministry, his visits to the coffeehouses became a passion rather than a habit. It was among his fulfillments rather than his necessities. If in his earlier days—and especially after his return from the war—he had found it difficult to spend an evening alone, he was now possessed by a real horror of solitude. Not that he wished to be part of a community. He just wanted to sit in the coffeehouse, nowhere else but in his coffeehouse.
>
> He had a few acquaintances, perhaps one or two friends. These were writers, painters, musicians, sculptors. I knew of no

more attentive reader, no more conscientious citizen, no more ardent theater-goer and no more devoted listener to music than Arnold. He was interested in all the arts. Among his pleasures was being near those who practised them. He certainly envied them. For it seemed to him that they alone had achieved something in life and had a right to be there, to be looked up to, to be esteemed and to hold power. Their utterances seemed to him to be so important that he just listened to them, without taking part in their conversation. Perhaps he found some comfort in sharing their evenings, although his days seemed so very different from theirs. On the other hand, perhaps he was cleverer than I imagined, and took comfort, when he saw the artists, in the fact that they talked about the same worries as the rest of the world. They, too, had no money. They, too, could not travel. They, too, played tarok and sixty-six and dominoes. They, too, drank coffee and dunked their rolls.

Arnold didn't play, but he was glad to look on. After a time he became for many of the players an indispensable spectator. . . . He also felt less at home at a table where they talked than at one where they played. For while the rules of a card game definitely require the presence of a spectator, the rules of conversation do not. Arnold's sensitive ear picked up a hundred times, even though no one ever put into words: What is this fellow Zipper actually doing here? For it was known that he neither painted, wrote, nor composed, and yet everyone who painted, wrote, or composed knew him. He never dabbled in politics, as did every other guest in the coffeehouse on the quiet, nor did he do newspaper work. Yet Arnold belonged to this coffeehouse and to no other.

. . . And Arnold listened. The coffeehouse drew him every evening, as the tavern does the drinker and the gaming rooms the gambler. He could no longer live without the sight of the small, round white tables and the square green ones; without the stout pillars which once, in the youth of this coffeehouse, must have underlined its brilliance and elegance, pillars which were now blackened by the smoke, as if by decades of sacrificial fires, and on which hung newspapers, like withered fruit, in shrivelled, yellow, clattering binders; without the niches dark with overcoats on overloaded stands, the lavatory in the corridor with its endless comings and goings, in front of which one met and greeted acquaintances, where one could stand for half an hour without noticing how the time flew by. He could not live without the blonde cashier at the counter, who knew everyone by name and distributed their mail to the regulars, whereas letters and cards that came for the ordinary "passing trade" were displayed in an impersonal, official, cool window; without the waiters, who never changed, never died, never asked the guests what they wanted but just brought their usual order; without the carbide lamps, which at that time had taken the place of gas and electricity and looked like will o' the wisps domesticated and brought into human service. . . . Sometimes the coffeehouse resembled a winter encampment of nomads, sometimes a bourgeois dining room, sometimes a great anteroom in a palace, and sometimes a warm heaven for the frozen. For it was warm, with an animal warmth, reinforced by glowing coals in three far stoves, through the bars of which came a red glow, so that they looked like entrances to a hell devoid of terror.

Only on entering this coffeehouse was Arnold free of his day. Here began his freedom, for, although the revolving doors never ceased moving, Arnold could be certain that inside this coffeehouse he would never encounter anyone who reminded him of his work or indeed of any work whatever.[11]

The availability of free time in an age of different rhythms and, more important, the willingness to make time to sit with friends, colleagues, and even adversaries or just by oneself for hours on end in a public place informed the old Vienna coffeehouse with a social and cultural significance that it has been unable to recapture in the second half of the twentieth century. Friedrich Torberg speaks of the changes that beset the Vienna coffeehouse once its underpinnings collapsed:

The reasons—political, social, and technical—are obvious. The regular patronage of these coffeehouses, like the intellectually and artistically interested public in general, was largely Jewish. Before 1938 almost a quarter of a million Jews lived in Vienna. Today they number barely 10,000. That is the one major cause, and there is no denying it. It asserts itself in other areas of public life as well, but in no other so lastingly and with such trenchant consequences as here. This isn't to say for a moment that there are no literary people, no intellectuals, no intellectually and artistically interested people in Vienna any more. Of course there are. But not only has the number of them drastically declined; so also have their possibilities for coffeehouse visits. This is where sociology comes into play. They are employed. They have things to do. They are only potential coffeehouse patrons, no longer practical ones. They bear all the requisites of a coffeehouse regular except themselves. They have no time. And having time is the most important, the most indispensable prerequisite of any coffeehouse culture (indeed, in the final analysis, of any culture). The regulars of the earlier literary coffeehouses were also employed, in part just sitting in the coffeehouse, in part with things they could take care of and wanted to in the coffeehouse. It was there they wrote and created. It was there they received and answered their mail. It was there they were called on the telephone, and if by chance they weren't there, the waiter took the message for them. It was there they met their friends and their enemies. If you wanted to talk with them, you had to go there. It was there they read their newspapers, there they discussed things, and there they lived. . . . They just slept in their dwelling places. Their true home was the coffeehouse.

Why isn't it that way anymore? Even for those who might constitutionally be suited for it? Is it because they can't work any longer in the coffeehouse? It is the fault of the coffeehouse itself?

It has to do with their work. It has to do with the technology that combined with politics and sociology into a sinister trifolium. It has to do with the fact that today's writers compose directly on a typewriter, which they can't take along with them into the coffeehouse; that they dictate their radio plays to a secretary, whom they also can't take with them into the coffeehouse (or not for purposes of dictation); that the executive producer of a television drama and the program director of the radio section "Cultural Word" can't come to the coffeehouse and prefer to be consulted in their offices and studios. And rightly so, since they have as little time as their authors and because of it receive just as much money. And, of course, they all have a telephone at home as well as in the office, so that they don't have to leave instructions for them to be rung up free of charge in the coffeehouse or use the six-minute time limit the single coin drop entitles them to for three conversations. Not only do they have their own telephone, most of them also have their own automobile. These are professional tools, no longer luxuries. Having time is a luxury. Even the poorest occupants of the old literary coffeehouses could afford this luxury. They were poor but happy. Earning money was regarded by them as almost dishonorable. When it came to paying a check—unless they were simply let off the hook—they had their patrons, who also aren't around any longer, and if they were, then they too wouldn't have any time. The inhabitants of today's coffeehouses are their own patrons. The coffeehouse is no longer the alpha and omega of their existence, but at best just the trimming. It plays no further role. It is a matter of indifference to them, pleasant perhaps but not indispensable. They can go to the coffeehouse, but they don't have to. When they enter, they do

the coffeehouse a favor, not themselves. It is no longer a necessity of life for them. It is no more the humus without which
they would dry up, without which they could neither prosper
nor bring forth anything.[12]

THE LITERARY COFFEEHOUSES

Griensteidl

The fame of the Griensteidl, Vienna's first true literary coffeehouse, was
established at the turn of the century. It was the gathering place of the
"Young Vienna" circle, among whom Austrian literary modernism was
born. The importance of "Young Vienna" was summed up by Stefan Zweig
in these words in his *World of Yesterday:*

> In our own city there appeared overnight the group known
> as "Young Vienna" with Arthur Schnitzler, Hermann Bahr,
> Richard Beer-Hofmann, Peter Altenberg, in whom the specific
> Austrian culture, through a refinement of all artistic means, had
> for the first time found European expression.[13]

If any further claim on immortalization was needed, that was provided by
Karl Kraus's withering satire on "Young Vienna," *The Demolished Literature.*
Although the Griensteidl entered Austrian literary history and legend
at the turn of the century, the coffeehouse was founded in 1847 by an
apothecary named Heinrich Griensteidl. It was located on the ground
floor of the Palais Herberstein at the corner of the Schaufflergasse and
the Herrengasse, just a stone's throw from the Hofburg. Within a year after
its founding, it became so identified with the revolutionary cause that it
acquired the nickname of "Café National." Even after the "Spring of
Nations" had come and gone, the Griensteidl continued to attract a liberal
clientele, unlike, say, the nearby Café Daum, which became instead a
conservative bastion. This association with the freethinking and revolutionary clung to the Griensteidl to the very end. The adoption of a constitution
by the Habsburgs became the occasion for joyous celebration there. And
when the new "Young Vienna" circle began meeting there more or less
regularly, their choice of locale seemed predetermined. Its charter membership consisted of its principal organizer, Hermann Bahr (1863–1934),
a chameleon of literary theories and styles, fresh from Paris and all dolled
up in the best Montmartre artsy style; the older and more down-to-earth
Arthur Schnitzler (1862–1931), the outstanding chronicler of turn-of-the-
century Vienna decadence, soon to scandalize the city with his dramatic

carousel of frivolous sex known as *Reigen* in German and usually *La Ronde* or *Round-Dance* in English; the tubercular Baudelairean Felix Dörmann (1870–1928), who transformed nerves and neurasthenia into high poetry; the sartorially elegant and fastidious Richard Beer-Hofmann (1866–1945), an archetypical turn-of-the-century dandy and a leading practitioner of Viennese late impressionism; the aristocratic Leopold von Andrian (full name Baron Leopold von Andrian-Werburg, 1875–1951), celebrated above all for a novel on then-modish narcissism under the title *Der Garten der Erkenntnis* (*The Garden of Knowledge,* 1895); the young schoolboy Hugo von Hofmannsthal (1874–1929), who under the pseudonym of Loris astonished all with his poetic gifts; the not always deliciously malicious Karl Kraus (1874–1936), with his slight hump and schoolmasterish appearance, a self-appointed crusader for justice and morality whose rapid disaffection with "Young Vienna" would result in a literary demolition worthy of the actual one visited on the coffeehouse itself; and the diminutive and sometimes irritatingly energetic Felix Salten (1869–1947), who won international literary fame in the 1920s as the author of the celebrated children's story *Bambi.*

In the early 1990s, a new Café Griensteidl was erected on the site of the original. But if the past can be retrieved in form, it is almost beyond retrieval in spirit. The unique aura of the first Griensteidl, recalled so vividly, for example, by the well-known political writer, novelist, and playwright Stefan Grossmann (1875–1935) in his book of memoirs *Ich war begeistert: Eine Lebensgeschichte* (*I Was Inspired: A Biography,* 1979), belongs now only to history:

> We young people boldly chose the Café Griensteidl. It was situated on the Michaeler Platz, directly across from the Hofburg. It still retained the charming character of the old Viennese coffeehouse. It was completely lacking in pomp, it had no marble, no velvet; its sole decoration consisted of huge, gold-framed mirrors. From the front rooms, in which chance guests could still manage to lose their way, you had to slip through a small Biedermeier arch if you wanted to reach the more hallowed inner chamber.
>
> Since the coffeehouse stood on the corner of the Herrengasse, there were window views on two fronts. In each of these niches, and in all the hallowed rear rooms stood so-called closed reserved tables. Toward the end of the '90s, the Griensteidl was an intellectual center of the city. Austria, that is to say young Austria, which consciously or unconsciously pondered a renaissance of the disintegrating state, was in this camp. In the sanctified rear rooms resided the politicians. Here

strolled the bearded historian of the war of 1866 [against Prussia], Heinrich Friedjung, monologizing back and forth. Here was the gaming table of Victor Adler and his old friend Engelbert Pernerstorfer, who was slowly slipping over from the German Nationalists to the Socialists. The third member of their group was a light-blond banker named Otto Wittelshöfer, a highly-respected figure in the world of finance who was surrounded by the aura of "secret comrade."

In another smoke-filled room, the greats of the Burg-theater, which was a stone's throw away, spent their nights or days. Our table, of course, couldn't be pitched in the all-holiest rooms to the rear. The waiter Heinrich, the benevolent stage director of the coffeehouse, had awarded us a window niche on the Herrengasse side.

The intellectuality of the Café Griensteidl manifested itself not only in the fact that it made available a huge number of domestic and foreign newspapers, but also in the fact that a number of literary weeklies and monthlies wandered from table to table. Being recognized in the Café Griensteidl was tanta-mount to laying the foundation of great fame. But how indif-ferent we young people were to fame or the lack of it. At that time the first work of the little Karl Kraus, who also was born in the Griensteidl, appeared in a Munich monthly, *Die Gesellschaft*. I remember one evening, when the two of us left the Griensteidl together, he slipped his arm under mine and quite seriously asked me: "What would you give to be as famous as I am?" I didn't want to laugh straight in his face, but when later on I had to read almost every week the pathological ex-cesses of vanity of this tragic dwarf, this first revealing experience kept coming to mind.[14]

Imperial

When the palace of Duke Philipp von Württemberg was turned into a hotel after 1873, the hotelier Johann Frohner almost immediately thereafter established a spacious coffeehouse on its premises. Located on the Kärntner Ring (no. 16), the Imperial acquired its own cachet as a literary coffee-house at the turn of the century when Karl Kraus moved there from the Central, ostensibly because of the noise in the latter establishment. His new *Stammtisch* soon acted as a magnet for the likes of Peter Altenberg, Hugo von Hofmannsthal, Rainer Maria Rilke, Franz Werfel, the popular humor-ist and cabaret performer Roda Roda (real name Alexander Rosenfeld, 1872–1945), and the well-known author of *The Golem*, Gustav Meyrink (1868–1932). Sigmund Freud frequented it and was not above holding psychoanalytical consultations at his table. Leo Trotsky, who was in exile in Vienna from 1907 to 1914, was also seen playing chess there on a number of occasions. It also attracted prominent musicians. Wagner is supposed to have composed there during his stay in Vienna in 1875. Brahms visited it, as did Gustav Mahler and the opera director Franz Schalk.

Central

Ater the closing of the Griensteidl in 1897 and before the opening of the Herrenhof in the revolutionary year 1918, the Café Central reigned supreme as *the* literary coffeehouse of turn-of-the-century Vienna. It was aptly named, for no other coffeehouse was as central to the literary culture of the period. Besides the old Griensteidl "Young Vienna" circle, for whom the Central became their new gathering place, much of its mystique accrued from the regular encampment there—and its place in the writings—of such coffeehouse denizens and wits as Peter Altenberg, Egon Friedell, and Alfred Polgar. Until he transferred his loyalty to the Imperial because it was quieter there than in the Central, the acidulous Karl Kraus was no less permanent a fixture. Younger writers such as the satirist Franz Blei (1871–1942), Anton Kuh, and Franz Werfel also succumbed to its lure and made it a part of their literary consciousness. So, too, did Otto Weininger, the author of the once celebrated but highly eccentric treatise on sex, women, and Jews, *Sex and Character*. Weininger's mental problems eventually got the best of him and he shot himself to death in 1903, the year in which his book was published, at the age of twenty-three.

One of the best accounts of the Central was written by a person whose place in turn-of-the-century Viennese literary culture was determined not because of her own achievements but because of her role in the life of Peter Altenberg. She was Helga Malmberg, from Munich originally, and Altenberg's longest—and longest suffering—romantic attachment. When Altenberg had sunk irretrievably into the paranoid self-pitying abyss of his neuroses and sanatorium replaced coffeehouse as his principal habitation, Malmberg at last gathered the strength of will to end their relationship. Years later, distanced by time and space from the events and personalities, she took stock of her bittersweet life in Vienna in a book called *Widerhall des Herzens: Ein Peter Altenberg-Buch* (*Echoes of the Heart: A Peter Altenberg Book*, 1961). Since she had spent so much time in the Central, in the company of its most legendary habitué, her observations about it carry the weight of intimacy:

> The habitual haunt of the literary world in the First District [of Vienna] was at the time the Café Central, a corner establishment on the Herrengasse. The architecture itself was original.

You first entered a dim anteroom with deep alcoves. A cool twilight always reigned here. It was the ideal lighting for recluses and eccentrics. Then you went through a narrow corridor and reached a kind of court with a skylight. A small staircase with wide steps led up to it. The large room was really a vault without a ceiling. The smoke evaporated here all the way up to the high glass roof. Unlike the anteroom, the court was light and airy. Here were the reserved tables of individual artists—absolutely off limits to anyone else—the chessplayers' island, the oasis of the dominoes enthusiasts, the corner where people played billiards. All these sections with their onlookers and kibitzers were separated from each other by a fair amount of space. Nobody disturbed anyone else. Artists of all kinds came together here: poets, writers, painters, sculptors, and at the same time those art-mad bourgeois circles which took an interest in everything new and unusual. These people gave off a light scent of the snobbish. Common to all, however, was an intellectual vivacity, an interest in life in its many different facets, and a passion for everything beautiful.

There were different tables that were rigidly demarcated from each other. To Peter Altenberg's circle belonged Egon Friedell and Adolf Loos. For a young writer to be invited to this table was a definite honor. But the table of the satirist Karl Kraus was even more exclusive. Karl Kraus later exchanged it for a table in the Café Imperial, since the lively atmosphere of the Central got on his nerves.

One table in the Café Central was devoted to young people. This was presided over by the affable, highly talented Karl Adler, the son of the labor leader Victor Adler. He was a radiant Siegfried-like figure. Nowadays he would surely be champion of a famous sports team. But at that time he breathed his life's air in a coffeehouse. There he sat, smoked, chatted with his friends, made great plans for the future, and wrote things that were never published. When one summer he visited Ea [von Allesch] at a friend's place in Switzerland, he said, with his ingenuous smile and referring to the loveliest Alpine range: "Certainly pretty here, but it's prettiest of all in the Central, right?"

How different was this generation from today's. Their yearning befitted an atmosphere of intellectuality. It signified their homeland.

Among these and many other celebrities stood an intermediary, a neutral personality, a beloved and important figure: the waiter Jean. He was a thin, dark man endowed with an unbelievable knowledge of human nature. He could keep all these people separate in his mind, he knew the most important thing about each and every one of them, and had an astonishing physiognomical memory. It all enabled him to accommodate himself to such a distinguished literary circle. Moreover, he was so well read that no new book escaped him. He especially followed the development of his favorite authors with the greatest interest. He knew exactly which newspapers and journals were read at the different tables and he was never wrong. A falsely placed evening paper could bring swift retribution. He attended to the artists with the greatest solicitousness and affection. This went so far that every now and then he "covered" for his charges when he knew they were short of funds or even loaned them small amounts. The artists thanked him with good-natured intimacy.[15]

The most dazzling part of the Central was the high glass-roofed inner court, the "Arkadenhof" or "arcades court" as it came to be known. The effect it could have on a visitor, as well as the atmosphere of the coffeehouse in general, is handsomely conveyed by Franz Werfel in his novel *Barbara oder die Frömmigkeit* (1929; published in English translation in 1931 under the title *The Pure in Heart*). The "Pillar Hall" (Säulensaal), as it is referred to in the novel, is seen through the eyes of the novel's "hero" Ferdinand when he enters it for the first time:

> "I must introduce you . . . Let's go into the Pillar Hall . . . I'll show you the way . . ."
>
> One might have thought, so important did these words sound in his mouth, that he wanted to bring him before some crucial and unapproachable eminence of mankind. The conception of "Pillar Hall," too, awakened the image of an exclusive seat of power. Without waiting for his consent, he dragged him from the big, babbling, cup-clattering room down a narrow passage, where the unreal coffee scent of the kitchen mingled with the real, ammoniated odor of the lavatory.
>
> Finally, the quite bewildered Ferdinand stood at the entrance to a vast and high court which, though it seemed to house only a shabby coffeehouse, not unjustly bore the name Pillar Room.
>
> The first impression remained with him forever. Why is this cavern so high? And how is it lighted? After so many years Ferdinand still wonders if his mental picture of those towering cupolas does not spring from some faulty recollection that confuses the outward appearance of the Pillar Hall with his own state of mind at the time. The uneasy sensation, in any case, of an absurd height of which one could have only a presentiment is with him even today. Something oddly ecclesiastical. A thick

cloud-drift of cigarette smoke (the suffocating odor of incense of this cathedral) sealed off the vault.

The light, too, bewildered the neophyte. The grey walls of the court, whose misanthropic official-Renaissance induced an all too infernal mood, had no external sources of illumination, not so much as a single dormer-window! All the electric bulbs together shone too dimly to hold their ground against the towering darkness. Besides, this was wartime and electricity had to be economized.

An inner room, the chess room, faced the street. A shameless beam of summer daylight streamed in from there, disturbing and offensive! This twilight, a painful amalgam of two worlds, a blend of unhealthy earth and sloppy heaven, weighed on the soul. The air just suited this light. The shaft of the Pillar Hall seemed set not in any ordinary building but in a mountain for the better protection of this sphere against any renovation and ventilation.

The clients suited the place, the light, the air. Only six or seven tables were occupied, but there was lively coming and going between them. Time and again somebody would get up, shuffle a few steps, and sink down again unceremoniously amidst the company at another table where, as a rule, he would mostly take no part in the conversation but just dawdle in obvious boredom. Some of these shapes moved in an inimitably slack way, in the same way as the neglect of their proper bourgeois attire was inimitably slack. From disgusted lips hung extinguished cigars and cigarettes from which the smokers seemed much too indifferent to take a drag. Almost all the faces were pale, sunken, or bloated. They sighed of inescapable tedium. But sometimes an electrifying temperament would break through the glassy-eyed masks. Torrents of hostile words would then come pouring out, the limp arms would thrash about excitedly, wittiness would sharpen sentences. But such flames turned quickly to ashes. . . .

Behind the colonnade of pillars, next to the wall, stood green-covered tables. It was from that quarter that the meditative, scornful, or triumphant sounds of the cardplayers emanated. Shortsighted writers' eyes, wrinkled intellects' brows, stared at the tarok cards. Outside in the field or in the barracks cardplaying was an appropriate activity, the expression of excruciating, aimless waiting. But here, the molelike crouching together seemed unpleasant. A somber statement of Engländer's surfaced in Ferdinand's memory: The secret of cardplaying is fear of death.[16]

Alfred Polgar, who knew it so well, once wrote a "Theory of the Café Central," and Anton Kuh, who made the passage from one coffeehouse to another, drew a comparison of it and its postwar successor in his "Central and Herrenhof." Both pieces are included in the present collection.

The Venetian-style cupola-topped court of the Central was originally built by Heinrich Ferstel in 1856 to accommodate a stock exchange. Twenty years later, the premises were transformed into a coffeehouse. When the revolution of 1918 swept over Vienna, a new coffeehouse, the Herrenhof, arose in the Herrengasse—where the Griensteidl had once stood and where the Central had for nearly two decades reigned supreme. As if to challenge that supremacy, the Herrenhof was built just across the street from the Central. Almost immediately, if Anton Kuh can be relied on, everyone of any political or revolutionary bent—which would then have embraced most of the younger generation of writers—migrated there from the Central. Those who remained behind, the old loyalists who remembered better days and were never guilty of fickleness in their coffeehouse preference, were dubbed "conservatives" and relegated to the scrap heap of history. The salad days of the Central were over.

Museum

Located at Friedrichstrasse 6, at the corner of Friedrichstrasse and Operngasse, the main distinction of the Café Museum was that it was designed by the always elegantly attired, indeed fashion-setting, architect Adolf Loos in 1899. It was his first major work in Vienna. Like most of Loos's designs, the coffeehouse reflected his preoccupation with simplicity and functionalism. The shunning of the ornamental, the conspicuous repudiation of the Austrian Baroque heritage—for which Loos was widely denounced and ridiculed at the time—was attributed by many to American influence.

Because of its clientele, both before and after the First World War, the Museum was soon dubbed the "Café Nihilism" by the prominent art critic Ludwig Hevesi (1843–1910), the editor of the *Wiener Fremdenblatt*. Before the war, the popular caricaturist and cabaret singer Carl Hollitzer virtually made his home there. Besides performing as a singer—mostly of folk and soldier's songs at the Cabaret Fledermaus—Hollitzer was the designer of the cabaret's famous tiles, each of which bore the caricature of some well-known Viennese personality. A boisterous, fun-loving artist, Hollitzer was usually surrounded by a small entourage consisting primarily of his lady friend, the dancer Gertrude Barrison, herself a leading performer at the Cabaret Fledermaus; Peter Altenberg, whose great loyalty to the Café Central did not prohibit his visiting other coffeehouses; the German dramatist and cabaret performer Frank Wedekind; and the popular Viennese actor Alexander Moissi. The Museum also enjoyed a certain repute for its musicians' table, which included Franz Léhar, before he became famous, Erich Wolfgang Korngold, Alban Berg, and Oscar Straus. Léhar had his own *Stammtisch* there, and even though he rarely visited the coffeehouse after his reputation was made, the owner of the establishment was so proud of the fact that the now-famous Léhar had been one of the Museum regulars he placed a small statue of the musician above his old table.[17] If painters were fewer in number, they were well represented by Oskar Kokoschka, whose early career owed much to Loos's support, Egon Schiele, and Gustav Schütt. A talented painter, Schütt was a longtime *Stammtisch* regular at the Museum. Admired for his art, he was also the source of a great deal of gossip. A theosophist become alcoholic, he needed to be only slightly inebriated (so Emil Szittya informs us) to get undressed, no matter what the company, and recite poems in medievial German and dance. During the First World War, he served on the Russian front, was captured, and imprisoned for a time in Siberia, where he succeeded in painting some of his most interesting works.[18]

The Café Museum lost much of its importance after the revolution of 1918. Emil Szittya, a contemporary observer, speaks of it in the early 1920s as being the central coffeehouse for "Hungarian communist émigrés," meaning communists who fled Hungary after the collapse of the regime of Béla Kun.[19] Nevertheless, it continued to be frequented in the interwar period by such literary luminaries as Robert Musil, Hermann Broch, Joseph Roth, Franz Werfel, and Elias Canetti.

The many allusions to the Café Museum, and, to a lesser extent, the Herrenhof, in Elias Canetti's *Das Augenspiel: Lebensgeschichte 1931–1937* (*The Play of the Eyes: Biography 1931–1937*), provide some insight into the kind of role the coffeehouse could play in a writer's life. The following are typical:

> I made the acquaintance of [Hermann] Broch's mistress Ea von Allesch at the Café Museum. (26)[20]
>
> At the Café Museum, where I went every day after moving back to town, there was a man whom I noticed because he was always sitting alone and never spoke to anyone. That in itself was not so unusual, lots of people went to cafés to be alone among many. (112)
>
> Soon after my return I ran into [Stefan] Zweig at the Café Imperial. (186)
>
> One afternoon in mid-October, at the Café Museum, I handed Dr. Sonne the book, which he had never seen in manu-

script, which I had never mentioned to him, of which he had heard only an isolated chapter at a reading. (206)

One afternoon at the Café Museum—we had just exchanged greetings and sat down—Sonne said without preamble, without apology, that he had read my novel; would I like to know what he thought of it? (208)

Just then a first review of the book appeared in the *Neue Freie Presse*. It was written in a tone of lavish enthusiasm by a writer whom I did not take seriously. Still, it had its effect, for when I went to the Café Herrenhof that same day (or possibly the day after), [Robert] Musil came up to me. (270)

Herrenhof

The Café Herrenhof was by far the most popular coffeehouse among Vienna's cultural elite during the interwar years. It was established by the coffeemaker Bela Waldmann right after the November 1918 revolution that transformed Austria into a republic. And tradition carrying the weight it does in Vienna, it was located on the same narrow street, the Herrengasse (no. 10), where the no longer extant Café Griensteidl had once stood and just a few steps from the Café Central, which it now displaced. Spacious and light, the coffeehouse was decorated throughout in Jugendstil pattern. The heart of it was a room illuminated by a yellow glass roof with a large number of loges arranged in the shape of stars. A larger space adjoined by a game room on the Walnerstrasse side appeared in the background. Prominent guests sat usually in alcoves by the windows toward the front of the establishment, particularly during the early afternoon hours. The real literary life of the coffeehouse unfolded later in the loges of the back room.[21]

Among the regulars who esconced themselves in the Herrenhof were such stellar members of the Viennese psychoanalytical establishment as Alfred Adler, Siegfried Bernfeld, Otto Gross, Jakob Levy Moreno, and Adolf Josef Storfer. Freud himself put in an appearance from time to time. Adler also frequented the Café Siller on the Danube Canal, and when he and Freud happened to be in the Herrenhof at the same time, Adler preferred sitting at a separate table.

The literary community represented at the Herrenhof included such established writers of interwar Vienna as Vicki Baum, Hermann Broch, Willy Haas, Gina Kaus, Anton Kuh, Robert Musil, Alfred Polgar, and Joseph Roth. Egon Friedell, Robert Neumann, and Hilde Spiel looked in from time to time. Of the younger writers, Elias Canetti and Heimito von Doderer were the most loyal to the establishment. The Prague contingent was especially prominent. Although it included Max Brod, Franz Werfel, and, on rarer occasions, Kafka, its leading spirit was Ernst Polak (1886–1947), a bank foreign currency clerk, who was married at the time to Kafka's epistolary sweetheart Milena Jesenská. Polak was considered by many as the chief attraction of the coffeehouse. As that keen chronicler, Milan Dubrovic, recalls, he was "not only one of the leading figures among the Herrenhof's regular guests, he was, one could say, the personification of the Herrenhof spirit."[22] Of a well-to-do Prague Jewish family, Polak had already become a well-known coffeehouse personality in that city before the First World War. Although he frequented both the Arco and the Continental, the most prominent coffeehouses at the time, it was above all at the Arco that he came to the center of a group of such leading representatives of Prague's German literary community as Max Brod, Franz Kafka, Franz Werfel, Willy Haas, Paul Kornfeld, and Johannes Uridzil. And it was in the Arco that his relationship with Milena Jesenská developed. While no artist himself, he thoroughly enjoyed the company of artists, stood them many a bill, advised them, and, according to Emil Szittya, also had the dubious distinction of having introduced some to cocaine.[23] Be that as it may, the strength of his personality and the warmth of his relations with writers earned him a place in their fiction. Anton Kuh once referred to Polak as the midwife of Werfel, Kornfeld, and Kafka. Kafka himself immortalized him in the figure of the department head Klamm in his novel *The Castle*. Heimito von Doderer accords him space in his memoirs, while Karl Kraus parodied him in his "magical operetta" *Literatur oder man wird doch da sehn* (*Literature, or You'll See for Yourself,* 1921). Leo Perutz, Arnold Höllriegel, both on the staff of *Die Stunde* (*The Hour*), which was widely read at the Herrenhof, and the novelist and playwright Otto Soyka (1882–1955) quarreled here daily. The former bank employee Lazy Löwenstein shone at different tables before he was discovered as Peter Lorre for the films.[24] Prominent among the intellectuals who were regular visitors to the Herrenhof were the social scientists Paul Lazarsfeld, Otto Neurath, and Hans Zeisl.

After the German annexation, on 19 March 1938, the Café Herrenhof was ordered placed under "Aryan management." With so many of its regulars, above all Jews, abandoning Vienna for safe havens elsewhere, the coffeehouse began taking on a deserted look. The legendary headwaiter Franz Hnatek, whom Friedrich Torberg immortalized in his "Requiem für einen Oberkellner" ("Requiem for a Head Waiter," 1958), strove to keep some semblance of continuity during the war years. When the allied troops landed in Normandy, as Torberg relates it in his "Requiem," Hnatek whispered to a regular: "Do you think, Herr Editor, that the other gentlemen will be returning soon?" After 1945, the front room was managed, with no small difficulty, by Albert Kainz and Hnatek. But only a handful of returnees showed up. Otto Soyka and the poet, essayist, and stage director Berthold Viertel (1885–1953) took up positions as the last landmarks of a bygone world. Soon after their deaths, in 1961, the Herrenhof was closed. It later reopened as a modernized "café-espresso."

THE COFFEEHOUSE AND KLEINKUNST

Kleinkunst in German refers to a so-called art of small forms, "little art," in other words. It is used most of the time to describe the kind of entertainment that characterized the programs of cabarets when that type of establishment first spread like wildfire across the European continent from 1881 to the First World War. In the merging of "high" and "low" art typical of the first "artistic" cabarets beginning with the legendary Chat Noir in Paris, small stages or performance areas easily accommodated puppet and marionette theaters, shadow shows, chanson singers, poetry readings, small-scale pantomimes, dramatic sketches, solo as well as small ensemble dancers, and the like. Cabaret programs were much like those of variety theaters and music halls. They consisted of several "numbers" of fairly short duration. The difference was that at least in the early cabarets, which were more elitist than commercial, the programs were put together and performed by artists and surpassed those of the variety theaters and music halls in quality. They were also often of an experimental nature and deserve to be regarded as another manifestation of the great transformation of artistic sensibility occurring at the turn of the century.

By "small forms" in literature, we generally understand various types of prose works of short length. These might include short stories, sketches, anecdotes, essays, reviews, feuilletons, and aphorisms. They were, to be sure, cultivated at a time when large novels, full-length plays, and fine poetry of every hue and stamp were being written. The emergence of literary *Kleinkunst,* to use the German term again, hardly spelled the end of the novel, novella, or drama. But the modernist upheaval in the arts beginning at the turn of the century created a climate of experimentation and innovation of far-reaching consequences for all literary creativity. Structural and linguistic transformation of conventional literary genres, from novel to poem, was also accompanied by a spurning of these genres by writers who were attracted to, and sought to make their niche in, the emerging world of literary small forms. If most of them seem to have long been overshadowed by the "big" writers of their time, which implies the continued preeminence of the established literary genres, the impression is misleading and stems in part from an academic stratification mostly unsympathetic to *Kleinkunst.*

Realistically speaking, a fresh look at the Austrian literary *Kleinkunst* of the period 1890–1938 is not going to result in any reevaluation of the achievements of such major figures as Hofmannsthal, Musil, Roth, Schnitzler, Doderer, or Werfel, for example. What it should accomplish is a better understanding of the range of literary activity and the proper place of *Kleinkunst* in the culture of the period. It may be convenient to believe that the practitioners of literary *Kleinkunst* were writers who simply lacked the talent or dedication to make names for themselves in the big genres. But this does not seem to have been the case. Was Karl Kraus, hailed as the greatest satirist of his time and one of the foremost in twentieth-century European literature, a lesser writer because, as prolific as he was, his literary home was that of *Kleinkunst*? And make no mistake about it, Kraus was—with the great exception of his extraordinary (and extraordinarily long) play *The Last Days of Mankind* (1922)—indeed a practitioner of *Kleinkunst*. *Die Fackel* (*The Torch*), a journal he published himself from 1901 to 1936, served as the principal outlet for his creative energies and was composed entirely of short pieces, mostly satirical in nature, and "glosses," essentially a form of journalistic derivation consisting of short, polemical, often ironic commentary on actual political and cultural events. Besides, Kraus wrote a large number of aphorisms, which became one of the favorite "small forms" at the turn of the century. Peter Altenberg wrote a number of them, usually under the title "Splitter" (splinters, fragments) and dealing for the most part with his sometimes idiosyncratic ideas about diet and hygiene. Egon Friedell, Alfred Polgar, and Anton Kuh—three other well-known *Kleinkunst* artists—also turned out a fair share of aphorisms. Of these four writers—Altenberg, Friedell, Polgar, and Kuh—their abiding preference for small forms has not precluded their recognition as well-regarded and popular writers. Altenberg's reputation especially has grown by leaps and bounds in recent years. As the literary impressionism with which he is so intimately identified, of which he was, in fact, a leading representative at the turn of the century, has been positively reassessed, his miniature prose pieces are hailed as "gems," "small masterpieces," and so on. Altenberg has become the focus of a great deal of new interest, not just in Austria, and it is not uncommon for him to be adulated now as one of the foremost writers in German of the late nineteenth and early twentieth centuries. Sensitive perhaps to the charge that he was frittering away his talent on trifles, on little prose sketches, Altenberg rose splendidly to the defense not only of his own literary preferences but of the art of small forms in general. Addressing in particular the phenomenon of cabaret, which had made its first appearance in Vienna in 1906 when the Nachtlicht (Nightlight) was opened, Altenberg wrote:

Cabaret— — —*theater of small forms* [Kleinkunsttheater], the art of achieving *in miniature* what the big things do *in the theater!* This something only very few people can do. For me, up to now, just Yvette Guilbert, Mela Mars, Marya Delvard in her best things, Dr. Egon Friedell, Coquelin ainé, Girardi, Otto Tressler, Niese. All of them could indeed make *everything* out of *nothing!*

You can write a novel of 200 pages and it can turn out superb. But you can also say the same thing in three pages and have it turn out just as superb. Nowadays there are many otherwise capable people who have no time to read 200 pages. It is to such people you give three pages in extract!

There are many people these days who can no longer endure a supper of ten courses. It is to just such people you give sanatogen and somatose. Why should they exert themselves to digest 200 pages? You give them three pages that fulfill the same purpose! That is the position of "cabaret" with respect to "theater." That is to say, how it should be. . . .

Ideally considered, the cabaret is thus a refuge of small big art! Not all birds are bearded vultures, sea-eagles, or condors who can rise up 12,000 feet in the glacial clear air in order to survey the entire expanse of earth below! There are also precious and charming little birds like the wren, the kingfisher, the hooded titmouse. They are perhaps more original, more remarkable, even more wonderful than the big birds! It is the same with respect to the *artists of small forms!* They do not rise up 12,000 feet above the earth like Ibsen, Gerhard Hauptmann, Hamsun, Strindberg, Maeterlinck. But they flit with indescribable grace over the earth, through meadow grass and thicket, and bring pleasure, too, through their "small art" of living life! So it was in their time with the "military music" of Detlev von Liliencron and the music of Oscar Straus. So was it with Straus's splendid round dance. Must all "pearls" be sunk in one-and-a-half-hour operettas and have to be fished out just by "skillful divers"?!?!

The cabaret spares the paying public this effort! It brings the "pearls" and lets the sludge and other things of no value run off — — —. Just the way the *pearl divers* do.[25]

The turn of the century—in Vienna and elsewhere—was a time of remarkable ferment in the arts. As the nineteenth century drew to an end, apprehension over what lay ahead became widespread. Change was occurring at a rapid tempo, the natural result of the relentless progress of human knowledge. Nowhere was this more evident than in science and technology. But political change was also in the wind. Cracks had begun to appear in the otherwise magnificent edifices of the great empires of Continental Europe—Austrian, German, Russian. Contempt for bourgeois culture, the common passion of the turn-of-the-century artist and intellectual, often accompanied a fervent desire for sweeping social transformation. This yearning was keenly perceived in the Habsburg Empire. The long, comfortable reign of Franz Joseph, the smugness of bourgeois liberalism, and the outward brilliance of Viennese society and culture in the twilight years of the Empire masked the rot below the surface.[26] Urban housing was frightfully inadequate, sanitation lagged far behind the times, exploitation of workers and women was rampant, the large ethnic minorities—Czechs, Poles, Ukrainians, South Slavs—were agitating ever more aggressively for greater representation, and anti-Semitism became more overt and threatening. Artists and intellectuals desperately sought to end the tyranny of convention and tradition. The status quo was unacceptable and change a necessity. Most would probably have preferred that it come peacefully in the evolutionary way propounded by positivist thinkers. But when change just crept along or seemed too little or when defenders of the status quo demonstrated considerable tenacity, the belief gained currency that the old order would be toppled only through some cataclysm or catastrophe, only through war or revolution or perhaps both. And indeed this is what came to pass. The First World War, to which many responded with a sense of relief and anticipation, as if a pent-up storm had finally broken, brought the destruction of the Habsburg Empire and the birth of a tiny Austrian republic in the postwar revolution of 1918.

Change is usually unsettling and dynamic change even more so. Yet the energies released in a period of rapid change often stimulate extraordinary creativity. So they did at the turn of the century and nowhere to the degree of extraordinary cultural achievement as in Vienna.

At first glance, it might seem that there would be little correlation between the emergence of an art of small forms and the changes overtaking society at the turn of the century. But the widespread sense of impermanence and inevitable change had aesthetic as well as attitudinal ramifications. The imposing structures and institutions of imperial society were no longer trusted. The dismantling to which history appeared to condemn them had an aesthetic correlative. And this expressed itself as a conscious turning away from, indeed at times as a dismantling of, larger structures in favor of smaller ones. It was a movement from the massive and imposing to the miniature and unassuming. We see this in the drama, for example, in the cultivation of a new type of short play. Neither a continuation nor revival of the traditional one-acter, it was instead a highly compressed dramatic work of emotional intensity to whose cultivation such writers as Strindberg and Maeterlinck, among others, devoted considerable energy. This growing preference for the short dramatic form was also paralleled virtually throughout Europe—from Barcelona to St. Petersburg—by the establishment of small, intimate, or chamber theaters. Indeed, this development, which engaged the energies of such disparate talents as Strindberg, Max Reinhardt, and Vsevolod Meyerhold, was one of the more interesting in the history of the stage. Artists' growing attraction at the turn of the century to such popular entertainments as puppet, marionette, and shadow shows as well as pantomimes resulted in their felicitous accommodation by the new, smaller performance environments of cabarets and chamber theaters.

A similar move to miniaturization occurred in music. Think, for example, of the short piano pieces of the 1880s and 1890s by Erik Satie or the pieces in his *Sports et divertissements* (*Sports and Entertainments*, 1914). Or of Arnold Schoenberg's symphonic poem *Pelleas and Melisande* (1902–3, after Maeterlinck); *Chamber Symphony*, op. 9 (1906); *Six Little Piano Pieces*, op. 19 (1911), reminiscent of the miniatures of Erik Satie from the same year; the song cycle *Fifteen Poems from The Book of the Hanging Gardens*, op. 15 (1908), based on the last part of the poet Stefan George's *Die Bücher der Hirten- und Preisgedichte, der Sagen und Sänge und der Hängenden Gärten* (*The Books of Eclogues and Eulogies, of Legends and Lays, and the Hanging Gardens*, 1895); the half-hour monodrama *Erwartung* (*Expectation*, 1909); the unfinished orchestral pieces of 1909; and the well-known *Pierrot Lunaire*, op. 21 (1912), set for *Sprechstimme* (speaking voice) and chamber ensemble. There were also Alban Berg's "Altenberg" Lieder, op. 4 (1912), for soprano and orchestra, in which he paid homage to Peter Altenberg. After Satie, Anton Webern was perhaps the most persistent "miniaturist" of early twentieth-century music. This is especially evident in such compositions as *Four Pieces* for violin and piano, op. 7; *Six Bagatelles* for string quartet, op. 9; *Five Pieces for Orchestra*, op. 10; and *Three Small Pieces* for cello and piano, op. 11. Equally deserving of mention are Maurice Ravel's one-act comic opera *L'Heure espagnole* (*The Spanish Hour*, 1907) and Igor Stravinsky's play with music and dance *L'Histoire du soldat* (*The Soldier's Tale*, 1918), which was composed for a chamber orchestra, and his one-act opera burlesque *Mavra* (1922).

Prose fiction paralleled the changes then taking place in drama, theater, and music. The novel was obviously not going to wither away or be tossed onto the scrap heap of literary history. But as it, too, fell victim to processes of subversion and fragmentation, hardly any aspect of composition proved resistant to change—style, narrative structure, perceptions of time and space, or the delineation of character. The works of Marcel Proust, James Joyce, Franz Kafka, Thomas Mann, and the Russian Symbolist Andrei Bely (above all, his novel *St. Petersburg* [1916, 1922]) strikingly exemplify the extent to which the structure of the novel could also be reshaped by the new aesthetics of the turn of the century.

The impulse to dismantle larger forms, either externally or internally, the impulse, that is, toward "miniaturization," to an art of small forms, prepared a fertile field for the intermarriage of coffeehouse and *Kleinkunst,* just as it had for that of cabaret and *Kleinkunst* in the same period. To begin with, the coffeehouse was a well-established Viennese institution before its emergence in the 1890s as a prime locus of literary culture with the "Young Vienna" circle. The bourgeois intelligentsia flocked to coffeehouses for much the same reasons that others did. They were, as we have seen, ideal places in which to while away idle time or sometimes not such idle time. There were friends to meet, people to chat with, gossip to be exchanged and circulated, and ideas to be argued. The coffeehouse was a superb place to keep in touch and be informed. The dissemination of information and opinion was also greatly aided by the availability of newspapers and journals from all over. Regular and especially prominent guests—writers such as Altenberg and Kraus, for example—had their special or reserved tables around which circles of friends and followers formed. Allegiances could obviously shift and the composition of a circle change, but a core group usually remained to maintain the circle's "character." The membership of a circle, ever subject to change, became in itself a source for gossip.

Conversation was the air that the literati and other artists breathed in the coffeehouses. It was gossipy and cliquish much of the time, as befitted the essentially small world of Viennese culture, where people tended to know each other or of each other. Conversation was also as witty as it was gossipy, since among the intelligentsia who gave the Vienna coffeehouse its distinct character talk was competitive. It was not so much that people were out to impress one another as that many of the regulars dealt in words, lived and breathed words. Virtually all the writers who rose to prominence as masters of *Kleinkunst* were in one way or another, at one time or another, involved in journalism. They were not only born communicators, but they were also paid reporters of and commentators on contemporary society. The popularity and prominence in journalism of the feuilleton, the value placed on style and wit, turned the coffeehouse into a kind of school and gladiatorial arena of wit-making and storytelling combined. Milan Dubrovic has found this apt comparison for the verbal pyrotechnics of the coffeehouse:

> Now and then our regular round table took on a star cast quality when the real preceptor of the table, Ernst Polak, together with Franz Werfel, Anton Kuh, Friedrich Torberg, and Gustav

Grüner were all present at the same time. Sometimes it came to a quip-spraying competition of ideas and opinions which were exchanged back and forth like balls in a ping-pong match. And as brilliantly as if a world championship were at stake. The aphoristic utterances and forms, which later appeared in books or else sank in the eddy of speech, were creations of the moment, beget from temperament and inspiration.[27]

The coffeehouse was also a hospitable environment and, in some cases, perhaps even a breeding ground for such *Kleinkunst* prose forms as the aphorism, anecdote, feuilleton, sketch, satire, parody, "gloss," and review. Brevity was not only in the air in a climate of changing artistic sensibility; it was also particularly well suited to the atmosphere of the coffeehouse. Competition was keen, attention easily diverted, and center stage capable of being commanded for any length of time only by such magnetic personalities as Peter Altenberg and Karl Kraus.

Writers who lived and breathed the coffeehouse atmosphere transposed that atmosphere of gossip, wit, storytelling, verbal one-upmanship, and criticism into the various forms of literary "small art." It was not that their talents limited them to the more abbreviated confines of *Kleinkunst*, but that this was truly their natural habitat. It was a sphere they chose and preferred to live in. It is a sphere we have to view on its own terms in order to recover a dimension of late nineteenth- and early twentieth-century Viennese society and culture which has for too long remained a preserve of the Viennese alone.

ABOUT THE TRANSLATIONS AND
THE ORGANIZATION OF THE BOOK

The translations will, in the final analysis, have to speak for themselves. The attempt was made to keep them accurate and yet as readable as possible in English, not always an easy task in light of the colloquial nature and idiom of many of the original texts and their topicality. Viennese dialect, which appears occasionally, is just handled as slang. It is, of course, impossible to do it justice in English. Anything needing explanation has been noted. Puns or verbal witticisms for which plausible English equivalents could not be found are explained in the notes with reference to the original German. With the exception of Karl Kraus's "Aus dem Papierkorb" ("From the Wastepaper Basket") and Hermann Bahr's "Die Überwindung des Naturalismus" ("The Overcoming of Naturalism"), all texts have been translated in their entirety whether originally published separately or as parts of collections. A few very minor deletions were made in Karl Kraus's *Die demolirte Literatur* (*The Demolished Literature*) because of the untranslatability of the original passages. The deletions are indicated in the text by ellipsis points and are explained in the notes. Punctuation generally follows standard English usage for greater readability. The one important exception, and a somewhat reluctant one, is represented by Peter Altenberg's sketches. In this instance, the original punctuation was followed closely because of its reflection of the author's literary as well as personal idiosyncrasies. Altenberg's dashes and dots and combinations of question marks and exclamation marks should be regarded as part of his style and may be best left as they are.

Since most of the authors were contemporaries, they are not presented in any strict chronological order. Bahr appears first because of his importance to that fin-de-siècle literary modernism in its coffeehouse setting against which Karl Kraus rails in *The Demolished Literature*. Kraus's assault on contemporary Viennese journalism, here represented by pieces satirizing Siegmund Münz and Felix Salten, logically follows after *The Demolished Literature*. Both for chronological reasons and because of his importance as a literary miniaturist and impressionist, Altenberg comes next. But chronology has not been the guiding principle in the order of the texts themselves. Here, partly in view of the number of Altenberg texts, a type of topical arrangement seemed more interesting. Because of his initial piece on Altenberg and his long-standing feud with Kraus, Felix Salten has been situated immediately after Altenberg. Egon Friedell and Alfred Polgar come next both because of their participation in the Altenberg "circle" and because of their own literary collaboration for a time. As the youngest of the "Vienna coffeehouse wits," Anton Kuh puts in an appearance after Friedell and Polgar. His publicly delivered diatribe against Karl Kraus, *Der Affe Zarathustras* (*Zarathustra's Ape*), like Kraus's *Demolished Literature,* is in terms of its length hardly characteristic of coffeehouse *Kleinkunst.* But in spirit, also like Kraus's text, it is wholly compatible with the gossip, satire, and wit-making (often at others' expense) of the coffeehouse milieu. It may be regarded as a kind of settling of scores with Kraus and, in a way, a belated response to the malice of *The Demolished Literature.* The texts, as it were, balance each other out, although Kuh's is certainly the nastier. Since the journalist Edmund Wengraf's little essay on the coffeehouse and literature is, in fact, an attack on the literary coffeehouse, it seemed, as a dissenting voice, an appropriate piece with which to end the collection.

A biographical sketch of each author precedes his texts. The length of the sketch was determined by the author's relative importance, unfamiliarity to the English reader, and material available on him. In the case of Wengraf, who is represented in the book only on the basis of his one essay and on whom next to nothing has been written, it is quite short. The notes to each biographical sketch contain as much information on secondary literature as possible.

A large selection of texts, such as the present, obviously represents a high degree of selectivity, if not subjectivity, on the part of the editor-translator. The pieces were chosen for various reasons, all of them valid: their prominence in the individual author's canon on the basis, to some extent, of anthologization; their relative popularity; their typicality for the Viennese coffeehouse environment; their exemplification of the *Kleinkunst* style; their literary-historical significance; their appeal; and their linguistic accessibility. It was out of consideration for the last that stories by Roda Roda were excluded. Although he excelled as a cabaret performer and developed his career more in Germany than in Austria, Roda Roda was certainly a familiar figure in the world of the Vienna coffeehouse. But his best stories, which typify the *Kleinkunst* style, either reflect his own experiences in the imperial Habsburg army or his intimate knowledge of the Slav and Magyar populations of the old empire. While entertaining in the original, their extensive use of dialect makes the best of them untranslatable. Significantly, two important new Austrian books of reminiscences and other writings about the coffeehouses—Milan Dubrovic's *Veruntreute Geschichte: Die Wiener Salons und Literatencafés* and Hans Veigl's *Lokale Legenden: Wiener Kaffeehausliteratur*— make no mention of Roda Roda. The only other writer for whom a case for inclusion might have been made but who has been omitted here is the Vienna-born Franz Blei (1871–1942). A prolific and sometimes entertaining writer, Blei was principally a critic and novelist known especially for his rather erotic writings about women and romance. The one major work of satire from which a few excerpts might have been drawn is his *Das grosse Bestiarium der Literatur* (*The Great Bestiary of Literature,* original edition 1920, published under the pseudonym Dr. Peregrinus Steinhövel, and enlarged edition, 1922). The *Bestiary* consists of short satirical portraits of mostly German and Austrian writers as members of the animal kingdom. The pieces dealing with the figures represented in this book are essentially too inconsequential to warrant their inclusion in translation and would, in any case, mean more to readers with a firsthand knowledge of the writers themselves. Blei, like Roda Roda, developed his literary career primarily in Germany. There are a half dozen or so passing references to him by Dubrovic, and Veigl, like Dubrovic, apparently not thinking of Blei in the mainstream, so to speak, of the Vienna coffeehouse literary world, ignores him, as he does Roda Roda.

1.   For a very good anthology of writings about the Vienna coffeehouse, see Hans Veigl, ed., *Lokale Legenden: Wiener Kaffeehausliteratur* (Vienna: Kremayr & Scheriau, 1991).

2.   Milan Dubrovic, *Veruntreute Geschichte: Die Wiener Salons und Literatencafés* (Vienna and Hamburg: Paul Zsolnay Verlag, 1985), 30–32.

3.   Hans Veigl, *Wiener Kaffeehausführer* (Vienna: Kremayr & Scheriau, 1989).

4.   For a very fine, comprehensive, and yet succinct introduction to Austrian turn-of-the-century literature, see the introduction in Donald G. Daviau, ed., *Major Figures of Turn-of-the-Century Austrian Literature* (Riverside, Calif.: Ariadne Press, 1991), i–lxiii.

5.   Robert S. Wistrich, *The Jews of Vienna in the Age of Franz Joseph* (Oxford: Oxford University Press, 1990), 63.

6.   On the early history of the Vienna coffeehouse, see especially Gustav Gugitz, *Das Wiener Kaffeehaus: Ein Stück Kultur- und Lokal Geschichte* (Vienna: Deutscher Verlag für Jugend und Volk, 1940). Gugitz's book was the first serious study of the Vienna coffeehouse. For a popular, anecdotal, and handsomely illustrated account, see Hans Weigel, ed., *Das Wiener Kaffeehaus* (Vienna: Molden Edition, 1978).

7.   John Stoye, *The Siege of Vienna* (New York: Holt, Rinehart and Winston, 1965), 188.

8.   Karl Teply, *Die Einführung des Kaffees in Wien: Georg Franz Koltschitzky, Johannes Diodato, Isaak de Luca* (Vienna: Kommissionsverlag Jugend und Volk Wien-München, 1980. My account here follows Teply.

9.   Friedrich Torberg, *Die Tante Jolesch oder Der Untergang des Abendlandes in Anekdoten* (Diessen: Langen Müller, 1975), 4th ed. The quotations are from 318–26. On Torberg himself, there is an interesting collection of essays published on the occasion of his seventieth birthday: *Der Weg war schon das Ziel: Festschrift für Friedrich Torberg zum 70. Geburtstag,* ed. Josef Strelka (Munich and Vienna: Langen Müller, 1978).

10.   On the Jews of Vienna in the period under discussion, see Marsha Rozenblit, *The Jews of Vienna 1867–1914: Assimilation and Identity* (Albany: State University of New York Press, 1983); Steven Beller, *Vienna and the Jews 1867–1938: A Cultural History* (Cambridge: Cambridge University Press, 1989; first paperback ed. 1990); and Robert S. Wistrich, *The Jews of Vienna in the Age of Franz Joseph.*

11.   Joseph Roth, *The Spider's Web and Zipper and his Father,* trans. John Hoare (London: Chatto & Windus, 1988), 174–78. I have made a few very minor changes in the translation based on the original in Joseph Roth, *Werke,* ed. Hermann Kesten (Berlin: Kiepenheuer & Witsch, 1975), 1:472–75.

12.   Torberg, *Die Tante Jolesch,* 326–28.

13.   Stefan Zweig, *The World of Yesterday* (New York: The Viking Press, 1943), 46.

14.   Stefan Grossmann, *Ich war begeistert: Eine Lebensgeschichte* (Königstein/Ts.: Scriptor Verlag, 1979), 54–56.

15.   Helga Malmberg, *Widerhall des Herzens: Ein Peter Altenberg-Buch* (Munich: Albert Langen-Georg Müller, 1961), 133–34.

16.   Franz Werfel, *Barbara oder die Frömmigkeit* (Berlin, Vienna, Leipzig: Paul Zsolnay Verlag, 1929), 424–26. The English translation by Geoffrey Dunlop, *The Pure in Heart* (New York: Simon and Schuster, 1931), 319–20, omits a few paragraphs of the German original.

17.   Emil Szittya, *Das Kuriositäten-Kabinett* (1923; reprint, Constance: See-Verlag, 1973), 288.

18.   Szittya, 292.

19.   Szittya, 292.

20. This and following excerpts are from Elias Canetti, *The Play of the Eyes*, trans. Ralph Manheim (New York: Farrar Straus Giroux, 1986).

21. I am following the description in Hans Veigl, *Wiener Kaffeehausführer*, 52.

22. Dubrovic, 49.

23. Szittya, 293.

24. Veigl, *Wiener Kaffeehausführer*, 53.

25. Peter Altenberg, "Peter Altenberg," *Bilderbögen des kleinen Lebens*, 3d ed. (Berlin: Erich Reiss Verlag, 1909), 164–65.

26. For engaging presentations, in English, of this period in Austrian and Viennese history, see especially Hilde Spiel, *Vienna's Golden Autumn: 1866–1938* (London: Weidenfeld and Nicolson, 1987) and Paul Hofmann, *The Viennese: Splendor, Twilight, and Exile* (New York: Anchor Books, Doubleday, 1988). The interwar period, particularly with reference to Austrian social democracy in Vienna, is very well covered in Helmut Gruber, *Red Vienna: Experiment in Working-Class Culture 1919–1934* (New York-Oxford: Oxford University Press, 1991. Also recommended by way of a more general view of the culture of Central Europe in the interwar and postwar periods is Claudio Magris, *Danube*, trans. from the Italian by Patrick Creagh (New York: Farrar Straus Giroux, 1989). See specially the chapter "Café Central," 165–215.

27. Dubrovic, 95–96.

HERMANN
BAHR
1863–1934

Photographs from Bahr's middle years show him as a burly, densely bearded man. With the eventual whitening of his mane he came to resemble Tolstoy in his prophetic aspect. Had Bahr not looked so in life, one would have tended to imagine him this way. He was a cultural figure of prodigious energies and talents, a powerful advocate and catalyst of change who approached what he regarded as a necessary transvaluation of Austrian society and culture with a true sense of missionary zeal. He was the leading advocate of the modernist movement in turn-of-the-century Austria and the driving force in the so-called Young Vienna circle of writers, whose embrace

of modernism ushered in a new era in Austrian literature. Once he identified with it, he became the leading organizer of the informal group and
its principal theorist. He was also a writer of extraordinary versatility and
productivity. Yet he has often been made light of because of his changes
of artistic direction, his undeniable tendentiousness, and the prolix nature
of much of his writing, in which talk weighs more heavily than any other
aspect of composition. Although scholarly interest in him is greater now
than it has been in a long time, and not just in his own country, hardly
any of his works have been reprinted and one can say in all fairness that
he is seldom read.[1] From that point of view he has fared perhaps the worst
of any of the leading writers of the Austrian fin de siècle.

Apart from the reasons already advanced for the neglect of Bahr or
his underestimation, his lifelong vilification at the hands of Karl Kraus
might also have done him harm. Even before Kraus broke with the "Young
Vienna" circle and undertook a demolition of it, Bahr had already become
a prime target of his.[2] In some ways Bahr was an easy target. He was a good
speaker, flamboyant, passionate, capable of arousing an audience. That
this could rouse Kraus's envy goes without saying. Bahr was also immensely
prolific, which would have been another reason for Kraus's animosity.
Bahr was also vulnerable on the basis of the changeability of his literary
and aesthetic views. Once an enthusiast of naturalism, he turned against
it and preached its overthrow. He spent time in Paris, assimilated the
"decadence," promoted it upon his return to Vienna, and eventually turned
away from it in favor of expressionism, which also gave way to something
more classical and traditional. Bahr's chameleon-like nature, which in fact
accorded with his concept of modernity, provided Kraus with plenty of
ammunition for ridicule. Moreover, Bahr's early modernist enthusiasms
expressed themselves in a lofty style of programmatic utterance which lent
itself to easy mockery. Matters worsened considerably when Kraus's sense
of ethics and morality were offended when he became convinced that he
had evidence of collusion between Bahr, as a drama critic, and Emmerich
Bukovics, the director of the theater whose productions Bahr reviewed on
a regular basis. The Bahr-Bukovics affair was nasty, involving, according
to Kraus, slanted reviews as well as a pay-off in the form of property. Kraus's
"revelations" in *Die Fackel* were calculated to be injurious.[3] But the outcome
was a libel suit brought by Bahr and Bukovics against Kraus in 1901 which
was decided in favor of the plaintiffs. Kraus not only lost the case but also
had to pay a fine of 1,800 crowns as well as 1,200 crowns in court costs.
Needless to say, Kraus never forgave Bahr for this perceived humiliation
and he resumed his campaign of vilification against him with renewed
vigor. Kraus also never forgave Bahr for coming from the Upper Austrian

provincial city of Linz. Hence Bahr's background was turned into another liability. When later in his career Bahr took up the banner of provincialism with his usual bearish embrace, this seemed to confirm Kraus's derogation of him as an educated provincial. Although Kraus clearly compromised his own principles by his relentless belittlement of Bahr, it would be hard to imagine that it had absolutely no bearing on the way Bahr himself came to be viewed later on. But Bahr's own weaknesses as a writer, despite his immense output and importance, must also be reckoned a factor in his neglect. Yet he remains so formidable a figure in turn-of-the-century Austrian culture that he cannot be taken lightly.

The son of a Linz notary of liberal persuasion, Bahr's academic pursuits shifted from classical philology to law and then to what was referred to at the time as political economy. As his interests changed, so did his university. He began in Vienna, transferred to Graz, from there to Czernowitz, and finally to Berlin. But Bahr's changes of university, which hints perhaps at his subsequent changes of sensibility, also contained an element of wanderlust. Bahr clearly enjoyed travel and lost no opportunity to do so. He was especially fond of Dalmatia and in his *Dalmatinische Reise* (*Travels in Dalmatia,* 1909) also addressed the concerns of that South Slav region which was then a part of the Habsburg Empire. An opportunity to accompany the German actors Emmanuel Reicher and Lotte Witt on a trip to St. Petersburg resulted in the fictionalized *Russische Reise* (*A Journey to Russia,* 1893), which is interesting for two reasons, primarily—Bahr's personal discovery of the great Italian actress Eleanora Duse, and the light the work sheds on the dying phase of Bahr's own decadence. From an artistic point of view, the most formative of his foreign sojourns was his year-long residence in Paris in 1888 and his return visit in the spring of 1890. There, in the French capital, the young provincial from Linz, Austria, threw himself with abandon into the turn-of-the-century decadence, assimilated it, and eventually came to Vienna to disseminate it in the context of a post-naturalist modernist revolution.

The next major event in the development of Bahr's modernist outlook was his work with the Freie Bühne in Berlin in 1890. After a trip to Russia in 1891, Bahr went on what was supposed to be a short visit back to Vienna. But his contacts with the group of writers usually characterized as "Young Vienna" and his recognition of the stirrings of a Viennese literary modernism personified in the figure, above all, of the very young Hugo von Hofmannsthal convinced him of the wisdom of prolonging his stay. The prophet, in other words, had a ready-made audience. And so, despite his professed dislike of a bureaucratic, bourgeois-dominated Vienna, Bahr remained there until 1912 in undoubtedly the most productive period of his life. In 1894, together with Heinrich Kanner and Isidor Singer, Bahr founded the Vienna weekly *Die Zeit (Time)*. Five years later, in October 1899, he took over the position of theater critic at the *Neues Wiener Tageblatt*. He joined Max Reinhardt in Berlin in 1906 for two seasons as director of the Deutsches Theater. When he returned to Vienna, he became the Burgtheater reviewer for the *Neues Wiener Journal*. In 1909 he married the Wagnerian singer Anna von Mildenburg after divorcing his first wife, the actress Rosa Joël (also known as Rosalie Jokl). Three years later he left what he had come to regard as an unappreciative Vienna for Salzburg, with which his name has subsequently been linked more intimately than with Vienna. Although born into the Catholic faith, Bahr renounced it in his decadent phase and remained an atheist for a number of years. He eventually reconverted to Catholicism in 1914, becoming a devoted churchgoer and advancing the cause of religion as an antidote to science and materialism in such later writings as the autobiographical novel *Himmelfahrt* (*Ascension,* 1916), the essay collection *Inventur* (*Inventory,* 1922), and the essay *Vernunft und Wissenschaft* (*Reason and Science,* 1917). In September 1918, he was given the prestigious post of head of a three-man directorate at the Vienna Burgtheater, but the arrangement proved unsatisfactory and in November the directorate was dissolved. Bahr remained with the theater another four months in the capacity of "First Dramaturg" with primary responsibility for choosing plays for production. From 1922 until his death twelve years later, he and his family lived exclusively in Munich, where his wife got a position teaching at the Academy for Music after failing, despite Bahr's intervention, to secure a similar position in Vienna.

Bahr's vast literary output breaks down into several categories. Among his novels, a dozen of which represent a cycle devoted to contemporary Austrian and especially Viennese society and culture, the most readable include his first novel, *Die gute Schule* (*The Good School,* 1890), which has a decadent theme based on his experiences in Paris; *Theater* (1897), which draws heavily on Bahr's own intimate knowledge of both the Berlin and Vienna stages; *Die Rahl* (*The Actress Rahl,* 1907), the first of the Austrian cycle which also deals with the world of the theater; and *Die Rotte Korahs* (*The Company of Korah,* 1919), an ambitious, quite interesting novel about Jews, Austrian attitudes toward them, and the nature of Austrian anti-Semitism. Although attracted to the nationalistic and anti-Semitic platform of Georg Ritter von Schönerer's German National party in his younger days, Bahr soon spurned it. But not content with merely a personal renunciation of anti-Semitism, he undertook a critical examination of the phenomenon in the Austrian context in several fictional and nonfictional writings. Of the latter, he is best known for *Der Antisemitismus: Ein internationales Interview* (1893). Concomitant with his vivisection of anti-Semitism, Bahr also introduced into his fiction a broader, more realistic, and more sympathetic portrayal of Austrian Jewish types. This is particularly true of such novels as *The Actress Rahl*, *The Company of Korah*, and *Österreich in Ewigkeit* (*Eternal Austria*, 1929), which deals, in part, with the rise of Hitler and the Nazis in Germany.

Through most of his career Bahr was deeply interested in the theater and actively involved in it as a reviewer, director, and consultant. Besides the theatrical background of such novels as *Theater* and *The Actress Rahl*, Bahr also wrote thirty-four works for the stage. While most of these are lightweight or tendentious in the manner of his novels, some are dramatically effective and have proven popular. These include *Die Wienerinnen* (*Viennese Women*, 1900), a putdown of turn-of-the-century Vienna modernity as social fad; the dialect comedy *Der Franzl* (*Franzl*, 1901), based on the life of the regional poet Franz Stelzhamer; *Der Krampus* (*The Bug-a-Boo*, 1902), which enlivens a traditional romantic plot with song and dance and a late eighteenth-century setting; *Sanna* (1905), which, like *The Bug-a-Boo*, features the figure of an old bureaucrat as domestic petty tyrant; the well-crafted one-act *Der arme Narr* (*The Poor Fool*, 1906); and the Schnitzlerian *Das Konzert* (*The Concert*, 1909), the most successful play by Bahr ever staged in the United States.

For those interested in the stage, Bahr's writings *about* theater may prove more appealing than those *for* the theater. Apart from four volumes of reviews published between 1898 and 1906, Bahr also wrote a historical survey of the Burgtheater, *Burgtheater* (1920); a study of tragedy under the title *Dialog vom Tragischen* (*A Dialogue about the Tragic*, 1904); and a book on acting, *Schauspielkunst* (*The Art of Acting*, 1923). Throughout his long involvement with the stage, Bahr was immensely interested in the actor and developed a concept of the theater in which the principal ingredient was the actor. This set him within the current of such early twentieth-century theatrical innovators as Gordon Craig in England and Vsevolod Meyerhold and Nikolai Evreinov in Russia, who sought to redirect the emphasis in the production from the literary text to the directorial vision or the primacy of the actor.

Bahr's reputation as a literary theorist and reformer whose ideas were informed with the vision of an attainable Austrian cultural greatness was based on his early essays on naturalism and modernism. These are contained in the collections *Zur Kritik der Moderne* (*On Modernism*, 1890), *Die Überwindung des Naturalismus* (*The Overcoming of Naturalism*, 1891), and *Studien zur Kritik der Moderne* (*Studies on Modernism*, 1894). It was as a prophet of modernity, a concept which in Bahr's usage was not restricted just to literature but embraced the whole of contemporary culture, that Bahr made his great impact on the turn-of-the-century Viennese artistic community. Acknowledging the contribution of naturalism toward a subversion of tradition, Bahr preached a liberating modernity of individuality and flexibility. Once unfettered from the conventions of the past, from the weight of "schools," the artist was encouraged to respond only to his own creative instincts and to cultivate a sensibility based on nerves capable of responding to the most delicate fleeting impressions. Modernism, or modernity, as understood by Bahr, would in time permeate the whole of Austrian culture and bring it out of its smug provincial cocoon onto the level of the mainstream European. With a modernistic art in the vanguard, Bahr believed, Austrian—not just Viennese—society and culture could be transformed and then better able to realize its potential for greatness. It was also through modernism that an Austrian culture distinct from the German could be achieved. Whatever his respect and admiration for German cultural achievement, Bahr refused to see the Austrian as merely an aspect of the German but rather as a separate and distinct culture with its own special attributes. The Austrian domestication of European modernism was Bahr's greatest accomplishment, and his later enthusiasm for the Expressionist movement (on which he wrote a study, *Expressionismus*, in 1916) came only after modernism had succeeded so well that it tended toward the shallow and modish.

Although Bahr cut a wide swath through the world of the turn-of-the-century Vienna cafés, he is not being included here primarily as a representative of the "Vienna coffeehouse wits." The writers of "Young Vienna" had already taken their first steps on the path of modernism when Bahr entered into their circle at the Café Griensteidl in 1891. His greater reputation as a writer at the time combined with his cosmopolitanism and persuasive skills facilitated his shaping of Austrian literary modernism at this critical juncture. An undeniable symbiosis came to exist, then, between this emergent Austrian literary modernism, which owed much to Bahr's inspiration and encouragement, and the Café Griensteidl, which as the favorite meeting place of the "Young Vienna" writers became in effect the seat of this modernism and Vienna's first fin-de-siècle literary coffeehouse. Kraus clearly had this relationship in mind when the imminent razing of the Griensteidl in 1897 provided the pretext for his own literary demolition of the coffeehouse and what it stood for. Kraus's attack in *The Demolished Literature* on "Young Vienna," modernism, and especially Hermann Bahr is a reasonable point of departure for a consideration of the writings of the "Vienna coffeehouse wits." But the thrust of Kraus's satire is better appreciated if we have some firsthand experience of the modernism advocated by Bahr, hence the inclusion here of excerpts from his major programmatic essay "The Overcoming of Naturalism."

Bahr's championship of modernism made him a logical supporter of the Secession, when that rupture occurred in the ranks of Austrian artists on 3 April 1897 under the leadership of Gustav Klimt. He threw himself into the cause of modernism in the visual arts with as much passion as he had in the case of literature and campaigned tirelessly in its behalf.[4] For Bahr, the Secession meant no more than the freedom of the individual artist to choose his own direction. It was in this spirit that he wrote a few essays in defense of lesser-known modernist painters, whose canvases in some instances provoked disbelief and ridicule both among critics and the public. "Rothe Bäume" ("Red Trees"), which is included here as a further exemplification of Bahr's advocacy of modernism, was written in defense of the painting of the same name that the artist Ludwig von Hofmann (1861–1945) showed at the exhibition mounted in 1895 at the Vienna Künstlerhaus (Artists' House) by breakaway young artists who officially founded the Secession two years later.

1.   The executors of the Bahr estate have long hampered the reprinting of his works, so that their unavailability in newer editions cannot be attributed mainly to a lack of interest in them. Nevertheless, until new editions become available, it is difficult to determine the extent of any new interest in Bahr as a writer outside the scholarly community. For a very good account in English of Bahr's life and career, see Donald G. Daviau, *Hermann Bahr* (Boston: Twayne Publishers, 1985). This is essentially an English version of Daviau's German study, *Der Mann von Übermorgen: Hermann Bahr 1863–1934* (Vienna: Österreichischer Bundesverlag, 1984). Daviau's shorter entry on Bahr in the *Dictionary of Literary Biography* (81) is also recommended; see Donald G. Daviau, "Hermann Bahr," *Austrian Fiction Writers 1875–1913*, ed. James Hardin and Donald G. Daviau (1989), 29–50. While of a more specialized nature, the essays in the *Hermann-Bahr-Symposion: "Der Herr aus Linz"* (Linz: Bruckner Haus, 1987) offer valuable information and insights.

2.   On the Bahr-Kraus relationship, see, for example, Hans Heinz Hahnl, "Hermann Bahr: Zielscheibe Zeitgenosse (Hermann Bahr und Karl Kraus)," *Hermann-Bahr-Symposion*, 113–19.

3.   See especially *Die Fackel*, no. 69, Ende Februar 1901, 1–14.

4.   On this, see especially Donald Daviau, "Hermann Bahr and the Secessionist Art Movement in Vienna," *The Turn of the Century German Literature and Art: 1890–1915*, ed. Gerald Chapple and Hans H. Schulte (Bonn: Bouvier, 1981), 433–62.

The Overcoming
of Naturalism

The supremacy of naturalism is over, its role is played, its spell is broken. Among the broad masses of the foolish who trot along behind a trend and usually first seize on every issue long after it has been settled, there may still be talk of it. But the vanguard of culture, the knowledgeable, the conquerors of the new values, turn away from it. New schools appear that want to have nothing more to do with the old slogans. They want to be free of naturalism and beyond naturalism.

There are now two questions that cannot be dismissed.

First, the question of what the new will be that is to overthrow naturalism.

Second, the question of the future destiny of naturalism. How it should adjust to such a change, what value it will hold for the next generation, and what it will finally mean in the totality of developments.

Many traces of the new are already apparent. They permit of a number of interpretations. For a while, it was psychology that took the place of naturalism. To abandon the images of the external world in order to search out instead the enigma of the lonely soul—this was the catchword. One plumbed the last secrets slumbering in the depths of man. But diagnosing these conditions of the human soul no longer satisfied the restless fever of evolution. Instead, they demanded lyrical expression by means of which their pressure could first be relieved. We had come to psychology through a consistent naturalism, since psychological reality can be grasped only by us. Once its impulses were accommodated, we finally progressed from psychology to the necessary overthrow of naturalism. From this resulted the forming of the individual out of himself instead of imitating someone else, searching out the mysterious instead of following the extraneous, and above all expressing that other existence wherein we feel differently and which we know as reality. At the end of the long journey in search of the eternally elusive truth, the old feeling of the song by Petőfi, "Dreams, mother, never lie," had become widespread.[1] And art, which for a time had become the marketplace of reality, once again became "the temple of dream," as Maurice Maeterlinck had called it. Aesthetics did a turnabout. The artist's nature was no longer to be a tool of reality in order to realize its image. On the contrary. Reality again became the raw material of the artist in order for him to proclaim his nature in intelligible and effective symbols.

At first glance, it seemed an obvious reaction—a return to the classicism we so wickedly maligned as well as to romanticism. The opponents of naturalism were right. Its whole splurge was just an episode, an episode of aberration. And had we immediately paid heed to the well-intentioned admonishers who never tired of casting suspicion on it and deploring it, we might have been spared the humiliation of the entire business and many a hangover. We would have remained with the old art and would have had no need of acquiring it only now as the very newest art.

We could, it is true, find various defenses for it, apologies of different sorts, and something nearly like a historical justification—even if naturalism were truly just a straying from the right path. We could say: granted, it was a deviation. But then it was one of those necessary, indispensable, and salutary deviations without which art cannot move further, cannot move ahead. Its goal, to be sure, was always and always will be to express an artistic nature and to summon it forth from itself toward power over all others with such energy that they will be subjugated and forced to follow it. But precisely for the sake of this power, it needs the right material in order to have an association with the others. In ancient times this was self-evident. But philosophical deformation lost it. Early man, however he undertook to express his inner being, could not do it any other way than by means of the things which in fact formed his inner being. Otherwise he had nothing in himself. He bore reality, the original form of reality, the way he received it, untransformed, and when he vented himself externally it could be only into reality. Every wish, every hope, every belief was mythology. But when the philosophical indoctrination concerning mankind arrived, that is, the instruction in thought, then the accumulated experiences of the soul were abbreviated to a set of symbols. Man learned to transform the concrete into the abstract and to preserve it as idea. And then postclassical idealism sometimes forgot that when a nature wishes to operate externally it must first reverse this process, moving from the abstract again back to the concrete. That is because the abstract, as an abbreviation and governor of the concrete, works only on him who has already possessed it for a long time. Hence naturalism became a useful and inevitable admonition. As such, one could support it even though the new art actually returned to the old.

But there is, after all, a difference between the old art and the new, if we examine it a bit more rigorously. To be sure, both the old art and the new art seek the expression of man. In that regard they are in agreement in their opposition to naturalism. But when classicism says "man," it means reason and feeling. And when romanticism says "man," it means passion and the senses. And when modernism says "man" it means the nerves. So much, then, for the great unanimity.

I believe, therefore, that naturalism will be overcome by means of a nervous romanticism or, perhaps better said, by means of a mysticism of the nerves. Then naturalism would no longer be a corrective for philosophical deformation. It would be instead the release of the modern, for only in this thirty-year friction of the soul against reality could the virtuosity of nervousness develop.

Naturalism can be regarded as a reflection by idealism on its lost means.

Idealism lost the material for ideal expression. Now the necessary gathering and supplying has taken place. All that remains is for the old tradition to be taken up again and continued.

Or naturalism can be regarded as the principal school of the nerves, one in which the artist is developing and perfecting entirely new feelers, a sensibility of the finest and most delicate nuances, a self-consciousness of the unconscious for which no example exists.

Naturalism is either a pause for the recuperation of the old art or it is a pause for the preparation of the new. In any case, it is an intermission.

The world had renewed itself. Everything has become entirely different, all around. It began with the observation of the external. That is the first direction restless curiosity turned. To portray the unfamiliar, the external, in fact, the new. First phase.

But it was precisely that way that man also renewed himself. He is what matters now. To say how he is—second phase. And more important, to assert what it is that he wants: the urgent, the impetuous, the licentious— wild lust, the many fevers, the great enigmas.

To be sure, psychology, too, is just prelude. It is merely the awakening of naturalism from this long self-alienation, the rediscovery of the joy of the exploration of the self, the harkening to one's own impulses. But it goes deeper: proclaiming oneself, the egotistical, the singular individuality, the wonderful new. And this is to be found in nervousness. Third phase of the modern.

The new idealism is distinguishable from the old in two ways. Its means are those of the real world, its aim is to carry out the orders of the nerves.

The old idealism is genuine rococo. It expresses natures. But natures were then understood to be reason, feeling, and ornament. Take Wilhelm Meister, for example.[2] But romantic idealism tosses reason out, hangs feeling on the stirrup of the racing senses and gallops off against ornament. It is disguised entirely in Gothic. But neither the old nor the romantic idealism give any thought to first transposing themselves out of themselves into reality. Without that, they feel sufficiently alive in naked inwardness.

The new idealism expresses the new human beings. They are nerves. Everything else has died out, withered and sterile. They experience only with the nerves, they react only from the nerves. Events transpire on the nerves and their effects proceed from the nerves. But language is rational or sensuous. That is why they can make use of it only as an idiom of flowers. Their manner of talking is always metaphor and symbol. They can often change it, since it is neither dangerous nor compulsive. And in the end it remains always disguise. The content of the new idealism is nerves, nerves, nerves and—costume. The decadence supplants the rococo and the Gothic masquerade. The form is reality, the quotidian external reality of the street, the reality of naturalism.

Where is the new idealism?

Its heralds are already here: Puvis de Chavanne, Degas, Bizet, Maurice Maeterlinck. Hope need not waver.

When nervousness becomes completely liberated and man, especially the artist, becomes entirely subordinate to the nerves, without regard for the rational and sensuous, then the lost joy will return to art. The imprisonment in the external and the bondage of reality cause great pain. But now there will be a joyful liberation and an optimistic, audacious young pride when nervousness feels sovereign and able to assume the tyrannical organization of its own world. Naturalism was a lamentation for the artist, since he had to serve it. But now he removes the tablets from the real and inscribes his own laws on them.

It will be something ebullient, hurrying, light-footed. The burden of logic and the weighty affliction of the senses are gone. Reality's ghastly delight in misery is going under. When the unfettered nerves are free to dream, a rosiness suffuses everything, a rustling, as from green shoots, can be heard, and there is dancing like that of the spring sun in the first morning wind; it is a winged, earth-freed ascent and soaring in azure voluptuousness.

"Die Überwindung des Naturalismus," 1891. Translation based on text as given in Hermann Bahr, *Zur Überwindung des Naturalismus: Theoretische Schriften 1887–1904,* ed. Gotthart Wunberg (Stuttgart: Kohlhammer Verlag, 1968), 85–89. For an interesting new look at "The Overcoming of Naturalism," see Andrew Barker, "Hermann Bahr und die Überwindung des Naturalismus," *Hermann-Bahr-Symposion: Der Herr aus Linz,* 9–14.

1.   Sándor Petöfi (1822–49), Hungarian Romantic and revolutionary poet.

2.   A reference to the eponymous hero of Goethe's *Wilhelm Meisters Lehrjahre* (*The Apprenticeship of Wilhelm Meister,* 1796).

RED TREES: ON THE EXHIBITION OF
THE SECESSIONISTS IN THE
VIENNA HOUSE OF ARTISTS

People say to me: "Now, see here, you mustn't do that. They shouldn't praise Ludwig von Hofmann. He paints red trees and a person doesn't know what's what! Everything has its limits, after all. Don't go talking us into *this one!*" And while they tolerate—indeed worship—mediocre, muddled, and shallow painters, this powerful, indescribably fine artist radiant with the secret essence of the beautiful is rebuked, even jeered, just because he paints red trees. They make no effort to understand his style. The red trees are enough to make him suspect and disgusting in everyone's eyes.

I would just like to assert, perhaps even demonstrate, that people can paint red trees, since that is neither against the laws nor against the customs of art but, on the contrary, is permissible and customary, and that today people ought to paint red trees if they want to serve the most recent evolutionary impulses and at last satisfy zealously and long-guarded desires.

The idea that people may paint red trees is rejected. Why? There can only be two prohibitions: based on the essence or on the practice of art. It may well be that red trees are contrary to the nature of art and contrary to an unalterable and eternal law of art. And it may well be that they are contrary to its customs and practices. In the event of the former, they would be punishable, but in the event of the latter, they would be a bold and risky innovation which would still have to establish its legitimacy.

Why should red trees be contrary to the essence of art? What law of art bans them? Why should they be unartistic? Because they are unreal, say people. One ought not to paint what isn't. They mean: what our senses don't tell us. Real trees are brown, so one should not paint trees any color but brown. The artistic must be based on the real. That is to say, one should not paint what does not exist empirically. These splendid people now want suddenly to decree that art must confine itself to the world of the senses, that it must create nothing out of itself but instead must only ape the appearance of things and must simply heed the real. What they want is to impose naturalism on art. That is ludicrous coming from those whom the naturalists otherwise cannot disparage, slander, or chide enough. These naturalists, who diligently degrade themselves to the level of plagiarizers of nature, must speak that way. But artists have not been afraid to change the material supplied them by the senses until it becomes a bearer and servant to their minds. Indeed, it is absolutely their nature and duty to amplify the world out of their own souls. Why shouldn't they do it, after all, with red trees if they want to? Whether externally the trees appear red to them or whether they have feelings that suggest red trees and do not lend themselves to better, clearer, or purer representation than as red trees is their business. Consider, if you will, Raphael or Leonardo. Their works are full of things that "don't exist." The figures behave with a dignity or love which is not of this world, in far-off, unreal places conjured wholly from the realm of dreams. Think of the pyramids of the holy families; think of the marvelous cliffs behind the Mona Lisa. "Composition" simply means making nature real in order for it to be able to speak its truth in an unimpeded way. But when it is permitted to help it with forms that are not in the senses but only in feeling, how can it be forbidden, if we are to explain life, to bring more delicate and more subtle or, on the other hand, much more exuberant colors into the world than it has in its own inanimate power to offer? Are the colors of the classics, after all, always real? The gold of Titian or the browns, the red shadows of the Bologna school? "How does it happen," asked Ruskin concerning the Cinquecentisti, "that the light falls only on the middle group and everything else remains in shadows? Of what materials does the world consist that these shadows are all of the same brown? Nature does not know the red-gold light and the warm blossoming flesh that so fascinates us in the pictures of the Venetians. The Cinquecentisti produced symphonies in brown, but did they ever paint green grass, yellow sand, or blue sky? All these golden and silver gallery shades are just pleasant lies." The naturalist has to speak so. The naturalist, for whom the artist is just an honest copyist of nature, must banish the red trees along with every other animation and inspiration of things. But whoever gave an artist the right to shape the sensuous, whoever suggested to an artist that in choosing among the gifts of the senses he take some and give away others, and whoever allowed an artist to "compose" cannot deny him the right to paint red trees. They are neither an innovation nor a sin. They are in the practice and essence of art.

Red trees may be painted. But should they be painted? It might still be possible that, if indeed they are permitted, they would be rather a pardonable whim and not any command of the art of today. What does the person seek who paints red trees? You can paint in order to render the appearance of things. But that is evidently not the case here, since trees do not appear red. You can also paint in order to summon the essence of things from their appearance, so that their roots can appear. But that also is not applicable here, since red trees lack substance. Or, finally, you can paint in order to express the spiritual in terms of the sensuous, feelings in their substantive equivalents, melancholy in the form of a gray donkey, or desire in the form of an exultant and frenetic rose. But that, too, is not the case, since red trees, as we know, are found nowhere in the material world. Yet when one does paint red trees, the spiritual is clearly brought into a sensuousness that at once wants loudly to proclaim itself as unsensuous and untenable, that wants to struggle against the senses and provoke them to violent protest, in a form intentionally offensive to appearances. Something manifestly spiritual will be painted whose sole purpose presumably is to express its arrogance to things, its desire to be different, better, and unique. The arrogance of a soul will be painted that is too proud to be caught sensuously and wants only to wink from behind the mask, to squint at the world, in order to stir its desires but then scurry away immediately at their approach.

The red trees are signals sent by lonely, arbitrary souls at odds with the senses which, next to this eternal abundance of their inner world, regard that other world on the outside as wretched, poor, and shabby. They would also like to shame it into confessing that and to make it feel their resentment. That is the feeling they create, and since it is a feeling that the most recent art indeed now prescribes, red trees are not only permitted today but commanded. For this art urges flight from the senses, disdain for the gifts of this world, and the ascendancy of the mystery and loneliness of the soul, just as previously that other art urged a ridding of souls, a stilling of the voices of the feelings, and the tyranny over everything of the senses. Think of how literature proceeds from the Zola-ists to the psychologists, to the mystics, into revery. It is the revenge of the souls on the senses, and what deeper abuses, profanations, and outrages for the senses can the souls find than the red trees? When souls and senses unite again some day and art again enters the last chamber where all separations fall and the feelings of their own accord kiss things, the red trees will no longer be needed. They are only torches outside in the courtyard. But for now let them radiate their great eagerness to force matter beneath the spirit.

The piece originally appeared in *Die Zeit* (Vienna) on 5 January 1895. It was later included in Bahr's collection of essays published in 1897 under the title *Renaissance*. Translation based on text as given in *Hermann Bahr: Zur Überwindung des Naturalismus*, 172–75.

K A R L
K R A U S
1 8 7 4 – 1 9 3 6

Let my style capture all the sounds of my times. This should make it an annoyance to my contemporaries. But later generations should hold it to their ears like a seashell in which there is the music of an ocean of mud.

THAT IS HOW KRAUS, WITH HIS USUAL PERSPICACITY, SUMMED UP THE SIGNIFICANCE OF HIS WRITING IN ONE OF HIS MANY APHORISMS. The annoyance he in fact caused his contemporaries is legendary. Fearless, uncompromising, high-principled, dogged, vindictive, Kraus, above all through the medium of his own journal, *Die Fackel* (*The Torch*), waged an extraordinary, indeed unique, campaign throughout his life for the highest standards of morality and ethics in Austrian public life. He disliked far more than he liked and his detractors were many. His relentless exposure of corruption wherever he thought he found it and his acrimonious but satirically masterful assault on the contemporary Viennese press for what he regarded as its abuse of responsibility and language ensured him high visibility in a city whose love of gossip about the prominent belied its status as a metropolis.

Although his first major literary work was a putdown of the coffee-house circle of modernists generally referred to as "Young Vienna," Kraus himself was a familiar figure on the Vienna coffeehouse scene. The impression his own writing may sometimes create of a reclusive, lifelong bachelor closeted in his study much of the day and night frenziedly churning out diatribes against corruption and injustice is anything but true. Although he never married, Kraus liked the company of women, had at least one great romance in his life (with the Baroness Sidonie Nadhérny), was sensitive, albeit inconsistently, to what we would today call feminist issues, and dealt with them extensively in *Die Fackel.* His attack on the "Young Vienna" group managed to alienate him from much of the literary community, but Kraus would not have regarded that as a great loss. He was temperamentally unsuited anyway for literary circles, cliques, or salons and preferred keeping his distance. However, he was not antisocial in the broad sense and had a following of loyal, even worshipful, admirers. Among his closest friends were the bohemian writer Peter Altenberg and the well-known architect Adolf Loos. Like any real Viennese he spent a fair amount of time in the coffeehouses and indeed held court at his own table. The atmosphere of the coffeehouse literary milieu as a whole undeniably found reflection in his own writing. Even if this may seem out of character, Kraus had a real sense of the theatrical and was fond of performing. In this, he was also a product of his environment.

Of the Vienna "coffeehouse wits" of the period 1890 to 1938, Kraus is certainly the best known both in the German-speaking world and abroad. He has been the subject of six full-length studies in English,[1] to say nothing of many articles and essays, and apart from Egon Friedell's *Cultural History of the Modern Age* his work is the best represented in English. Much of his huge antimilitaristic play, *Die letzten Tage der Menschheit* (*The Last Days of Mankind,* 1922), two small collections of various writings including some of his poetry, and a selection of his aphorisms have been translated.[2] However, in light of Kraus's great literary productivity, little, in fact, has been published in English. Since he has been so extensively studied, this is obviously not a matter of neglect. The problem is essentially one of language. Kraus prided himself on the excellence of his German ("My language is the common prostitute that I turn into a virgin," he once wrote) and took almost perverse delight in taking to task those writers—journalists, above all—who failed to meet his own high standards. Because of his mastery of German, Kraus can often be extremely difficult to translate, and there are those who consider him for the most part untranslatable.

Adding to the linguistic and stylistic difficulties encountered in trying to transpose Kraus into English, there is also the matter of his topicality. Kraus was a great moralist and satirist. He hated war and spared no words in condemning it. He had no use for sham, pretense, or posturing of any kind. Social double standards, hypocrisy, corruption, and injustice on all levels only excited his ire and provided material for some of his most acerbic satire. But whatever the universal dimension of his moral outrage, Kraus spoke to his own time, society, and culture. The overwhelming topicality of much of his writing raises a formidable barrier to the translator. Forgetting for the moment the linguistic obstacles, Kraus's topicality demands a better than average knowledge of the Vienna and Austria of his time. One can hardly blame a translator—only too well aware of the alienating nature of a large number of footnotes—for steering clear of all but the most broadly appealing of Kraus's works.

The overwhelming majority of Kraus's writings appeared in a journal of his own founding. It became probably the most famous (and to many, infamous) journal in Viennese literary history. Aided by a well-to-do father when he was twenty-five years old and scornful of conventional literary outlets, Kraus set himself up in business with a private publishing tool, the journal known as *Die Fackel*. Since most of his writing was moralistic and satirical, hence nonfictional, and of modest length in the spirit of *Kleinkunst*, it was easily accommodated by this type of publication.

The name Kraus chose for his journal—*Die Fackel*—was appropriate. Kraus saw himself as the trail-blazing, torch-bearing advocate of honesty and decency in society and culture. So complete was his identity with his journal that he was often referred to—good-naturedly and derisively—as "Fackelkraus" or "Fackel-Kraus" (Torch Kraus).

Kraus began publishing *Die Fackel* on 1 April 1899. His original intention was for it to appear thrice monthly. But as time went on, publication tended to be more irregular. That made little difference to its readers. The little journal, with its distinctive red cover, was a huge success from the very beginning. Within its first two weeks it reached an unheard-of circulation of 30,000 copies, and by the time the last issue appeared in February 1936—four months before Kraus's death—some 37 volumes totaling 922 numbers and over 30,000 pages had been published. (See also page 298 for a discussion of *Die Fackel's* temporary suspension.)

Independently wealthy, beholden to no one, with his own journal at his command, Kraus could write pretty much what he pleased. *Die Fackel* very soon became a forum for moral admonishment, satire, and the exposure of social injustice as perceived by its editor-author. Although his net of righteous indignation was cast widely, Kraus had his favorite targets. The literary pretensions of the "Young Vienna" circle, in which Hermann Bahr was the prime mover, had already felt the sting of Kraus's lash even before *Die Fackel* saw the light of day. In 1893, Kraus made Bahr the target of a biting satire under the title *Die Überwindung des Hermann Bahr* (*The Overcoming of Hermann Bahr*), inspired, of course, by Bahr's own book of essays on modernism, *Die Überwindung des Naturalismus* (*The Overcoming of Naturalism*, 1891). *Die Demolirte Literatur* (*The Demolished Literature*), a mocking assault on the "Young Vienna" writers and the coffeehouse literary culture of the time, which Kraus knew well from the inside, first appeared in the *Wiener Rundschau* in 1896 and as a separate pamphlet in 1897. It was, in fact, Kraus's first major publication.

Once *Die Fackel* was launched, the field of Kraus's satire obviously widened. But Kraus never lost an opportunity to sail into any "Young Vienna" writer who remained steadfast in those literary attitudes and mannerisms which Kraus had castigated in *The Demolished Literature*. Chief among them was Bahr, against whom Kraus continued a tireless campaign of ridicule. To Kraus, Bahr offended in any number of ways. His important organizational role in "Young Vienna"; his early embrace of and eventual repudiation of decadence; his flamboyance; his shifting literary enthusiasms, his "trendiness," if you will; his impressive productivity; his theater reviews as well as his own dramatic writing; his questionable relationship with Emmerich von Bukovics, the director of Vienna's Deutsches Volkstheater; Bahr's origins in provincial Linz and his later advocacy of regional as opposed to urban culture—all aroused Kraus's ire and, one suspects, envy in some respects.

Much of Kraus's venom, especially after *Die Fackel* had come into being, was spewed at contemporary Viennese journalism. Two of his aphorisms make his attitude toward the press crystal clear: "Journalism just seems to serve the present. In reality it destroys the intellectual receptivity of posterity," and "Newspapers have approximately the same relationship to life as fortune tellers do to metaphysics."[3] Kraus believed he had ample reason for running herd on newspapers and newspaper writers. The hypocrisy and venality of the press, which was controlled at the time by a handful of print barons, mirrored the rot that lay beneath the surface of Habsburg society in its twilight years. Worse yet, it was, Kraus believed, the newspapers themselves with their own low moral standards that bore considerable responsibility for shaping, indeed manipulating public opinion, often in self-serving ways. To Kraus, this was nowhere more obvious than in the chauvinism and war hysteria whipped up by the big Vienna papers both before and during the First World War.

Kraus held another brief against the leading Vienna papers. Besides contributing to a lowering of moral standards, they were also responsible for a lowering of German literary standards. Kraus was right in his element here. Given his own rigorous linguistic and stylistic standards, the grammatically and stylistically sloppy, cliché-ridden habits of journalists irritated him no end. His lifelong campaign against them assumed all the character of a holy war.

Kraus focused much of his scorn on the genre of the feuilleton. Its prominence in the contemporary Viennese press as well as its glibness and superficiality made it a natural target. "Writing a feuilleton," wrote Kraus, "is like twisting curls on a bald head."[4] So hostile was Kraus to the feuilleton that his efforts to discredit it took in not only the form itself and its leading practitioners, but the outstanding German nineteenth-century poet Heinrich Heine. In his denunciatory essay *Heine und die Folgen* (*Heine and the Consequences,* 1910), Kraus blamed Heine for the very introduction of the feuilleton into Germany from its native France. Kraus also held Heine responsible for the debasing of the German language through his encouragement of journalism. This is the gist of one of his best-known aphorisms: "Heinrich Heine so loosened the corset of the German language that today every salesman can fondle her breasts."[5]

In exposing the low moral standards of the major Vienna newspapers, Kraus left no stone unturned to bring to light questionable business practices, ethical lapses, and downright corruption. The behavior of the press both before and during the First World War filled him with disgust. Its chauvinistic embrace of the war, the unreality with which it depicted it, and its suppression of the evidence of war-profiteering led Kraus to write the most extraordinary of his dramatic works, *The Last Days of Mankind,* on which he worked for several years and finally completed in 1922. Despite its inordinate length and difficulty of production, the work remains one of the most powerful expressions of antimilitarism in European literature. More than any other work by Kraus it became the basis of his considerable, even greater prestige in the postwar period.

There was hardly a prominent newspaper owner, editor, or journalist who did not have wounds to lick by the time Kraus got through with him. In the case of the shady Hungarian print baron Imre (or Emmerich in German) Békessy, Kraus mounted a relentless campaign that eventually succeeded in driving him out of Vienna and Austria. The highlight of the campaign was his series of public lectures before nearly a thousand people in the Vienna Concert House in the spring and summer of 1925, in which not only did he denounce Békessy but also called for the expulsion of the "low-life" from Vienna. How fearless Kraus dared to be is exemplified in his related campaign against the Vienna chief of police (and later for a while Austrian prime minister), Johannes Schober, whom Kraus accused of working in collusion with Békessy. His play *Die Unüberwindlichen* (*The Unconquerable*, 1927–28), is a documentary based on Schober's presumed corruption.

Kraus's pursuit of Moritz Benedikt, the proprietor of the all-powerful *Neue Freie Presse* (*New Free Press*), whose chauvinism and militarism enflamed Kraus's wrath, was only slightly less vigorous. That Kraus's vendetta against the press could be excessive is seen in his attacks on Isidor Singer, the co-owner and co-editor with Heinrich Kanner of the liberal and pacifist newspaper *Die Zeit*. In this instance, Singer's chief crime was simply running a newspaper, which in Kraus's eyes was enough to condemn him.

Kraus's sometimes exaggerated moral outrage was accompanied (as it often is) by a great sense of self-righteousness and vindictiveness. Kraus had no qualms about personalizing his attacks and, where Jewish figures were concerned, about using his wrath as an outlet for what can only be described as a kind of Jewish anti-Jewishness. Kraus was uncomfortable with his own Jewishness, to such an extent that he eventually converted to Roman Catholicism, which he subsequently also formally abandoned. But that was not enough for him. He never lost an opportunity to expose the Jew behind an assumed non-Jewish name or to knock the putative Jewish features, mannerisms, or style of speech of his adversaries.

Specialists on Kraus, confronted with Kraus's importance as a writer and the interest in him, have tried in various ways to bring a sympathetic understanding to what is usually referred to as Kraus's Jewish self-hatred. But however well intentioned the efforts not just to understand and explain but to rationalize this aspect of Kraus's personality and career, there is no getting around its essential meanness and pettiness. Of the contemporary writers of whom Kraus had little if anything positive to say—apart from Bahr, who was not Jewish—his greatest malice was reserved for such fellow Jews as the German publicist Maximilian Harden, of whom Kraus had once been an admirer, the prominent German critic Alfred Kerr, Franz Werfel (the author of the immensely popular *The Song of Bernadette*), and Felix Salten. We have already taken note of his diatribe against Heine, a Jew, for his role in the spread of the feuilleton. Kraus's attitude toward Zionism, which arose in his own time as the creation of a fellow Viennese Jew, Theodor Herzl, was one of undying hostility. Herzl, like another early Viennese Zionist leader, the writer Max Nordau, was a frequent target of Kraus's malice. But what made Herzl an even more appealing object of derision was his prominence as one of Vienna's best writers of feuilletons before he shifted his energies to the Zionist cause.

Salten, a Hungarian Jew whose real name was Zsiga (Germanized as Siegmund) Salzmann, ranked high in Kraus's personal demonology. The original basis for Kraus's contempt for Salten was the latter's reputation as the most prominent feuilleton writer of the period. He was, in fact, a gifted practitioner of the genre and was widely admired for the elegance of his style. Since the feuilleton as a literary form was anathema to Kraus, Salten was in a sense doomed from the start. But Kraus had other reasons for venting his spleen against Salten. Feisty by temperament, Salten responded to the thinly veiled attack on him in *The Demolished Literature* by giving Kraus a beating. Needless to say, Kraus never got over it. To add insult to injury, Salten wrote for Békessy's papers, and when the fury of Kraus's campaign against Békessy mounted, he, like other writers in the Hungarian's employ (Anton Kuh, for example), joined the counteroffensive against Kraus. Kraus never forgave them. Forgiving, anyway, was not in his nature. Salten was also a Habsburg loyalist and as such easily became an apologist for the war—another, worse strike against him. When Salten's worldwide fame as the author of *Bambi* eclipsed his reputation as the foremost feuilletonist of contemporary Austria, it was more than Kraus could bear. It would be difficult to imagine that envy of the literary successes of a fellow Jew "masking" behind a Christian-sounding name played no role, subconsciously or otherwise, in the intensity, malice, and duration of Kraus's campaign against Salten. When Salten followed up his phenomenally successful *Bambi* with another animal story, *Fünfzehn Hasen* (*Fifteen Rabbits*), Kraus derided the new work in *Die Fackel* for the "Jewish" speech mannerisms of some of Salten's rabbits!

The vehemence of Kraus's attacks in *Die Fackel,* especially against individuals, hardly endeared him to many people. Once the novelty of the journal began to wear off, it lost readers. But Kraus still had a large and loyal following, bolstered if anything in the period of the postwar Austrian republic by his uncompromising stand against the war and his embrace of pacifism. There were also those who shared his feelings about the influence of the press.

Kraus's mystique as a fearless champion of morality and honesty in public life as well as his own incorruptibility was not developed wholly on the basis of his writings or the popularity of *Die Fackel.* Kraus also had a formidable and enviable reputation as a public speaker. By the time of his death of heart failure on 12 June 1936, Kraus had given some 700 lectures and readings, the last just a little over two months before his death, on 2 April. Besides lecturing on issues addressed by pieces in *Die Fackel,* Kraus also delighted audiences with his "Theater der Dichtung" (Literary Theater). These were mainly readings of his own dramatic works as well as those by other writers (among them, the nineteenth-century Austrian comic dramatists Nestroy and Raimund, Goethe, Shakespeare, and Wedekind). He also gave solo performances of operettas by Offenbach and recited sketches by Peter Altenberg. To judge from accounts of his appearances, they must have been spellbinding. One of the most incisive of such accounts comes from the Bulgarian-born Austrian Nobel Prize winner for literature, Elias Canetti. In an essay on Kraus from 1965 and included in the collection *Das Gewissen der Worte* (*The Conscience of Words*), Canetti vividly recalls his own adulation of Kraus—which was common among many young people in Vienna in the early years after the First World War—and the experience of a Kraus public lecture in 1924:

> In spring 1924—I had only just returned to Vienna a few weeks earlier—friends took me to my first lecture by Karl Kraus. The huge concert-house auditorium was jammed. I sat far in back, able to see very little at that distance: a small, rather frail man, slightly hunched, with a face that came to a point below, of an incredible agility, the movements of whom I did not understand, they had something of an unknown creature to them, a newly discovered animal, I could not have said which. His voice was sharp and agitated and easily dominated the auditorium in sudden and frequent intensifications.
>
> I could, however, very carefully observe the people around me. The auditorium had a mood that I knew from large political meetings: as though everything the speaker had to say was familiar and expected. The newcomer had been away from Vienna for eight years. . . . And for him, everything, down to the last detail, was new and astonishing because all the things that were said and passionately spoken with great emphasis as very important, referred to countless particulars of public and also private life. First of all, it was overpowering to feel that so much was happening in a city, so much that was worth being underscored, that concerned everybody. War and its aftermath, vice, murder, profiteering, hypocrisy, even typographical errors were pulled from some kind of context with the same vehemence, named, pilloried and then hurled in some sort of fury over a thousand people, who understood every word, disapproving, acclaiming, laughing, cheering. . . .
>
> All charges were presented in a strangely cemented diction that had something of legal paragraphs, never stopped, never ran out, sounding as if it had begun years ago and could be prolonged in the exact same way for many years more. The proximity to the legal sphere was also palpable in the presumption of an established and absolutely certain and inviolable law. It was clear what was good and it was clear what was bad. It was as hard and natural as granite, which no one could have scratched or notched. . . .
>
> He was the oldest of all paradoxes: this man who loathed so much, the most steadfast scorner in world literature since the

Spaniard Quevedo and since Swift, a kind of scourge of God for guilt-ridden mankind—this man let *everybody* speak. He was incapable of sacrificing even the least, the lowliest, the emptiest voice. His greatness consisted in the way he, all alone, literally alone, confronted, heard, eavesdropped on, attacked, and whiplashed the world, to the extent that he knew it, his entire world, in all its representatives (and it had countless representatives). He was thus the opposite of the writers, the huge majority of writers, who butter people up in order to be loved and lauded by them. We certainly need not waste any time discussing the necessity of such figures as he, precisely because there is such a lack of them.

In this essay, I am putting the main accent on the *living* Kraus, that is to say, Kraus as he was when speaking to many people at once. It cannot be repeated often enough: The real, the rousing, the tormenting, the shattering Karl Kraus, the Kraus who became part of our very being, who moved and shook us, so that we needed years to gather enough strength and stand up against him—the real Karl Kraus was the *speaker*. There has never existed such a speaker in my lifetime—not in any European language that I know.[6]

While admiring Kraus, Canetti was also aware of his imperiousness, to which he himself like so many others succumbed and against which he eventually rebelled:

> The heart of the matter was that he had appropriated all judging and did not permit anyone whose model he was to do any judging of his own. Anyone attached to him very quickly noticed in himself the result of this prohibition.

1.   Frank Field, *The Last Days of Mankind: Karl Kraus and His Vienna* (London: Macmillan, 1967); Wilma Abeles Iggers, *Karl Kraus: A Viennese Critic of the Twentieth Century* (The Hague: Martinus Nijhoff, 1967); Harry Zohn, *Karl Kraus* (New York: Twayne World Authors, 1971); Thomas Szasz, *Karl Kraus and the Soul-Doctors: A Pioneer Critic and His Criticism of Psychiatry and Psychoanalysis* (Baton Rouge: Louisiana State University Press, 1977); Kari Grimstad, *Masks of the Prophet: The Theatrical World of Karl Kraus* (Toronto: University of Toronto Press, 1982); Edward Timms, *Karl Kraus, Apocalyptic Satirist: Culture and Catastrophe in Habsburg Vienna* (New Haven, Conn.: Yale University Press, 1986).

Although there is a substantial literature on Kraus in German, a definitive study of his life and work has yet to appear. Among the more interesting German works, mention may be made of Leopold Liegler, *Karl Kraus und sein Werk* (Vienna: R. Lanyi, 1920); Werner Kraft, *Karl Kraus—Beiträge zum Verständnis seines Werkes* (Salzburg: Otto Müller Verlag, 1956) and *Das Ja des Neinsagers: Karl Kraus und seine geistige Welt* (Munich: Richard Boorberg Verlag, 1974); Paul Schick, *Karl Kraus in Selbstzeugnissen und Bilddokumenten* (Reinbek bei Hamburg: Rowohlt Verlag, 1965); Helmut Arntzen, *Karl Kraus und die Presse* (Munich: Wilhelm Fink Verlag, 1975); Nike Wagner, *Geist und Geschlecht: Karl Kraus und die Erotik der Wiener*

Moderne (Frankfurt am Main: Suhrkamp Verlag, 1982); Michael Horowitz, *Karl Kraus* (Vienna: Verlag Orac, 1986); Joseph P. Strelka, ed., *Karl Kraus: Diener der Sprache, Meister des Ethos* (Tübingen: Francke Verlag, 1990).

2.   The following works by Kraus are available in English: *Poems,* trans. Albert Bloch (Boston: Four Seas Press, 1930); *The Last Days of Mankind,* abr. Frederick Ungar, trans. Alexander Gode and Sue Ellen Wright (New York: Frederick Ungar Publishing Co., 1974); *In These Great Times: A Karl Kraus Reader,* ed. Harry Zohn, trans. Joseph Fabry and others (Montreal: Engendra Press, 1976; Chicago: The University of Chicago Press, 1984); *Half-Truths & One-and-a-Half Truths: Karl Kraus Selected Aphorisms,* ed. and trans. Harry Zohn (Montreal: Engendra Press, 1976): *No Compromise: Selected Writings,* ed. Frederick Ungar, trans. Sheema Z. Buehne and others (New York: Frederick Ungar Publishing Co., 1977).

3.   Karl Kraus, from *Sprüche und Widersprüche,* in *Beim Wort genommen* (Munich: Kösel-Verlag, 1955), 76, 77.

4.   Karl Kraus, *Beim Wort genommen,* 118.

5.   Karl Kraus, *Beim Wort genommen,* 241.

6.   Elias Canetti, *The Conscience of Words,* trans. Joachim Neugroschel (New York: The Seabury Press, 1979), 30–33. See also the description of Karl Kraus's three-hundredth lecture in Vienna's Great Concert House Hall on 17 April 1924 in Canetti's *The Torch in My Ear* [*Die Fackel im Ohr*], trans. Joachim Neugroschel (New York: Farrar Straus Giroux, 1982), 68–74.

7.   Canetti, *The Conscience of Words,* 36.

THE DEMOLISHED LITERATURE

Vienna is now being demolished into a metropolis. Together with the old houses the last pillars of our memories are falling, and soon an irreverent spade will have also leveled the venerable Café Griensteidl to the ground. This was the decision of its proprietors, the consequences of which cannot be foreseen. Our literature is bracing itself for a period of homelessness; the threads of artistic creativity are being cruelly severed. Men of letters might henceforth abandon themselves to pleasant sociability at home. But professional life, work with its manifold nervous crises and upsets, took place in that coffeehouse, which like no other appeared suited to represent the true center of literary activity. More than mere preference assured the old establishment its place of honor in literary history. Who does not remember the almost crushing profusion of newspapers and journals that made the visit to our coffeehouse a virtual necessity for those writers who had no craving for coffee? Need reference be made to all the volumes of Meyer's *Conversations-Lexikon*, which, deposited in an easily accessible place, made it possible for each man of letters to acquire an education? Or to the wealth of writing material that was always at hand for an unforeseen inspiration? The younger writers especially will miss terribly the intimate old Viennese interior, which always managed to make up in inspiration what it lacked in comfort. Only the great draft that blew back and forth through this coffeehouse idyll was perceived by the sensitive regular guests as a stylistic infelicity, and of late the cases of young writers paying for their strenuous productivity with rheumatism have multiplied. It should also be evident that in such an exceptional coffeehouse even the disposition of the waiters had to exhibit a streak of the literary. The waiters here adapted to the milieu in their evolution. A certain affiliation with the artistic endeavors of the guests was already stamped on their physiognomy, the haughty awareness, no doubt, that they were contributing in their own way to a literary movement. The ability to become absorbed in the individuality of any guest without sacrificing their own individuality raised these waiters high above all their professional colleagues. You may not believe in a coffee-brewers association that delivers your mail, but imagine the German writers' society appointing one. A line of prominent waiters like those who worked in this coffeehouse indicates the development of domestic intellectual life. An outmoded generation of writers beheld Franz the Worthy, whose memory is still preserved in countless anecdotes. He radiated style and authority when, without having to be asked, he used to hand over to a passerby who turned up again after twenty years the same newspaper that the person had requested when he was a young man. Franz, the

Imperial and Royal Court-Waiter, created a tradition that today is being thrown overboard by the young. With the death of the old waiter, whose privy councilor's title might have been ill suited to the storm and stress of the Nineties, a new era began.

Franz, who had hobnobbed with Grillparzer[1] and Bauernfeld,[2] lived long enough to see how naturalism made its triumphant advance from Berlin to the Café Griensteidl and was jubilantly taken up by some regulars as a vigorous reaction against an aesthete epigonism. Since then, the Café Griensteidl belongs to modern art. A new generation of waiters stood ready to familiarize itself with the complicated apparatus of artistic trends that superseded each other in succession. Those members of the waiters' fraternity who had hitherto served an antiquated literature as informers were now employed in the service of a modern movement characterized by the transvaluation of all values. They understood this, keeping pace with the times, and soon satisfied the demands of a heightened sensitivity. The moody creatures who now sprang up like mushrooms after a rain desired strange color compositions for ice cream and coffee.[3] The longing for inner experiences asserted itself, with the result that the introduction of absinthe as an effective beverage for the nerves became a necessity. If the indigenous literature of Paris and Germany was to maintain its momentum, the coffeehouse had to model itself on [the decorations of] Tortoni[4] and the Kaiserhof.[5]

Once down-to-earth realism had been set aside, the Griensteidl stood under the banner of symbolism. "Rarified nerves!" now became the slogan of the day. People began observing the "condition of the soul" and wanted to flee the ordinary plainness of things. One of the most important catchwords, however, was "life," and people got together nightly in order to come to terms with life or, if the going got hot and heavy, to try to figure it out.

Launching the new literary movement, undertaking the many difficult conquests, and, finally, impressing on coffeehouse life the stamp of a personality fell to a certain gentleman from Linz.[6] In point of fact, he soon succeeded in exerting a decisive influence on the youth and in collecting around himself a hardy band of followers. A Linz custom, implying genius by means of ringlets cascading over the brow, immediately found enthusiastic imitators; the moderns wanted it emphatically understood that they were in no way behind the times.[7] The bold seeker of new sensations from Linz immediately forbade his disciples from partaking further of the "imperial flesh of naturalism," recommending instead the "baked ducats of symbolism." Through such expedient directives, he knew how to maintain his position as the leading habitué. His manner of writing was easily mastered by the literary youth. To the youngest critics he opened up the columns of his newly founded paper, which every week presented the trailblazer and his imitators in closest proximity and even today demonstrates a faulty unity of style through the heterogeneity of ciphers. Then, when he did not as yet possess the mellow composure of Goethe, it was still difficult for beginners to follow him through the thicket of his oddly ornate and elaborately branched Un-German. Today, where he imitates Goethe, he finds the greatest number of followers, and there is hardly a pupil of his who would be confused about the difference between an "authority" and a "throng."

Here is a specimen of his writing, reasonably true to life, from the time when the Frenchified style of the Master was not yet saturated with elements of Goethe's language. Concerning the work of a Griensteidl guest and his performance at the Deutsches Volkstheater,[8] he might have expressed himself so:

> The more frequently one enters this Deutsches Volkstheater—where quotation marks surround every price—the more violent the annoyance with the performance, with this Herr Kadelburg[9] with the elegance of a paperhanger, and with this public with faces you see stuffed with sausage at the amusement park. Schnitzler is known. I have explained the special style of Schnitzler just as recently I have demonstrated the impulses of youngest Austria. The caustic remark of the furtive and willfully comic Julius Bauer[10] is fitting where he is really better known as Isidor Fuchs:[11] "A little official has nothing, but he has it confidently." He would like to play the *viveur* [pleasure seeker], but with a Viennese accent, not in the manner of the French, as might have been shown him by Pierre Blanchard or some other French proper name which only I know if I want to ignore Ferry Beraton,[12] who also gets it from me. This is the art of nerves, from the nerves on the nerves, and one must then think of Berti Goldschmidt[13] and the *psychologie blasée* of Stendahl and Huysmans, of the Goncourts and Lavedan,[14] and of Loris[15] and Maurice Barrés and, finally, of Portoriche. This is art with the sensitive nose for the smell of things, one that is like a last drop of champagne and feels like the clinging fawning of faded old silk, but always retaining a bit of the pleasant Viennese coziness of Canaletto.[16] He gives languid moods which surpass the art of Watteau and Fragonard, with the tender grace of forms and the half-veiled contours which still do not quite fit together. But there is still effervescence. His art seeks harmony. A residue remains. That is the short sentences. I can't help it. There are audacious, impetuous, and confused impulses exerting pressure. But the

confident shaper of intimate experience that demands art soon
asserts himself. And now the performance. Much asks little. Some
suc-ceeds. Sandrock[17] was again an exquisite marvel of pure
power and beauty. But her noble art was alone. Only Herr Nhil[18]
can measure himself against her; perhaps also the confident-
growing Giampietro,[19] and Tewele,[20] if he could get rid of his
nose. With the others, I was reminded of Iglau, where it runs
into Leitomischl. It was disgraceful and offensive. The direction
was indeed wanting. Artistic instincts came to ruin. A better
paperhanger and Kadelburg cannot help. The assured manner
of the sharp Martinelli[21] would have been more in order, his
pensive and measuring technique which comes off so well. Herr
Kutschera[22] allows his heroes to be forgotten like a fop. I will
never be able to forget or get over Fräulein Hell,[23] who always
wails so. That is why the young and talented Bauer[24] plays off
against her older colleague, that dear, pale girl who is so moving.

But how Herr Broda[25] played Moritzky[26] the whole of
Vienna should have seen. The way he crawled into the character
of this Moritzky, without anything superfluous, is something
entirely new, beyond the Spaniard Vico and the Dutchman
Boomeester. He provided the redemption and consecration of
the evening. He is a mixture of Kainz[27] and the secretive Duse.[28]
Words fail me. But the formula had to be sought for the vague
and confused sensations inspired by the great uniqueness of
Broda's art.

Each one of his reviews poured forth upon the land a torrent of personal
names. The luminaries of art whom he introduced were known by name
only by *him*. He had often picked them out of Spanish theater handbills
or even Portuguese street signs. Even today, he continues to give unveri-
fiable facts the appearance of something experienced, to establish firm
links between things that he really hopes to bring about. It is, to speak
in his style along with Goethe, an extraordinary file index which he does
not have but which has him.

As a critic, he soon drew general attention to himself. He interested
people. Even though you might not always agree with his tone, you still
had to admit that he was one of those people who brings clarification, who
independently of the misunderstanding of others always has his own
prejudice. The shallow impressionism to which this discriminating dawdler
surrendered himself bordered on the homey. Pleasing was the lack of
humor, which disguised a rare absence of any point of view but yet discreetly hinted that a reproach was no purposeful attack but just vague
provocation. People applauded when in his own way he raised a protest
against good taste and recalled the Dionysian need of students to run a

stick against the roll shutters of arches. In such a manner he often sowed his wild oats and teased the watchmen of the public literary order.

Storm and Stress was one day relieved of its Weimar refinement.[29] The time for maturity had come for him, a blasé smugness informed his words, and a "lovely generosity" spoke from the directives that he issued from on high to the youth of the country. But so quickly did the youth make the decision to emulate him that the youngest began speaking of the "young artists," and when one day the first work by a nineteen-year-old appeared, a twenty-year-old patron cried out, "I don't mind at all that the young people are now coming up in the world a little!" And that crowd of authorities whose attitudes are just secondhand and who receive their affectations by subscription are now professing an Olympian worldview. Moreover, the calm artist's eye, with which some "pure artists" were wont to overlook economic matters, betrayed the Goethe-natures all too plainly. In short, everything owed the Café Griensteidl was now straightened out. He who really did not belong to literature but was permitted to listen in on conversations and make cues began to feel like Eckermann. But the Leader, who acted as though Weimar and not Urfahr was the suburb of Linz, continued to expand his horizons and became so versatile it was widely feared that in the end he was going to take up chromatics and optics. Unsatisfied, moreover, with an imprecise knowledge of the theater, he is now undertaking to misunderstand the visual arts and even to generalize abstract philosophical subjects more thoroughly. For the benevolent tone in which this foremost authority speaks to his crowd the words are characteristic that he once wrote in a treatise on the value of physical exercise: " . . . and so despite my preference generally for sitting or lying around meditatively, I can frequently be observed strolling in our fair city, just like Father Horace, comfortably sauntering about, droll stories in mind, without any schedule."

Through contact with his pupils it is well known that the gentleman from Linz has always stood up for them selflessly. Without him, many a young nontalent would have run aground and been forgotten. And there are not a few who can take pride in the fact that they were discovered by him. They bear the indelible brand of his prediction that in four weeks' time Europe would be speaking about them. "The way I know Europe," he once said, "Europe between the Volga and the Loire has no secrets from me." But then it appeared that, even with this modest qualification, it did indeed have a secret from him. Even after the four-week deadline was generously extended, it absolutely could not be budged to make any declaration concerning the discoveries that had been made in the Café Griensteidl. But perhaps it was the very circumstance that they remained unknown after such a clamorous production that made a name for these youngest writers.

The fact that one of them was still attending secondary school inspired the Discoverer to the exclamation: "Goethe at the school desk!"[30] A rush was on to win the youngster for the coffeehouse, and his parents themselves conducted him there. They were anxious to show that he inherited his stature and the serious direction of his life from his father and from his mother his cheerful disposition and his enthusiasm for storytelling. His movements then assumed the character of the Eternal, his correspondence that of an "exchange of letters." He set to work writing a fragment, and it was owing to its maturity that it was prepared for his literary estate. In dignified verses he also instructed his heirs to lavish the consecrated oil from the hands of the dead old woman on eagle, lamb, and peacock. Then he rehearsed his "last words."

One of the most delicate blossoms of the decadence sprouted in the Café Griensteidl in the form of a young baron who, it is said, traced his affectation back to the Crusades.[31] The gentleman from Linz liked the style of the young man, who wandered into the coffeehouse one day by chance. When the latter got carried away into making the remark, "Goethe is quite clever," the former thought: Here lies a wealth of affectation that should not be lost to literature. Thus was awakened in the young man the consciousness of his sensitivity, which was sufficient to stimulate him to productive creativity. There then came a vision tinged with memories of Kalksburg;[32] and as the product of an intellectual narrowness which, padded with ideas associated with the word "Viennese," is known as "pure artistry," a novel arose called *The Kindergarten of Ignorance*.[33]

No wonder the Discoverer liked it. He placed the author alongside Goethe, whom he had the occasion to celebrate anew, and he was glad that appreciation for the master who was unknown to him had come about from the overestimation of the dilettante who was known to him. Goethe had to furnish the Café Griensteidl with the building material for a fresh renown and the phraseology of a new art. As it turned out, the basic artistic-philosophical principles of "extracting the exceptional from the common" and "thrusting the individual into the eternal" were repeatedly compromised and represented ostentatiously as modern slogans, applicable to the latest literary sensation. After all, the gentleman from Linz wanted to claim the general interest for an exceptional talentlessness, and the disgrace, which was indeed individual, he knew how to thrust into the eternal.

Goethe subsequently continued to provide him important services. The gentleman from Linz's file cabinet grew, developed, and reached maturity. Even today he is still in the habit of using the fairly well-known anecdote about the dog Bello against the naturalism that he himself once supported. And as the question of literary ownership became more acute, he thought he would have to appeal to Goethe for the artistic transfiguration of plagiarism. In fulfillment of the long-held wishes of the communist guests of the Café Griensteidl, the literary thief was granted dispensation on 20 June 1896. Freedom from censorship and the lifting of the ban on colportage [the peddling of religious books] could hardly have fructified the domestic literature any better.

It may boldly be observed that the sphere of activity acquired by the gentleman from Linz covers three or, in the case of a popular coffeehouse, four tables. From the hall dressing table on, his popularity begins to fall off. It was here that those literati took their stand who, unwilling to acknowledge unconditionally his absolutist dictatorship of taste, soon renounced him and established themselves as independent poseurs. In the meantime, the influence of the man who, where he did not directly plead the cause of nontalent, had nevertheless prepared a fertile field for coming mediocrities should not be forgotten ungratefully. Those who welcomed such an impulse in any case went the way of their own development while he was busy with the overestimation of new talent. It has not been easy for them. They have to thank their own energy for their present neurasthenia. Self-made men of affectation,[34] they had to first earn their blaséness. It is indeed touching to observe aristocratic writers, whose nobility encompasses many degenerations, brushing aside class distinctions and without any pride trafficking with the upstarts of the Decadence.[35] And it is precisely these people who are the real treasure of that Young Austria which foreigners are accustomed to identifying as modern Viennese art. Vienna is the spiritual hotbed of these poets, for whom a benevolent destiny has already placed the sweet little girl of the outer districts in the crib,[36] and they are so easily satisfied that they hope to get by their whole lives with a few Vienna images.

The modern movement, which a decade ago emanated from the North,[37] has produced among us only purely technical variations. Our young art, which seeks its salvation indeed in the renunciation of the intellectual battles of the time, has been spared the internal action of a new style that helped expand subject matter and brought social problems into play. If a poverty of ideas expects to revel in images, then Viennicity has to pay the piper, and local patriotism awakens to a new, more responsive existence.

Despite the numerous coffeehouse sessions held for the purpose of achieving an appropriate formulation of the concept "artistic personality" [Künstlermensch], a good many of these writers never produced anything.

Before they had agreed on a definition, none of them wanted to risk the effort. Besides, several of them had long ago made names for themselves as regular guests and they were loath to forfeit them through their work. The Griensteidl has definitely become the gathering place for people who want to fritter away their abilities, and one shouldn't wonder at the sterility of talented people who sit so packed in together in a coffeehouse that they mutually hinder each other's development.

Until now, an affected attitude toward art has been mandatory in these circles. The particular ability of the Young Vienna poets lies in their adopting the airs of the bon-vivant most when they can live on the impressions of an evening at Ronacher's[38] for weeks on end, enjoy the antics of a clown with relish, and drag out the oldest jokes every time they get together. The same spirit, when it flees from such a life of plenty into contemplative solitariness, finds consolation in the thought of the "quiet lanes on a Sunday afternoon" and the "unspeakably melancholic aspect of a Prater inn on weekdays"—ever-recurrent sentimental delusions that fill this touching but narrow horizon. In Vienna, too, they have taken over several locales, where they nurture their very own individual worlds of sensation. Thus must the Fischerstiege [Fisherman's Stairs], the Heiligenkreuzerhof [Holy Cross Square], the Votivkirche [Votive Church], and the Karlskirche [Karl's Church] fulfill their needs. "The Karlskirche is mine!" one of them screamed one day when his neighbor at table wanted to contest the issue. When the latter remained content with the Vienna river banks, the border dispute of moods was peacefully settled.

He who plunges deepest into such shallowness and is the most absorbed in this vacuity, the writer who made the "sweet young girl" suitable for the Burgtheater,[39] knew how to preserve a quiet unpretentiousness of megalomania amidst deafening surroundings. Too good-natured to approach a problem head-on, he concocted a little world of gay blades and pleasure-loving working girls in order to ascend once in a while from these depths to false tragedy. Then when something like death occurs—please don't be frightened; the pistols are loaded with blanks[40]—*dying* is nothing compared to living and not seeing!

Incapable of engaging themselves in life, these purveyors of sensitivity occasionally squirm out of the snail-like shells of their so-called egos, but only for the sake of raptly observing each other's coquettish gyrations. A sense of style based on French models affords them a naive pleasure in the design of their next habitat, that of their own person. Here is a writer who has so much success to show in the area of fashion that he can confidently enter a competition with the prettiest of his readers.[41] For years he has been working on the third line of a novel, since he ponders every word in several changes of dress. A Persian cloth manufacturer supplies him with the best material. He fusses with his clothes with the utmost diligence and burnishes them down to the finest and most subtle detail. His shirts are stunning, and since he is very productive, he follows one exotic pattern after another in breathtaking succession. Always with an eye for beauty and the greatest exactitude of each and every pose, he succeeds in uniting everything around him in tasteful effect, since, by way of example, he traffics only with such young people whose garb accords with his own of the day. A harmony of friendship so created, he then enters into it with his whole heart and soul. Well-hung drapery is an experience to him, and when he speaks, he takes great pains to use his upper lip in a decorative way. Thus it is that he himself drapes his milieu and comfortably papers his life.

In his circle, he has a very critical function to discharge. His task is to inspect the wardrobe of each incoming man of letters and to undertake all necessary adjustments. Our poet often succeeds in this with a few characteristic strokes. Here he is at work, himself putting the finishing touches on something, there issuing the appropriate instructions, giving pertinent tips and practical advice; here he completes the fragmentary beauty of a bicycle outfit, there he pronounces by means of a reproachful glance the impossibility of a complete trousering. His rebukes are terse: "That won't last," or "People don't wear that kind of thing anymore," or "A person can't work with you"; his praise is equally to the point: "That can stay." And one can put up with this criticism calmly, since our poet does not hesitate to make similar observations about nature itself. Beholding a certain landscape, he is supposed to have repeatedly declared, "This has to be a bit stylized!" and only rarely dispensed his usual praise: "That can stay."

This poet now goes so far in his endeavors that even his own set no longer understands him. The youngsters with their insignificant shirts can't follow the train of thought of his polychromatic vest. So must he bear the cross of the lonely individual, and when this genius who is not understood by his own time is overheard in his solitude, you can't help but feel awestruck. For a very long time he has known how to be preoccupied with himself, how to concentrate just on himself. Far from the maddening throng, he sits for hours at a time in front of a mirror—*enfin seul* [at last alone] with his necktie! . . . But he will also prevail, and in proper recognition of his merits it will one day be said of him:

> He was a poet who did not dress himself according to the fashion—a singular talent which also expressed itself in the thoroughly independent style of his low-cut shoes. To this sensitive nature, a false collar, one which was not sewn right onto the

shirt, choked off inspiration. His gift of keen observation, which was strengthened through a finely polished monocle, overlooked no sartorial shortcoming. The sensations a chic necktie was capable of arousing in him also enabled him to play havoc with a handkerchief that hung too far out of a coat pocket. The most intensive moods, the most original thoughts, which would have helped others achieve literary successes, he had tucked away in his fine belts. This poet was unique. God save us from his epigones!

You see, it isn't always just the common interests on which guests of the literary coffeehouse can count; some of them indeed also put on a universal human comedy. If you overlook their insignificance, you'll delight in their effectiveness. The smallest achiever who wants to win recognition in the battle of the coffeehouse existence and struggles for a solid position at the table of the mature literati ought not to be disregarded. The development of emerging talentlessness supplies an abundance of observations. It is quite piquant to peer through a coffeehouse window and see how today's novice tries to propel himself by means of somebody already established as of yesterday.

Conspicuous above all is a writer who from modest beginnings contrived to become a friend of the Burgtheater author.[42] He is a parvenu of gestures who has learned everything from his literary tablemates and owes them his knowledge of the most important poses. If the others have already routinized this affectation, he still exhibits the great effort that is taking its toll of his nerves. For all that, he has today fortunately managed to scrape up a few nerves that permit him the exercise of an unassuming sensitivity. He thus places special value on not being able to bear it when somebody scratches a knife on a plate. It is from such events, which in others provoke only a normal degree of discomfort, that he finds the stimulus to artistic creativity. Here lie the style and strengths of his talent. He did not have to go far to find his material.

He writes always on what his friends are working. And since the Young Vienna school has unanimously chosen the theme of dying and has united its energies in endeavoring to wrest from death a few novels, we see him zealously absorbed in the sensation of sentimentality concerning funerals, cemetery wreaths, and the bereaved. You have to imagine his literary production this way: A witty gossip of sorts, he keeps a whole collection of the stories of one of his more accredited friends in reserve and so never has to use more than a tenth of them. Although he apparently came by his personality cheaply at some sale, pure artistic genius hasn't yet paid off in the long run. He, who was always enjoined in his circle to look down his nose at newspaper writers, soon put into the the harbor of journalism, but with the firm resolve as an erstwhile man of letters to rise above the niveau of his numerous colleagues. Fortunately, the intonation of modern style still remained in his ears from before, his friends had sent him on his way with some defenseless observations, and he hastily snatched up a few corrupt witticisms that had fallen from the table. Besides, possessed of a good dose of self-assurance and understanding that where he could not rely on his friends he would have to write Un-German on his own, he began his profession. The first thing he did was inquire of a watchman about the condition of the theater whose tradition he had determined to oppose. It must be confessed that down to today he has in fact seen the most important plays of Schiller and Shakespeare. Why, he now asks, does the management tarry so long with the history plays? *Hamlet*, for example, he saw for the first time on the occasion of a recasting. As a conscientious reviewer, he did not fail to request the manuscript from the director's office ahead of time. Then, in the lapidary style in which he often liked to express his shallowness, he is supposed to have cried out recently, enraptured (as much as his dignity permitted him): "You'll have to keep your eye on Wolter!"[43] He has always proven to be a plucky, independent critic who makes no concessions either above or below, and indeed while himself disregarding all rules of grammar, is always ready to take an energetic stand against just such abuses.

His reformist zeal is engaging when, overcoming a deep-seated prejudice, he praised the actor Martinelli for a "broad, comfortable geniality." As an ironist he has always stood on his own quotation marks. When his target happened to be the notorious Vienna comedians' clique, the quotation marks threatened to run short at the printer's, for he has always been able to pump this particular subject for ever-new pages utterly devoid of interest. Some foreign words seemed so new to him that he thought he had to try them out over and over again. He always maintained, for example, that Herr Reimers[44] speaks *ad spectatores* [to the audience] and that Fräulein Bleibtreu[45] is caryatidic.[46] Perhaps it was a case of rather too strongly emphasizing expressions usually encountered for the first time only in high school and already mastered after four classes. One day he ordered a reviewer's copy of Muther's *History of Nineteenth-Century Painting* and so became an art historian. When shortly thereafter the Muther affair began and the renowned art historian was frequently accused of plagiarism, it was said that Muther also made use of our reviewer.

Although journalistic service has taken its toll of him, our man of letters has still managed to preserve his individuality right down to the present. He still succeeds in confusing the dative and the accusative cases with undiminished youthful enthusiasm. At the outset, he had to contend, to be sure, with the opposition of the compositors who, as we all know, want to be wiser than the author and like to make corrections, since they regard as Un-German the most original expression of an artistic personality. But soon they learned to respect the individuality of our author and his talent prevailed. Unimpeded, he could now kick up his heels and could be recognized even in unsigned articles. When, for example, in an aging actress he missed that "hot breath" that "blows *to one* (Einem . . . anweht) only from a maiden's innocent bosom," it would have been quite superfluous to append his signature. He obviously *encounters people* (begegnet er die Leute), but he can transform even this accusative and come to a quite unexpected result when he eventually speaks about people with whom *one has an encounter* (von Leuten . . . die Einem begegnen), and so through a slip hits upon the right thing. On the occasion of last year's Sonnenthal jubilee,[47] in keeping with the importance of the honoree, he acquitted himself of a variety of muddled case endings. . . .[48] When the commentary touched upon theatrical novices, he was as indulgent as ever, declaring in his own elegant way that it would be reproachful "to set *one au niveau* [on a par] with the dilettante."[49] When the newspaper where he is employed once carried the telegraphic report that the "Serbian-Montenegran alliance along with the nuptial speculations dependent *to* it" remains in question,[50] you couldn't help come to the opinion that he, too, was composing telegrams. However, this amounts to a definite overestimation of his sphere of activity, since the purview of our friend encompasses exclusively the confusion of the dative case with the accusative, and not with the genitive, and then only in the theater and art sections.

No one would seriously maintain that these and similar grammatical idiosyncrasies could handicap *one's* literary career.[51] Wholly by means of the pretensions with which he advances his superficiality, a writer is always in a position to impress a reader.[52]

What extends beyond the literary frame should be of no interest to us. There are those who do not want to confess to the views that he advocated. But there are many who are even more believing. This strengthens him in his confidence and emboldens him to new deeds. The stage conquests of his friends have intoxicated him, and the goal now of all his aspirations is: To be performed! And sure enough, we see him taking a short byway behind the wings of the Burgtheater . . .

And now, away from him who has received an unexpected preference here to other tablemates who are already waiting and have begun complaining about the partiality of the service. The pale composer of an Athenian box-office play who has been spoiled by success is clearly impatient.[53] Although his inability either to ride a bicycle or play skittles seriously obstructed the director of the Imperial Theater from discovering his talent, he succeeded in getting a foothold in the Burgtheater. This is as it should be in view of the fact that his work represents a most felicitous combination of the misunderstood Greek and unfathomed modern spirits. For the Viennicity of his milieu, he is endowed with an unspeakably Bukovinian style that manifests itself in particular in the considerable adroitness with which he employs the ten-foot iambic meter. His play creates the impression of having being written upon the invitation of [Georg] Büchmann.[54] It contains a series of exceptionally tedious familiar quotations on the order of: "The yearning for happiness is more than happiness," or "How little the people know their own mind!" . . .[55] The renown of a Grillparzer-epigone so flatters him that in order to justify it, at least in part, he is now said to have his eye on a government position and, moreover, to be rigidly adhering to his master's biography. Had he not already outgrown the old-Austrian tradition, on no account would he let it elude him. After all the excitement and exertions of the premiere, may he now be allowed to experience in peace what he created in his play!

Who is that sprightly young man who has approached the gentlemen of the Circle with all kinds of questions?[56] One of those curious phenomena of the coffeehouse world, he created the impression in this manner that he was a permanent fixture at the Griensteidl despite the fact that nobody ever saw him sitting there. His connection with literature is limited to the service of conducting writers home at night. If one of the gentlemen happens to have some success to boast of, our young man becomes egomaniacal and often downright arrogant through the praise that others receive. Along with his literary colleagues, he, too, received much encouragement from Goethe:

> He came to the coffeehouse
> Just to be seen.
> And instead of imbibing
> Wanted to preen.

The result was that he is now the most regular of regulars. The waiters have already become used to this state of affairs. At the outset, when the others ordered something, he had to keep on repeating: "Nothing for me." Old Heinrich has already been initiated and says, as soon as he sees him: "The usual, sir?" Only rarely does it happen that Heinrich grumbles gently into his beard: "The coffeehouse isn't here just for you to get stimulated." Nevertheless, our guest can be satisfied with the service. He would have something to complain about, after all, were it too attentive. Nobody bothers to help him remove his hat and heavy winter coat, and he is permitted to hold forth for hours on end on the importance of his auditors. There he stands, lapping up enthusiasm, gesticulating wildly. He would have become a big fool even if he had been born without hands . . .

The Young Vienna portrait gallery possesses one fine study of great promise as a sufferer's countenance. This decadent (lyricists' section) has become approved for the literary table through three imposing volumes of poetry in which he demonstrated that he has frayed nerves.[57] "Neurotica" was confiscated and created "Sensations," the latter finally becoming a laughing-stock. The true gift of poetry, the ability to extract undreamt-of inspiration from insignificant phenomena, was never denied him. He always composed poetry on a much higher level than he experienced life, and if you inquired into the muses of his ecstasies, you would be amazed to discover how really meager a flame a demonic woman is when she is courted by a modern lyricist. At one time, he purported to love "Everything strange and sick." The critics believed, however, that the seat of his suffering was to be found in his reading of Baudelaire and prescribed the strictest diet and forbade him any affectation. But out of fear of succumbing to incurable health, he paid no heed to these measures. Hectic verses filled him with a sense of satisfaction, and he acquired literary weapons that bore his name: a tired old heart, a cold withered soul, and a struggle with consumptive tuberculosis, all entwined with rarified nerves. Success relieves him of all sense of responsibility and, while still in his youth, he is today already an experienced old man.

At long last, a true neurotic![58] How well indeed he fits into this milieu of feigned morphinism. He is no artist, just a slick librettist who sets a good example for others in this respect. Exhausted, thoroughly shaken by all the excitement of theatrical rehearsals, he takes his place in the coffeehouse with a lot of hustle and bustle. "Waiter," he snaps, "the satirical papers, and be quick about it! I'm not here for my pleasure, you know!" While his modern tablemates are preoccupied with bringing change to intellectual life, we see him opening the way for commerce into literature. His connections to the stage may be those of an energetic theater agent, but he displays a phenomenal productivity that extends across most of Vienna's stages. After every one of his operettas you think he's finally spent himself. Truly an Antaean of nontalent,[59] he forever draws new strength from his failures. He almost never appears alone on a theater bill, and it must be delicious to see the two partners at work. The personalities so complement each other that what one lacks in humor the other makes up for by an absence of imagination. Since the latter is talentless with a passion, the former has to live from it. Yet business seems to look after its own man. Today he owns a villa beautifully situated on the Attersee, with a view of the Waldberg.

A certain person, who through his versatility affords a pleasant diversion, attaches himself to this circle of young men who do not know how to write but always have their hearts set just on this one profession.[60] Although he thinks of himself as a painter, he cannot paint. When he was already in his more mature years, he also set out to express his lack of talent as a writer, but not without first laying the solid foundation of a thorough lack of education. Long before he attracted attention through his peculiar connections to German grammar, he could already point to numerous fiascoes as a visual artist. There is a familiar saying that is right on target about the person who would like to combine in one hand the two pursuits of painting and literature: The writers know quite well that he is no good painter, and the painters have no delusions anymore about him being a good writer. When applied to our friend, the saying falls apart. For a long time he derived his style from Linz, from where, as we well know, all efforts at literary reform have for several years issued forth. The violence he has already done to the German language after just a little training defies comparison. When it came to introducing foreign personal names into convoluted German prose, he put the master to shame. Some of his periods will remain unforgettable. The sensation of a divorce affair and the flaming protest that the heroine published against her persecutor reached its zenith only when our writer took pen in hand and wrote the ringing words: "The courthouse where the case is being heard hung for many years like a Damocles sword over the head of the persecuted." A small article on Hanslick's seventieth birthday—and the complete edition of his paper was out of print.[61] Hanslick, he wrote at the time, "was born in Prague, on the early trail of his future." He sang the praises of the feuilletonist in this manner:

> That evanescent section of the paper where, when he directs his pen with abundant skill whither the feuilleton is created beneath the bottom line of the first page, the mind is afforded the opportunity of recovering from the woe-beridden burden of the editorials and the weighty matters of politics and where it ought to be able to wander in lovely fields and refresh itself informatively. And if one attempted to say how he happened to succeed where so many writers with their cheerful words turn outrage and abuse into a boring, deadly, and widely mocked thing, a comparison would be hard to find.

Here is an excerpt from an impressionistic description of the funeral services of some important man:

> Shrill and ghastly cries for help arose. I see bodies lying on the street and people's feet almost trampling them. I see children with expressions of horror. Why is it that children are always dragged into crowds? Why are the small trembling bodies of infants not spared and why are they brought into the obvious danger of being crushed? . . .
>
> Boys and men were hanging from the branches of trees. People try in vain to drive them away. They keep on climbing up. The curious take up positions even atop the fence of the Public Garden. They really cannot see anything, but they still remain where they are. That is the way they want it . . .

Privy Councillor Kozarek appears . . .

> Hats flew from heads before the hearse with its splendid white horses in their gold-covered caparisons . . .
>
> The gleaming swords swept within a hair's breadth of the faces of the onlookers . . .

But he met with particular approval when he took the opportunity once to express himself on the "viscid speech organs of Herr Kutschera."

The syntactic reforms he introduced into our writing made the man popular. But also in terms of what he wrote, through the outlook and tone of his articles, he always acted with the intention of providing a type of popular entertainment. The charming delusions he was used to producing, the grotesque presumptions in which the "genial Viennese wonder" indulged himself, exerted a considerable attraction. There is no important discovery that would have been made without *his* cooperation, no artistic personality who did not receive his first encouragement from *him*. Everything owes its genesis to *him*, he was the one who "made" everybody. It was he who at once recognized Mascagni's[62] greatness: "I did my best in order to help him with favorable reviews. . . . So I was of use to him, as they say; I have always been of use to others as well, even today." It was a long time before a German dramatist won his support. "Finally," he proclaimed, "did Hermann Sudermann[63] succeed in completely convincing me!"

Where the writer, either through Un-German or megalomania, absorbs the whole of the public's interest, nothing is left over for the painter. Only he could give the still life a meaningful impetus and win a name for himself as a first-rate painter of howlers. The portraitist has for a long time already been viewed with distrust. This made him so sensitive that, deeply wounded, he took his leave of an association whose chairman he had painted. Ultimately, only more deceased people came to be drawn by him. No reproach can touch him in such cases insofar as he has the excuse of the features distorted by death itself.

There are issues, worth the sweat of the noble, that hold the company at a neighboring table in suspense. No literary false note upsets the pure stage craze of these people; no Young Vienna artist goes astray here. On the 24th of April, who played the fat man in *The Wild Duck* in the Regensburg Stadttheater? When did Herr Rottmann make his last appearance in the Burgtheater?[64] These and similar subjects, usually heatedly discussed, must recede into the background when the vital question arises: Are there free tickets today? Every actor has a theater enthusiast at his side who listens to him with the same respect that the actor himself pays the critic of the table. There are, in fact, pathetic outer-city mimes who preserve the tradition of the Burgtheater in the Josefstadt. We find stage celebrities here who can look back on service in a theater box of long duration and who acquired a certain reputation as spectator-players of the Burgtheater.

There are also tables whose relationship to literature is at best only very casual. Here sit people whose talent expresses itself in marginal comments and glosses with which they supply the various journals lying about the literary coffeehouse. Many of them write for the leading domestic and foreign reviews. These authors do not sign their full names and as a result remain unfamiliar to the public at large. Nevertheless, each one of them possesses his own striking individuality. There is one, for example, who over a period of years and through the changes of direction to which this coffeehouse was subject held to his point of view; the one comment you read from him even today is "Jew!"

Not even this peak of productivity was attained by a group of young people to whom the pretext that they were easily responsive to moods ceded some small place in the hangout of modern writers. Several of them were able to make themselves useful to the extent that they mediated the traffic between the individual tables, brought the guests theater news, and actually spared many even the reading of journals. Several again appeared to take great pains to imitate the free customs of Parisian bohemians. The intention was honorable, but the talent too meager for indolence. When one day this society appeared no more, Heinrich the waiter asserted, in his usual delicate way, that the gentlemen owed more than just proof of literary talent.

All others will now part with heavy heart from the beloved scene of their activity. A great exodus is being prepared. The wrecking crew is banging on the windowpanes. The moment has come. All the literary implements—lack of talent, premature mellowness, poses, megalomania, sweet young girls, neckties, affectation, false datives, monocles, and rarified nerves—will be hastily gathered up. Everything has to go. Hesitant poets will be gently escorted out. Plucked from a gloomy corner, they shrink from the day whose light blinds them, from the life whose richness will oppress them. Against this light the monocle is but a weak defense; life will break the crutches of affectation . . .

Where is our young literature heading now? And what is its future Griensteidl?

Die demolirte Literatur, 1897. Translation based on text as given in vol. 4 of *Reihe Deutsche Satiren*, ed. Karl Riha. Karl Kraus, "Die demolirte Literatur," ed., with an afterword, by Dieter Kimpel (Steinbach: Anabas-Verlag Günter Kämpf KG, 1972).

1.   Franz Grillparzer (1791–1872), outstanding Austrian dramatist.

2.   Eduard von Bauernfeld (1802–90), prominent comedy actor of the period and a friend of Grillparzer's. He performed often at the Imperial Court Theater in Vienna and was ennobled in 1872.

3.   "Melange," in the German; the designation for a common coffee and cream blend in the Vienna coffeehouses.

4.   A reference to the Café Glacier in Paris, Boulevard des Italiens 22.

5.   The Café Kaiserhof in the Hotel Kaiserhof in Berlin on the Zietenplatz. The café, which was promoted as a Vienna-style coffeehouse, was a gathering place for literary people at the time.

6.   Kraus is referring to the writer Hermann Bahr, who is usually thought of as the moving spirit of the "Young Vienna" circle.

7.   A play of words in the original. Kraus writes: ". . . dass ihnen der Zopf nicht hinten hang," which means literally "that their tresses didn't fall rearwards." *Zopf* has the figurative meaning of "obsolete, antiquated custom."

8.   After the Vienna Stadttheater (City Theater) burnt down toward the end of 1885, the effort was made to establish a German popular theater to take its place. The first performance before a public in the new theater took place on 14 September 1889. The "Griensteidl guest" Kraus refers to here was Arthur Schnitzler, and the specific work by Schnitzler, the play *Das Märchen* (*The Fairy Tale*), which had its premiere at the Deutsches Volkstheater (German Popular Theater) on 1 December 1893.

9.   Gustav Kadelburg (1851–1925), a very popular actor in both Austria and Germany.

10.   Julius Bauer was the editor of the *Illustriertes Wiener Extrablatt* at the time.

11.   Isidor Fuchs, a Viennese writer and journalist of the second half of the nineteenth century.

12.   Ferry Beraton (real name Ferdinand Perathoner; 1859–1900). Actor, medical student, salesman, painter, poet, and art critic.

13.   Adalbert von Goldschmidt (1848–1906). A member of a prominent family with close ties to the Rothschild bank, he studied music, concentrating above all on the oratorio. His greatest musical success was the oratorio *Die sieben Todsünden* (*The Seven Deadly Sins*), which was performed for the first time in Vienna in December 1877.

14.   Henri Lavedan (1859–1940), a well-known Parisian journalist and writer of popular comedies.

15.   The pseudonym under which Hugo von Hofmannsthal published his first poetry in June 1890. It was taken from the name of a Russian general, Count Loris-Melikov, who died in 1888.

16.   The name used by two Venetian painters, Antonio Canale (1697–1768) and his nephew, Bernardo Bellotto (1720–1780), who are much admired for their luminous

canvases of city scenes. Bellotto is especially highly regarded for his superbly detailed and accurate paintings of such cities as Dresden, Vienna, and Warsaw.

17. Adele Sandrock (1863–1937), a well-known German actress.

18. Robert Nhil (real name, Reinhold Steegmüller; 1858–?), a German actor who, like Sandrock, performed in the Deutsches Volkstheater in Vienna.

19. Joseph Giampietro (1866–1913), a popular comic actor who also performed at the Vienna Deutsches Volkstheater.

20. Franz Tewele (1843–?), like Giampietro, a Vienna-born actor. He had a particular fondness for the Viennese operetta, folk plays, and French comedies of manners. He toured North America in 1882 and from 1890 performed regularly at the Deutsches Volkstheater.

21. Ludwig Martinelli (1832–1913), a well-regarded Austrian actor of Italian noble origin. He also performed at the Vienna Deutsches Volkstheater.

22. Viktor Kutschera (1863–1933), a Viennese actor who performed regularly at the Deutsches Volkstheater.

23. Adele Hell (1865–?), a Vienna-born actress who performed in Austria and Germany and later became affiliated with the Deutsches Theater.

24. Ida Bauer (1873–?), an Austrian actress who performed at the Deutsches Volkstheater and won critical acclaim for her Shakespearean roles at the Hamburg Stadttheater in 1898.

25. Moritz Broda (1842–1910), a Dresden-born actor who also played at the Deutsches Volkstheater.

26. A figure in Schnitzler's *The Fairy Tale*.

27. Josef Kainz (1858–1910), one of the most famous of Austrian actors.

28. Eleonora Duse (1859–1924), the celebrated Italian actress.

29. Located on the Ilm River, in the Erfurt district in southeastern Germany, Weimar has played an exceptionally important role in German culture and politics. In the sixteenth century, it became the capital of the duchy (after 1815, grand duchy) of Saxe-Weimar. Its fame as a cultural center is closely linked with the career of Goethe, whose association with the ducal court began in 1775. In German political history, Weimar won renown as the seat of the National Assembly, which in 1919 established the republican government that came to be known as the Weimar Republic.

30. Kraus is referring here to Hugo von Hofmannsthal, who wrote his first literary work at the age of sixteen.

31. A reference to Leopold Andrian (full name: Leopold von Andrian-Werburg).

32. A village in Lower Austria where Leopold Andrian spent some of his youth.

33. Kraus is referring to Leopold Andrian's most famous literary work, the auto-biographical novel *Der Garten der Erkenntnis* (*The Garden of Knowledge*, 1895).

34. "Selfmade-men" appears in English in the German text.

35. An apparent reference to Ferdinand von Baumgartner (1875–?), whose literary promise was based on a novel named "Franzi"—about an aristocratic girl—which circulated in manuscript.

36. The "sweet young girl" (*das süsse Mädel*, in German)—who was generally of lower social origin and from Vienna's outer-city working-class districts and with whom dalliances (marriage excluded, however) were fashionable, especially among army officers, the well born, and artists—was a common figure in turn-of-the-century Austrian literature. Schnitzler's prose fiction and plays offer perhaps the best definition of the type.

37. Kraus is referring to so-called Berlin naturalism.

38. A popular Viennese variety theater of the period.

39. Kraus is speaking here of Schnitzler.

40. "Die Pistolen sind mit Temperamentlosigkeit geladen," in the original. This means, literally: "The pistols are loaded with a lack of vivacity."

41. A reference to the writer Richard Beer-Hofmann.

42. Kraus is now launching an attack on Felix Salten. The "Burgtheater author" is, of course, Arthur Schnitzler.

43. The German-born actress Charlotte Wolter (1834–97), who was a leading lady at the Vienna Burgtheater from her debut there on 12 June 1862 until the time of her death.

44. Georg Reimers (1860–1936), an actor who became stage manager of the Vienna Burgtheater in 1920, an honorary member of the theater in 1922, and director of chorus as well as professor in 1925.

45. Hedwig Bleibtreu (1886–1958), an Austrian actress who performed widely in Germany as well as Austria. In 1883, she became a member of the Burgtheater.

46. The caryatids were priestesses of Artemis at Caryae in Laconia. The term is also used to indicate a draped female figure supporting an entablature.

47. A reference to the actor Adolf von Sonnenthal (1834–1909), who later in life also held major administrative positions at the Vienna Burgtheater.

48. Kraus gives a few more examples of Salten's putatively faulty grammar, this time involving confusion over the dative and accusative cases of the personal pronoun "er" (he)—"ihm" and "ihn," respectively. I have omitted these lines because they would make no sense in English given the grammatical differences between German and English.

49. In German: "*Einem* nur auf Niveau mit dem Dilettanten setzen." In correct usage, it would be "einen" (accusative of "einer") instead of "einem" (dative).

50. In the original, the grammatical error involves the preposition "mitsamt" (together with), which is followed by the dative case, not the genitive as quoted by Kraus. The German text reads: "serbisch-montenegrinische Verbindung mitsamt *des* [instead of "dem"] daranhängenden Heirathsgedankens."

51. Kraus, mocking Salten, himself uses the dative case of "einer" (someone) instead of the proper accusative after the verb "behindern" (handicap).

52. The sentence again mocks Salten by having the accusative case where the dative should be ("mit die" instead of "mit der") and the dative where the accusative should be ("auf dem . . . wirken" instead of "auf den").

53. A reference to Leo Eberman (1863–1914), the author of two tragedies, *Zwei Welten* (*Two Worlds*), with a Jewish ghetto setting, and *Die Athenerin* (*The Athenian Woman*). The production of the latter at the Vienna Burgtheater on 19 September 1896 was a considerable success.

54. Georg Büchmann (1822–89), a Berlin linguist who in 1864 published a collection of familiar quotations under the title *Geflügelte Worte*.

55. A line involving an obscure reference to an Austrian historian primarily of the Thirty Years War, Anton Gindely (1829–92), has been omitted here.

56. A reference to Leo Feld (real name, Leo Hirschfeld; 1869–1924), a journalist and dramatist of no great distinction.

57. Kraus is speaking about Felix Dörmann (real name, Felix Biedermann; 1870–1928), whose reputation as a leading poet of the Austrian turn of the century rests primarily on three early volumes of poetry: *Neurotica* (1891), *Sensationen* (1892), and *Gelächter*

(*Laughter,* 1902). There is a good discussion of the volume *Sensationen* in Jens Malte Fischer, *Fin de siècle: Kommentar zu einer Epoche* (Munich: Winkler Verlag, 1978), 114–24.

58. This seems to be an allusion to Viktor Léon (real name, Viktor Hirschfeld, Leo Feld's brother; 1858–1940). He is best known for the operetta librettos on which he collaborated, among them the one he and L. Stein wrote for Franz Léhar's *The Merry Widow* (1905).

59. Antaean was a giant defeated by Hercules.

60. A reference to Ferry Beraton. See note 12.

61. Eduard Hanslick (1824–1904) was a prominent and influential Viennese music critic.

62. The Italian composer Pietro Mascagni (1863–1945), whose greatest success was *Cavalleria rusticana* (1890).

63. Hermann Sudermann (1857–1928), prolific and widely translated German novelist and dramatist whose works deal primarily with contemporary social issues. The fame brought him by his play *Die Ehre* (*Honor,* 1890) convinced him of the wisdom of concentrating on dramatic writing.

64. Alexander Rottmann (1869–1916), a Hungarian-born actor who performed widely in the German-speaking world. He was best known for his appearance in heroic, manly roles, chiefly as the leading figure in Goethe's *Egmont.*

KRAUS NEVER LOST AN OPPORTUNITY TO VENT HIS SPLEEN AT THE LOW STANDARDS OF
VIENNESE JOURNALISM AND AT THE SAME TIME THE POPULARITY AND INFLUENCE ENJOYED
BY LEADING JOURNALISTS, ABOVE ALL THE WRITERS OF FEUILLETONS. And if they happened to be Jewish—as perhaps the majority of them were at the time—
malice and wit combined. Two of his favorite targets were Siegmund Münz
(1859–1934) and Felix Salten (1869–1945). "An Evening with the Bulgarian Royal Couple" and the three pieces that follow it comprise a small cycle
inspired by Münz's travels through, and reporting from, the Balkans during
the period 1892 to the First World War, when he worked for the *Neue Freie
Presse* as both a political correspondent and feuilletonist. After receiving
his doctor of philosophy degree from the University of Vienna in 1885,
Münz spent the next three years in Rome, where he wrote for several
Austrian and German newspapers. From 1889 to 1891, he divided his time
between Milan, Venice, and Florence. His prominence above all as a
political correspondent came with his employment with the *Neue Freie
Presse,* for which he not only covered sensitive areas such as the Balkans
but also attracted considerable attention with sensationalist interviews with
foreign heads of state and other dignitaries. On the basis especially of such
interviews, Münz developed an international reputation and was published
in a number of German, Italian, French, and English reviews. Münz's
familiarity with statesmen and world leaders also stood him in good stead
when he contributed political essays to the *Neues Wiener Journal* and cultivated the genre of the political portrait. Kraus's attacks on Münz concentrate on his reports from the Balkans, which, in Kraus's judgment, were
surrounded by a greater degree of idiocy than any of his other high-level
reportage. Moreover, they nearly provoked a war between Greece and
Turkey, which was grist for Kraus's mill, since recklessness and irrespon-
sibility were high on his list of Viennese journalism's most flagrant faults.
The pieces on Münz, all originally published in *Die Fackel,* are also interesting for the ironic way Kraus has woven into them parallels with Schiller's
play *Don Carlos* (final version 1805), with Münz playing the role of a latter-
day Marquis of Posa (a Knight of Malta and confidant of king, queen, and
prince), whose enlightened humanitarian ideals clash with the absolutist
outlook of King Philip II of Spain and who, to save Prince Carlos, pretends
that it is he, not the prince, who loves the queen.[1]

1.   There is a brief but interesting discussion of this aspect of the Münz satires in
Edward Timms, *Karl Kraus. Apocalyptic Satirist: Culture and Catastrophe in Habsburg Vienna,*
160–64. Timms regards these anti-Münz satires as among Kraus's best works. He writes:
"Kraus's response to the writings of Münz represents one of his most finely balanced
achievements" (162).

An Evening with the
Bulgarian Royal Couple

The *Neue Freie Presse,* which today is of the opinion that it can make a lot of fuss in the world with the intrusiveness, presumption, and stupidity of the '80s, filled four pages of its Sunday edition with a description of how the king of Bulgaria interviewed Siegmund Münz. This conversation between Münz and Majesty, which consisted of nothing other than the fact that Herr Münz found Sofia more modern but Constantinople, on the other hand, more antiquated, in many ways recalls the well-known interview that the Marquis Posa had with King Philip.[1] The difference is that the liberal hopes that Posa attached to the conversation, only to be later disappointed, Münz finds already fulfilled in King Ferdinand, without his having to first convert him to the ideals of the bourgeois world order.[2] On the contrary. The king at once said to him: "I very much regret the death of your colleague Schütz."[3]

The conversation might have taken place otherwise, as in Posa's time and as has been customary between a citizen of the world and a potentate from time immemorial—except for when the king of Spain allowed himself to be sounded out mainly on the important question of the freedom of thought and just at the very end ordered his visitor: "Seek out my son; explore the queen's mind." Herr Münz, meanwhile, was at once summoned to the family dinner party and had hardly arrived in Sofia when he was already on the heels of the queen and Crown Prince Boris. A certain parallel also emerges in that, as the Marquis Posa recounted, he had just come from Flanders and Brabant and had bumped up against burned human bones, while Herr Münz was coming from Leipnik[4] but kept on maintaining that he was in fact coming from Constantinople and missed in Sofia the picturesque traces of the past, everything here being so cultivated that he has the impression he "is in some new Hungarian provincial city and finds the place ever so much less Oriental."

Herr Münz means to say that the Bulgarians are a robust people, a great people and also a good people, everything you could want, and that the country has so many rich blossoming provinces. But "on the way here to Sofia, Your Majesty, I saw very few smokestacks. Industry in Bulgaria does not appear to be any more developed than in Turkey." Free speech, to be sure. Münz can't be a sovereign's footman. The king "stared at his opposite number" just the way that other monarch gazed at the good marquis, now with a look of amazement, now with astonishment, anticipation, and surprise. But Münz doesn't have to educate his king any further. "In the king, I had before me," he discerns, "a man of temperament and self-confidence and I would esteem him the same way even if he were not a king." It is indeed understandable that it ill becomes a journalist who sets store by his reputation and to whom every aspect of a royal court is alien to become blinded under the influence of a friendly reception by the brilliance of a crown to such an extent that he might want to overesteem its bearer in any way that might mislead the public. *Hail the majesty of the king—hail the complete independence of journalists!* Hey, hey! Münz cannot be a footman! Nothing to be done about it. (The king is moved.) Upon rising from the table, the nicest thing Münz could have said is: "My heart is full—the emotion too great, standing before you to whom I should like to open it."

But then he was dragged into conversation by the king. And here for the first time do we see revealed the entire difference between Posa and Münz, between the surprise the former and the satisfaction the latter must have felt. For while Posa sought gradually to bring King Philip around to permitting bourgeois felicity to become reconciled with sovereign nobility, Münz observed to his pleasant surprise that the king of Bulgaria— what a king-commoner!—is a peasant king, that "from the first day on he grasped the healthy kernel with the hard shell," became politically democratized, and utterly abandoned himself to the coarse Bulgarian national spirit. He still uses his cane, since he contracted gout in this climate, but above all to bring to an end an interview that threatens to last too long. It is never employed, however, for absolutist purposes. Otherwise he seems to place the greatest value on the presence of Münz, who is in no position to answer all the questions hurled at him by the royal family.

Münz is beset like a long-lost son. With all the other potentates of Europe he is treated like a child of the reigning dynasty; here, however, a quite special interest seems to attach to his endeavors. "How did you like Constantinople?" the king begins. "What were your impressions? You don't like everything in Constantinople?" . . . "And what impression did the troops make on you?" (Münz responded to this question by maintaining that he was no soldier, but the troops did in fact evoke his pleasure.) And the queen still wants to know: "And what impression did Constantinople make on you?" (Münz also replied to her question obligingly and fully asserting that he is a modern man of culture.) But the king asks: "Did you see the sultan?". . . "And what impression did the sultan make on you?" ("From the tired lines of his face," answered Münz, "I read a long tale of woe.") . . . "And what other impressions did you have of Constantinople? Did you see many people, the ministers, the deputies?" ("I had to see so many people," Münz answered, becoming a trifle impatient, noticeably terse, but tactful, "that I had little time left for such matters.") The unspoken question of Crown Prince Boris—And didn't you see little Kohn?—

by which the crown prince obviously meant the Constantinople correspondent of the *Neue Freie Presse,* Münz answered with another question, by which he clearly wanted to digress from politics. Namely, whether the crown prince, when he was in Bayreuth, did not become fatigued from the excessive length of the performances. "Not at all," said the crown prince, who, on the contrary, had trained by his visit to Bayreuth for Münz's visit to Sofia. And the queen now wished to bring the conversation to an end, since, evidently under the impression of the personality, she muttered to herself: "Yes, the Orient has its charm." Herr Münz parried modestly, saying: "Your Majesty has also come to know the Orient in its worst horrors." But as the queen was about to exclaim a courtly oh! he explained what he meant: "Your Majesty passed through Manchuria like a Samaritan." The queen again replied unassumingly: "A person has duties whatever his or her station in life." The misunderstanding was thus clarified. Herr Münz had Manchuria in mind, and the queen, the *Neue Freie Presse.* How close Münz is to the Bulgarian royal family is demonstrated by the fact that he "was in the position to tell the king" that years ago he had spent a pleasant week among friends in Ketschendorf Castle near Koburg and knows the crypt in which the king's parents lie. Whereupon at dessert the crown prince "presented him with a bonbon with a picture on it of his two sisters" and "asked him to take it with him as a memento of the occasion." The description of the royal banquet provided by Herr Münz wholly accords with the type of a king who has become entirely democratized. "The table was richly covered with flowers. Several pieces of old Sèvres came to our attention . . . The king, who is involved in everything . . ." No wonder he grasps the healthy kernel with the hard shell. The dining habits of Herr Münz can also be assumed from this description, for otherwise it would be inconceivable that the king, to whom after all the *Neue Freie Presse* is grateful for this full report, did not touch on this point. To be sure, this was inappropriate to the style of such an encounter, which accorded with the finest of world-historical forms.

As soon as Münz appeared, it was clear to the king that here was a head in which the world was represented differently than in other human heads. Münz admired the portraits of the king's parents that Herr von Angeli had painted. You could clearly hear the king suppressing the words "Odd sort of gusher!" Münz asserted that "in all Constantinople he never saw such plaster as in Sofia." The king (aside): "By God, he's reaching my very soul!" The Bulgarians "have to struggle with nature," said Herr Posa, and "a fury of construction can be seen everywhere." "A thankless task, their construction," thought Marquis Münz, "the hard struggle with nature has been waged for nothing." Since he didn't stop explaining to the king the difference between Sofia and Constantinople, the king might have been asked finally to recall the quotation: "No more on that subject, young man!"

The king pointedly refrained from making one observation. Herr Münz courageously declared that he missed industry in Sofia and foolhardily made the offer of an Austrian loan. The king for sure did not cut him short with the words: "You are a Protestant!" Otherwise Herr Münz most likely would have had to answer: "Your faith, Sire, is not mine!" The king instead spoke of the fact that "it had not been easy for him, as a foreigner, in Bulgaria," since the allusion in Schiller to the "crowned stranger" has again been deleted in later editions. Discrepancies here and there. On Herr Münz's part, there remained unspoken the thought "Leave me as I am. What would I be to you, Sire, if you, too, bought me off?" However, a special telegram from Sofia contains a remark with which the king concluded this memorable conversation. Court Marshal Draganov entered and the king exclaimed: "Under no circumstances, Draganov, will the idiot ever again be shown in, announced or unannounced!"[5]

"Ein Abend beim bulgarischen Königspaare," 1910. Original text in *Die Fackel*, no. 301–302, 3. Mai 1910, 47–51.

    1.   A reference to 3.3 of the 1805 version of Schiller's *Don Carlos*.

    2.   Ferdinand (1861–1948), who ruled Bulgaria from 1908 to 1918, was a grand-nephew of Ernest I of Saxe-Coburg-Gotha.

    3.   Friedrich Schütz was a colleague of Münz's at the *Neue Freie Presse* who also found himself the object of Kraus's scorn, particularly for his theater reviews.

    4.   The small Moravian town in which Münz was born.

    5.   A parody of the last line of 3.3 of *Don Carlos* in which King Philip instructs Count Lerma that henceforth the Marquis of Posa will be admitted unannounced.

S. M.

The journalistic success attained by the king of Bulgaria through his interview with Siegmund Münz did not allow the king of Romania to sleep. He competed for a similar interview and soon had the opportunity to greet S. Mz., who was now calling himself simply S. M., in Bucharest. The first thing we hear is: "Our yacht is anchored alongside the quay." But it's just a delusion. We're not on the Upper Danube, but actually in the vicinity of the Black Sea. A Romanian princess appears on the beach reminding S. M. of Ovid: "Even the Roman emperor's daughter Julia, in whom the aging poet was passionately in love, couldn't have been any lovelier than this Princess Bibesco strolling by herself and lost in conversation with the waves, which were rolling gently today but seldom ever rage angrily . . ." Enough! The king is waiting. Münz presents his credentials. But why?

People know who he is. However, the "Brahmins of Bucharest society were crowding in on all sides." It was, in fact, the king's birthday, and he had asked to see Münz. "We were afraid of remaining unnoticed in the sea of names." There was nothing to fear. The king was waiting and knew what was in store for him.

Münz had previously met Herr Jonescu, "a famous surgeon who had discovered a way to undertake the most serious operation on a fully conscious patient by means of a spinal injection." The king could thus calmly welcome Münz. But the latter was still temporizing. He paid a visit to the opera, where he espied in a box "an Oriental beauty enveloped in magical enchantment, a pallid Salambô figure, and like the heroine of the Goncourts' novel she, too, appeared at a masked ball." *Salambô* happens to be by Flaubert, but no matter. "In contrast to the one bathed in the southern glow of the Orient's colors stands the purer, more symmetrical Germanic beauty of the crown princess. There in another box sits the blonde, rosy-cheeked, and blue-eyed crown princess in the luminous magic of her still fresh . . ." Enough! The king is waiting. But Münz still pokes around Bucharest a bit more. Again, as in Sofia, he compares the cityscape with that of Constantinople, and not with that of Leipnik. "Since we are coming from Constantinople, our demands on the spell of the East, on the romanticism of decay, on the charm of the contemplative, remain unsatisfied." Münz is quite demanding. He confesses: "Strong aspirations without the scent of fairy tale are perceptible here." What do you know!

After this, they were received by the minister for foreign affairs. "They" because throughout the entire trip Münz accompanied a Sir Max Wächter, who was carrying a lot of superfluous baggage with him, namely, a plan for an economically based European federation. Herr Wächter was presenting his plan to the rulers and ministers of all the Balkan states. All of them had the same thing to say: "We can have only the greatest sympathy for this, but we are a small country," which Herr Münz keeps on reporting to us. The Balkans send geegaw peddlers to Europe, and Europe takes revenge by sending back Sir Max Wächter, who time and again offers an economically based federation. And the king waits. At last!

"He immediately drew me into a friendly conversation." These kings always do this in order to quickly overcome the first unpleasant impression. "Only at the beginning of our conversation did I have the opportunity to look the king straight in the eye a bit." But the king preferred seeing Herr Münz in the dark, and "just at the moment he got up to leave did the electric lights blaze up." Here Münz made a noteworthy observation. "I had not seen the king for years. *Since then he got older . . .*"

The interview itself went splendidly. The king wanted to find out everything he could; indeed, he was perhaps even more curious than the

Bulgarian one. "With great friendliness, the king inquired about the places I had visited on my previous trip to the Orient of several weeks' duration and asked me if I was in Romania for the first time and how I liked it. I told the king by way of a reply that I was in Romania for the first time and that I feel very much at home because of the Latin sounds of the language." Interesting that he calls these sounds "Latin." But immediately thereafter he laid his cards on the table: "I must confess to Your Majesty that here I have the feeling of being incomparably nearer to Vienna than to Constantinople." His memory was also anchored right alongside the quay. But then things took a diplomatic turn. "Your Majesty has the indisputable reputation of being a bulwark of peace in southeastern Europe," and "Your Majesty is regarded as a guarantor of the status quo in the Balkans." It was then the king's turn to speak again. He was of the opinion, he declared, that the public tends to attach too much importance to meetings between monarchs. "The king presented his views in a quite straightforward way without any note of didacticism." What else would you expect! But the interview between His Majesty of Romania and His Münz of the *Neue Freie* is also likely to be given too much importance. It was of an entirely personal character. The king just wanted to know this and that. The Bulgarian had asked about Constantinople. The king of Romania "inquired about the impressions I had formed in Sofia." One is anxious to know how the Balkan sovereigns are going to sort it all out. But the Romanian himself compared Bucharest and Sofia. "I regret having to say that the number of illiterates in Romania is greater than in the Kingdom of Bulgaria." However, that was no insult, since Münz was now in Romania and no longer in Bulgaria.

Münz was very tactful in directing the conversation to Jew-baiting, for which he placed the blame on backwardness. "The Jewish question has been one of the gravest concerns of my reign," the king said, at the same time openly glancing at his watch, "and it continues to concern me." Münz failed to get the message and appealed to humanity: "Given Your Majesty's wise understanding, it should follow that . . . well, you know, equal rights . . . all your subjects." The king sensed at that point that an editorial was in the making and quickly nipped it in the bud. "The Jewish question is not a question of religion to us; it is an economic question. The Romanian is by nature tolerant. But it is the economic preponderance of the Jews to which the national mood is opposed. Agrarian banks have been established. Help protect the Romanian element against pernicious exploitation." The agrarian banks, that is, not the *Neue Freie Presse*, which clearly did not take note of this remark of the king's and which will direct Münz henceforth to leave the audience room immediately should the king of Romania again express such views, which could then slip through during printing. But Münz tried just this once to influence the king: "Your Majesty, the objective understanding of monarchs, who walk the peaks of mankind, often mitigates the people's sufferings." Bravo!

The king changed his tune. "And how often this responsibility really is incumbent upon us!" he acknowledges. For the most part, Münz knows how to catch his attention with original figures of speech. How is the king progressing with his memoirs? "It would be most desirable if Your Majesty could again take up the broken threads of the narrative." Or: "In Romania's foreign policy, I asserted, we recognize the wise guiding hand of the skilled helmsman who for more than four decades has ruled the country." "Have you looked about Bucharest?" the king replied. And then: "Are you going on to Sinaia?" And finally: "*I know the queen would also like to see you.*" The audience had lasted an hour and a quarter.

"The queen received me a few moments later and kept me with her until after eight-thirty." A whole hour. "But the conversation was too substantive and important for me to able to reproduce it within the framework of these reports . . ." 5 May 1910. Until today, 27 May, nothing has appeared. The *Neue Freie Presse* can and still does bring out Münz-receptions without end!

The Turkish successor to the throne, Yussuf Izzedin Efendi, must also believe it. We meet Münz again in Constantinople, where his demands on the magic of the East will be completely satisfied. In the waiting room, he saw "an old Oriental and a young one." (Münz is a man well in his forties.) "The old one is the Orient to a *T* . . . He rings his hands, shuts his eyes, moves his lips." Münz takes it for a prayer. But the man is really cursing. The East is defending itself. The old man hopes Münz will go away. "He bows down, straightens himself up again, and again throws himself to the ground, and so it continues well more than a dozen times, an unending rotation of contrition and deliverance . . ."

Münz is finally escorted away. After all, the successor to the throne is waiting. His first meeting has been with Sir Max Wächter. Is an economically based European federation agreeable? No, thanks. The successor to the throne then addresses the following statement to Münz: "I have high regard for the great value of the press. It is one of the most effective means of serving human progress, and your vigilant eye is often successfully directed to preserving the liberal institutions that are absolutely necessary to this progress." Münz "gives the impression of being satisfied with this declaration." The successor to the throne continued: "Our constitution is the banner of our progress." He spoke like a fez manufacturer who publishes an appeal in the *Neue Freie Presse* as a municipal council candidate for the first eligible voter of [Vienna's] First District.

The real interview then began. "Are you in Constantinople for the first time? And how do you like it here?" "The first time, Imperial Highness," answered Münz, "and I am overcome by the beauty of this city, which is so unique in the world. But may I be permitted a frank word? It would be most desirable for this splendid city to develop in a modern direction . . ." Among the facilities named by Münz as definitely lacking in Constantinople was the telephone. The successor to the throne said: "*Please be patient with us*. I do hope that when you come back here in ten years' time you will be able to see . . ." Earlier, what the successor to the throne had hoped for was not to see Münz in Constantinople. The successor to the throne held out the prospect of progress. Münz immediately raised the issue of investments. "May one anticipate, Imperial Highness, that foreigners, too, will be permitted to participate in the economic development of Turkey?" The successor to the throne brushed this aside and declared that "the constitution [is] the guarantee of the equality of all nations and religions." Münz lit up. "Thus non-Turks and non-Muslims, Imperial Highness, will also enjoy the security of the constitution . . ." He says "security," the other says "shelter." He says "equal obligations and equal rights of all citizens," the other says "authorized safeguarding of national and religious differences." Münz then declared that General von der Goltz Pasha wrote for the *Neue Freie Presse*. The successor to the throne asked: "Did you see a military review during your stay in Constantinople?" Münz had nothing but praise for the military. The successor to the throne was glad that, unlike Sir Max Wächter, he was not "for the abolition of armies." "And the prince smiled and rubbed his hands together." Münz proceeded to explain Herr Wächter's program and spoke of the status quo. Whereupon the successor to the throne also spoke about status quo and added: "There is nothing as important as serving progress in time of peace through the strengthening of the constitution." The successor to the throne kept repeating the word "constitution" over and over again and, to be sure, in this European form, not in the Turkish translation.

But now Sir Max Wächter was about to be received by the sultan and would relate everything to Münz, and he in turn, to us. When Münz accompanied him on his way, he observed a new spectacle: Three boys entered carrying something or other. "Unexperienced in the customs of the imperial palace, I thought it had to do with the preliminaries of some religious function." But it was just black coffee being served. "And when I held the cup in my hand, I noticed to my astonishment that the golden saucer was entirely studded with diamonds." Münz was even more aston-ished when he learned later from somebody in the know that "until the very present, not a single one of the golden diamond-studded cups is missing from the imperial service." And indeed until now there were only editorial writers but no economists in the seraglio.

The audience concerning the economically based federation came to an end. As they rode past the parliament, Münz quoted: "The place is burnt down!" But for a long time memories of the conversation with the successor to the throne accompanied him, "especially the memory of how he kept on repeating the foreign word 'constitution' over and over again . . ." The Bosphorous is becoming foul, the Balkans are exploding, and the sovereigns are finally concluding an economically based federa-tion, since they have no other way of getting the *Neue Freie Presse* to refrain from sending Münz to them anymore.

"S.M.," 1910. Original text in *Die Fackel*, no. 303/304, 31 Mai 1910, 6–12.

THE QUESTION OF CRETE

Münz, whom the Greek royal family was to be saddled with next, heard that they were on Corfu and determined not to let the opportunity slip by. He betook himself to Corfu, immediately dragged the king into con-versation, and the result was that it almost came to war between Greece and Turkey. No joke. The king's subjects who have any dealings with Herr Münz have to be prepared for any eventuality. In the foreground an idiot presents his calling card, and behind him the cannons are already talking. But they are not talking to Herr Münz, who wouldn't hear what they're saying. He is too preoccupied already writing his column and thinking mostly not about cannon balls but about the renowned [pastry] balls of the ritual kitchen, which have never yet torn a hole in the belly of anybody from Leipnik. To the rear, far away, in Turkey, people are fighting each other. That's what happens when one of our colleagues gets the chance.

His Majesty Münz was thus on Corfu. The general adjutant was unable to "bid him even be seated." It was the king's name day. The general adjutant had a choice between the Te Deum and Münz. He chose the Te Deum. Münz had a recommendation to a certain Herr Theotokis, across whose breast "was draped the wide blue ribbon of the order of the Greek Savior." This gentleman, therefore, was impervious to harm. In fact, hardly did the conversation begin "when suddenly Mr. Mac Kinnan, the first officer of the yacht *Rovenska*, which had borne us here across the Ionian waters, burst in and shouted to us almost breathlessly: 'A royal message!'"

What was it that caused our otherwise so imperturbable Scottish friend to adopt such a frenzied tempo? An invitation from His Majesty to Majesty Münz. The king spake, the page ran, and Mr. Theotokis was saved.

Münz put him off until afternoon and went to the king. The king told him everything that was on his mind. First, a question in confidence: "Did you hear that for a moment thought was given to summoning another dynasty?" Münz shook his head; but he must have known it. The king: "Can *you* satisfy everybody? You assume a smaller responsibility and therefore need to satisfy a smaller circle of people." Who says so? Well, maybe; there are more Greeks than subscribers to the *Neue Freie Presse,* but they're scattered over the whole world. The king now asked Münz—guess what! Well, we guessed it: "The king asked me if I was in Greece for the first time and how I liked it in Athens." There seemed to be an agreement among Balkan sovereigns mainly to ask Münz whether he had been here or there and how he liked it. Unaware that he was being humored, he asserted that he was in Constantinople, in Sofia, in Bucharest "for the first time in my life, Majesty!" And he continued like the educated man in the "local train studies" who always travels from Vienna to Baden: "I can hardly emphasize enough how fortunate I was to be able to celebrate a reunion, so to speak, with the enchanted places on which the glory of antiquity lies, a reunion insofar as we had already been beholding it all in our minds from early youth on. But I also very much liked the modern aspect of Athens—the splendid palaces donated by Greek patriots for public use, the clean pretty streets, a first-class hotel. Comfort of every kind in Athens."

And then the king availed himself of the opportunity, as long as Münz was already there, to sound him out on the Cretan question. "I have been on the throne since 1863, and from the very first hour I have had the Cretan question on my back," the king said literally and thought that since Münz was in fact in this part of the world, he could settle the matter *prima vista.* Münz responded at once with a very political observation, to which the king said: "So you, too, are reproaching us . . . My answer to you is . . ." And sure enough, the words "status quo" are uttered. "You were, I hear, on Crete? What was achieved there until the arrival of the Greek high commissioner? Nothing, absolutely nothing." "I can only agree with Your Majesty. With respect to all traffic conditions, the situation is straight out of the Middle Ages." (We learned later that while he was on Crete, Münz was told: "We can't even traffic with each other there normally.") Münz then asked the king if there were other islands that are Greek but still belong to Turkey. The king shrugged his shoulders and replied that he wanted only Crete. Münz: "Your Majesty, a thoroughly proper desire, it seems to me, wholly in accord with my own sentiments." The king experienced a strong sense of gratification. "After about a half-hour's conversation, the king discharged me, accompanied me through the opposite chamber, and made an allusion to the fact that he would be glad to see me again on Corfu." At all events, he gave me greetings for an especially charming and beautiful lady of Vienna society." (Münz is discreet and names no names.)

Meanwhile, the king of England died. "I was now certain," said Münz, "that our invitation to the court, which we had received the day before, would be recalled at the last moment." But he failed to take his popularity into account. This can cope with any and all court mourning. Soon he heard "that the invitation was still in effect; it would take place, explained the general adjutant, only once and with the smallest circle of people in attendance . . ." Münz just had to be there.

Münz on Corfu; the king didn't have to repeat it twice. Conversation at the table was, to be sure, "rather forced," but it took place. What king of England? When Münz of the press was in Greece for the very first time in his life, disinviting him to a family dinner would have been such a sensational violation of international hospitality that the thought of risking it wasn't entertained even once. A war with Turkey on account of Münz— sure; but not one with the *Neue Freie Presse!*

The king, "entirely taciturn, from time to time directed the conversation to me." "Once he said: 'Regretfully, I saw you yesterday in a box in the theater.' 'Why, Majesty, regretfully?'" And the king did not reply as anticipated: "Because I saw you in the theater." Instead, he said: "Because the production left much to be desired." At this point Münz made a very sensitive observation: "But it did indeed afford me pleasure to hear for the first time in my life the sounds of the Greek language from the stage, even if just in the translation of the *Waltzertraum*. With all due respects, Majesty, to the talents of the composer, my fellow countryman. But we had the better of the bargain when the Greeks gave us their tragedies and took our operettas in exchange." Bravo! That is why the crown prince was introduced to him.

"The crown prince is a clever individual, which you can barely tell from looking at him . . . he speaks good German." Münz doesn't. The crown prince yields nothing to the king in outspokenness and complained to Münz about his exclusion from the chief command. Münz consoled him: "The future king of the Hellenes will still have a great mission even if he is no longer now the head of the army." "The crown prince praised the virtues of the Greeks but complained that they have little liking for discipline, unlike the Germans, for example, the nation of iron discipline." He remarked: "The Greeks are strange." The crown prince was not allowed to ride a bicycle, skate, or play tennis. Münz said: "That surprises me, Your Royal Highness. Sport is, after all, a legacy to mankind of Greek culture, which gave careful thought to the highest physical development." You can see it was just the right time for the conversation to be interrupted by the appearance of the queen.

Now almost the entire openhearted family had gathered about Münz. The queen, too, immediately "urged" something "on him." To wit, "not to leave Corfu without having made some excursions into the surrounding areas." Perhaps she really had in mind for him to take some trips around Corfu and then leave the island. "This is a real paradise," she said, and then began quoting Baedecker: "There are splendid roads everywhere, on which you can travel comfortably not only by carriage but also by automobile."

But then a ticklish subject arose. "The queen thought that she missed a Viennese accent in my German pronunciation." She was right on target. "I replied that I came from Moravia, from a region where the German and Slavic populations bordered on each other." "There are Czechs, I believe," the queen said mischievously, "who live next to the Germans there." The queen then touched on "the power of the sun, which, in the form of sunbaths, can cure certain illnesses." The queen is, you know, a good Samaritan by calling. "She thinks in very humane terms." "She knows the horrors of war from her own observations. She saw at first hand the consequences of the Greek-Turkish campaign . . ." Of the past one. But now she could see at first hand the cause of the future one, namely Herr Münz.

At this point, Sir Wächter joined the conversation, that gentleman who, as we know, wanted to create a federation based on economic grounds. Finally, Prince George also had the desire to meet Münz, came up to him, and posed several questions to him, such as: "Do the Turks have even the slightest claim to Crete? Did they ever accomplish anything there? And aren't even the Mohammedans on Crete Greeks?" Instead of saying simply: "What do you want from me?" or "Do I know?" or "I should have your troubles!" or whatever one usually says in such situations, Münz got embroiled in debates. After finally catching on to the continuous allusions of various members of the royal family to Crete and Cretans and the giggling of the prince, whom the queen kept jabbing in the ribs, he thought it best to withdraw. But the queen called after him: "And please don't forget to give my warmest greetings to the charming Frau . . . . in Vienna." (Münz is discreet and names no names.) The king wanted to make a return visit to him on the yacht, "but the death of King Edward caused him to forgo it." So that was out. But the crown prince insisted on it. "At the stroke of five" he came to tea (otherwise there wouldn't have been any five o'clock tea). Several barques sailed up and gave Münz a "veritable Neapolitan serenade." It was very nice. "The crown prince ended his visit after two and a half hours" and headed back to the castle, to which Münz made a point of accompanying him . . .

"When we awakened the next day, we saw Father Etna smoking his morning pipe." This is a very euphemistic description of what Father Etna did when he saw Münz. In the evening—that is, "as day retreated into darkness"—Münz strolled "with heavy heart among the ruins of Messina," not without being able to express the thought of "how close enchantment and death, splendor and ruin, are to each other in life." No doubt, life is just a mess. But the most frightful contrast is between an interview and a war. A king becomes talkative in the presence of a traveling fool and the next thing you know Europe is in flames.

"Constantinople, 8 June. The communiqués of the *Neue Freie Presse* concerning the statements made to a staff member of this paper by King George of Greece were discussed yesterday in official quarters." A formal denial is demanded, a boycott against Greece is threatened. The king vacillated. The *Neue Freie Presse* sticks to its guns. The column "The Statements of King George to a Staff Member of the *Neue Freie Presse*" is continuing. The grand vizier exhorts the Greek emissaries to revoke the king's statements concerning the annexation of Crete. *Tanin* (*The Dawn*) demands "an official denial or war."[1] The Greek subjects living in Turkey are being threatened with expulsion. A boycott committee was also established in Salonika and a blockade of Greek shipping imposed. Anger is growing. Demands are being heard for the convocation of a congress of all Berlin Treaty powers. The king's statements are being called a "frightful suicide." The rumor is going around that massacres of Greeks have been planned. Münz is on his way back to the paper. The king vacillates. The *Neue Freie Presse* sticks to its guns. Will the king decide for war or against the *Neue Freie Presse?* He is opting for denial. The retaliatory measures are being rescinded. The situation stabilizes. *Tanin* declares that henceforth no responsible leader in Greece will issue any declarations offensive to Turkey. Shame, cries the *Neue Freie Presse:* "The noteworthy story of how *King George should be compelled, under the pressure of international complications, to issue a formal denial of the statements made through our correspondent,* has been reported by us repeatedly. *Tanin,* nevertheless, speaks of a previously published denial of which we are unaware. Until now, this denial has not reached us. Our correspondent scrupulously reported what the king said to him and his reports *remain reliable,* whether the denial appears or not. The Editors."

The paper insists on war. Its famous impudence will also emerge victorious from this campaign. It is not abandoning Münz. He leaves the Balkans convinced of the faithful performance of his duty. He has spoken with many kings, but none of them ever dared subsequently deny something he never said in the first place! . . . One wonders how the king wriggled out of it. A rumor is making the rounds that he brought off a diplomatic masterpiece. The whole thing was a misunderstanding. Everything was reliably reported except that it didn't have anything to do with the Cretan question but rather with the question of whether or not cretinism is curable.

"Die kretensische Frage," 1910. Original text in *Die Fackel*, no. 305/306, 20. Juli 1910, 11–16.

    1.   *Tanin* was a leading Turkish newspaper of the time.

Don Münz

What have we missed for a whole year? Dismissed by the king of Romania on 22 April 1910, at 7:15 in the evening, Münz, as a result of an intrigue on the part of the palace lady Eboli (who was played by Barsescu[1]), got the key to the queen's quarters and disappeared inside. He reserved the right to come back to the episode in a special article. That was on 5 May, and I wrote: "The *Neue Freie Presse* is able to publish it and even makes a point of it." We've now been waiting a whole year. There must have been some riotous scenes, but on 9 April 1911, he restrained himself no longer and told his story.

    The queen, it seems, was lying on a chaise longue, clad entirely in white, as Münz entered. "Her eyes shone with a brilliant lustre . . . She was sufficiently dignified so that one could not forget that she was the queen, but her manner was so human, so natural, so sparkling that it was easy to believe one was far from the court." Then a motif from [Schiller's] *Wallenstein* intruded on the scene between Elizabeth and Don Münz so long desired by the parties themselves as well as by the public. He found none other than Sir Max Wächter with her. He had expounded on his well-known plan for an economically based European federation in other circles, and "among none of the other sovereigns to whom he had presented his plan for an economically based European federation did the English gentleman find such an enthusiastic response as with the queen of Romania." She was "at once excited about the matter" and in her idealism forgot "how endlessly difficult feasibly ideal plans are and how things get botched in the execution." And since, by way of contrast, thoughts live easily together, we are thus in the midst of Wallenstein, and the queen actually said when S. M. entered: "There is no reason at all for Sir Max to leave us." It can't be, she just refuses to believe that Max can leave her when Münz comes. Man is, after all, cut from common cloth. She lay there, expecting no assault, but that is exactly the fate of the beautiful on earth. Grave is the sight of need. There are moments in life. The world is narrow and the brain weak. What can you do? Drink tea. "She sipped it lying down. From time to time, as she chatted, I had to hand her a sandwich." But besides that, he also handed her two books, whereupon she said: "I'll devour that," a remark which Münz applied to the books.

While the queen thus observed Münz before her, she began to talk about the blind and to extol her fate. For not only has she repaid destiny handsomely, she also promises them much. The queen proposes that the state should bring all its sightless people together in a single city: "There should also be there some tradespeople who would look after the sale of the blind people's work so that they can live from the proceeds, marry, and support their children." The queen speaks like a book and like one by Carmen Sylva.[2] (Humanity is as blind as justice. She places the sightless manufacturers under the protection of merchants who can see. The city of the sightless would be well provided for if a few farsighted tradesmen took the enterprise into their own hands!)

Münz was in raptures over her ideas. And equally excited by her willingness "to speak about the relationship to monarchs and courts." ("He and the queen are one. The venom of the innovators, heretofore concealed, seeps into both their breasts.") She surely intends it differently than he. "I often ask myself what people really get out of it when they come face to face with royal personages in lamentably formal circumstances, what possible use all the fainthearted crawling is to them. There is just one explanation for it, and that is that they evidently feel themselves uplifted by such behavior. Such people believe, I imagine, that a glimmer of the presumed lustre of the majesties falls on them . . ." So says the queen. But Münz, who again had to hand her a sandwich, calls it frankness and fair-mindedness.

She speaks of the king and complains "how little she is able to enjoy the king, who from morning until evening is burdened with affairs of state." Only when he was sick did he belong to her entirely; that was because she massaged him. "The queen spoke of the king in the warmest terms and praised the fact that his loyalty was beyond doubt. Münz then interjected: "Would you like to commit your memories to paper, Majesty?" The suggestion was gratifying to her, she rang, and a book entitled *My Household Nook* was brought in. These were her memoirs, and instead of a loftier kind of gossip they are "memoirs, so to speak, of the soul." "When the queen read aloud the chapter titled 'Bernays,' I remarked: 'Your Majesty means, I assume, Michael Bernays?'"[3] The queen responded with a gesture of her hand which seemed to say, annoyedly: "I do not bother with people of such ilk." "She exclaimed as well: 'What? Michael? Heavens, no! Jacob Bernays!'"[4]

Münz received a copy containing a bookplate "depicting the queen stepping pensively among the tree trunks of a forest." Below, she had written the dedication: "We wander through the world and sometimes, besides trees, even encounter—spirits! Carmen Sylva." Münz had to control himself. ("Am I not strong, Elizabeth?") But what did she have against Michael Bernays? Jacob was the better authority on Aristotle. "But he never dined with us." And why not? Since he was also the better Jew. The queen gives him his due. (Münz is enlightened and will really not be deterred from supping with the queen of Romania.)

She expresses herself disparagingly with respect to people who become baptized. "The queen spoke in a voice that penetrated a person's very soul." With two poems that she then read aloud, "she grasped your heart." But Münz was absolutely crushed when the queen again spoke of religion and made a point of boasting that intellectually distinguished people turn completely away from her. (He could now calmly remain for supper.) The Jewish ones especially she was only too happy to let go their own way. (No, he couldn't remain for supper after all!)

Since until now the queen had tried her hand just at the feuilleton, S. M. endeavored to draw her out for the lead article. He keeps on referring to her husband as "the Hohenzollern" or even as "the Hohenzollern on the Romanian royal throne" and delivers the following period in her presence: "When I saw the two Spanish diplomats in their gold-covered uniforms on their way to the palace in order to present their credentials to the Hohenzollern on the Romanian royal throne, there stood plainly before me the episode from the year 1870 which initiated the Franco-German war. The candidacy of the Hohenzollern, the brother of King Karol, for the Spanish royal throne was vividly before me—the small cause of a big effect. All that came to life before me when I saw those men in Spanish court dress moving toward the palace of the Hohenzollern in the Calle Victorei." The queen seems doubtful that Münz is aware of the meaning of the Spanish word "calle," which is the same as "street." She is also opposed to formalities and prefers to talk about another Spanish envoy. "He grasped my hand, kissed it ecstatically, and thanked me warmly for all the encouragement that his deceased spouse, a Cuban, who was a soulmate of mine, had derived from my writings."

"It grew late." (Be quiet! Didn't you hear something? The queen: I hear nothing but the terrible bell tolling for our separation.) "The queen was informed that the supper was ready." (Am I not strong, Elizabeth?) "The queen expressed the intention of seeing me *the next day*. But to my regret, I had previously made all necessary preparations in order to leave that night on the Orient Express." Did the queen suspect it? "I took my leave of her with the impression that in one of the forward outposts of civilization in the East I came across a woman with the greatest yearning for knowledge and with humane ideals that even in the farthest West strive for fulfillment." And which unfortunately can be completely attained with the Orient Express. "Good night, then," calls the Infante, "you will receive from Vienna my article which will make public the secret of our relations . . . From now on I want nothing hidden between us. You need not fear the eyes of the world. This is my last foolishness." (The king, accompanied by the editor of *Die Fackel* and his grandees, appears in the background without being noticed.) "It is your last!" . . . (Coldly and quietly to the editor.) "Do what you must!"

"Don Münz," 1911. Original text in *Die Fackel*, no. 321–322, 29. April 1911, 1–5.

    1.   The princess Eboli is a character in Schiller's *Don Carlos*. Agatha Barsescu (1864–1939) was a Romanian actress who rose to prominence at the Vienna Burgtheater. Her career was promoted especially by Adolf Wilbrandt during his directorship of the Burgtheater from 1881 to 1887. The well-known critic Ludwig Speidel once dubbed her "the luck of the Burgtheater."

    2.   A reference to Elizabeth (1843–1916), queen of Romania, consort of King Karol I. She was of German birth, but after her marriage to Karol in 1869, she identified with the Romanian people and immersed herself in their culture. Under the pseudonym Carmen Sylva, she wrote a number of works in German, French, English, and Romanian. The one referred to here is *Pensées d'une reine* (A Queen's Thoughts, 1882).

    3.   Michael Bernays (1834–97) was a German literary historian who wrote principally on Goethe and Shakespeare.

    4.   Jacob Bernays (1824–81) was a well-known German classical philologist.

FELIX SALTEN WAS ONE OF KRAUS'S FAVORITE WHIPPING BOYS FROM AS EARLY AS *THE DEMOLISHED LITERATURE*. A very successful and popular writer of feuilletons, criticism, and fiction, who at least on one occasion physically assaulted him, Salten represented to Kraus everything that was morally reprehensible in contemporary Viennese journalism. To Salten's further discredit—in Kraus's estimation—was his professional association with papers owned by the shady Hungarian newspaper entrepreneur Imre Békessy, whom Kraus campaigned to drive out of Vienna. Kraus never lost an opportunity to deride Salten in *Die Fackel*. The following two selections are typical. In

"From the Wastepaper Basket" ("Aus dem Papierkorb," 1909), Kraus takes aim at Salten's predilection for writing about the imperial family and aristocracy as well as his obvious desire to enjoy their recognition. The following piece, "Rabbits with Jewish Dialect" ("Jüdelnde Hasen," 1929) was inspired by Salten's extraordinary fame as the author of *Bambi*.

In 1929, a year after the publication of *Bambi*, Salten came out with a new work of fiction about animals, *Fünfzehn Hasen: Schicksale in Wald und Feld* (*Fifteen Rabbits: Fate in Forest and Field*), originally issued by the Vienna publisher Zsolnay. An English translation of it under the title *Fifteen Rabbits: A Celebration of Life* was published by Simon and Schuster in 1930. Anxious to deflate Salten after the huge success of *Bambi*, Kraus wrote the following piece for *Die Fackel* mocking the "Jewish" speech habits of Salten's rabbits. "Exposing" Jewish writers and other prominent figures with changed names (like Salten) as well as ridiculing the putative Jewish mannerisms in their speech (which Kraus does in his anti-Salten "Rabbits with Jewish Dialect") was a favorite pastime of Kraus and an outlet for negative feelings about his own Jewishness. Kraus also could not resist the temptation in "Rabbits with Jewish Dialect" to deride Salten further by mentioning the pornographic novel *Josefine Mutzenbacher*, which was published anonymously but is usually attributed to Salten.

FROM THE WASTEPAPER BASKET

. . . [Felix Salten] has truly become intimately bound up with the Habsburg tradition like no other feuilletonist in Austria. The intimacy that allows him to participate in all the fortunes of the imperial family so that *Die Zeit* was the first paper to publicize Leopold Wölfling's early history and to exhibit his photographs in the communiqué room, this great connoisseurship, also enabled him to say an authoritative word concerning the elevation of rank of the princess Hohenberg.[1] Astonishing above all was the impartiality that permitted one in the court sphere of domestic journalists to voice his unconditional yea to the marriage of the successor to the throne: "We neither determine so exactly nor reckon that the Choteks have borne the count's coronet barely two hundred years, nor do we weigh the prerogatives of equal birth too carefully." Prepared to subordinate the interests of the family to considerations of state, he acknowledges that "this marriage remains an enduring event" and that it "remains important for us in Austria, for our present as well as for our future."

He must certainly have appreciated the fact that a Countess Chotek cannot become an archduchess of Austria and why she cannot become one. But with genuine sympathy he "measured the road she had traversed since the day of her wedding: Your Grace . . . Serene Highness . . . Duchess . . . Majesty . . ." And today, looking back, he can speak of the difficulties, of the "endless expenditure of tact and tactics, of energy and the power of resistance" that it must have cost. "We knew nothing of it, but now we realize it," he declares modestly, with restrained feeling, in order, through exhaustive enumeration, to ease the heart of a duchess. We didn't know it. "Only now do we note that it was in no way anything self-evident, and so on and so on." "Only now can we recall what it meant that the archduke and his wife for years occupied an ordinary box in the Burgtheater and that now he takes his place with her in the royal box." Rose Bernd, as we know, wasn't permitted anymore into the Burgtheater, but the sigh "What she must have suffered!" suggests itself to us in the present case.[2] "It lasted for nine long years," says Salten not without bitterness, "and it could not have been easy." Well now, come, come . . . And more than once we are reminded "what this woman's nature is" and can only "surmise that she possesses unusual qualities, that she is a strong and unique personality." And within the confines of such suppositions one can but guess. "Behind all that there must be a great strength of will, an iron resolve of character, or an irresistible goodness, a thousandfold knowledge of life, a remarkable refinement of instinct, or also naturalness, or even utter passivity, single-mindedness, or imperturbable trust in luck. We simply do not know." The searching mind resigns in the face of the last two attributes.

Who can resolve the problem of the duchess von Hohenberg? "Legitimate interests passionately favor this woman." Will she win out or will she not win out? We simply do not know. "Perhaps the battle is already over. We are incapable of passing judgment on that, either. We do not know what else must occur in order for the wife of the successor to the throne to be permitted publicly to exercise all the rights to which she is, in human terms, entitled, and so forth."

In a word, we see that we can know nothing. Therefore, let us hope! "In the days ahead, she will have and she must have the greatest influence and the leading voice with the emperor." And even if she should not share his title, "the children who will call our future monarch 'father' will call her 'mother.'" Thus are we dismissed by the deeply pessimistic thinker with a tenderhearted allusion to the outcome. Of course not without closing with one of the maxims taken from his outlook on life: "The future of Austria belongs to the duchess von Hohenberg. But nobody knows what the future will bring." This is Herr Felix Salten. You can say that his soul is a willing resonance for everything great and beautiful of the modern Prometheuses.

But we do an injustice to an able man. We pull him back from immortality in order to put him to use here on earth. And, finally, we

separate the social function of journalism from the superfluities of literature. Such an insight can find no better example. The best journalist of
Vienna can at any hour comment as easily on the interesting aspects of
a countess's career as he can on the flight of a balloon, as easily on a session
of Parliament as he can on a court ball. In western Hungary at night you
can bet that within a half an hour the gypsy primate will be on hand
together with his entire orchestra. He's awakened, gropes for his fiddle,
rouses the cymbalist, everybody hops out of bed, into the carts, and in half
an hour things liven up—it's merry, melancholic, uninhibited, demonic,
and whatever else you can think of. These are unheard-of practical advan-
tages that only a person who neither knows nor shares the needs of the
world is capable of underestimating. To be always ready is everything. If
only the world itself were not unjust! It says that a certain person is the
best journalist there is, and he is that without a doubt. But it never says,
so and so is the most important bank manager. And yet he serves the world
as well as the other and has nothing whatsoever to do with the vanities
of literature.

One could live with the perfect feuilletonists, were it not for their
quest for immortality. They know how to use foreign words, they have
everything at hand that they don't have in their heads, and they are often
tasteful. If you want to have a display window decorated, you don't call
a lyric poet. He might be able to do it as well, but the fact is that he doesn't.
The window dresser is the one who does. This establishes his social position, which the lyric poet rightly envies him. Even a window dresser can
pass down to posterity. But only if a lyric poet writes a poem about him.

"Aus dem Papierkorb," 1909. Original text in *Die Fackel*, no. 289, 25. Oktober 1909, 10–13.

1.   A reference to Sophie Chotek (1868–1914), with whom the Archduke Franz
Ferdinand (1863–1914), the eldest son of Emperor Franz Joseph's younger brother,
contracted a morganatic marriage in 1900. Opposed to the marriage, Franz Joseph
finally accepted it on the condition that the couple promise never to seek the throne for
any of their children. Shunned in imperial society, Sophie Chotek held the title of
princess until 1909, after which she became Duchess of Hohenberg. The issue alluded
to in Salten's piece is the campaign to elevate her to an archduchess. Both she and Franz
Ferdinand were assassinated in Sarajevo in 1914, thereby providing the spark that
ignited the First World War.

2.   An allusion to the German dramatist Gerhart Hauptmann's play *Rose Bernd*
(1903), about an unwed mother who commits infanticide. The play was banned in Vienna.

RABBITS WITH JEWISH DIALECT

Not all who know and esteem the extensive range of activity of our Felix
Salten are probably familiar with the fact that he still has enough time to

cultivate hunting. Many are aware, of course, that he succeeded in eaves-
dropping on the animal soul, but they would certainly not imagine that
the way to his typewriter led through that exhausting experience. And if
they now believe a legitimist capable of handling a firearm, they would
not at all believe that a Zionist could bend a deer's hair. Nevertheless it
is so, and Salten is closer to the thick forest, which he sometimes penetrates
with his rifle, than it seems and than one would believe possible of a
confessor of Moses. In any case, he's there because of the greenery.[1] Just
as in [Weber's opera] *Der Freischütz*, he can sing: "What on earth can
compare to the hunter's pleasure?" although as the author of *Josefine
Mutzenbacher* he certainly was in no position to plait the bridal wreath. He
was introduced, as they say, to the secrets of the forest by Békessy, who
was a mighty Nimrod before the Lord. While somebody like myself was
still sitting at his writing table, lying in ambush for many a noble beast,
the two of them went roaming through wood and field or waited at the
hunting platform they lacked in their journalistic endeavors. One would
sooner have imagined a different weapon in Békessy's hand than the barrel
aimed at deer from whom nothing more than the loss of life is concealed.
Salten, who indeed must satisfy more refined literary demands, did not
let the opportunity slip by of mastering their language before the last
animal disappeared. As clearly emerges from the rabbit novel he is publishing in the *Neue Freie Presse*, it couldn't have been difficult for him to
understand this language, since, as it turns out, the rabbits speak in Jewish
dialect. One of them, who is called "Iwner" and might easily have been
taken by Békessy as a knitted goods salesman from the quay, answers the
timid question of a friend named "Hops" with a whole series of his own
questions. It goes like this:

> "And . . . He?"
>
> Iwner blinked disdainfully. "Big deal! What's he got to do
> with us already? Doesn't mean a thing!"
>
> Hops grumbled: "Nnaa . . . that seems exaggerated to me
> . . . it's plain thoughtless!"
>
> Iwner replied quickly: "Thoughtless? Who's talking about
> thoughtless? A person shouldn't be thoughtless even a second !
> Don't forget it!"
>
> Cringing, his head in his front paws, Hops murmured: "I
> always say the same thing."
>
> "Well?" Iwner snapped. "Well? Day and night, every hour,
> there's constant danger here in the forest! You know it yourself!
> There's a threat in the bushes, in the open field, there's danger
> always and everywhere. But we're still living! What do you want
> from him? Since when is he coming into the forest? Him? Big

deal! He doesn't belong to the forest! He's not from the forest! You can hear his step even when he creeps softly. He's clumsy. You catch his scent. You can avoid him. The way he comes so awkwardly, the way he acts, he's the least dangerous."[2]

(To be continued)

This can get good. This rabbit, who is clearly no youngster and knows his way around, talks like a book the Zsolnay Publishing House is putting out. And Iwner's opinion of the one whose step can be heard when he creeps so softly is surely justified. Nothing gets by the instinct of animals. But it is amazing how they assimilated the enemy's speech. Perhaps mimicry as a defense against persecution? One easily gets used to Jewish dialect being used in time of danger; when they are among themselves, they know how to talk German. However it may be, one is eager for the continuation. When He puts in his appearance there may really be a merry howling!

"Jüdelnde Hasen," 1929. Original text in *Die Fackel*, no. 820–826, Ende Oktober 1929, 45–46.

1.   An untranslatable pun in the original. Kraus writes: "des Mooses wegen" (because of the moss). *Moos* (moss) in German slang also means "money." The idea is that Salten's interest in nature has a financial side to it.

2.   This is the same passage in Whittaker Chambers' English translation, which was originally published by Simon and Schuster in 1930 and was reissued by the Delacorte Press (New York) in 1976:

> "And . . . He?"
> Iwner blinked contemptuously.
> "Oh, He's highly important, I'm sure. What does he have to do with us? He simply plays no role at all."
> Hops objected. "No, no," he said, "that's going a little too far for me. That's altogether too irresponsible!"
> "Irresponsible," retorted Iwner quickly. "Who's talking about irresponsibility? One can't afford to be irresponsible for a single second. Just mark my word!"
> His head lowered, and laid on his forepaws, Hops muttered, "That's just what I've been saying!"
> "Well then?" Iwner went on. "Well then? Day and night, at every hour, there's constant danger in the forest! But you know that! There's a threat in every bush, in the open fields. There's danger always and everywhere. Yet we go on living! What do you want of him? When does He ever come into the forest? He? Nonsense! He doesn't belong to the forest. You can hear his step no matter how softly he sneaks. He's so clumsy. Then, there's his scent. We can avoid him. He comes so seldom and acts so clumsily that he's the least danger of all." (Felix Salten, *Fifteen Rabbits*, trans. Whittaker Chambers [New York: Delacorte Press, 1976], 149–50)

P E T E R
A L T E N B E R G
1 8 5 9 – 1 9 1 9

PETER ALTENBERG, OR P. A., AS HE PREFERRED TO BE CALLED, WAS BORN RICHARD ENGLÄNDER. There was little in his family background to suggest that he was destined to become the embodiment of the turn-of-the-century bohemian and a writer whose reputation in his own country has reached legendary proportions.[1] His father, Moritz, was a cultured and successful Viennese wholesaler of Yugoslav peasant goods with a penchant for French literature (Hugo was his favorite author), which his son inherited, and his mother was an adoring parent. Much of what we know of Altenberg's family and his early years comes from his sketches. Although he never wrote memoirs or maintained diaries in any orderly fashion, his attachment to his family and the fond recollection of his childhood and youth provided inspiration for much of his writing. This was particularly true of his later years. The more critical he grew of the society around him and the more distant he felt from it, the more frequent became his flights into the past. His early years were a happy, secure period in his life, and they became a refuge, psychically, when a self-abusive life-style and growing mental instability raised havoc with his nerves. In contrast to the pettiness, meanspiritedness, and insincerity he saw all around him as an adult, childhood loomed large in his thought as a kind of fairy tale of affection and devotion. It was out of deference to his generally happy youth that he adopted the pen name "Peter Altenberg"; about the time he began his studies at the University of Vienna, he enjoyed visiting with a friend in the little town of Altenberg on the Danube. It was there that he became enamored of the thirteen-year-old Bertha Lecher, his friend's sister. She was nicknamed "Peter" by her brothers. As if to immortalize the idyll of early love, Richard Engländer combined Bertha's nickname and the name of the town in which she first entered his life to produce the pseudonym "Peter Altenberg."

Perhaps the earliest indication of a future departure from the ordinary occurred when Altenberg was ten years old and already a gymnasium student. He came down with a severe inflammation in his foot that kept him in bed for the better part of a year. He recalls that so concerned was his mother that she moved her own bed next to his in order to watch over him at night and in the afternoon sang songs of Schubert in an adjacent room to comfort him. Altenberg eventually recovered from his illness, but it is possible that the episode left him with a lasting concern for health that later became obsessive. It may also have laid the groundwork for a nervous condition destined to worsen as time went on.

After completing his secondary-school studies, Altenberg enrolled in the University of Vienna in 1877 with the intention of studying law. But by the summer semester 1879, his interest in law had waned and he shifted instead to medicine. This, too, was broken off within a year in an emerging pattern of instability. An attempt to learn the book trade by apprenticing in a prominent Stuttgart bookshop (Julius Weise's Hofbuchhandlung) from late autumn 1880 to the beginning of the new year also came to naught. The circumstances by which he came to Stuttgart in the first place are unknown. But he left because the work seemed boring and stifling. With borrowed money (again adumbrating a future pattern), he retreated to a favorite childhood family summer resort, the Hotel Thalhof in Reichenau bei Payerbach, below the spectacular mountains around Semmering a few hours to the south of Vienna. The entire area, with

Semmering as its hub, was quite fashionable among affluent Viennese at the turn of the century as a cool haven from summertime city heat and dust. The natural beauty of the region acted on Altenberg as a kind of therapy, and he returned to it both physically and in his writing on many occasions.

Further attempts at the resumption of formal learning on Altenberg's part—such as undertaking legal studies in Graz in 1881 and again in Vienna the following year—proved futile. When in 1883 his father decided to seek professional counsel concerning his son's inability to stay a course of study or work, he was informed following a psychiatric examination that because of nervous hypersensitivity (neurasthenia gravis), his son was constitutionally unfit for any steady employment. Thus relieved of further pressure from his family to continue his studies and prepare for some career, Altenberg drifted into a bohemian way of life to which his own nature may in fact have predisposed him. He loosened his relations with his family and became estranged from them except for the period approximately from 1898 to 1902, when he lived with his brother Georg, who took over their father's business.

After he parted company with his brother, Altenberg began the pattern of residence in small inexpensive centrally located Vienna hotels that he maintained until his death. Wanting little in the way of material things and creature comforts, Altenberg furnished a small room with his favorite possessions, chief of which was a huge collection of picture post-cards (which obviated the necessity for extensive travel). His longest hotel encampment was in the London at Wallnerstrasse 17 in Vienna's First District. The last several years of his life—apart from the time he came to spend in sanatoria—found him in the Graben-Hotel on Dorotheergasse, right off the Graben, in the heart of Vienna. Since the Graben-Hotel was his place of residence in his later years, when he was already known as a writer and the Altenberg legend had already developed significantly, it is the one with which he is most often associated. The hotel is still in existence in the same location and honors Altenberg's memory with a wall plaque as well as a restaurant named after him.

Once settled into his hotel life-style, Altenberg soon began acquiring a reputation for his bohemianism. His hotel room was used essentially as a place to sleep whenever he found his way back, usually in the wee hours of the morning, from the coffeehouses which increasingly became his true habitat. But Altenberg's attachment to the coffeehouse was such that he could be found there at almost any hour of the day or night. The Löwenbräu, in the vicinity of the Burgtheater, the Griensteidl, and then the Central, on the Herrengasse, just a short walk from the Hofburg, became his favorite haunts. Part of the Altenberg legend revolves around his coffeehouse routine, above all at the Central, where he spent so much time that it served as an address for him. Little wonder that the renovated Café Central today features a full-sized likeness of Altenberg seated at a table to the immediate right of the main entrance.

Altenberg's bohemian way of life consisted in the main of spending much of the day in a coffeehouse, where he soon became known for his stories, for drinking heavily, for consorting with prostitutes, for befriending the "little people" in Vienna's inner city—waiters, chambermaids, coachmen, flower sellers, children, young girls especially—and for viewing the life around him with an extraordinary power of observation. We have no idea exactly when he began writing, but until his "discovery" his attitude toward it was casual. Attracted to the myriad of small things that make up everyday ordinary existence and with a deep feeling for the beauties of nature, Altenberg drank everything in with his keen eyes and at some point made the apparently easy transition from visual to verbal notation. Possessed of highly sensitive nerves—so much so, as we saw earlier, that he was declared medically unfit for regular employment—Altenberg was thus temperamentally suited to the fashionable literary impressionism of the turn of the century. The fleetingness and randomness of the impressionistic style, its attentiveness to nature and color, its fixation on details and minutiae, its inclination toward the concise and aphoristic, accorded with his nature. Even when he wrote theater and cabaret reviews or began promulgating his often idiosyncratic ideas about diet, nutrition, and dress, Altenberg never moved much beyond the diminutive confines of the very small sketch of anywhere from a paragraph to a half-dozen pages in length. So remarkably talented was he at this type of prose miniature, so much did this type of writing become an extension of his being that he was—and is—acknowledged as its unparalleled master. He never wrote novels or plays, despite his interest in the stage, never exhibited much interest in the essay, and with respect to poetry wrote only short prose poems that are barely distinguishable from his sketches and reflect the interest in the genre of the poem in prose, especially in France, in the turn of the century. At the beginning of his career as a published author, in 1896, he gave evidence of an ability to think in terms of larger structures by linking related sketches into sketch cycles. There are four such cycles in his first book of sketches, *Wie ich es sehe* (*As I See It,* 1896), of which only two consist of a dozen or more sketches. With subsequent publications, Altenberg abandoned the sketch cycle linkage, preferring to let his hundreds of individual sketches sort themselves thematically.

If there is any unifying element in Altenberg's writings, apart from style, it is Altenberg himself, who, whatever persona he adopts—the

unnamed "poet," the "young man," the "revolutionary," or just "P. A."—
is always immediately identifiable. With a psychologically plausible narcissism and egocentricity that are also characteristic of turn-of-the-century art,
Altenberg and his subjective responses to the world around him are always
at the center of his art. The title of his first published collection of sketches,
As I See It, tells it all—it is the world as Altenberg himself sees it, and the
emphasis, as he himself makes clear in several instances, must fall on the
verb "to see." In the light of the writing itself, it is difficult to resist the
temptation to shift the emphasis to "I," but to Altenberg what mattered
most was the *seeing*, his power of observation, which is the shaping agent
of his many sketches.

Since virtually everything Altenberg wrote relates to himself and his
perceptions, it is from his own words that we learn about his first writing
and his "discovery." These passages are found for the most part in the
sketches "Wie ich 'Schriftsteller' wurde" ("How I Became a 'Writer,'"
included in his posthumous collection *Mein Lebensabend* [*The Evening of My
Life*, 1919]), "So wurde ich" ("How I Came to Be," *Semmering 1912*, 1913),
and "Wie ich mir Karl Kraus 'gewann'" ("How I 'Won Over' Karl Kraus,"
Vita Ipsa, 1918).

As Altenberg tells it, he wrote his first sketch toward the end of
September 1894. He was thirty-five years old at the time and was inspired
by two young girls he met during a summer vacation in Gmunden in Lower
Austria. The sketch was titled "Neun und elf" (Nine and Eleven), referring
to the girls' ages. He was still, as he puts it, a "pure nobody." Not long
afterward, apparently, he made the acquaintance of Karl Kraus, who took
an immediate liking to him. It was a fondness from which Kraus never
retreated despite the considerable differences between the two men. The
painter Oskar Kokoschka, another familiar coffeehouse figure of the time,
knew them both and offers this description of their relationship in his
autobiography:

> The lyric poet Peter Altenberg—whose real name was
> Peter Engländer [*sic*]—was a lifelong friend of both Kraus and
> Loos. Altenberg looked like a seal, or rather a newborn seal-pup
> that has just been put into the sea; such was his habitual expres-
> sion of astonishment. He could be full of sparkling gaiety at one
> moment, and surly and miserable the next. To make us laugh,
> Kraus sometimes used to goad him into one of the childlike
> outbursts of anger which were so easily provoked. Especially
> when as a joke they got Altenberg's rich patron Herr von Lieben
> to delay payment of the weekly pension which Altenberg re-
> garded as his by right of custom. But Karl Kraus was his truest
> benefactor all his life. Altenberg was a bohemian, and always

lived from hand to mouth in the same shady little hotel in the city centre, frequented by prostitutes whose poet laureate he became. Thanks to them there was always a bottle of slivovitz under the bed, and his room was papered with their postcards and pictures. He was a dreamer who, in his checked shirt and brightly coloured homespun jacket, looked like a clown.[2]

However he became aware of Altenberg's fledgling literary efforts, Kraus was impressed enough to surreptitiously get hold of a number of his manuscripts from the various boxes and drawers in which they were tucked away in Altenberg's tiny Vienna hotel room. He bundled them together and in the summer of 1895 sent the package to the venerable Berlin publishing house of S. Fischer, with whom Kraus had contacts. Fischer at the time was developing a reputation for its support of modernism. The novelty and freshness of Altenberg's style persuaded the Fischers that a new talent was on the verge of being discovered, and they chose to publish a collection of Altenberg's sketches under the title *Wie ich es sehe.* The book came out in 1896 and was an immediate success.

The publication of *As I See It* was preceded by the appearance on 21 January 1896 of Altenberg's sketch "Lokale Chronik" ("Local Chronicle") in the Vienna weekly *Liebelei.* This was the first sketch by Altenberg to appear in print. He recalls in "How I Came To Be" that he was sitting in the Café Central writing "Local Chronicle" when in came the leading lights of the "Young Vienna" circle—Schnitzler, Hofmannsthal, Salten, Beer-Hofmann, and Bahr. Previously unaware that Altenberg wrote, Schnitzler asked to see what he was working on. As if anticipating what was to happen not long afterward at the Fischer Verlag in Berlin, there was an immediate sense on Schnitzler's part that he, too, had unearthed a new Austrian literary talent. After the chance encounter at the Central, Richard Beer-Hofmann organized a "literary supper" in Altenberg's honor the following Sunday at which his "Local Chronicle" was read by his host "for dessert," as Altenberg remembers the occasion. A few days later, Bahr invited him to contribute to his newly founded weekly, *Die Zeit.* Peter Altenberg's literary talent was now about to depart obscurity.

The response by the Vienna literary community to Altenberg's *As I See It* when it first appeared in 1896 was extraordinarily enthusiastic. Reviewing the book under the title "Ein neues Wiener Buch" ("A New Viennese Book") that same year, Hugo von Hofmannsthal did his best to capture the appeal of Altenberg's sketches but acknowledged their virtually indescribable uniqueness.

Fame and the growing status of an authentic Vienna legend effected little change on Altenberg outwardly. He dressed in the same eccentric way we see in a number of photographs of him—bold checkered trousers or suits, floppy "artist's" neckties, sandals over bare feet, a long, loose-fitting raglan-sleeved tweed topcoat, a wide, colorful tweed beret with a pompom on the top. He continued to sleep in his tiny hotel room and spend most of his days in Vienna in coffeehouses. His affection for the "little people" remained the same. He seemed the same old Peter Altenberg.

After *As I See It*, Altenberg published another ten volumes of his sketches between 1897 and 1919, the year of his death. These include: *Ashantee* (1897); *Was der Tag mir zuträgt* (*What the Day Tells Me*, 1901); *Pròdrômôs* (1906), which is actually a collection of prescriptions, recipes, and aphorisms related to health; *Die Auswahl aus meinen Büchern* (*The Selection from My Books*, 1908); *Märchen des Lebens* (*Fairy Tales of Life*, 1908); *Bilderbögen des kleinen Lebens* (*Picture-Sheets of the Small Life*, 1909); *Neues Altes* (*New Old*, 1911); *Semmering 1912* (1913); *Fechsung* (*Harvest*, 1915); *Nachfechsung* (*Late Harvest*, 1916); and *Vita Ipsa* (1918). *Mein Lebensabend* (*The Evening of My Life*, 1919) appeared posthumously. Altenberg's literary legacy, or *Nachlass*, which was edited by his fellow coffeehouse denizen Alfred Polgar, was published in 1925, also by S. Fischer Verlag, the steadfast publisher of every collection of Altenberg's sketches except one (*Picture-Sheets of the Small Life*, which was published by the Erich Reiss Verlag of Berlin).

Once Altenberg broke with the series or cycles of sketches characteristic of most of *As I See It*, his subsequent collections—with two exceptions—were just collections of sketches often thematically and stylistically related but without the underlying structural unity of *As I See It*. There was also a certain redundancy. Sketches from previous collections were incorporated into later ones, sometimes with small changes, sometimes with none. The exceptions—and then not entirely—were *Ashantee* (1897) and *Pròdrômôs* (1906). Originally a separate publication, most of the sketches comprising *Ashantee* were incorporated into later editions of *As I See It*. The inspiration for *Ashantee* was the establishment in the Vienna Zoo of an authentic West African Ashanti tribal village in conjunction with a hunting exhibition. Altenberg was drawn to the village out of curiosity and the desire for new impressions; he was also anxious to try out some of the English he knew. He visited it on a number of occasions and became friends especially with its children and young women. The sketches inspired by the Ashanti people he met in Vienna do form a series, albeit simpler than the larger ones in *As I See It*. Perhaps a more important facet of the collection is Altenberg's ability to relate to the exotic African tribespeople. Free of any sense of superiority as a European, Altenberg viewed the Ashanti as an object lesson in the virtues of living in greater harmony with nature, of being content with the simple joys, of having no need for what he regarded as the excesses and superfluities of everyday European life. The Ashanti were admirable because of their honesty and directness, and to Altenberg, who loathed pretense and artificiality, these were true virtues.

As his reputation and public recognition grew, Altenberg became more didactic in the expression of his views about nutrition and health. His ideas clearly accorded with his outlook on life, but the repetition of the same prescriptions from one work to another could become tedious and alienating. The more he reiterated them, the more he appeared like an overzealous preacher. To Altenberg, the proper care of the body—which meant, above all, proper diet (the eating of easily digested foods, for example) and proper sleep (a subject on which he could be fanatic)—strengthened an individual's vitality and inner resources and enhanced the possibility of spiritual and moral regeneration. Unwholesome diet and inadequate sleep, the abuse of the body, of the human organism, was sinful, from Altenberg's point of view, and lay behind unwholesome attitudes toward life and toward others. Contemptuous of artificiality in any form, Altenberg also preached a liberation from the constraints of dress, especially among women. Tightfitting clothes, high neck collars, even shoes were to be abandoned in favor of loose garb that permitted freer movement of the body and ultimately the mind as well. Not only did Altenberg come to advocate sandals, especially wooden clogs, but insisted they be worn over naked feet, whatever the season. This practice as well as his insistence on sleeping next to an open window, again irrespective of season, later contributed to his physical demise. Although Altenberg's ideas about nutrition and health are scattered throughout his writings, they reach a crescendo in *Pròdrômôs*, which consists entirely of prescriptions and aphorisms on everything from minutiae of diet to recommendations on fountain pens. As idiosyncratic—and tediously repetitive—as he may appear in *Pròdrômôs* and elsewhere on the subject of health, it would be unfair to dismiss Altenberg as a mere crank. His attitude toward the care of the body was but an aspect of his worldview and should best be considered in that context.

Altenberg's peak years were 1896, when *As I See It* appeared, to 1910, when his nerves began deteriorating to such an extent that he had to undergo treatment in the Fango hydrotherapy sanatorium in Vienna from 6 February to 10 May of that year. After the extraordinary success of *As I See It*, Altenberg published *Ashantee, What the Day Tells Me, Pròdrômôs, Fairy Tales of Life, The Selection from My Books*, and *Picture-Sheets of the Small Life* within that fourteen-year period. He had also become a contributor to several prominent Austrian and German newspapers and journals, among them the Munich *Jugend* and *Simplicissimus*, the Berlin *Neue Rundschau* and *Schaubühne*, the Vienna *Extrapost, Der liebe Augustin,* and *Wiener Allgemeine Zeitung,* and Karl Kraus's *Die Fackel.* Much of Altenberg's journalistic writing took the form of theater reviews, of which his coverage of the Vienna variety theater and the early cabaret are the most interesting in view of his own firsthand knowledge of these performance milieux. In October 1903, Altenberg, together with the architect Adolf Loos, also became involved in the elegant new art journal *Kunst: Monatsschrift für Kunst und alles Andere* (*Art: A Monthly for Art and All Else*). Altenberg became the editor of the short-lived journal but relinquished the post in February 1904. However, he continued to contribute to it until the June/July 1904 issue.

Altenberg's admission into the Fango sanatorium on 6 February 1910 as a result of his worsening nervous condition marked the beginning of long periods of confinement until his death on 8 January 1919. He was in Fango from early February until nearly mid-May 1910, then in the Fries sanatorium in Inzersdorf, just outside Vienna, until the middle of August. He was not long out of Fries when he was back again in December 1910 and remained there until September 1911. During his first stay in Inzersdorf, in August 1910, friends and admirers of his in Vienna, including Karl Kraus, mounted a public drive to raise money to defray his expenses. Not only had his health deteriorated; so, too, had his finances.

The remarkable thing about the last nine years or so of Altenberg's life was his ability to continue writing despite the evident breakdown of his nervous system and his mental instability. Not only did he succeed in publishing another five collections of sketches (*New Old, Semmering 1912, Harvest, Late Harvest, Vita Ipsa*), but he had already assembled a sixth, *The Evening of My Life,* which was published some three months after his death. He also resumed contributing to a few Vienna papers. As keen an observer as ever of the life around him, Altenberg even made his own illness and sanatoria visits the subject of a number of sketches. Taken as a whole, these represent an interesting if obviously at times depressing body of works. Altenberg's self-absorption is sometimes humorous, sometimes ironic, often complaining, self-pitying, and despairing. There were times when he was suspicious of everyone and everything around him, and there were times when he expressed a desire for death.

His situation turned worse when he made life so emotionally unbearable for his female companion, Helga Malmberg, with whom he began a friendship in 1906, that she finally broke with him definitively in 1911 while he was at Inzersdorf. Always attracted to and attractive to women, especially very young women, Altenberg was splendidly sensitive to the feminine psyche and, in a sense, could think like a woman. Even if in his later sketches an earlier exaltation of the female of the species gives way to expressions of frustration, remorse, and bitterness, he never completely abandoned his previous idealization of women, his belief that women were spiritually superior to men, or his appreciation of the beauty of the feminine form. This liking for women, however, never culminated in marriage, and Altenberg remained a bachelor throughout his life. He was troubadour-like in his celebration of women, and there is no reason to doubt his sexual experience. But he had a profound need to spiritualize woman and to see in her the spiritual redeemer of man. Looking beyond the gratification of erotic desires and the conventionalities of bourgeois marriage, Altenberg envisaged a new, spiritually revitalized relationship between men and women capable of serving as a model for society as a whole. It would be extremely difficult to believe that this outlook did not, at least in part, shape his personal relations with women. When Altenberg addresses the matter of sex, it is almost always to vituperate against the sexual exploitation of women, of which he saw enough in the Vienna of his own time. And no matter how frequently and adoringly he writes about young girls, it would be an injustice to impute prurient motives to him. If they existed at all, they appear to have been scrupulously controlled and sublimated.

After leaving Inzersdorf in the fall of 1911 and with Helga Malmberg no longer around to look after him, Altenberg repaired to his beloved Semmering, where he installed himself until the middle of 1912 in an annex of the once-fashionable Hotel Panhans. The mountain scenery, the fresh air, the strolls through the woods, and the occasional contacts with other guests collectively acted as a therapy enabling Altenberg to continue writing with a renewed vigor. One of his better collections of sketches, *Semmering 1912*, dates from this period.

By the end of 1912, Altenberg was again institutionalized. On 10 December he entered the Am Steinhof mental hospital in Vienna, where he remained until 28 April 1913. His departure from the hospital came primarily at the urging of Adolf Loos, who thought that a trip with him, his second wife, Bessie, and a few other friends to the Lido in Venice would do him more good than a prolonged stay in a hospital. Altenberg remained in Venice nearly six months, a sojourn reflected in the Venetian sketches in his *Harvest* collection, published in 1915.

After his return to Vienna, Altenberg took up residence in the Graben Hotel, where he lived until his death. The last five years of his life were devoted to writing, propagating his views on health, and fighting periods of depression and frequent sleeplessness. A romantic interest in the form of Paula Schweizer Deman—who figures in a number of his later sketches—

entered his life in 1914 but, like Helga Malmberg before her, she, too, eventually left Altenberg to marry another man. The war years had no great impact on the writer. He was sympathetic to the Austrian-German cause and wrote several sketches on war-related themes, but he never dwelled on it at length nor seemed to have been in any way deeply touched by it. His *Nachlass,* or literary legacy, contains a series of diary-like entries chronicling his failing health and general state of mind. True to his own precepts on health, he insisted on dragging about Vienna through all seasons without a hat, his bare feet—usually undried following a bath— sheathed just in wooden clogs, unencumbered by underclothes, and sleeping in the nude alongside an open window. Even two broken wrists, the result of a fall on slippery pavement at the doorstep of his hotel while wearing his clogs, failed to deter him. At one in the morning on 19 December 1918, a glass of wine spilled onto his bedsheet. Undisturbed, he slept in the wetness, his window opened wide as usual. The next morning he experienced a return bout of the bronchitis from which he suffered in his youth. The condition worsened into a severe inflammation of the lungs. Friends who called on him at the Graben-Hotel at nine in the evening on 6 January 1919 found him in a delirious condition. They had him taken immediately to the hospital. Although it was suspected that Altenberg was suffering from an excessive dose of paraldehyde, which he had been taking for years for his chronic insomnia, a stomach pumping proved negative. Shortly thereafter, the proper diagnosis was rendered: severe inflammation of the lungs and edema. Two days later, Altenberg was dead. He was buried in a "grave of honor" of the city of Vienna in the Central Cemetery. The religious ceremony was Roman Catholic in view of Altenberg's conversion in 1900 from the Judaism into which he was born. The funeral oration was delivered by Karl Kraus. When it became public, Altenberg's will came as something of a surprise. Although he had a reputation for impecuniousness and often accepted money from admirers for such basics as the rent on his hotel room, Altenberg left an estate of about 100,000 crowns, all of which went to the Children's Aid Society.

A few months after his death, in April 1919, Altenberg's *The Evening of My Life* was published by S. Fischer. An *Altenberg-Buch,* edited by Egon Friedell and consisting for the most part of letters by Altenberg to various people as well as pieces by other writers about him (reminiscences, reviews, testimonials), was published in 1922 by the Verlag der Wiener Graphischen Werkstätte of Vienna and Leipzig. This was followed in 1925 by the publication by S. Fischer of his *Nachlass* (*Literary Legacy*) in an edition prepared by Alfred Polgar. In 1930, another selection of his works, prepared by his sister, Marie Mauthner, was published by Richard Lanyi. Two years later the Anton Schroll Verlag of Vienna came out with a collection edited by Karl Kraus.

The Altenberg legend owes as much to his literary style as to his personality. In its time it was regarded as distinctly new and refreshing, something for which there were really no antecedents in German-language literature. When one thinks of turn-of-the-century *Kleinkunst*, of the "short prose" so characteristic of the period, and of the literary culture of the coffeehouse milieu, Altenberg is invariably the first writer who comes to mind. His world was that of the "little things," whose virtue he proclaims in many of his sketches—the ordinary things of life—items of dress, for example—one usually takes for granted, the myriad of nuances in the colors and textures of nature, the "little people" who so often go unnoticed, and, above all, children, whose innocence, vitality, naturalness, and play instinct he so admired. Not only did Altenberg cultivate the small prose form, the sketch, but it was ideally suited to his subjects. He was a writer who thrived on smallness, who wrote in small, cramped quarters, including the little marble-topped tables of coffeehouses, in the belief that it was in smallness that bigness was to be found.

Altenberg's appetite for life was prodigious and explains the importance he attached to vitality. Bourgeois smugness and stagnation, contentment with the habitual, and the hypocrisy of appearances all represented to him a kind of death in life, uncreativity, spiritual withering. The antidote was movement (*Bewegung, Beweglichkeit*), a term that looms large in his thought and suggests healthy vitality, a sound spirit in a sound body. It was for this reason that he so celebrated the dancer and saw in Grete Wiesenthal, for example, a leading Viennese dancer of his time, the embodiment of his ideas about movement and vitality. Seen from the perspective of his attitude toward life in general, even a prescriptive book such as *Pròdrômôs* and his many sketches on health and nutrition should not be dismissed out of hand as the ravings of a crank. Their repetitiousness can, however, become maddening. When his own health deteriorated—in large measure because of his own self-abuse—and he lamented the lack of movement imposed on him by circumstances, Altenberg slipped easily into a depressing self-pity, bitterness, and remorse. Yet as painful, and embarrassing, as much of Altenberg's later writing is, the many sketches examining the phenomena of sickness, insomnia, and nervous breakdown, and the psychology of the patient and those around him, exert their own sometimes compelling fascination.

Altenberg's reputation as a writer has never been greater. There is a substantial and growing scholarly literature on him, primarily in German, new editions of his works are appearing, and he has been translated into other languages.[3] Although he figures as a character in several literary works (Schnitzler's unfinished play, *Das Wort* [*The Word*], for example), perhaps the finest tribute to him to date is the well-known Austrian composer Alban Berg's *Fünf Orchesterlieder nach Ansichtskarten-Texten von Peter Altenberg,* op. 4 (*Five Orchestral Songs Based on Picture-Postcard Texts by Peter Altenberg*). The first public performance of two of the songs, in the auditorium of Vienna's Great Music Society (Wiener Grosse Musikverein) on 31 March 1913, provoked a scandal. The work was poorly understood and mocked. Stravinsky subsequently praised it as "one of the most perfect works of this century," and its reputation, like that of the provocative artist who inspired it, is now secure.

1.   Although there is no formal biography of Altenberg as such, there is much valuable information in the following works: Hedwig Prohaska, "Peter Altenberg: Versuch einer Monographie" (Ph.D. diss., University of Vienna, 1948); Helga Malmberg, *Widerhall des Herzens: Ein Peter-Altenberg-Buch* (Munich: Langen & Müller, 1961); Herbert Ahl, "Extrakte des Lebens: Peter Altenberg," *Literarische Portraits* (Munich-Vienna: Albert Langen-Georg Müller, 1962); Richard von Schaukal, "Seele: Zu Peter Altenbergs Gedächtnis" and "Peter Altenberg: Zum 75. Geburtstag," *Über Dichter* (Munich-Vienna: Albert Langen-Georg Müller, 1966); Egon Friedell, *Kulturgeschichte der Neuzeit: Die Krisis der europäischen Seele von der schwarzen Pest bis zum ersten Weltkrieg* (Munich: Verlag C. H. Beck, 1974 [original edition in three vols., 1927–31]), 1456–58; Gisela von Wysocki, *Peter Altenberg: Bilder und Geschichten des befreiten Lebens* (Munich-Vienna: Hanser Verlag, 1979); Camillo Schaefer, *Peter Altenberg: Ein biographischer Essay,* 2d augmented edition, Freibord Sonderreihe no. 10 (Vienna, 1980); Hans Christian Kosler, ed., *Peter Altenberg: Leben und Werk in Texten und Bildern* (Munich: Matthes & Seitz Verlag, 1981); Maria Gelsi, *Peter Altenberg: La strategia della rinuncia* (Rome: Edizioni dell'Atene, 1982); Barbara Z. Schoenberg, "The Art of Peter Altenberg: Bedside Chronicles of a Dying World" (Ph.D. diss., University of California, Los Angeles, 1984); Josephine M. N. Simpson, *Peter Altenberg: A Neglected Writer of the Viennese Jahrhundertwende* (Frankfurt am Main: Peter Lang, 1987); Hans Bisanz, *Peter Altenberg: Mein äusseres Ideal* (Vienna: Brandstaetter, 1987).

The periodical literature on Altenberg contains several interesting articles in English: Andrew Barker, "Peter Altenberg's Literary Catalysis," in Mark G. Ward, ed., *From Vormärz to Fin de Siècle: Essays in Nineteenth Century Austrian Literature* (Blairgowrie: Lochee Publications Ltd., 1986), 91–106; Andrew W. Barker, "Ein Lichtbringender und Leuchtender, ein Dichter und Prophet: Responses to Peter Altenberg in Turn-of-the-Century Vienna, " *Modern Austrian Literature: Journal of the International Arthur Schnitzler Research Association* 22, nos. 3/4 (1989): 1–14 (this article, like the preceding one by Barker, deals with Altenberg's reception in Austria); Barbara Z. Schoenberg, "'Woman-Defender' and 'Woman-Offender,' Peter Altenberg and Otto Weininger: Two Literary Stances vis-à-vis Bourgeois Culture in the Viennese 'Belle Époque,'" *Modern Austrian Literature* 20, no. 2 (1987): 51–69; Barbara Z. Schoenberg, "The Influence of the French Prose Poem on Peter Altenberg," *Modern Austrian Literature* 22, nos. 3/4 (1989): 15–32; Andrew Barker, "Aus einem Skizzenbuch: Five Unpublished Sketches by Peter Altenberg," in Edward Timms and Ritchie Robertson, eds., *Vienna 1900: From Altenberg to Wittgenstein* (Edinburgh:

Edinburgh University Press, 1990), 28–45; Leo A. Lensing, "Peter Altenberg's Fabricated Photographs: Literature and Photography in Fin-de-Siècle Vienna," in *Vienna 1900: From Altenberg to Wittgenstein,* 47–72. This last article is an exceptionally interesting analysis of Altenberg's photo collection. Altenberg's activity as a theatrical reviewer is the subject of a detailed essay by Robert Werba, "Ein Aussenseiter der Theaterkritik: Peter Altenberg und das Wiener Theaterjahr 1898/99," *Mask und Kothurn* 20, no. 2 (1974): 163–90.

    Interesting reminiscences of Altenberg by contemporaries include: Lina Loos, "Peter Altenbergs Flugversuche," *Der Querschnitt* (Berlin: Im Propyläen-Verlag, 1929), 9: 97–98; Lina Loos, *Das Buch ohne Titel: Erlebte Geschichten,* ed. Adolf Opel and Herbert Schimek (Vienna: Hermann Böhlaus Nachf., 1986); Berthold Viertel, "Erinnerung an Peter Altenberg," *Dichtungen und Dokumente* (Munich: Kösel-Verlag, 1956), 311–18; Franz Theodor Csokor, ed., *Du silberne Dame du: Briefe von und an Lina Loos* (Vienna-Hamburg: Paul Zsolnay Verlag, 1966); Stefan Grossmann, "Mit Peter Altenberg," *Ich war begeistert: Eine Lebensgeschichte* (Königstein/Ts.: Scriptor Verlag, 1979), 106–16.

    2.   Oskar Kokoschka, *My Life,* trans. David Britt (New York: Macmillan, 1974), 40.

    3.   Altenberg has been translated into French (three collections), Italian, Czech (two collections), Ukrainian, Hebrew, Esperanto, and English. The sole English collection of some of his sketches on women was done by the Austrian-born satirist and humorist Alexander King and published under the title *Peter Altenberg's Evocations of Love* (New York: Simon and Schuster, 1960). The translations are rather free, with no indication of the texts from which they were taken.

How I Came to Be

In the thirty-fourth year of my impious life—a daily newspaper can't possibly give the particulars—I was sitting in the Café Central, Vienna, Herrengasse, in a room with golden embossed English wallpaper. I had in front me the *Express* with the photograph of a fifteen-year-old girl who disappeared forever on the way to a piano lesson. Her name was Johanna W. Consequently, deeply moved, I was writing my sketch "Local Chronicle" on quarto paper. In came Arthur Schnitzler, Hugo von Hofmannsthal, Felix Salten, Richard Beer-Hofmann, and Hermann Bahr. Arthur Schnitzler said to me: "I had no idea that you wrote! And on quarto paper, a portrait in front of you—now that is suspicious!" And he took my sketch "Local Chronicle" for himself. The next Sunday Richard Beer-Hofmann arranged a "literary supper" and for dessert read aloud my sketch. Three days later Hermann Bahr wrote to me: "I heard your sketch about a missing fifteen-year-old girl read at Herr Richard Beer-Hofmann's. Urgently request contributions from you for my newly founded weekly, *Time!*" Later on Karl Kraus, also known as Torch-Kraus because he flings the torch of his brilliant and droll wrath at the corrupt world in order to scorch it or at least "purify it by fire," sent a package of my sketches to my present publisher, S. Fischer, Berlin W., Bülowstrasse 90, with the recommendation that I am an original, a genius, somebody different, a nebbish. S. Fischer printed me and so I came to be! Just think of the coincidences on which a person's destiny depends! Isn't it so? Had I that time in the Café Central written out a bill for all the coffee I hadn't paid for in months, Arthur Schnitzler might not have taken an interest in me, Richard Beer-Hofmann might not have given a literary soirée, and Hermann Bahr might not have written to me. At all events, Karl Kraus might indeed have sent my package of sketches to S. Fischer, since he is "his own man," an "uninfluenceable." All together, however, "made" me. And what did I become? A sponger!

"So wurde ich," 1913. Original text in *Semmering 1912,* 5th and 6th enlarged ed. (Berlin: S. Fischer Verlag, 1919), 35–36.

How I Became a "Writer"

In the summer of 1894, while in Gmunden, two adorable girls, nine and eleven years old, attached themselves to me with a passion. The end of September the family returned to Vienna. On the night of the tearful departure of Alice and Auguste I wrote the first sketch of my life, at the age of thirty-five, under the title: "Nine and Eleven." This became the first sketch in my book *As I See It.* In the seventeenth year of her life the older one, Alice, suffered cerebral apoplexy while strolling on Kärntnerstrasse. She passed away immediately and painlessly. As we were riding back from the funeral to the family's apartment, the mother said to me: "Perhaps we paid too little attention to her great affection for our poet!"

"Don't start getting eccentric again, Betty!" said the father, "One shouldn't even think of such things; I would please ask you to keep that in mind!"

"Wie ich 'Schriftseller' wurde," 1919. Original text in *Mein Lebensabend,* 1st–8th ed. (Berlin: S. Fischer Verlag, 1919), 9.

IN MUNICH

For several days now I have been in Munich for the first time. I have seen nothing, absolutely nothing, marked out in the guide books, no monuments, no paintings. I am not interested in things that were. I am interested in things that *are,* that *will be!* But see! The window displays of fine shops were radiant with the "new art" intended to turn everybody who has become shrivelled in life into a kind of fanatic man-of-art when he looks at it for hours on end back in the lair of his own country. Europeans, where are you tarrying?!? Without inner joy you are still placing Meissen figurines and vases in carved cupboards! You are deceiving only yourselves!

You are living without ties to the magnificent colors and forms of nature itself, you say "ah!" at things that are strange and unappealing to you, you feed on phrases, on history, you buy vases with flowers that never existed! You have eyes that cannot enjoy anything in and of itself but instead are ruled by names and labels! And so, since you make no use of these noblest of organs, you do not extract the treasures of these two rich inexhaustible eyes, you remain miserable, empty, sad, and seek instead to draw on the pleasure of other organs which are and yet already are no longer! Then come long desolate hours which have to be killed with these poisons "drinking," "playing" — — !

Behold, the new, modern artist wants to unite you with nature and its deep splendors! He wants to make your eyes responsive to the brilliance of life itself as opposed to the deceptive forms of the imagination that have lost their effectiveness! Hear the roar of *sources,* not *cascades!* Your eyes should fall in love with things, should celebrate a wedding, a noble union, with them!

But you tarry in the distance, collecting trash! You see how close nature still is in the boy who creeps up to the splendid Apollo butterfly on mountain thistle!?! Or the young girl binding a small bunch of meadow flowers! *But later comes life, and makes one blind and empty?!* Then they play lawn tennis in the fields, in nature! Lawn tennis! Hot cheeks with cold souls!

Learn from the Japanese! When the cherry blossoms are in bloom, people come out to see them and for hours at a time stand silently before the rosy-white splendor. No benches or tables are set up for people to stuff themselves and guzzle on. The artistic folk stand silently before the rosy-white splendor, for hours at a time! Rooms are decorated with little bamboo baskets of fine flowers hung on neat, delicate, light-yellow mats. Men and women come in, observe the baskets of flowers, go their way, and quietly resume their daily routine. But what kind of trash do you have on your desks, on your walls?! You *have* it, that's all there is to it! What is there to look at?! You *possess* it, but you don't love it!

Why don't you instead place under glass the real works of art of nature, wonderfully exotic beetles or precious mussels in pale colors! These colors of beetles, mussels, butterflies, and stones, the true forms of blossoms and leaves, are now captured for you in arts and crafts by the "new artists." They place them in window displays, present you with magnificent nature, which nobody will ever tire of observing who has just once looked at them with those eyes that are linked to soul and mind, which indeed themselves have become the beholding mind and the observing spirit!

What do you all buy?! Shame on you! Possessions!? God, possessions must be like the possessions of one's skin or one's hands! They belong to me, are indispensable, maintain, as it were, the collective organism, are exquisite parts of it, the exterior covering the epidermis! Whatever stands on my table, on my walls, belongs to me like my skin and my hair. It lives with me, in me, of me. Without it I would be almost a rudimentary, something stunted, poorer. For example: my girl friend, the "dark lady," and Burne-Jones's picture: "A girl is sitting in a garden by the shore, her hands upon an old book, leaning back. Two angels play music, and her hands upon the old book, leaning back, the girl dreams, in the garden by the shore, soaring away from book and garden, whither, whither?!" This picture and the "entranced lady" above whose bed it hung were *one and the same!* Who understood the picture, understood her; who understood her, understood the picture. No other one could hang above her bed. It belonged to her, to her, like her own hands and hair. The lady pricks her ears—whither, whither?!

New people, it is with such things that belong to you, that are a part of your being, that you must surround yourselves! The new artist creates out of his genius the things that are for your souls! That truly appertain to you! Paint your walls just white and place in a corner or against a wall one of those splendid bowls that have the brilliance of flying humming-birds, setting suns, and sea foam!

I saw a vase here, light brown with gold flashes and dark stripes. Then a yellowish one, blanched the color of milk. Then a completely translucent one shaped like a huge honeycomb with cells, wax-yellow in color. And another like the green wings of ephemera. A dark-blue one that changed into the colors of early morning, from night to morning, and again became darker, nightlike. Then spherical light-brown clumps of glass on glass bamboo stalks, superb creations. Gallè glasses; light-brown flowers appear to come nebulously out of the glass itself and yet not out of it, evaporating.

Do not allow such vases to be forgotten once back in your own lairs! People have the most tender affection for such vases! When they enter a room, they greet them. And when they depart, they bid them farewell. Intimate pleasures!

Paint your walls white, in all simplicity, and place things there that you can love like a brother or a sister, not cold, strange things! That way you will be wealthy and never lonely!

I have been in Munich now for several days, for the first time, and have seen nothing, absolutely nothing marked out in the guide books, no monuments, no paintings. I am not interested in things that *were*. I am interested in things that *are*, that *will be!* From the window displays of fine shops the "new art" shone to me as I made my solitary way through the streets!

"In München," 1901. Original text in *Was der Tag mir zuträgt: Fünfundsechszig neue Studien* (Berlin: S. Fischer Verlag, 1924), 305–9.

LITTLE THINGS

For a long time now I have been judging people on the basis of *minute details.* I am sorry to say I cannot wait for the "big events" in life through which they "reveal" themselves. I must be able to discern these "revelations" on the basis of the smallest events! For example, the cane or parasol handle he or she selects. The necktie, the material of a dress, the hat, the dog he or she keeps, a thousand insignificant little things, even down to, or really up to, the cuff links! For *everything* is an essay about the person who *chose* them and *enjoys* wearing them! He reveals himself to us! "He wrote a good book, but he wore crudely tooled, artificial-looking cuff links!" That says it. Something is wrong somewhere in the "state of the soul!" It's not *important* that some beloved woman deceived us! Destiny will *surely* punish her *mercilessly* with *deep disappointment!* But *what matters most* is her first *coquettish, passionate* glance! I can compete with the one who *deceived* me, *totally,* but not with the one who shot a *covetous* look *from afar!* Little things murder! *Fulfillment* can always be overcome, but never *anticipation!* That is why I put store in the *little things* of life, in neckties, parasol handles, cane handles, discrete remarks, pearls that roll under tables and nobody ever finds! The momentous things in life have *no significance at all!* They tell us no more about existence than what we already know! That is because in *great need* they *all* function *exactly alike!* But it is in details alone that the important distinctions appear! For example, what flowers a man gives his most dearly beloved! Or what belt buckle he selects for her among hundreds! Which pears from France, or grapefruits from America, he brings her home; which brown-speckled Canada apples he chooses for her among hundreds. That demonstrates many more intimacies than the orgies of so-called love! Aesthetics, understanding, and love must, after all, constitute a triple alliance. One should be able to compose a *symphony of ordinary existence* out of "little things!" Instead of waiting for big ones to happen! The *very smallest* thing is *big!* The squeaking of a mouse in a trap is a terrible tragedy! Somebody once said to me: "The *most awful thing* is a young rabbit dragged into a fox hole. Day and night the little foxes slowly gnaw on its still-living body with their needle-sharp teeth!" Those are the tragedies of existence!

Little things take the place in life of the "big events!" That is their value, if one can grasp it!

"Kleinigkeiten," 1909. Original text in *Bilderbögen des kleinen Lebens,* 3d ed. (Berlin-Westend: Erich Reiss Verlag, 1909), 182–83.

PERFECTION

Nowadays, perfection is a thoroughly misunderstood word. People say: Gustav Klimt, the perfect modern painter; Frau Bahr-Mildenburg, the perfect Wagner performer; Otto Wagner, the perfect architect; Peter Altenberg, the perfect writer of sketches; Karl Kraus, the perfect "aggressor, mocker, annihilator!" But every person can be perfect, in everything! An orange seller can be perfect if he can tell with unerring accuracy from the outside, right through the skin, as it were, the taste, succulence, and sweetness of each orange or mandarin! A chestnut roaster can be perfect if he has the feeling for when and in what circumstances his chestnuts are roasted to a lovely even golden yellow, without getting any brownish black hard spots. A bartender can be perfect, an affectionate woman, a short-haired fox terrier, a shirt cleaner, a salesclerk, in the way he waits on people, a cook, a stenographer, in short: all, everybody, so long as they achieve the most perfect in whatever they do or are! May the noted companies of universal fame perish; long live the unknown who sing divinely when washing or dressing without being engaged by the Court Opera! Long live the exceptional weavers and cloth manufacturers, long live the Croatian, Bosnian, Hungarian, Scottish, Irish, Danish, and Swedish cottage industry! Perfection is as perfection does!

"Vollkommenheit," 1913. Original text in *Semmering 1912,* 5th and 6th enlarged ed. (Berlin: S. Fischer Verlag, 1919), 46.

Peter Altenberg as Collector

The *International Collectors' Newsletter* has just published in No. 13 an interesting poll about the value of collecting. The journal has contributions from, among others, Minister of Education Count Stürgkh, Alfred Lichtwark, Alma Tadema, Harden, Paul Heyse, Max Kalbeck, Eduard Pötzl, Felix Salten, Balduin Groller, and Ginzkey. Peter Altenberg gave the following interesting answer to the question about his collecting hobby: "It is quite noteworthy that it is indeed to me that you turn in this matter. For you absolutely could not know that I, a truly poor man, have been a simply fanatical collector for many years and that, just like the millionaires, I have managed to acquire, through many sacrifices, a dearly beloved, protected, and superb picture gallery: 1,500 picture postcards, 20 hellers apiece, in two splendid little Japanese boxes with six compartments each. They are exclusively *photographic* pictures of landscapes, women, children, and animals. Several weeks ago I discovered that the really cultivated person in life has to divest himself of his treasures in order to be able to enjoy the *deepest single* pleasure of giving, of donating to his beneficiaries in his lifetime. That is why I sent both Japanese boxes with the 1,500 picture postcards collected since 1897 to a young lady in Hamburg, who alone of all women can appreciate this present. Since then I have been collecting all the more keenly, all the more passionately in order to complete my friend's collection. — — Here, then, are two of the most salutary distractions from the perilous plummet of one's own ego: first, the pleasure of collecting itself, and second, the pleasure it can bring to *somebody else* just as appreciative! Collecting means being able to concentrate on something outside of one's own personality that is, however, neither as dangerous nor as ungrateful as a woman one loves . . ."

"Peter Altenberg als Sammler," 1911. Original text in *Neues Altes,* 3d ed. (Berlin: S. Fischer Verlag, 1911), 191–92.

PICTURE POSTCARDS

The architect Adolf Loos returned from Cracow and said: "Peter, isn't it unusual in your artist's life that you will never see this *ancient* and still *eternally modern* work of art, the 'Wawel' hill, this national shrine of the Poles in indestructible stone?"

I then began to enthuse over the "Wawel," this Polish national shrine, in an exalted way! I described the wonderful, melancholic, fantastic and at the same time simple corners, alcoves, passageways, views, and so on, and so on.

He said: "As if you had been there, Peter! But almost more impressive!"

I answered modestly: "There is a modern living Polish painter who throughout his young life (or is he older?) exclusively paints *details of the 'Wawel' hill!* And I *have* picture postcards of all these paintings, 50 hellers apiece!

"Ansichtskarten," 1919. Original text in *Mein Lebensabend,* 1st–8th ed. (Berlin: S. Fischer Verlag, 1924), 224–25.

PICTURE POSTCARDS

Whoever understands and loves my 10,000 picture postcards, which I have collected for 20 years, has really no further need of trudging laboriously through the "famous" picture collections. He gets everything "in extract" if he is just mentally and spiritually fit for it. Otherwise he must unfortunately settle for the *accredited* "celebrities" in the galleries, which to me are insipid and worthless from the word go!

I fanatically love nature *at first hand* (God's) or the brilliant, that is, *nearly* equal nature of the simple *near-to-nature* artist. But the "stylized will," the nature-*abusing* urgency of the moderns, the businesslike and megalo-maniacal-obscene way they now exploit *apparent* trends for purposes of their own vanity and megalomania as the *"alleged modern generation,"* is a stupid infamy to be sure only of those who fall into it. For the so-called young artist of the rising generation wishes only to surrender himself as quickly and comfortably as possible to its immanent "instinct for self-preservation" and perhaps, even before he has his school diploma, to achieve what others do only after painfully consuming, nay, wasting a long, valuable existence. "Nature" isn't enough for them, a pity. They want to play "nature" themselves, a pity. But are they it? *No!*

"Ansichtskarten," 1919. Original text in *Mein Lebensabend,* 1st –8th ed. (Berlin: S. Fischer Verlag, 1919), 269–70.

The Hotel Room

At three in the morning the birds began singing softly, in a suggestive way. My cares grew and grew. It began in the brain as with a rolling stone, dragged along all hopefulness, all capacity for life, became a ravaging avalanche, and buried the ability to meet the day and the pitiless imperious hour! And chance! A mild storm lashed the treetops in front of my window. For absolutely no reason at all I burdened and troubled the life of the sweet Madam J. One of my benefactors also refused to pay my paltry rent as of next month. Somewhere he heard something about me and my views. They were too radical and unsympathetic for him. My *aesthetic ideal*, Fräulein W., has for a long time belonged to those who can pay it. I, who pursued the "mystic cult of beauty" with her, was always too inelegantly attired, incomprehensible, and in general insane for her taste. When I sank to my knee, deeply, deeply moved by her noblest physical perfection, she said that I was perversely inclined and that I shouldn't blame her! My hotel room grows light, my soul darkens. It is becoming morning.

The singing of the birds in the treetops becomes more distinct, traces of melodies are present. Tepid storms carry the fragrance of meadows. This would be the most appropriate hour to hang oneself on the cross-bar — — —.

"Das Hotelzimmer," 1908. Original text in *Märchen des Lebens,* 7th–8th ed. (Berlin: S. Fischer Verlag, 1924), 51.

Decorating a Room

To build your own nest, a truly high-reaching nest, exquisite, different from all others! Like a bird painstakingly assembling its own, twig by twig! And each nest is different, entirely different, and somehow assumes the *character* of its owner, its resident. Indeed, the birds don't have the misfortune, to be sure, of having architects for interior decoration in the bird world who for 10,000 marks will produce a "pretty" lodging for you! My one-window room on the fifth floor of the Grabenhotel is my "nest," collected twig by twig over twenty years. The walls entirely covered with photos: Princess Elisabeth Windisch-Grätz at the age of five; the same with her four angelic children; Franz Schubert and Hugo Wolf; Beethoven and Tolstoy; Richard Wagner and Goethe; Japanese "wading birds"; Mt. Fuji; a large crucifix from the Bolzano woodcarving school; Gustav Klimt's "Schubert-Idyll"; Castle Orth in Winter; Ciseri's "Interment." Photos of: Bertha L., Klara P., Nâh-Baduh from Accrâ, Paula Sch., Grete H., Kamilla G., Fräulein Mayen, Fräulein Mewes, and my thirty-three beloved clay vases and sixty-four Japanese "small art" things, all sponged from "admirers." In

short, everything bespeaking my being, my taste, my inner "experiences."
A nest! When I think who will sometime inherit this beloved room lock,
stock, and barrel, dying really doesn't make me any too happy! But on
the other hand, Paula Sch., Amen!

"Zimmereinrichtung," 1918. Original text in *Vita Ipsa,* 8th–10th ed. (Berlin: S. Fischer
Verlag, 1919), 60–61. For a quite interesting analysis of Peter Altenberg's photo
collection, see Leo A. Lensing, "Peter Altenberg's Fabricated Photographs: Literature
and Photography in Fin-de-Siècle Vienna," in Edward Timms and Ritchie Robertson,
eds.,*Vienna 1900: From Altenberg to Wittgenstein* (Edinburgh: Edinburgh University Press,
1990), 47–72.

CHECKPOINT

I take my breakfast at a kiosk in the Graben. It's situated in the open and
you can see constantly busy people. However, my barber is on
Teinfaltstrasse, thus rather far from my breakfast place. But I only pay him
30 hellers and 10 hellers tip. Now on 7 May at ten in the morning it was
already unbelievably muggy. A thunderstorm was expected no later than
two. Without any real reason I was dead tired, sat rather satisfied at my
kiosk on the Graben, and observed all the busy people. The route to my
cheap barber on Teinfaltstrasse struck me as an extremely fatiguing journey: Graben, Kohlmarkt, Herrengasse, Teinfaltstrasse. Opposite me was
the gleaming plaque: Charles Uhl, Court Barber. I knew that there it costs
60 hellers and 20 hellers tip, hence 40 hellers more than at my barber.
But the savings in energy?! The *heightened tone* of the nerves because of the
convenience?! The cool street and steps?! I went to Charles Uhl, Court
Barber. On the elegant steps I ran into a wealthy friend who once lent
me a hundred crowns in one of my plights.

"You here in this house, noteworthy. Where are you going then?"
asked the Great Inquisitor.

"I'm going to my barber," I said.

"Aha?! That's my barber, too. Didn't you have the little one on
Teinfaltstrasse before?!"

"Yes, before — — —."

"I see, before, before?!?"

"No, please, this isn't my usual barber. In this oppressive heat today
it just seemed too far all the way to Teinfaltstrasse."

"I see, so it was too far for you?! Well, as a matter of fact, yes, today,
too, since morning the heat's been oppressive. By the way — — —."

"Any time I can be in a position to," I said and climbed up to the
court barber.

"Die Kontrolle," 1908. Original text in *Märchen des Lebens,* 7th–8th ed. (Berlin: S. Fischer
Verlag, 1924), 67–68.

So Should It Always Be

A gentleman strode up to me in the coffeehouse and said: "I'm a fanatic admirer of yours."

"Very kind," I said. "Perhaps then you wouldn't mind standing a fine champagne?"

"With the greatest of pleasure."

We drank three glasses of G. and H. Mumm, extra dry, sweet.

It became seven in the morning. I went to the central baths, 27 degrees centigrade, porcelain tubs. A young woman with aristocratically delicate hands sat at the cash register. I said to her with my eyes: "Sweetest cashier —" And: "One ought to be allowed to purchase you as well — — —."

Then I breakfasted in a charcuterie. Cold smoked sturgeon from the Volga, 12 hellers a serving. Crayfish from Ostende. Large green olives from Spain, ten pieces 60 hellers. Prague ham, 6 hellers a serving, 90 hellers. Two bananas, gold-yellow-black flecked, from Africa, 30 hellers apiece, 60 hellers.

Then I bought a blue phototype picture postcard: "Path along the lake." In a winter landscape.

I imagined it set in a five-centimeter-wide ash-wood frame.

Because of these reveries I got home at nine-thirty in the morning. The young housemaid who led me to the lift said to me: "Herr Altenberg must have been knocked around again last night — — —."

"Yes indeed," I said, "you know, the philistine world order!"

She thought: "Well, he paid 40 hellers for the lift though it's already counted into the rent — — —."

"So sollte es immer sein," 1911. Original text in *Neues Altes,* 3d ed. (Berlin: S. Fischer Verlag, 1911), 83–84.

Reserved Table

A reserved table is a table at which in the evening the rudeness, impudence, and egoism of your fellowmen reach immeasurable proportions! A *slop-spout* for everything that burdens the busy machine of life during the day and irritates it!

I have, therefore, adopted, for the sake of some eventual relief, a *small tariff* for my favors.

Anecdotes from the nursery and wonderful experiences with one's children: 70 hellers!

Attempts by a man to make a fool out of, mock, or present his spouse or sweetheart as a "dumbbell": 1 crown 20! Revenge by both sexes for something that upset them during the day: 80 hellers! The *ostentatious* attempt on the part of a gentleman to justify all the stupidities a lady might say: 1 crown 40! Conversations concerning hygiene that do not comply with my *Pròdrômôs:* 90 hellers![1]

Attempts at conquering a soul which, like all souls, belongs to me, 3 crowns 80! For sitting next to a woman who appeals to me: 5 crowns! On the first evening my tariff was introduced, Herr T. paid:

70 hellers

1 crown, 20 hellers

80 hellers

1 crown, 40 hellers

90 hellers

3 crowns, 80 hellers

5 crowns - hellers
_____

13 crowns, 80 hellers

"Stammtisch," 1913. Original text in *Fechsung,* 3d and 4th ed.(Berlin: S. Fischer Verlag, 1915), 60.

1. Altenberg's idiosyncratic book about hygiene and diet, published in 1906.

RESERVED TABLE

All his friends want to make Peter *jealous. Friends?* Ha ha.

Something *special* should happen, therefore, not the insipid *commonplace.*

Is anybody to blame, after all?

You sit *united,* hence really *disunited,* at the table from 9 at night until 12.

Art, politics, literature are quickly disposed of.

What then? People *try* to lure Peter's lady friend, *of the moment,* away from him!

Also a kind of diverting game of dice, or lotto, or dominoes.

Only one wasn't playing along.

He paid *too close* heed to the feelings of Peter and of *her* who was the object of this psychic trade.

Then Peter said: "*You,* my dear friend, are much more *dangerous* than all the idiots we see engrossed in their cards. See to it that you make a timely disappearance from my table! The others can *play* at the dreary insipid game of favor!"

"Stammtisch," 1918. Original text in *Vita Ipsa,* 8th–10th ed. (Berlin: S. Fischer Verlag, 1919), 97–98.

The Reserved Table

Herr Peter left his third mug of "Löwenbräu" standing, quit his table earlier than usual. To her, to her, to her!

"Oh Peter, what do you get out of it? She has a natty young husband and maybe somebody else as well. What do you get out of it?"

What I get out of it is the driving force within myself to be able to leave something I enjoy, my reserved table and beer!"

To make a church out of a woman! What good did it do me to reduce the *stone epic* of the cathedral, the candles tall as lampposts, the scent of consecration fumes to her *essence?!?* There is only one true *impotence,* and that is to be able no longer to endow things with the richness of one's own soul!

"Der Stammtisch," 1918. Original text in *Mein Lebensabend,* 1st–8th ed. (Berlin: S. Fischer Verlag, 1919), 186–87.

Rules for My Reserved Table

Cutting fingernails at the table is forbidden, even with a proper set of scissors of the old type carried on one's person. But especially no cutting of fingernails with the modern clipper, since the sharply clipped nails can then easily fly into the beer glasses, and fishing them out is fraught with difficulty!

The word "butt" or the like should be avoided if possible. But if that proves to be impossible, then it should be brought forth more or less in a whisper!

Conversations of an entirely private nature, concerning personal ambition, vanity, delusions of grandeur, and "putting on airs," should not run more than three hours. Otherwise the perpetrator will have to stand a French champagne! Each glass extends the time limit of the conversation until the glass is empty!

Reports of personal indigestion together with detailed descriptions lacking any universal point of view must be transmitted to those seated nearby in short, terse phrases. Moreover, the sympathy of the listener must be discreetly conveyed in such a way as to repress his natural happiness over a friend's misfortune!

Political conversations must not go beyond the phrase: "I think things are stirring in America!"

Conversations about Goethe must not degenerate into a horrible baiting of Hugo von Hofmannsthal!

Ladies at our table who have to go "somewhere" from time to time must demand 20 hellers from their husbands or lovers loudly and clearly, since *this transaction* at least pleasantly reminds us of the "girls for sale!"

It is improper to test match heads for any length of time on a porcelain rubbing surface, since it is irrelevant to the question of the "development of mankind," to which everything at this table, after all, is subservient!

Young waiters must be defended against all their impudent remarks only by the person who can prove that he really is "homosexual!"

Conversations of a general nature must possess a perfidious hidden point against somebody at our table. It's like condiments in food; they help you digest it better!

Romantic couples must come to our table, for that is an infallible indication that they do not wish to spend at least *these* hours with each other alone. A defeat, thus, *coram publico* [in the eyes of the public]. Besides, perhaps the lady can be enticed away!

"Regeln für meinen Stammtisch," 1919. Original text in *Mein Lebensabend*, 1st–8th ed. (Berlin: S. Fischer Verlag, 1919), 44–45.

EPISODE

Two elegant young people introduced themselves self-consciously:

"For a long time we've been enthusiastic admirers of your works and request the honor of your drinking champagne with us at our table — — —."

"Gentlemen, I am very very ill and therefore ask that you guarantee me in advance that you will conduct yourselves with the utmost propriety!"

"But Herr Altenberg, would we otherwise venture to request the honor of your company?"

Two hours later: "Peterl, old man, the two of us, we're just ordinary naive human beings, but you've got sophistication, after all, you really understand this stuff about you know what. Beggin' your pardon, but we really got the hots for the one over there at the third table. Come on, give us a hand—play the intermediary!"

I stood up and said: "Gentlemen, you are forgetting your promised guarantees! I must seriously remind you of them — — —."

"What guarantees—we want to have some fun for our money!"

I then got up abruptly, went over to the lady and brought her back to my table. An interval of uneasy embarrassment ensued. Then I said: "You've got your enjoyment for your money! Apropos, you still owe me two glasses of champagne for my mediation! Pay up then! But I will drink them alone at another table!"

"Episode," 1911. Original text in *Neues Altes,* 3d ed. (Berlin: S. Fischer Verlag, 1911), 169.

PERFUME

As a child I found in a drawer in my beloved, wonderfully beautiful mother's writing table, which was made of mahogany and cut glass, an empty little bottle that still retained the strong fragrance of a certain perfume that was unknown to me.

I often used to sneak in and sniff it.

I associated this perfume with every love, tenderness, friendship, longing, and sadness there is.

But everything related to my mother. Later on, fate overtook us like an unexpected horde of Huns and rained heavy blows down on us.

And one day I dragged from perfumery to perfumery, hoping by means of tiny sample vials of the perfume from the writing table of my beloved deceased mother to discover its name. And at long last I did: Peau d'Espagne, Pinaud, Paris.

I then recalled the times when mother was the only womanly being who could bring me joy and sorrow, longing and despair, but who time and again forgave me everything, and who always looked after me, and perhaps even secretly in the evening before going to bed prayed for my future happiness . . .

Later on, many young women on childish-sweet whims used to send me their favorite perfumes and thanked me warmly for the prescription I discovered of rubbing every perfume directly onto the naked skin of the entire body right after a bath so that it would work like a true personal skin cleansing! But all these perfumes were like the fragrances of lovely but poisonous exotic flowers. Only Essence Peau d'Espagne, Pinaud, Paris, brought me melancholic joys although my mother was no longer alive and could no longer pardon my sins!

"Parfum," 1911. Original text in *Neues Altes,* 3d ed. (Berlin: S. Fischer Verlag, 1911), 169.

DOMESTIC SERVANTS

The Nursemaid

The nursemaid with the light-blond silken hair opened the front door. "Oh—," she said, "Nobody's at home, the mistress and master went for a drive with the little boy."

"I'll wait for them," said the young man.

He sat down on a wooden chair in the kitchen.

Everything gleamed, the blue-gray tiles, the heavy brass faucet, the water pipe, the red-brown mosaic floor with the dull white and blue spots — — — and the silken hair of the girl.

Yellow-green muscatel grapes hung on a chord in the open window.

The young girl stood leaning against the door.

"How was it in the country, Emilie — — ?"

He knew that she loved the country and longed for it — — —.

Then he said: "It's a lovely autumn evening today — — —!"

"Oh, in the city — — —?" she said.

It became very quiet.

Only the drops of water on the gleaming brass faucet were striking the marble basin — — — pláp, pláp, pláp.

"Do you ever have a day off!" he said.

"What for? Who should I go to? I have no one — — —."

"You have a very good life here," he said. "You're very fond of the kid, and your master and mistress are fine and good people, especially your mistress."

"Yes," she said.

She was eighteen years old, with a pink complexion and an ideal figure. Everybody around her was fond of her, especially the child, oh, the — — —! That is why whenever anybody said to her, "You have a very good life here," she said, "Oh yes."

The young man thought: "There must be ten thousand unborn desires spinning around in such a young organism — — —!"

He said: "What do you do evenings when the child's asleep?"

"Nothing — — —," she said.

"The little one falls asleep about eight, doesn't he — — —?!" he said.

She said nothing.

Then she said, her eyes lowered: "If I had the master's newspaper from yesterday — — —! But that takes light — — —."

The next day her young mistress said to her: "Emilie, you can always take the newspaper into your room in the evening — — —. I bought a high Japanese folding screen so that the baby won't be bothered by the light from your lamp."

"My lamp — — —?!"

"Yes, I bought you a reading lamp."

"Oh, m'lady — — —," said the young girl and blanched.

But the young man from yesterday thought: "There must be ten thousand unborn desires spinning around in such a young organism. Bring one to birth, to fruition — — — and only nine-thousand-nine-hundred-ninety-nine remain!"

The Housemaid

The young woman with the gold-brown hair received her from her mamma. Among the splendid wedding gifts was, as it turned out, the most valuable "Marianne, housemaid."

"Of course, she does have her little faults — — —," said Mamma.

But she herself had no idea what these were.

It was more a suspicion of the imperfection of everything mortal — — —. Be that as it may, she was a girl of "deep tact," as the brother of the young woman put it.

"She can tell everything you're thinking from your eyes — — —," said a lady who had come on a visit.

"She of course has her little faults — — —," said Mamma.

"No, she doesn't — —," said the gold-brown daughter with a very hurt look on her face.

She received this girl as a wedding present.

"Here is your room, Marianne — — —," she said and opened a small paradise and smiled. There were even flowers in it.

"Oh, m'lady — — —," said the poor girl.

The relatives said: "She is like the child in the house — —. But she deserves it."

Marianne was good, aristocratic, reserved, and hard-working — —.

She even cooked. But only when asked to.

She occasionally read, tended her flowers, sewed — —.

Or she looked down at the large courtyard, where the carriages were being washed, and above, over the roofs, where a fine white tower stood and the blue sky — — —.

In the second year the young gold-brown woman thought: "Marianne is changing. She's beginning to think. Can a person live just on being 'like the child in the house?' She has an adorable little room, good wages, clothes — —. What is it? For what is man born? We're taking advantage of her! Maybe she loves my brother or some other fine, well-born person

— —? Maybe she sits up crying at night in her little paradise. Maybe she's jealous of my happiness, my peace of mind?!"

In fact, Marianne had begun to think — — —.

She envied one person— — the hairdresser!

"To be a hairdresser, free, independent — — —!"

She regarded this being like the goddess of freedom — — —.

Where did she come from? Where is she rushing — —?!

She rang, burst in, did hair, told stories, gossiped like a member of the family, took her money, and was on her way — — —.

"She has no time to think — —," thought Marianne.

At least that's what was appealing to her — —.

It was drive in this life, a struggle with galloping time, with the mysteries of ladies' hair, with life itself — — —!

Marianne looked down at the courtyard, where the carriages were being washed, or above, over the roofs, where the fine white tower stood and the blue sky — —.

One day the hairdresser failed to appear — — —.

She had worn herself out, simply worn herself out.

Nobody said a word about it — — —.

Only the gold-brown woman said more gently than ever: "Marianne — — —."

The next day another hairdresser showed up.

She rang, burst in, did hair, told stories, gossiped like a member of the family, took her money, and was on her way — —.

Marianne looked down at the courtyard, where the carriages were being washed, or above, over the roofs, where the fine white tower stood and the blue sky — — —.

Now she no longer envied anybody — — —.

"Maybe that's happiness — — —," she thought.

One day the gold-brown woman said: "Marianne, my brother told me that nobody can make a Sachertorte like you. The glaze is like a batter — —."

Happiness — — — that was happiness!

"Dienstboten," 1896: "Das Kindermädchen" and "Das Stubenmädchen." Original text in *Wie ich es sehe,* 16th–18th enlarged ed. (Berlin: S. Fischer Verlag, 1922), 71–76.

LATE-SUMMER AFTERNOON

"I can only attract, not fascinate — — —," she said.

She wore a wide light-blue dress with tiny white dots, a brown straw hat with white carnations — — —.

"There's a pretty path through the woods up there — — —," he said, "little fields of thistle and lilac flowers and birch trees all over. You just go straight ahead, and down below the river whips up white foam — —."

She looked at him the way one says: "Would you like to be with me and inhale the scent of my dress — — —!?"

But they did not follow the straight path with the little glades of thistle, lilac flowers, and birch trees, but instead they drank coffee en grand société in the dewy meadow at a reddish-brown table and then played badminton — —.

The young girl's hair became damp, and delicate little ringlets cascaded over her temples — —.

She was very pretty — — —.

It began to rain — — —.

The unmowed meadows gave off a strong fragrance like woodruff in May. The brown paths began to glisten like glazier's putty. The pebble heaps on the street were washed clean, and the poplars trembled and drank rain — — —.

She carried the pretty straw hat with the white carnations in her hand, and he held the umbrella above her brown hair like a good, careful mamma.

Then they went into the piano room of the casino.

A bare, dark room that had the smell of a cellar — — —.

The girl's brother was playing Chopin, étude A major.

It was like waves of the sea that sing, glide up, and dissolve — — —.

It grew very dark.

Outside at the window the leaves of chestnut trees bowed before the gusts of wind and the storm went sh sh sh — —. A gas lamp shone in the distance — — —.

Inside, the A major étude glided up, abated on hearts, and dissolved — — —.

The gentleman and the lady smoked — —.

Only the glowing tips of their cigarettes were visible — —.

He was sitting very near her and was trembling — — —.

"Let's dance — — —," she said.

Outside, the leaves of chestnut trees bowed before the gusts of wind, the cigarettes shone at the window sills, the brother kept on playing, and the two danced slowly in the dark, silent all the while — — —.

Later she said: "What is the name of the étude that you played before — — —?"

"Chopin A major — — —," said the piano player. Then he added: "Robert Schumann has wonderful things to say about it. Why do you ask?"

"Just like that — — —."

But the young man was as if in another world — —. He also felt something wonderful about the étude in A major, but he couldn't express it like Schumann — — —. He just said softly to the girl: "My kindly queen — — —!"

"Spätsommer-Nachmittag," 1896. Original text in *Wie ich es sehe*, 16th–18th enlarged ed. (Berlin: S. Fischer Verlag, 1922), 31–33.

THE TWINS

They were exactly alike — — —.

They had blond hair of spun gold, delicate breasts, and fine white hands and feet.

Nobody could tell them apart.

Once a gentleman said: "Oh, I can tell you apart — — —!"

One had a blond tortoiseshell comb, the other a dark-yellow one, in their blond hair of spun gold.

They went out and came back in — — —.

Smiling, one of them handed the gentleman the two tortoiseshell combs, the blond and the dark-yellow.

The gentleman kissed her — — — and was vanquished!

"How could Herr Z. settle on that one?" a lady once asked.

"He could indeed not," answered Herr A., "he in fact took the other one!"

That was a bad joke and all laughed. Especially the first one.

But later he really did take—the other one!

She turned pink!

But the other turned pale — — — —.

Then one could tell them apart—this one and the other!

"Die Zwillinge," 1896. Original text in *Wie ich es sehe*, 16th–18th enlarged ed. (Berlin: S. Fischer Verlag, 1922), 202.

DIALOGUE

He and she are sitting on a bench in a street lined with linden trees.

She: Would you like to kiss me?

He: Yes, Miss — — —.

She: On the hand — — ?!
He: No, Miss.
She: On the mouth — — ?!
He: No, Miss.
She: Oh, you're indecent — —!
He: I have in mind "on the hem of your dress!"
She turns pale — — —.

"Dialog," 1896. Original text in *Wie ich es sehe,* 16th–18th enlarged ed. (Berlin: S. Fischer Verlag, 1922), 129.

NINETEEN

She lived in the splendid hotel on the lakeshore.

In the evening, she dined beneath the green pergolas glimmering in the electric light.

The day was long — — until the evening.

She got up late — — . Then she sat on a bench on the shady promenade.

After dining, she retired to her cool room.

Around five, or six, she went for a walk with her parents and her siblings.

In the evening, the family dined beneath the green pergolas glimmering in the electric light.

The day was long until the evening — — — .

Once in a while, a young fellow who loved her came on a visit — — — .

The hours he spent there on her account she devoted to him wearily and quietly. He took her rowing out onto the lake — — he felt himself to be very lucky.

She sat in the stern.

She sat there as if in a velvet or silk armchair in an opulent, stuffy municipal chamber — — — .

She was wearing a lovely dress of rust-red silk with a wide knitted dark-golden belt and a Florentine straw hat with white violets and a long silk chord, which was tied beneath her chin in a bow.

The lake lay in the subdued colors of evening — — — . The scent of leaves wafted from the woods.

The gray castle on the lake and the white castle on land were bathed in mist — — .

White-green pearls glided down the oars — — .

The oars sang: plúk-prlúk, plúk-prlúk, plúk-prlúk — — — .

On the day before her departure, in autumn, she received a bouquet of lovely dark roses.

On the enclosed card was written:

"To the ideal of human beauty."

A "Greek"

Night.

She slipped off her nightdress and stood stark naked before the large mirror.

It was the "ideal of human beauty."

The table was redolent with the fragrance of the roses — — — .

For a moment, the musty, weary boredom left her and, like a jubilant young conqueror, hope seized her — — .

As she sat in the carriage and rode off into autumn and then into winter, in shivering boredom, she thought: "Pericles, Sophocles, Themistocles, Socrates — — — ."

She had then a vague perception of the beautiful immortal spirit of Greece — — — .

"Neunzehn," 1896. Original text in *Wie ich es sehe*, 16th–18th enlarged ed. (Berlin: S. Fischer Verlag, 1922), 8–9.

THEATER EVENING

She couldn't take the poodle with her into the theater. So the poodle remained with me in the coffeehouse and we awaited the mistress.

He set himself down in such a way that he could keep an eye on the entrance, and I regarded it as very proper, if indeed a bit excessive, since, if you please, it was 7:30, and we had to wait until 11:15.

And so we sat there and waited.

Every carriage that sped by aroused his hopes, and each time I said to him: "It's not possible, she can't be here now, just think, it's not possible!"

Sometimes I said to him: "Our beautiful, kind mistress — — —!"

He was simply sick from longing and turned his head in my direction: "Is she coming or isn't she?"

"She's coming, she's coming — — —," I answered.

Once he gave up his post, came up to me, laid his paws on my knee, and I kissed him.

It's as if he said to me: "Just tell me the truth, I can take anything!"

At 10 o'clock he began whining.

I said to him: "You think, my dear, I'm not anxious too? You have to control yourself!"

He set no store by self-control and kept on whining.

Then he began softly weeping.

"Is she coming or isn't she?!"

"She's coming, she's coming — — —."

He now stretched out flat on the floor, and I sat somewhat bent over in my chair.

He no longer whined but glanced at the entrance, while I stared straight ahead.

It was 11:15.

There she came. She came with her sweet, soft, gliding steps, very calm and composed, and greeted us in her gentle way.

The poodle exulted, sang, and jumped up.

I removed her silk cloak and hung it on a hook.

Then we sat down.

"Were you worried?" she said.

As if one said: "How are you, darling?" Or: "Your devoted N. N.!"

But I thought: Longing, longing, that streams and streams and streams from the hearts of men and animals, what becomes of you? Do you perhaps evaporate into the cosmos like water in clouds? Just as the air is filled with mist, so must the world be filled and heavy with longings that came and found no soul to take them in! What happens to you, the best, the most tender in the world, longing, if you come upon no souls to imbibe you, avidly, to exploit you for their own power?!?

Longing, longing, that pours forth from man and animal into the world, pours forth, pours forth, what becomes of you?

"Theater-Abend," 1901. Original text in *Was der Tag mir zuträgt: Fünfundsechzig neue Studien* (Berlin: S. Fischer Verlag, 1924), 34–36.

JAPANESE PAPER, VEGETABLE FIBER

He had already given her everything that a most tender and affectionate soul could think of — — — . Now he was at the end of his affectionate imagination and all that was left him was to repeat himself — — — . She had accepted everything in admirable modern understanding, for she felt that it was effective medicine for his sick soul to keep on making presents of unusual things — — — . She accepted it as an obligation toward a heart that people had made ill, however unintentionally. And so she also put up no resistance toward such presents, which in other circumstances might have had too intimate a character, such as a parasol, gloves, belt buckles, handkerchiefs, and so on, and so on, and so on — — — . But now he had come to the end of both reality and fantasy, as far as his money permitted — — — . Then he came across an advertisement in a newspaper for an authentic Japanese toilet paper, made of Japanese vegetable fiber, exceptionally delicate yet firm in texture. A packet of it cost, to be sure, one crown eighty hellers, whereas the best domestic brands could be had for a crown — — — . He bought ten packets and sent them to her. At first, she was quite shocked, offended, and angry. But gradually, natural thoughts gained the upper hand. And she wrote back simply: "Now, my most tactful one, it is going to be truly difficult for you to think of something else that could make my life easy — — — ."

"Japanisches Papier, Pflanzenfaser," 1909. Original text in *Bilderbögen des kleinen Lebens,* 3d ed. (Berlin-Westend: Erich Weiss Verlag, 1909), 99.

Dogs

I hate women, not just because of the fake neckties they wear, or because of their fake umbrella handles, their fake hats, their fake cuff links, and so on. I hate them of late because of the costly "plant-dogs" they purchase in order to carry on with them a kind of mendacious animal romanticism.

When she was fifteen years old, my wonderfully lovely sister found a terribly starved animal, an absolute fright, on the Bergstrasse in the direction of Kaiserbrunn. But she took fantastic care of it. And when, one summer morning, she found it drowned in the tank of the small, fragrant vegetable garden, she went to bed and refused any nourishment for eight days.

Nowadays, they spend a good few thousand on prize-winning Russian greyhounds, first-class jumpers who, as we know, can leap over unheard-of high barriers but can't even muster the sense of smell to find their way back alone to the residence of their apparently beloved mistress!

Heartless idiots favor themselves with externally pretty animals, shameful masks of ideals, a reflection of their own empty personalities, draped in modern attire! Like themselves!

In the old days, the most loyal friend of man was favored, the white or black poodle who was always ready to sacrifice himself.

But today, people love the infamously treacherous dachshund, the grotesque clown fox terrier, and the stupid, heartless, and blasé Russian greyhound.

Today, people go for color and form. But the melancholic and guileless eye has become indifferent to you! It will certainly take revenge on you! The "aesthetic," too, can come only from the mysterious depths of the heart. Otherwise it is a blossom that decays and withers in its own shameless cold! Only the heart has eternally invigorating tropical warmth. Beauty alone murders!

"Hunde," 1911. Original text in *Neues Altes*, 3d ed. (Berlin: S. Fischer Verlag, 1911), 43–44.

FLIRT

"I'm sitting for the first time with a poet," she said, shuddering, as it were, within herself.

He said: "You have splendid hands, Fräulein — — — ."

She thought: "A true poet — — —!"

Then he said: "You're pale; you seem exhausted. You must never, never, never let yourself be awakened from sleep in the morning. Who wakes you up?!"

"Mamma."

"Sleep is the true, perhaps only charitable gift we have of an otherwise hard and pitiless nature!"

She thought: "How he expresses himself! A true poet!"

Then he said: "I'd like to be a preacher—but just for the sanctity of sleep—like Jesus Christ was for universal things, and Liebknecht and Tolstoy for others! The exalted prophet of the holy right of the human system to abundant self-ending sleep! *Woe unto you, criminal, murderer, destroyer,* who awakes a person asleep whom nature has set about healing and liberating, and so disturbs and thwarts nature's holy plans!

"A mother who awakes her daughter from sleep is no mother!

"One thing should be holy to you—*nature in her mysterious work* of replenishing what the pitiless struggle of the day has wrenched from the exhausted organism! Amen."

The young woman thought: "A prophet; a fanatic — — — too bad!"

Later, he said to her: "Woman!? Who earned this title of honor?!? When I asked a girl what kind of rice is the noblest, she was struck dumb and didn't know what to say! A lady once said to me: "My dear sir, we always have the finest rice, isn't that so, Karl?! Not at all bad, wouldn't you say?!?" But she had no idea what distinguishes the "finest rice"!

The young woman thought: "A cook — — — too bad!"

Then she said: "Well, what distinguishes it?!?"

He: "Every kernel of rice should be perfectly translucent, like fine alabaster, with no dull or cloudy places. When you cook it, it should stay very soft and yet retain its complete shape, as if it were still hard and uncooked! Firm and tender at the same time. Like refined people."

She said quite sadly: "Must a 'woman' just be able to understand rice?!?"

"No," he said. "But rice, one of the finest, most tender, and most easily digestible foods, *a source of warmth for life's coldness,* represents, one could say, the holy world of *substitutes* for lost energies! To help a man regain his strength, his stature, his passions, his highest functioning—to want to help him so, to be able to help him so—that is what it means to be a 'woman!' A true woman!"

The young woman thought: "I don't understand that at all. A fool — — — too bad!"

Then they spoke about the glass lemon squeezer, "Columbus's egg," as he called it. That is to say, he spoke, and she yawned inwardly, appreciative and knowing. "When you think of how it used to be in the old days, it's frightful. You could get a cramp in your thumb, and half the juice remained sitting in the lemon while the unnecessary seeds were in the glass. But now, with the glass lemon squeezer for 50 hellers, the juice flows like a clear brooklet into the lower groove while the useless seeds remain in the upper one. And the skin itself is dry on the inside like the Gobi Desert. Now a usurer and a floozy can really say: 'I squeezed him like a lemon!'"

The young girl's friends were terribly envious that the poet conversed with her aside so long and so intently.

One of them said: "What could they be talking about?! I have absolutely no idea."

Another said: "Maybe about Maeterlinck, or at the most still about Ibsen."

The third said: "About love!"

The fourth: "About adultery, of course."

But the youngest thought: "What difference does it make *what* you talk about with a poet—you're talking with a *poet!*"

"Flirt," 1913. Original text in *Was der Tag mir zuträgt: Fünfundsechzig neue Studien* (Berlin: S. Fischer Verlag, 1924), 60–63.

VENICE

Maria Mazzucato is the prettiest girl in Venice. She works in a tiny milliner's shop in the Merceria Capilleri. From early on till evening, she sits trying on hats for women, the lot of whom are not as pretty as she is. She is an aesthetic union of Otéro,[1] Grete Wiesenthal, and Duse. She is sixteen years old and very thin and tall, in other words—perfection personified. I wrote her a picture postcard (calme du soir): "Venise a été cet été une ville vraiment très intéressante et originale: elle a contenu la princesse de Terra Nova, Mitzi Thumb, et Maria Mazzucato! Les palazzi, mais mon Dieu, c'est mort, c'est enseveli! Et les vieux tableaux, mais, j'en préfère les jeunes et vivants!" [This summer, Venice has been a truly interesting and original city, for it contained the princess of Terra Nova, Mitzi Thumb, and Maria Mazzucato. But the palaces, my God—they make you think of just death and burial! And the old paintings! But I prefer the young and living!]

Maria Mazzucato *refused* to accept a farewell present, as a memento, a splendid leather handbag. She said: "As a memento?! But I have your picture postcard!" As a result, I exchanged the handbag for a stunning yellow-speckled tortoiseshell paper knife for my desk. How good that she *refused* it. First of all, she is going to have pangs of conscience and a little regret while I, well, I have a lovely paper knife! Yesterday I cut something open with it. I was really quite satisfied with the lovely paper knife.

The same evening, I saw a very small singer in the "Folies Bergères": La Eutimia. She was quite young, absolutely flawlessly built, yellowish complexion and black hair. With a deep, sweet voice she sang the marvellous songs "Fili doro, a retirata," "Una sola volta," and "Marechiare." After the performance, she took up a position in the narrow aisle and said to every man: "Twenty centesimi, if you please!" I gave her five lire. I said to her: "May I bring you a lovely leather handbag tomorrow?!" "By all means, sir, I'd be delighted!"

Then I took my lovely tortoiseshell paper knife and again exchanged it for the lovely handbag. "Ah," said the salesclerk who waited on me, "did the lady prefer the handbag after all?!" "Yes!" I said, "she changed her mind!"

"Venedig," 1915. Original text in *Fechsung*, 3d and 4th ed. (Berlin: S. Fischer Verlag, 1915), 53–54.

1.   The popular variety theater and cabaret dancer known as La belle Otéro or Caroline Otéro (real name: Caroline Carasson, 1868–1965).

The Primitive

All-night coffeehouse, four in the morning.

Seven drifters are sitting at a table awaiting the morning, the golden, rosy morning, the way the tourists do on Mt. Schafberg or Mt. Rigi.

But here, rest assured, there is no mountain air.

The drifter is the engine "man" derailed from the track. It begins to stumble, races here and there, does unnecessary things, expends energy—for what?—falls all over itself, and lies there like a drunk in street filth.

These people sit there, spend money, gab and gab, argue everything with the greatest seriousness, and are hopelessly drunk.

And straightaway they make bets and get all hot and bothered.

The coachmen sit at another table. They all possess a calm, internalized roughness. Rarely, if ever, does the storm erupt. It's as if everything were all laced up. I believe that it's all let out on the horses. "You scum!" A kick in the stomach. But the real scum is sitting indoors, in the coffeehouse—or somewhere else. The poor beast is just the representative. All the passions are directed at this scum "horse."

A young woman with a splendid pale face is leaning on the table at which a young, pale man is sitting.

"What's the matter with you?" said the young man, gently touching her beautiful white hand.

"I'm afraid," said the young woman.

"What does that fellow over there want from you?!"

"Nothing—! I think he's going to beat me as soon as I leave here. I'm afraid to go home. I don't need anybody to love me. I need money, pretty clothes. But he's going to beat me — — —."

"Come with me," said the young man and got up.

He had a deep sympathy for those who utter the true, honest word of the heart, even if it is brutal, like nature itself.

"I don't need anybody to love me—I need money, pretty clothes." That delighted him. He adored this woman, for whom speech and her entire organism were identical. Indeed, the entire organism itself had become sound, not an instrument like the flute or the clarinet that anybody at all can play, one way or another. And then puts it away. One is no longer a flutist. Nobody sees you for what you are. You wipe your lips, and that's that. You are a musician, not a human being! The human being cannot dispose of his music or wipe his lips — — —. He must always sing of his humanness, even if so softly that another person can barely hear it. If it's brutal — — — sing brutally!

But these cultivated people play whatever you want.

Above all, let your word be Truth! It is thence that beauty can blossom—*can*.

Anyway, that is what he was thinking of. The basis "Truth" was enough for him.

"That is the way I am," she said, and that delighted him.

He then thought: "This is the earth in the Cretaceous Age. What more?!"

So he became her knight, her protector.

She clung to him, nestled against him, from fear of "Petrucchio."[1] "I don't need anybody to love me," she murmured.

It was five in the morning.

Should I describe morning in the streets?!

This poor, shabby, early-world humanity, which delivers up sweet bed warmth to the cold morning air for 30, 40, or 60 kreuzer?!

A splendid aroma wafts from the bakeshops.

What else can one say?! One is not in a very cheerful mood.

This is in contrast to those who can await the sun when it pours white light and tepid rays onto the streets — — —.

He takes the young woman home with him.

His room was small, but it possessed an "individuality." To begin with, it always gave off a strong aroma of quince, which lay in a wooden bucket in a corner. In the second place, it was as clean as a Dutch flat and there were lovely wide curtains on the windows, embroidered *à jour,* like old, yellowish Brussels lace. In the third place, a superb engraving by E. v. Gebhardt, *The Last Supper,* hung over the bed.[2] A thick gold coin containing a splendidly engraved bust of Spinoza was glued above the head of Judas, standing in the half-open doorway.

"*This one* cancels out *the other's* disgrace. He covers him with his pure gold and rights the wrong."

That was the sense of it.

The young man took fragrant pinewood and lay the tinder in the wide, light-green fireplace. Then he lit it and loosely placed good hardwood on top of it.

A gentle warmth soon spread throughout the room and then it became hot and cozy.

The young woman sat stark naked in the corner next to the fireplace.

The young man sat at a table, opposite her, and wrote in a notebook: De pudore. Modesty! Perhaps it is the perception of the gulf between what we should and could be physically, and what we still are. We fret over our own ego, which in the stress of life becomes stunted. This worry is called "modesty." Don't look at me the way I am! We feel ashamed because of everything that destroys our ego and obstructs its development. It is the anxiety that we are still not the "last," the "God-like" — — —.

But what do you conceal when you have become your own ideal, when you are radiant in the "idea become deed?!"

Then you are in paradise, as you were once, and you show yourself naked!

The "beautiful" kills "shame!"

It is perhaps a feeling, placed within us, which we overcome through our perfection.

When you are what you should be, let your raiment fall, conqueror!

"What are you writing there?" said the young woman.

He read it to her, explained it. "It comes from you," he said. "I only transcribed it."

She said: "You know, I love my body and I treat it as something holy. I care about this form a great deal and respect it. It needs, for example, a long sleep that ends of itself, simple, easily digested nourishment, and a thousand other things. When I get up in the morning, my room is already bathed in a good, warm fragrance of wood burning. There is a large tub with cold spring water in the middle of the room. I jump eagerly out of bed into the water and lie in it for five minutes. Then I go back to bed. Ah, I steam myself there—a thousand lives flow in me! Then I get up. It makes me very happy — — —. Later on, I drink chicken bouillon with three egg yolks cooked in it, followed by a little salt-water fish, and finally Roquefort. I drink only water, and I don't smoke. 'You are the model of an egoist,' a man said to me once. But to whom do I bring pleasure, to me or to others who then think: *'When you are what you should be, let your raiment fall, conqueror!'?!*"

She stood laughing in her splendor—!

He kissed her on the mouth.

"You have spirit," he said. But it was his own.

He said: "Your breath is like the aroma of cooked, still warm, peeled sweet almonds."

He thought: "This breath is the consequence of the total organism. I love you because of this breath. It is a sign of divinity, a true breath of divinity: 'Everything about us can become so pure!'"

The "heavenly ecstasy" over perfection overcame him. It is like the shout of joy of the climber when he reaches the sunny mountain peak—there is no going any higher! Thence the calm, the peace, the sense of good fortune! The fulfilled wish of God—there is nothing holier! And this wish also applies to that "ponderous bearer of the soul." He can become beautiful! One observes a beautiful form, seeks to give it eternity—but the imperfect—may ruination befall it—dishonors it! What does it matter?!

This ideal body, this purest breath, dissolve the shabby feeling of passion, of desire, in the great perception of the world redeemed.

And so they went to bed like brother and sister.

When she awoke, he was sitting in front of her. It was three in the afternoon. She was pink all over.

The room lay in the warm aroma of fragrant, crackling sprucewood.

In the middle stood a gleaming tub of cold spring water.

A light-gray sea-bass lay in a shallow bowl on the table covered with white cloth. Aspic, like wine-colored topaz, glittered in another small glass bowl—.

A white-green piece of Roquefort lay on a small silver platter.

"Oh," said the late riser, surprised. "You are good!"

She bathed for five minutes. Then this blooming, ideal body steamed in bed.

Then she sat down naked at the table and began to eat.

He waited on her like the royal huntsman waits on the king.

For the first time in her life, this "primitive" experienced a man as a human being — — —. What was holy to her was holy to him — — — — her beautiful body. She felt a kind of justification of his care. It was like a whiff of Greek antiquity — — —. There was a connection between the way he understood things and the way she did. It was not a comedy that one was playing for the other's benefit. It was freedom, understanding. That is why she felt for him as she did! Indeed, through his complicated explanation of the primitive in her, he was almost an educator. He gave the "beautiful unconscious" a philosophical basis, a psychological interpretation. He "discovered" the primitive! It was called: "What does it matter? You have God's beauty!"

We cannot shape people in our own likeness, only in their own. Their ideal lies concealed in them, not in us!

One could almost say: Teaching means "listening to organic growth."

But these others want to bend, crack, cut down, undo, break, destroy—!

But whom are they destroying? Themselves! And then they bemoan their "murdered ideal!"

When it was time for her to go, the young woman said: "Give me this gold coin on the picture as a present — — —."

That was cupidity and curiosity combined.

He took the picture out of its frame and removed the coin. She then glimpsed the head of Judas.

"Also a destroyer — — —!" she said.

"What do you mean 'also'?! It's always the same. He lies within us and so, too, does 'the other one.' But that is what people don't understand. There is always one in us who betrays, sells out, and murders the 'ideal man' in us — — —!"

She took the coin with Spinoza's bust.

"Adieu," she said and kissed him on the mouth.

He again sensed this breath that had the fragrance of hot, peeled sweet almonds.

"Adieu," he said.

And then he hung the picture back on the wall above his bed.

The deathly sad noble ones again sat with the deathly tired, hounded, noblest of them of all, this blossom of all mankind. And Judas stood, pale, in the half-open doorway through which the early light of dawn glimmered. Morning was beginning — — —.

But it was not morning that was dawning—it was night falling!

"Die Primitive," 1896. Original text in Peter Altenberg, *Wie ich es sehe*, 16th–18th enlarged ed. (Berlin: S. Fischer Verlag, 1922), 120–28.

    1.   The character in Shakespeare's *Taming of the Shrew*.

    2.   The reference is to a work by Edmund von Gebhardt (1838–1925), a well-known religious painter of the so-called Düsseldorf school.

FROM *PRÒDRÔMÔS*

The spiritual evolution of mankind depends exclusively on the *activity* of the laws of dietetics and hygiene!

We are monsters. But we already *know* how we can become gods! It is a long, long road. But God has time! That is one of His qualities! He can count on unlimited hours! Today?! Tomorrow?! The day after tomorrow?!? No, He is optimistic; in *millions of years!*

Nature in us must be replaced by the *spirit!* For the spirit is nothing other than nature come to a *consciousness of itself!* Nature, conducted by the brain of man from the shades of night into the daylight of its own spirit! Nature brought to peace through absolutes! World and mind become *identities!*

For girls and women during m . . . .

Maternity diet, convalescent diet! If possible, remain in a restful position, by an always open window, day and night fresh air!

M . . . . is a weakening of the organism. Woe to her whom it does not weaken. She thinks she can pass over it to her *regular activity!* But m . . . . takes revenge for disdain — — — .

When somebody says: "It doesn't bother me — —," I always think: "But what good did it ever do you if you avoid it — — ?!?"

I bought a very pretty small carved elephant for a lovely seven-year-old girl who I heard had a quite exceptional and exclusive love for animals (she never played with puppets but with animals made of paper).

She received it at lunch. She paled from excitement. She could only say: "I can't eat any more — — — ." And she went to her room.

What kind of a present do you have to give a grown woman for her to utter the holy words of the soul: "I can't eat any more — — —"?!?

One winter night I accosted a very young, delicate, and beautiful fallen woman and expressed my admiration for her face. She became churlish and said: "Hey, take somebody else for a fool, not me!" I refused to be deterred from admiring her sweet beauty. Then she said: "Well, if you're really serious, prove it to me and buy me the prettiest gingerbread heart there is in a shop on St. Stephen's Square." "By all means," I replied. She got the prettiest heart. It cost two crowns. "Well, I won't detain you any longer," I said.

"That's all right, my work doesn't please me any more today. Walk me back to my door; I'm going home now with my lovely gingerbread heart. This is my luckiest night."

"And what if I went to bed with you?!?"

"Then that would be something very different. No, please leave me alone today with my luck — — — ."

I met a young woman who loved her canary the way every man would like to be loved by his deified creature in his ideal reveries! It was the model of a true reciprocal love!

He used to keep looking at her with a tenderness that threatened to burst his heart. His little black eyes cried of love and tenderness. His little feet danced and his wings trembled from tenderness. And his mistress drank in this unbelievable love and became strong and happy and confident!

And then the most beloved little bird died a tragic death. The girl's mother accidentally stepped on him. And he was done for! Everything was done for. Irreparably. From then on she lived like somebody dying.

"When he looked at me with those darling little black eyes of his — — — .

But the eyes of men have the look of moneylenders, the look of crafty businessmen.

Why am I grieving?!? I, I alone among thousands thus came to know the essence of love — — — ."

Calisthenics to a rhythmical piano accompaniment (American military marches), tremendously precise, executed *lightning fast*, elevate gymnastics to a "hygienic dance." *Dance-gymnastics.*

Lovely women—wear socks, summer and winter long, and *absolutely no underwear!* That makes you robust and pink-cheeked!

Clothing—*prohibitor* of the wonderful bond of "human skin" and "atmospheric air!"

One cannot wear too little!

The only criterion is the police and penal law!

"I have on as little as the police allow!"

Lesbian love. Here one knows exactly what transpires, what occurs in another. For one is one's own self, projected in a second, identical person! The *mystery* of the ego experienced in this mystery of the *non*-ego! She experiences her own bliss in another person who is at the same time the identical ego.

The highest altruism!

"I feel my own bliss in a foreign organism — — —!" she says.

I Drink Tea

Six o'clock in the evening approaches. I feel it approaching. Not as intensively as children feel Christmas Eve approaching. But still. At six on the dot I drink tea, a festive enjoyment without disappointments in this woe-burdened existence. Something that makes you feel sure you have your own peaceful happiness in your own power. It is completely independent of fate. I begin to feel happy as soon as I pour the good spring water into my pretty white half-liter nickel pot. Then I wait for the boiling, the song of the water. I have a large hemispherical bowl of brick-red Wedgewood. The tea comes from the Café Central; it smells like Alpine meadows, like brussels sprouts and grass burnt by the sun.

The tea is golden-yellow-straw-yellow, never brownish, light and unpressed. Along with it I smoke a cigarette, "Chelmis, Hyskos." I drink very, very slowly. The tea is an internal stimulating nerve bath. It enables you to take things easier. You think that a woman ought to have such an effect. But she never does. She still lacks the culture of harmonious gentleness to have the effect of a fine, warm, golden-yellow tea. She believes that to be that way, she would perhaps lose her power. But at six o'clock in the evening my tea never loses its power over me. I long for it daily the same way and lovingly wed it to my organism.

The Mouse

I moved into the quiet small room, fifth floor, of the good, old hotel, with two pairs of socks and two huge bottles of slivovitz for unseen eventualities.

"Shall I have your baggage fetched?!?" asked the bellboy.

"I don't have any," I said simply.

Then he said: "Do you wish electrical lighting?!"

"Yes."

"It costs fifty hellers a night. But you can also have plain candles if you like." he said, in view of the prevailing circumstances.

"No, I prefer electrical lighting."

Around midnight, I heard the sounds of wallpaper being torn and scratched. Then a mouse came in, climbed up onto my washstand and entered the washbasin, executed various well-mannered maneuvers, and immediately thereafter returned to the floor, since porcelain was incompatible. Generally, though, he had no firm, far-reaching plans and finally regarded the darkness beneath the stand as rather advantageous under the circumstances.

In the morning, I said to the chambermaid: "There was a mouse in my room last night. Lovely housekeeping!"

"We have no mice here. Where would a mouse come from here? Nobody can accuse us of anything like that!"

I then said to the bellboy: "Your chambermaid is a saucy creature. Last night there was a mouse in the room."

"We have no mice here. Where would a mouse come from here? Nobody can accuse us of anything like that!"

When I entered the hotel lobby, the porter, the bootblack, the other two chamber maids, and the manager of the establishment all regarded me the way one regards somebody who checks in with two pairs of socks, two slivovitz bottles, and already sees mice that aren't there.

My book *What the Day Tells Me* lay open on my table, and I once surprised the chambermaid reading it.

In these unpleasant circumstances, my credibility with respect to mice was somewhat undermined. Because of it I had, after all, acquired a certain aura, and people no longer argued with me, took no notice of my little weaknesses, closed an eye to them, and conducted themselves exceptionally obligingly, the way one does with an invalid or, on the other hand, as one does toward those whom one respects.

Be that as it may, the mouse appeared every night, scratched the wallpaper, and climbed frequently onto the washtable.

One night, I bought a mousetrap along with some ham, walked ostentatiously with the instrument in hand past the porter, the bootblack, the manager of the establishment, the bellboy, and the three chambermaids, and set the trap in the room. The next morning, the mouse was in it.

I then thought of carrying the mousetrap down quite nonchalantly. Let the matter speak for itself!

But on the staircase it occurred to me how upset people become when you find them guilty of something, like a mouse being discovered in a guestroom of a hotel in which there simply "are no mice!" Moreover, my aura of a person without baggage, with two pairs of socks, two bottles of slivovitz, a book called *What the Day Tells Me,* and who sees mice at night, would be considerably shaken, and I would at once be relegated to the embarrassing category of a tiresome and highly ordinary guest. As a result of these considerations, I deposited the mouse in one of those rather appropriate places for such purposes and placed my mousetrap on the floor of my room, again empty.

From then on I was treated all the more considerately, nobody showed the slightest wish in such circumstances to annoy me, and all indulged me like a sick child. When I finally took my leave, it was in the friendliest of atmospheres, although I took with me as baggage just two pairs of socks, two empty bottles of slivovitz, and a mousetrap!

Pròdrômôs, 1906. Original texts in *Pròdrômôs,* 4th and 5th eds. (Berlin: S. Fischer Verlag, 1919), 18–19, 28, 43, 43–44, 65–66, 70, 71, 106, 153–54,162–65.

THE KIDNEY

I always count it among the truest and, to me, sincerely touching sacrifices that a man can make to a beloved woman, when with roast kidney he lets *her* have the kidney, assuming, of course, that he himself likes eating it. But who doesn't like eating kidney?! Kidney is, after all, such an accurate thermometer in matters of love. For example: "Otto, why aren't you eating the kidney?!" — "I am going to eat it, and with the greatest pleasure, which is why I leave it for last!" — "Oh, I see," replies Hermine, disappointed. Or: "But Max, you're not eating the kidney!" and already has stuck it in her little mouth, while in Max's mouth the only thing sticking are the words: "Not at all!" Or: "There's love for you, he's devouring the kidney himself, just have a look!" However, those gentlemen who make the "sacrifice of the kidney" do it for the most part rather *tastelessly,* in that they imagine they now have a claim to gratitude and loyalty for the rest of their lives! No, that isn't so. The ladies accept the dainty morsels given them, but they have the right idea that such sacrifices are richly rewarded through the feeling of a higher dignity that a person receives from himself! Why overvalue the matter?!

"Die Niere," 1913. Original text in *Semmering 1912,* 5th and 6th enlarged ed. (Berlin: S. Fischer Verlag, 1919), 147.

Vienna's Hygiene

Since 9 March 1917, my fifty-eighth birthday, I have been wearing wooden sandals over naked feet. Since then I have been experiencing, suffering "Vienna's sins" against the *poor lungs* and, considerably less significant, against my naked feet! Feet can be washed ten times a day, but *lungs?!?* From seven in the morning on, *all* the stores treat the sidewalk and the street like depositing places for the *dust* from *dusters, door-mats,* and *carpets!* The "beloved" dogs are lovingly *trained* to use the sidewalks as toilets! "Shaking dust down on passersby" from windows is forbidden by the police, but the same "crime," committed from shops on the ground floor—which is even more direct—is evidently permitted, otherwise *everybody* wouldn't do it! Nowadays one shouldn't have to still rely upon *"obvious decency"* with respect to one's innocent unknown fellow creature; *draconic ordinances* with heavy fines are more in order. Whirling street dust and dung in the air *dry,* the way our streetcleaners do, instead of first wetting them down with *watering-cans* and converting them into a *harmless* mush, is also a *crime* against the lungs and against my naked feet.

Every good *innovation* in itself also engenders more correct views of conservative inveterate vices. *Our* way of treating streets and sidewalks as "dung pits" is a "hygienic crime!" It's not everybody's business to want to help others; but I want to. Shrugging it off as "nothing's right" to avoid at once becoming a "Danton, Marat, Robespierre" of public hygiene is too irresponsible. As I said, I can wash my naked feet ten times a day; but what about your *naked helpless lungs?!?* For *street dust-dumpers* 100 crowns dusted out for the "war blind!" No, 200 crowns! "Hygienic cleanliness" is a type of unconscious *"physiological genius,"* but Vienna doesn't *possess it at all.* It possesses, instead, a "divine gift of grace," *"good-natured nonchalance!"* A centimeter-thick layer of dust covers the Volksgarten [People's Garden] and it is constantly being *whirled about* by passersby and children. Cartloads of *sand from the Danube* and continuous *handspray-watering* could create a *"paradise,"* but nobody takes the trouble. One can only say: *holy Town Hall park* and *"the grounds* of the Minorite Church!" There the air is at least as clean and dustfree as it can possibly be in any big city. You have to first go about with *naked feet* in order *to understand* and *to hate* the crime against other people's *lungs!*

"Wiens Hygiene," 1919. Original text in *Mein Lebensabend,* 1st–8th ed. (Berlin: S. Fischer Verlag, 1919), 101–3.

LETTER TO GRETE WIESENTHAL,
THE DANCER

Safeguard your digestive system, this *center* of your life force, from unrestrained resolution, like a sick woman in labor must do *out of necessity* —— and you will stay light and mobile, flying and floating, dancing and rejoicing!

Help it along with the holy purgative: *Rhamnin,* Cortex Rhamni Frangulae, a tablespoon full before breakfast!

An ideal substitute for every cold bath: menthol rubbing alcohol, in a large *atomizer,* sprayed over the *entire body* like a rain shower. Evenings before going to sleep, mornings on awaking!

Arm exercises, *up, down,* and *sideways, to the tempo* of the brisk *march of the Bersaglieri,* to the accompaniment of piano, clarinet, and small drum (Sousa marches!).

Dance gymnastics!

Forward! Get a move on! Precise! Like the clatter of machine guns, rat-ta-tat!

Your devoted Peter Altenberg.

P. S. One becomes a *dancer* through *gymnastics!* Through dance alone, *never!*

"Brief an Grete Wiesenthal, die Tänzerin," 1915. Original text in *Fechsung,* 3d and 4th ed. (Berlin: S. Fischer Verlag, 1915), 58–59.

LETTER TO THE DANCER

1 July [1918]

Dear Fräulein Grete!

You will *understandably* regard me as insane. For five months now, since February, I have been laid up with two broken wrists, without eating, without being able to wash myself, in my *coffin-closet* (Vienna I., Grabenhotel). As a result of the deepest *aversion to life* I took an excessive quantity of sleeping medicine (instead of my usual single liqueurglass full, forty!). It destroyed me *completely.* Professor Baron Wagner von Jauregg (an *admirer* of my works) heard of this unprecedented occurrence and came to visit me. He informed me that I stood inevitably before the gates of *delirium or cancer* (*the death of tissue through paralysis of the nervous system!*). As soon as he left, I *immediately no longer knew* that this sleeping medicine existed at all. I *mysteriously-inexplicably* saved myself within the space of a single night, where otherwise *withdrawal treatments* of six weeks to eight months would be absolutely necessary! As Professor Wagner reported in the company of the physicians, this was the *first case* of this happening since sleeping medicine has been available. Since 26 June, I have been saved, restored to my *earlier elasticity,* as if by means of a *mystery of faith, physiological Christianity!*

On 3/9/1919 I shall celebrate my sixtieth birthday. I have the intention, *consequently* and above all in consequence of my frightful material circumstances, to make my appearance as your *dancing partner!* I imagine it this way: Costume—silk Lido cap, Lido tights, *sandals over bare feet* (this is how I walk about Vienna until December), short pants, *bare* underbones! Between your individual numbers, which I will accompany with *gestures,* I will dance solo Ashanti dances to wholly *primitive, enchanting* rhythms voiced by me and composed by me (any conductor can arrange it for orchestra in five minutes, it's just *children's music*). For the finale, however, you and I will dance an *artistic* six-step! I sit in the "Graben-kiosk" every day from 9 o'clock in the morning until 12 noon. Please look me up there!

Yours,
Peter Altenberg
Vienna I., Grabenhotel

"Brief an die Tänzerin," 1919. Original text in *Mein Lebensabend*, 1st–8th ed. (Berlin: S. Fischer Verlag, 1919), 287–88.

MENTAL HOSPITAL
(BUT NOT THE ONE I WAS IN!)

Morning Visit

The doctor sits, like a public prosecutor with a serious and inquiring look on his face, at a huge desk.

The offender (patient) enters.

"Please sit down — — —."

Pause, during which the public prosecutor (doctor) examines the criminal for signs of paralysis or simulation — — —.

"Well, my dear Peter Altenberg, I have known you for a long time of course from your interesting books, and hence permit myself, with somebody as renowned as yourself, to dispense with the conventional title 'Herr.' Your admirers, by the way, just call you 'P. A.,' isn't that so!? I have not as yet hazarded this *abbreviation of distinction* — — —.

"But down to business! Well, my dear Peter Altenberg, what are we going to have for breakfast, eh?!?"

"We?! I don't know. But I myself have coffee, light coffee with milk — — — ."

"Coffee?! Is that so?! Coffee, light coffee with milk — — — ?!? Fine, coffee — — —!"

"Yes, it's my usual drink, which I have been accustomed to for the past thirty years — — — ."

"That's fine. But you are here, after all, in order to *disaccustom* yourself from your previous life-style, which apparently up to now has ill served you. Even more so, to acquire, however gradually, the *necessary energy* to undertake such *changes* in your usual, indeed perhaps *all too usual* life-style! Well, let's stay with the coffee with milk for the time being. But how do you explain this decided aversion to tea, for example?! You can also drink tea diluted with milk — — — ?!"

"Yes, but I'm used to drinking coffee with milk — —."

"Herr Altenberg, do you have any definite reason to regard the drinking of tea in the morning as unsuitable for your nerves?!?"

"Sure, because it doesn't taste good to me — — — ."

"Aha, that's just what I wanted to know. Well then, my dear sir, what do you take along with your so beloved and *apparently indispensable* coffee with milk?!?"

"Along with?! Nothing!"

"Well, you must have something *solid* with it! Just plain coffee doesn't really have any taste — — —."

"No, I don't want anything with it; I like just *plain* coffee with milk — — —."

"Well, I regret to say, my esteemed sir, that that simply won't do here. You will have to make the great *concession* of having two rolls with butter — — —."

"I hate butter, I hate rolls, but I hate rolls with butter even more!"

"Well, I feel confident that we will yet *overcome* this hatred! I have already achieved *more difficult feats,* my dear — — —. Now, if you would be so kind as to betake yourself calmly to your breakfast on the veranda. One other thing: Are you in the habit of taking a rest after breakfast?!?"

"Depends — — — ."

"There's no such thing as 'depends.' Either you rest or you move about — — — ."

"In that case, then, I shall rest — — —."

"No, you shall take a walk for half an hour — — —!"

The offender staggers out of the office and heads, for the *commencement of his imprisonment,* to the veranda for his breakfast, fortified with two rolls with butter.

A few days later. The public prosecutor: "Well, you see, my dear illustrious author, your expression is already a lot more relaxed, I dare say, a lot more human, less preoccupied with fixed ideas — — —. Did the two rolls with butter do you any harm, eh?! You see!"

No, they hadn't harmed him at all, since every day he distributed them in the chickencoop — — —.

Afternoon Visit

"Herr Peter Altenberg is requested immediately in the director's office — — — ."

"Please have a seat. I strictly forbade you any alcohol consumption — — — ."

"Yes, Herr Director — — — ."

"Do you recognize this bunch of empty slivovitz bottles?!?"

"Yes, they're mine — — — ."

"They were found today underneath your bed — — — ."

"Well, where else would you expect to find them?! That's where I deposited them — — ."

"How did you get hold of this poison in my establishment?!"

"I bribed somebody. For two crowns, his honorable conscience wouldn't approve of it. So I offered him three crowns."

"You are not being held responsible in the entire matter, but the disloyal attendant is the guilty party! I am going to call him to account even though he's been here for twenty-five years and, *so far as I could tell,* has always conducted himself in an exemplary manner — — — ."

"Herr Director, it was just yesterday you told me that my being in your establishment and following a regular solid life here has made me twenty years younger and that I'm almost no longer recognizable?!?"

"I said that for *pedagogical reasons,* in order to bolster your self-confidence — — —."

"Herr Director, may I be allowed later to retrieve the empty slivovitz bottles from you?!? You know, I get six hellers back on each one — — ."

Director to the dishonest employee: "Anton, how could you, after twenty-five years of blameless service, accept a bribe to provide a patient, and a well-known writer with peculiarities to boot, with so much liquor?!?"

"But Herr Director, if I hadn't already done that for years with hundreds of alcoholics, they'd have all left here the third day and we wouldn't have had anybody in our sanatorium!"

"So be it, Anton, but from now on see to it at least that the empty bottles aren't found — — — ."

"Herr Director, the attendant Franz did it to me out of revenge because I make so much on the side — — — ."

Director to the attendant Franz: "Franz, you look after your own affairs, hear! You earn enough letting our alcoholics 'make out' a little with our female hysterics — — —. Each person has his own jurisdiction. There has to be order in a sanatorium!"

"Sanatorium für Nervenkranke," 1919. Original text in *Semmering 1912,* 5th and 6th enlarged ed. (Berlin: S. Fischer Verlag, 1919), 78–82.

FELIX SALTEN
1869–1945

SALTEN HAS THREE DIFFERENT REPUTATIONS.[1] Internationally, he has a permanent place in world literature for something that has nothing whatsoever to do with the Vienna coffeehouse. Wherever children read and wherever people love animals, Salten will be celebrated as the author of *Bambi* (1923). Subtitled *A Life in the Woods,* the charming tale of a deer was published in English translation in 1928 with a foreword by John Galsworthy.[2] It was subsequently made into a film by Walt Disney in 1942, and that more than the book itself assures Salten's immortality.

Whatever the popularity of *Bambi* in his native Austria, Salten also enjoys a certain notoriety as the anonymous author of a pornographic classic by the name of *Josefine Mutzenbacher: Die Lebensgeschichte einer wienerischen Dirne* (*Josefine Mutzenbacher: The Story of a Vienna Whore*, 1906).[3] No one can say for sure that it was written by Salten, and it has sometimes been attributed to Schnitzler (as something one might expect from the author of *Liebelei* [*The Game of Love*] and *Reigen* [*The Round-Dance*]). But the consensus has been and remains that it was written by Salten. For those who knew him it was more in character than *Bambi*.

Salten's third reputation, or distinction of sorts, owes everything to Karl Kraus. The two writers shared an animosity that assumed legendary proportions in their own time. That Kraus could irritate with his moral self-righteousness and self-appointed guardianship of the German language goes without saying. But Kraus so managed to get on Salten's nerves that Salten once could not restrain himself from attacking him physically, and in public, despite his own frailty and smallness of stature. Thereafter, whenever and wherever he had the chance, Kraus mocked and belittled Salten. Above all in *Die Fackel*, Salten looms large as the embodiment of everything bad about the Viennese journalism of the day. Kraus holds Salten up not only as an example of the abuse of German typical of the press but, during the First World War, also as the kind of facile, glib, irresponsible writer whose contribution to war hysteria was anything but negligible.

Felix Salten, whose real name was Siegmund Salzmann, was born in Budapest in 1869. The family was Jewish and had settled in Vienna when Salten was only four weeks old. After completing his secondary-school education in Vienna, Salten had hoped to go on to the university to study philology. But his parents' poor financial situation made that out of the question. Instead, at sixteen, he became a clerk in a relative's insurance company. It was about that time that he began writing, as much to relieve the tedium of his job as to express himself artistically. His earliest efforts were short pieces written for the *Allgemeine Kunst-Chronik* (*Universal Art Chronicle*) then being published by Wilhelm Lauser. Salten also became a member of the modernist literary society known as the "Freie Bühne" (Free Stage) and contributed to such modernist journals as *Moderne Dichtung* (*Modern Creativity*), *Moderne Rundschau* (*Modern Review*), and the *Wiener Literaturzeitung* (*Vienna Literary Journal*). He also joined the staff of the paper *An der schönen blauen Donau* (*On the Beautiful Blue Danube*), which had artistic ambitions.

It was not long before Salten's writing attracted the attention of the major Vienna newspapers, and in 1893 he accepted the very visible and prestigious position of Burgtheater reviewer and art critic for the *Wiener*

Allgemeine Zeitung. He held the position until 1898. It was during this period that he became a part of the Café Griensteidl "Young Vienna" circle and enjoyed a close relationship above all with Schnitzler. We have already identified Salten as one of the prime targets of Karl Kraus's malice in *The Demolished Literature.*

By 1900, Salten had become so well known as a journalist of talent that he was writing for virtually all the leading Austrian as well as German newspapers. In 1906, four years after his marriage to the actress Ottilie Metzeles (who performed under the pseudonym Metzl), he became editor-in-chief of the *Berliner Morgenpost* and took up residence in the German capital. The position afforded him the opportunity to visit England on several occasions, where he met such political figures as Lloyd George and Winston Churchill. Strongly attracted to and skilled at the genre of the feuilleton, and well aware of its prominence in the world of contemporary Viennese journalism, Salten leaped at the chance to become feuilleton editor for the Vienna *Die Zeit*, with which he had collaborated since 1894. It was about 1910 that he returned to Vienna to take up his new duties.

By the time the First World War broke out, Salten's literary reputation was formidable. Apart from his preeminence as a writer of feuilletons and whatever renown he acquired on the basis of his putative authorship of *Josefine Mutzenbacher*, he had also published a novella with the title *Die Gedanktafel der Prinzessin Anna* (*The Memorial Tablet of Princess Anna*, 1901); the novel *Olga Frohgemuth* (1911); a highly regarded collection of his best feuilletons representing a cross section of Habsburg society, *Das österreichische Antlitz* (*The Face of Austria*, 1910); and a popular little book about the Prater amusement park (*Wurstelprater*), which came out in 1911.

During the war, Salten, like several other well-known Austrian writers, saw action principally in the propaganda service of the War Archives in Vienna. In 1914, he reached the pinnacle of an Austrian feuilletonist's career when he became the Sunday feuilletonist for the *Neue Freie Presse*. The position assured him high visibility, great influence, and a comfortable income. It also earned him the undying wrath of Karl Kraus, who now truly became his nemesis. Angered by what he regarded as his spurious use of the feuilleton to beat the drums for the patriotic cause, Kraus made Salten a frequent target of ridicule in *Die Fackel.*

With the end of the war, Salten's journalistic preeminence—Kraus's assaults on him notwithstanding—afforded him secure circumstances in which to resume the writing of fiction even more intensively than before the war. The richest harvest of this activity was the international celebrity he acquired with the publication of *Bambi* in 1923.

Once he hit on the genre of the animal tale capable of bringing pleasure to children and adults alike, Salten was too shrewd a writer to want to abandon it in a hurry. *Bambi* was thus followed by *Fünfzehn Hasen: Schicksale in Wald und Feld* (*Fifteen Rabbits: Fate in Forest and Field,* 1930); *Gute Gesellschaft: Erlebnisse mit Tieren* (*Good Company: Adventures with Animals,* 1930); *Die Jugend des Eichenhörnchens Perri* (*Perri: The Youth of a Squirrel,* 1938); *Renni der Retter* (*Renni, the Rescuer: A Dog of the Battlefield,* 1940); and *Bambis Kinder* (*Bambi's Children,* 1939).[4] Besides his feuilletons and fiction, Salten also wrote extensively on the theater. His essays appear principally in two collections: *Wiener Theater 1848–1898* (*Vienna Theater, 1848–1898;* also under the title *Die Pflege der Kunst in Österreich 1848–1898* [*The Cultivation of Art in Austria . . .*], 1900), and *Schauen und Spielen: Studien zur Kritik des modernen Theaters* (*Plays and Players: Studies on the Modern Theater,* 1921). He was also the author of a book of literary and other portraits published by Fischer in Berlin in 1913 under the title *Gestalten und Erscheinungen* (*Figures and Fancies*).

In recognition of his literary prominence, Salten was elected president of the Austrian P.E.N. club in 1928. Two years later, riding the crest of international fame, he made his first and only trip to the United States when he came for a three-month visit sponsored by the Carnegie Endowment. He subsequently published a book based on his experiences under the title *Fünf Minuten Amerika* (*America in Five Minutes,* 1931).

Not long after his return to Europe, Salten's further activity as the head of the Austrian P.E.N. embroiled him in unwelcome controversy. Although hardly indifferent to the ascendancy of the Nazis in Germany on 30 June 1933, Salten advocated what some regarded as an attitude of cautious appeasement toward writers of the Third Reich at an international meeting of the P.E.N. held 25–28 May of that fateful year in Ragusa (Dubrovnik), Yugoslavia.[5] His stance led to a schism in the P.E.N. club movement and his resignation of the presidency of the Austrian chapter in 1934. The German annexation of Austria in 1938 represented a real danger to Salten. Not only was he a Jew but also an ardent Zionist who had published an account of a trip to Palestine in 1925 under the title *Neue Menschen auf alter Erde: Eine Palästinafahrt* (*New People on Old Soil: A Journey to Palestine*). Facilitated by his daughter Anna-Katherina, who was a Swiss citizen at the time, Salten, accompanied by his wife and their loyal housekeeper Pepi, succeeded in emigrating to Switzerland before harm could befall them. By 1939, they were living full-time in Zurich. They never saw Vienna again. Salten's wife, Ottilie, died in 1942 and Salten himself followed her three years later. He was seventy-six. Both he and his wife are buried in Zurich's Friesenberg Cemetery.

Felix Salten's celebrity as the author of *Bambi* has long since faded, and the campaign to discredit him by Karl Kraus—who is now considerably better known—may create a negative impression of his overall career. But

he was highly regarded in his own time both by the public and by the
international literary community. The *New York Times* carried a laudatory
obituary on 9 October 1945 that identified him principally as the author
of *Bambi* but also mentioned his German translation of *Abie's Irish Rose*,
which in Max Reinhardt's production in 1927 was "the season's biggest
hit in the Austrian capital."[6] His sixtieth birthday, in 1929, was widely feted,
and testimonials came in from everywhere. It was on that occasion that
Hugo von Hofmannsthal wrote an appreciation of Salten that remains
perhaps the most incisive summation of his literary achievement:

> F. S. For almost forty years now these initials indicate an
> activity that knows no rest, the incessant reacting to existence of
> a unique artistic individual who cannot be fit into any rubric.
>
> Writer, yes—the model of a writer. He was that already as a
> young boy, and his early confidence was just as astonishing as his
> vivacity, and he is that today, and his vivacity is just as astonishing
> as his mature confidence. He has a lot of, and little, "métier"—you
> be the judge. He writes much and easily, or perhaps with diffi-
> culty, but it appears easy, but one never has the sense that his
> métier overcomes him. We never feel him taxed for a period, for
> an image, for a turn of phrase. What makes his style strong is the
> direct life, the rhythm that comes from the inner emotion. He
> may be wrong on many occasions, from willfulness that hurts, but
> it is only near the very core of the ego, of the true un-overrefined
> egoistical ego, that so much liveliness can constantly renew itself.
>
> Artist—through and through, and from the very roots, and
> passionate. But even in those stories in which the artistic, the
> thoroughly creative, is very strong, something else is stronger—
> spontaneity. Stronger than the figures portrayed, stronger than
> the invented plot is the sympathy with youth, with old age, with
> illness, the sympathy of pride, of strength, of misery, of animal
> existence.
>
> Critic? An indefatigable one, one of the most renowned and
> influential. But one will look in vain in his criticism for firm
> standards, for principles, the firm convictions, the abstracted
> experiences that constitute the strength of criticism in the nar-
> rower sense. His negative reviews (a rare phenomenon) occupy
> by far the smaller space—and even they are not the application
> of a theory but pure spontaneity. The least abstract mind that
> one can imagine; the most direct sensibility that one can suppose.
>
> Politician—yes and no. None of the obligations, none of
> the rigidities that this position carries with it. And yet ever such,
> ever the new politician, from vivacity, from pugnacity, from the
> will toward a final showdown.

A Viennese—this famous Viennese writer; yes and no. He never submitted to any formula, including any Viennese ones. A citizen of the time perhaps more than a citizen of any country. But he is not bound by time any more than by space. Even in this respect a kind of ubiquity suits him: the just-contemporary, that is one of the confining formulas that are remote to him.

Life is a struggle between pure vitality and forms. This is what Goethe had in mind when he declared that all forms, even the highest, are characterized by something paralyzing, something fatal. We are ever in danger of losing life to institutions, to abstractions, to words (they, too, are forms). The initials F. S. will for a long time yet and often be the sign of direct, absolute liveliness.

A mass of experiences has accrued to it, but it is youthfully amalgamated. It affects the person who bears it not as a burden but as a reserve of imagination. An almost incomparable rhythmic vitality makes itself felt today as it did twenty and forty years ago, and both initials indicate a seat of primary life heat that has not yet cooled.[7]

1.   The only full-length study on Salten that I am aware of is an unpublished dissertation by Kurt Riedmüller, "Felix Salten als Mensch, Dichter und Kritiker" (Vienna, 1949). For a good short account of his life and career in English, see Lore Muerfel Dormer, "Felix Salten," in Donald G. Daviau, ed., *Major Figures of Turn-of-the-Century Austrian Literature*, 407–40. The appended selected bibliography by Gregor Ackermann (436–40) is especially helpful.

2.   The translation was by Whittaker Chambers, who translated other works by Salten, and was published by Grosset and Dunlap of New York.

3.   For an English translation, see *The Memoirs of Josephine Mutzenbacher*, trans. Rudolf Schleifer, intro. Hilary E. Holt (North Hollywood, Calif.: Brandon House, 1967).

4.   Translations into English: *Fifteen Rabbits: A Celebration of Life,* trans. Whittaker Chambers (New York: Simon and Schuster, 1930); *Perri: The Youth of a Squirrel,* trans. Barrows Mussey (Indianapolis: Bobbs-Merrill, 1938); *Renni, the Rescuer: A Dog of the Battlefield,* trans. Kenneth C. Kaufman (Indianapolis: Bobbs-Merrill, 1940); *Bambi's Children: The Story of a Forest Family,* trans. Barthold Fles (Indianapolis, New York: Bobbs-Merrill, 1939).

5.   On the Ragusa meeting, see especially Dormer, "Felix Salten," 413–16.

6.   *The New York Times,* Tuesday, 9 October 1945, 22.

7.   Hugo von Hofmannsthal, *Gesammelte Werke: Reden und Aufsätze III: 1925–1929, Aufzeichnungen,* ed. Bernd Schoeller and Ingeborg Beyer-Ahlert, in consultation with Rudolf Hirsch (Frankfurt am Main: Fischer Taschenbuch Verlag, 1980), 230–31.

PETER ALTENBERG

Is it not curious how he wanders about on the periphery of the everyday, on the outer edges of the bourgeois life? Whores' hangouts, brothels, bohemian dives, variety theaters, cabarets? Around people who cater to the brutal curiosity, the dull amusement, the thoughtless pleasures of the sated. Around people who become upset, unbearable, scorned, and whom he idolizes. There he revels in subtle delights and expires in fits of exquisite and tender despair. There were the Muscovite singers of the Nevsky-Russotin troupe to whom he surrendered his soul; there was the Spanish dancer Carmen Aguileras, to whom he also surrendered his soul; the Ashanti girl, Nah Bâdúh, to whom he likewise surrendered his soul; then the Nagel sisters, who sing Viennese lieder; then Leopoldine, Gusti, Anna, Helene, Gabriele, to whom he surrendered his soul time and again.

He enters into the frantic music, the beer stench, the clinking of glasses, the screaming, laughing, and crying of a night-spot, strides with his soft steps and with his soft smile through the tumult, and ten, twelve, twenty girls greet him one after the other: "Hi, Altenberg! . . . Oh, Peter, how are you?" They greet him not as some habitué, not as some valued customer, but as a friend or, better said, rather the way an honorary member is greeted in some association. Familiarly and deferentially. Familiarly, because he belongs to it, and deferentially because he is an honorary member.

You stand with him on the corner of a street. Graben or Kärntner-strasse. Late at night. He argues, gets excited, shouts. The coachmen listen in from their station, move closer, form a circle, grin. Then one of them says in a deep bass: "My respects, Herr von Altenberg . . ."   In order to show off before us that he knows him. The others repeat it, intimately and respectfully. It is nearly an ovation. The policeman comes by thinking that there's a riot. His features say: ah sooo . . . He smiles, salutes: "My respects, Herr von Altenberg."

Three in the morning in the square, where the market women are sitting, selling vegetables and flowers. He strolls about in the midst of all the bustle, breathing the scent of strawberries, mignonette, gillyflowers, spinach, artichokes, and green peas, and the fragrance of rising day and the freshly sprinkled street dust. He searches out, fondles with his eyes the bedewed flowers, the heaped-up green mountains of vegetables, and the pretty daughters of the market women, the fourteen- and fifteen-year-olds. The mothers and their daughters nod at him: "'Mornin' t'ya, Herr von Altenberg . . ."

Peter Altenberg wants the human soul to come out on top. He wrote this himself once and it expresses his nature splendidly. He is almost fifty years old. That is a stage to reflect on a great deal and to think over many things, and so I am reading his books.

I read what one of the Spanish women once said to him. A singer or a dancer, perhaps just one of those who roves gypsylike through the American bars and chantant-promenoirs of Europe, in any case one of the many to whom he gave his soul: "Votre lettre . . . je comprends, que vous me comprenez . . . c'est tout ce qu'il nous faut . . . c'est plus!"

I read how he waited in the coffeehouse with his sweetheart's poodle until she came out of the theater: "He sat himself down in such a way that he could keep an eye on the entrance, and I regarded it as very proper, if indeed a bit excessive, since, if you please, it was 7:30, and we had to wait until 11:15. So we sat there and waited. Every coach that sped by aroused his hopes, and each time I said to him: 'It's not possible, she can't be here now, just think, it's not possible!' He was simply sick from longing, and turned his head in my direction: 'Is she coming or isn't she?'—'She's coming, she's coming . . .' I answered. Once he gave up his post, came up to me, laid his paws on my knee, and I kissed him. It's as if he had said to me: 'Just tell me the truth, I can take anything!' At 10 o'clock he began whining. I said to him: 'You think, my dear, I'm not anxious, too? You have to control yourself!' He set no store by self-control and kept on whining . . . !"

I read about his hotel room: "At three in the morning the birds began softly singing, in a suggestive way. My cares grew and grew. It began in the brain as with a rolling stone, dragged along all hopefulness, all capacity for life, became a raging avalanche, and buried the ability to meet the day and the pitiless imperious hour! A mild storm lashed the treetops in front of my window . . . !" And then the conclusion: "The singing of the birds in the treetops becomes more distinct, traces of melodies are present. Tepid storms carry the fragrance of meadows. This would be the most appropriate time to hang oneself on the cross-bar . . ."

I read the little piece about the marches: "There are three marches that are transformed by the music into a fearlessness of death and blood lust: the march of Lorraine, the Stars and Stripes, and the procession of the gladiators. They must be played with a short and frightful resoluteness!—The instruments advance straight to their death! The little drum and clarinet are heroes! Die for the fatherland! Bottoms up! You really must see the battalions that leave the instinct of self-preservation far behind them. On, on, on! A terrible sickness has seized the brain, the nervous system: 'You or I, dog!' No other way!"

Then from a grandfather's diary: "Severe arteriosclerosis . . . The young woman will live, the one who said to me: 'I don't think my coming made anybody as happy as you!' —The mountain meadows in R. will smell sweet and sparkle, especially after a rain in the evening. Nobody ever stood before you as inspired as I am. —My sweet, unassuming, far too tender, shy, withdrawn granddaughter, you always feel it: 'My grandfather understands me better than anyone . . . ' I'd like to implore you from the grave: 'Wait for somebody who'll understand you like your deceased grandfather! But you won't be able to wait for him.' Amen . . . Severe arteriosclerosis . . . Be well!"

Then the Café de l'Opera in the Prater: "Yes indeed, there is a special relationship between these things: gentleman, lady; mandolin strumming, birch tree, plane tree, ash tree; white arc-lamps and the cool night fragrance of meadows. It's something apart from life. It doesn't creep in like brackish water. It's a wonderful mixture which makes us gayer and light. So I sit harmlessly and prick my ears. I envy no one. I buy a rose and give it to Signorina Maria as a present. I light a splendid cigarette. How delightful the mandolins are made, like hollow resounding pears! How the birch tree leaves glisten! How calmly the plane tree stands! And how the delicate fingers of leaves on the ash tree tremble."

I read all these small works, these small sermons, speeches, and poems. Many of them are like steel projectiles, so solidly locked in themselves, so complete and precise in their form. And they pierce the breast like a projectile. One is struck and bleeds from them. Many are like crystals and precious stones, glittering in all the colored reflections of the colored light of life, radiating with captured rays of sun and blazing with a secret inner fire. Many are like ripe fruit, warm from the breath of summer, swollen and sweet, and full of the fragrance of foliage and garden. I read all these small works and they are captivating in the rhythm of their speech, in their tempo, in their impetuously tossed together sentences, which have so much plasticity and pictorial power. This language is wonderfully personal and recalls no other. Only occasionally, ever so softly, does a tone remind you of Andersen. And if you know that Altenberg's father was mad about Victor Hugo and fanatically in love with French culture, but only when you know that, then you notice that in his youth this poet heard the verve and the graceful pathos of French conversational art and that a faint echo of it is audible in his rhetoric. Otherwise this language recalls nothing. . . .[1] It's as if you heard him speak, as if these exclamations, these encapsulated springy, unsnapped, pointelike closing figures of speech sprang directly from the haste and excitement of his thought and temperament. There is something compelling in his form. This seemingly asthmatic eloquence, this pulsing of all arteries in his prose, this brisk, snappy pithiness, operates seductively and tempts to emulation. But he himself calls this authenticity his own. He prefixed his first book with the motto: "Mon verre n'est pas grand, mais je bois dans mon verre!" With time, many others also drink from this glass. But no matter.

He chose this motto from Alfred de Musset when he began. He was some thirty years old at the time and ripe and ready. He has not changed since then, and what people call artistic development is not in his nature. He will never create a large work, compose and construct slowly; never will he spin, tie, and untie the threads of some plot, never create forms and fates in his imagination. That is because, unlike other artists, he doesn't carry a part or a piece—a "scrap," he'd say—of life home with him. He doesn't tear a piece out of life in order to digest it, in order to transform it, to elevate it, and to weave his whole ego into it. He sees life unfold before him like a unique, frightful, and magnificent spectacle and he has no time to miss anything while confined with himself and his own work. He is so moved, enthralled, and intoxicated by this spectacle, that he doesn't move from his place a single moment. The profundity of the world reveals itself to him in words spoken by passersby, in the burst of laughter or sudden paleness of a whore. The dark abysses of the tragic open up to him in the sigh of a disappointed youth, in the look an aging woman directs toward one blossoming. He says: "Fine, warm, golden-yellow tea" and discovers immense distances, exotic landscapes, immense possibilities of existence. He becomes rapt and deeply moved by the pink, healthy body of a child and trembles before the bright unswerving eyes of a thirteen-year-old as before something divine. His deepest need is to sit still and to behold life and while beholding it to be drawn to it or to grieve. And then it is his deepest need to address these short letters to life. At times they are letters of commendation that are soaked through with his rapture in a touching way. At other times they are insulting letters in which a choking rage dissolves into stammering. He will always write only these little prose pieces; all his books contain only such small prose pieces, and subsequent books which may yet appear from him will contain nothing different. But among them there are many small masterpieces. An extraordinary power of flight resides in them, and they will transport him over the years to generations that are still to come. For Altenberg possesses an astounding strength. While others with the stamina of a long breath write works that are already forgotten the next day, he with his short breath can say things that are simply unforgettable.

He sits in the whores' hangouts, in the bordellos, in the variety theaters, in the bohemian coffeehouses and wants the human soul to come out on top. Those are his own words. Indeed, that is the wish of just about all poets and also of all priests. The poets don't always emphasize it very explicitly, striving instead, consciously or unconsciously, to contribute something to the achievement of this goal. The priests preach it and proclaim it incessantly and know prescriptions of infallible help to the soul's coming out on top. Altenberg does both. He preaches, and he composes; he offers prescriptions, he reasons with and yells at life, reprimands it like a priest and then throws himself again into its arms unconditionally, bewilderingly, overwhelmed, like an artist.

He sees a female acrobat, a fencer, a young dancer full of verve in every movement, or a purebred collie, or a Tiffany glass, or a fresh meadow flower, and with a constricted voice trembling from excitement cries out: "That is the greatest! *The greatest!*" At this moment it is to him really the greatest. As if life held in store for Altenberg a new surprise, something new to attract his attention, as if it suddenly offered him this gift in order to allure him, and as if presents were now being lavishly bestowed on him, as if he were gifted above all others. But it is also as if in this one second he were again embracing the whole wealth of existence.

He sees a woman, and at that moment she is the only one to whom he offers his soul. "I have seen her face," he says. Every other face fades from view in him, sinks, and only this one exists. It is for him now the fulfillment of his dream of female beauty; it is for him now the highest achievement of creative nature and the occasion to address to life another letter of praise, another enthusiastic expression of gratitude. He often surrenders his soul for a few days, often for just half an hour. But when he surrenders it, he does so fully, without reservation, and as if he were doing it for the very first time.

He sits with the young men who are buying themselves girls, and he says to them: "Don't you believe that you now you have all rights to this creature! Just see how pretty this girl is. Don't take her in the brutal craving of your instinct. Don't take her with the insolent thought in mind that you're going to be soiled by her. Consider her melancholy and her cheerfulness; consider her lot. Don't be like animals!" The young people think to themselves: "He's cracked!" But they do change their tone toward the girls. The human soul came out on top.

Many young men throng to him; many older ones sit at his table and listen to him. Over the years many took hold of him one after the other, didn't let go of him, couldn't exist without his words of encouragement, without his gentle talk, without his fits of rage and blustering insults. Spoiled women and pining girls reach out to him over his books and over social restraints, clamor for his personal nearness, his words, sensing in him an unfamiliar new tenderness, a selfless adoration, a kind of deliverance, a kind of restorative or enlightenment.

The people in the night-spots, the prostitutes, the dull-witted drinkers and revelers, the waiters, the coachmen, the policemen, the proprietors, all talk to him. He tells them: "Take care of your digestion! Have respect for your sleep!" He tells them: "The only perversity there is is weakening and decreasing your vitality!" All these people naturally don't understand him, but they do understand that he somehow loves them, that he wishes them only well, and they love him in turn. They smile when he talks to them at length, they wink at each other, they shrug their shoulders, but they don't stop listening to him, they don't take their leave of him. In [Zola's] *Germinal* the pit horse sniffs the other young animal lowered into the mine straight from the meadows and senses the free air and the sun in his fresh smell. Similarly, these people who are trapped in their alcohol stench, in noise, in night music, in the drunkenness and fog of their world, pick up from Altenberg something of the scent of innocence that was lost to them, the scent of the poetry that they no longer know, and they are happy when he comes and they bow to him when he leaves.

In this world he is rather like the pilgrim Luka in [Gorky's] *Lower Depths* or the old Akim in [Tolstoy's] *Power of Darkness*. He is indigenous here and yet comes from elsewhere. He sends down roots here, and yet a flame burns in him which has not been kindled on these lamps here below. Among all the adult and burdened and disfigured by existence he is as perfect as a child. Those friends who understand him look at each other and smile when they hear him rail against life and oppose it like a child. And they smile again when they observe the extent to which he is nonetheless involved in the realities of this life and how naively he looks after his own. Most cultivated people are amused by his eccentric appearance, poke fun at his little masterpieces, regard him as crazy or as somebody who puts himself at the disposal of fools, possibly dangerous to society, and in any case very depraved. Dr. Egon Friedell relates Altenberg anecdotes in the Cabaret Fledermaus. Whenever he begins: "It has been my lot to play the same role in the life of the poet Altenberg that Eckermann played in the life of Goethe," the audience roars and thinks that Altenberg is now going to get his due. They think it's a joke when Dr. Friedell says, "the poet Altenberg." Because they believe that it is really quite impossible to call him a poet. They also roar at the anecdotes themselves and have no idea how cleverly these have been concocted. The uproarious hilarity that Dr. Friedell always excites with his Altenberg stories is surely a false, a misleading hilarity. For the people do not understand that the entire value of these splendid little stories lies in the fact that from them the touching and unique figure of Altenberg emerges full of life, that through them Altenberg's nature becomes illuminated and at times transfigured with a clear and uncommon psychological humor. People see him from afar. They see his works from the distance of their bourgeois perspective distorted by eroded truths, just the way they see his person from afar when he happens to pass them on the street or when he is in fact in the auditorium when Dr. Friedell is talking about him. They also think, after gaping at him, that he looks dissolute, neglected, and almost ragged. And they don't know with what care this soft light clothing that barely adds weight to his body is chosen. They don't know what a well-groomed, white, radiant face he has, what fine animated features he has, what beautiful penetrating eyes. They don't know that he has the slenderest, most aristocratic alabaster hands, and that his voice sounds gentle, melodious, and noble.

Is it not curious how he wanders about on the periphery of the everyday, on the outer edges of the bourgeois life, on the borderline where the well-ordered ends, where many things commonly regarded as irrefutable become doubtful! He is now fifty years old, and in today's Vienna he is one of the most interesting, most subtle, and most touching individuals. To all knowledgeable people in Europe he is a beloved and admired poet, an instrument in the great spiritual orchestra whose special sound remains penetrating and distinguishable from a thousand voices . . . and for the pleasure-seeking public at Maxim's, at the Café Central, and at the Cabaret Fledermaus, a curiosity, a ridiculous showpiece for curious middle-class people. But one day Altenberg reminiscences and Altenberg biographies will be written. Then those who read these books will believe that the whole of Vienna understood, admired, and celebrated this original. And they will say: A pity we didn't know him better, we too would have celebrated and admired him. One day somebody will show that outside, on the outer edges of the everyday, through Altenberg's works, the human soul came out on top. And it will be accepted because it is the simple truth. Only today nobody would believe it.

Original text in Felix Salten, *Das österreichische Antlitz: Essays* (Berlin: S. Fischer Verlag, 1910), 99–113.

1.   I have omitted a few lines here in which Salten quotes examples of Altenberg's speech.

THE VIENNA ROUTE

The old man writes in his diary:

Today was a splendid day. Full of sunshine and warmth, and the fragrance of violets was everywhere in the streets. The fact that today happens to be my sixtieth birthday might of course depress me. But say what you will, I am in quite a good mood. And I find that it is very pleasant to have a birthday in spring when it becomes so warm and when the streets give off the scent of fresh flowers. What more could one want? I went for a walk as usual. First through the Inner City. Then past the Opera on the Ring and back again. After that I took myself to a coffeehouse.

So, sixty years. I should best pass over it in silence. But since it has long been my custom on such occasions to drag out the ending of a year somewhat and to write down a few of my thoughts, I have no intention of doing otherwise today. Although . . . I really don't have a lot to say. The pages of all the years lie here, and should I want to read them over now, perhaps I would always find the same thing in them. I led a very regular life, and when one is a bachelor, not many things happen. I feel a certain shyness in taking these pages in hand now. They would in the end induce in me a sentimental state of mind, and there is no point to that. I am still quite excited by the lovely day.

Soon it will be possible again to sit in the open. Two coffee booths have already been set up on the Graben; a pair of tables were even occupied. But I still didn't want to risk it. There were also so many people running about the city today, you couldn't move. And the pretty girls you see, it's a real joy. You really don't know which to look at first. Troops of them marching about. And how charming it is, so many of these young pink faces and laughing eyes! For forty years, day after day, I follow the same path through the Inner City and across the Ring, and I always see these many pretty girls. Unbelievable where they all come from.

To be sure, they too don't remain young forever. Don't imagine it. Otherwise I'd have to grow old all by myself, and for that I'd be flattering myself in vain. But everything follows its prescribed course. That shouldn't really surprise you. I noticed that in the Baroness Ruttersdorf when I saw her today. God, how she looks! Her hair is already snow-white and she's completely fallen apart. I stood still and followed her with my eyes. As if after thirty years I was seeing her for the first time.

Thirty years ago I stood and followed her with my eyes more often. She was a young girl and pretty at the time. Even today I get giddy when I recall how pretty she was. At the time, I was madly in love with her. But this feeling has been extinguished in me for a long time now. Well yes, I did experience some things after all. Of course, I did not know her personally. How could it have been otherwise? I was a quite insignificant official. A lot more insignificant than I am today. And what would my income have been then, thirty years ago? Sixty or seventy guldens a month, certainly no more. But what do you want . . . ? I was a young man! And so at the time she filled my entire existence. I was quite well aware of the fact that on Sundays she went to the Schotten Church. I also knew when

I would encounter her afternoons in the city. If I cared to bring out the pages from that period, there would be a lot about her in them. I know how I followed her and how I imagined that I would suddenly become a millionaire, or that I would become a minister of state in two years, or that I was writing a play and would become famous, so that everybody would stare at me when I crossed the street and people would scramble just to get near me, and then . . . well, and then . . . It was so wonderful to imagine it so exactly, in so lifelike a way as if it were real, as if it could happen tomorrow. I lost myself completely in these reveries and owed them many happy hours.

But now I am sixty years old. And she is an old woman. I observed her entire life. At the time, she was a Countess Nussbach. I knew her father, too, the old general. He had thick white hair the way his daughter does now. Then she married Baron Ruttersdorf. Then she went for walks with her children. What adorable children they were, especially the oldest boy, Ferdinand. Then her father died and she inherited the palace on the Wieden. Then her husband had the affair with the Hungarian singer and there was talk that they would get divorced. Then Ferdinand shot himself to death. He was a lieutenant in the Windischgrätz dragoons. And then her husband passed away. If I had spoken to her today and told her that I know her whole life's story and that I loved her, what eyes she would have made! But of course one can't do that, and I am also not the type for it. But who knows how nicely we might talk with one another now.

I do believe that I would be able to speak with such a woman without making any gaffes. And I think, too, that my clothes are elegant enough for me to get by in better circles. I have always paid heed to proper manners and I always set great store by good clothes. The first thing I did when I was on a regular salary was to work out a schedule of monthly payments with a tailor. And since then I have always been very handsomely attired. I also made a point of frequenting the finest establishments. Obviously only coffeehouses, since restaurants are really too expensive for my means. But that's really not the issue. What, after all, do you get out of a restaurant? You eat, get up, and go away again. For this purpose my hotel on the Piaristengasse, where I am a regular customer and where for decades I have been dining every day at three o'clock after leaving the office, suits me well enough. But with the coffeehouse, it's a different matter. And in the Café Imperial or in Pucher I was always taken for a baron.

Obviously, I did not engage the Baroness Ruttersdorf in conversation and will, to be sure, never address her. Not in this life. Perhaps if we should ever meet in another world, then we would indeed have plenty of things to talk about and maybe she would even enjoy talking to me more than with her husband. But in this world the old boy has the edge. In the other world, though, I would have quite a lot of people to talk to, if I wanted to, beginning with everybody I spent my whole life observing.

Whether this is also the case in another city, in Berlin or in London, I have no idea. But among us it is this way. You see people who are interesting, you observe how they live. You live with them and you don't need to be wealthy or titled or a big shot. I most certainly do not belong to the aristocracy, but nevertheless I know them all. I knew them when they were young, observe them as they grow old, watch their children grow up, and follow the same patterns all over again. I never had enough money to go to art exhibitions whenever I felt like it yet I knew the important works as well as Makart.[1] I recall as if it were today how he used to ride about the Ring in a carriage, a quite small, thin man. I also almost never attended the theater but yet I knew and saw everybody: Wolter, who married Count O'Sullivan, and Geistinger, and how Girardi became famous, and all of them together. How come I know them, I couldn't even tell you. Perhaps you develop the knack going about the city day in and day out for so many years. You simply find out the famous faces, and then all of a sudden you know the names. And then you see the people again and again until at last you can tell from their faces, their walk, and their bearing everything going on inside them. As often as I walked my route over this long period of time, I was always excited and amused, I was always splendidly entertained, I always had the feeling that I was moving in some exquisite society. And for that you really need no riches. What more could you want?

When I recall how as a young man I learned, little by little, how to open my eyes . . . I grew up in quite modest circumstances, but yet I always understood what lovely things there are in the world. On a Sunday, when the city was at its quietest, I could have roamed around for hours at a time and looked at the old palaces—the portals and the view that opens up in the spacious courtyards, and then the high windows and the figures above them. Then the narrow alleyways like the ones around the University. How long I always stood on the Burgplatz before the entrance to the Schweizerhof. How well I knew the Burgplatz. On early winter evenings, for example, when snow covers the entire Burgplatz like a broad white carpet, when the gray facades glimmer, and when everything here seems so strange as if in another world. Or on afternoons in the middle of the summer when you know that the emperor is absent from the city and that whatever goes on is just servants carrying out orders. When this square with the guardhouse and sentries and the shuttered windows has something indolent and soporific about it. And then the summer evenings outside on the outer Burgplatz, when the sky is so very far, and when in the distance the roofs of the suburbs shine. How much I learned to see from the time I was a young man and got into the habit of going for a walk every day after the office. And how much I could relate. But I would just like to observe that during those young years it was indeed because of these walks that many qualities in me developed. The Burgplatz, for example, the Graben, the Kohlmarkt . . . it was there that I achieved a sense of good manners, and quite unconsciously at that; an inclination toward a better way of life and a certain sensitivity toward the ordinary and the tasteless.

I would like to observe that the people whom I saw daily exercised a certain constraint on me. I would have been embarrassed to have appeared among them in an unusual or obtrusive manner. After leaving my office and eating, I ran to the city to see the brilliant life. A young man must have his pleasure, after all. And that was a pleasure for me and it still remains one. The joy I took in luxury grew stronger in me with every passing day. And all I had to do to enjoy this luxury was just to go walking.

Let us take the carriage. I myself have ridden in a carriage only three or four times, but I understand that it is very pleasant the way a vehicle like that rolls along easily, the way the horses trot a regular pace, the way it turns a corner, rushes by, and then disappears. But I have just to look at it to enjoy the amenities that such a conveyance can afford. And as attentively as I observe it even today, it still gives me pleasure.

Let us take the Burgtheater and the Opera. I can count on my fingers the number of times I was in them. But on innumerable occasions I stood in the Opera vestibule after the performance and took in the spectacle of the fashionable world. And when I went home after watching the splendid throng of lovely women and elegant gentlemen streaming down the majestic stairways from the loges and the spectacle of all the busy lackeys, it was as if I myself were returning from some brilliant affair.

In summer, when you no longer have any outer clothing to store in the cloakroom, I often went to the Burgtheater, admired the staircases, strolled about the large foyer amidst the swarm of people there. And when the intermission was over, people rushed back into the auditorium. But I went my way and again had had my pleasure. Had I constantly traveled in a carriage, had I frequently gone to the theater, in a word, had I been so wealthy, who knows if in time everything would not have become dull for me. But this way I always tasted the best froth of things, pictured all pleasures in my imagination even more splendidly than they perhaps really are, and so today nothing has lost any of its charm for me.

As a young man I often used to run about the city and used to believe that something wonderful was going to come my way, something splendid was suddenly going to happen to me. Something connected with lovely women, with luxury and good fortune, with palaces, music, or the like.

This sometimes impatient expectation obviously became quite blunted with time. After all, I am sixty years old today. But even today when I promenade about the Inner City, when I wend my way through the rushing of the Ringstrasse, when so many lovely women's faces glide past me, it seems to me as if some hidden possibility still existed somewhere, as if something noteworthy and festive could still befall me. This is certainly silly, I do realize it, but time passes so quickly, and yet one feels oneself so excited and so content.

I am sixty years old, and I know that much has already passed me by. I am a poor devil. I know that too. And I have achieved nothing. Many people will say that I really have no reason to be so content. Many people will say that I might have put my years to better use, that I might have gone much further through greater industry, through higher aspirations. And I have to agree with them. Even more so, since I know better than anybody else that I did not lack talent, a solid foundation, and skills. I must say that today, when it is already too late, I could have become something in the world. Something big perhaps. For sure, something much bigger than what I became. But I must say that, everything considered, I am not unhappy. Perhaps as a poor devil, I might have been very discontent and very unhappy in another city. I am unable to judge that, since I have no idea of conditions elsewhere, nor do I know if elsewhere I might have felt excluded on account of my poverty and low position. But here I never ever felt excluded. On the contrary, I have always had the feeling, or at least the illusion, that I never needed any greater participation in all the luxury, in all the beauty, and in all the intimacy of the city. Perhaps elsewhere I might not have stopped trying to reach higher. It's hard to say. I only know that when I reached home in the evening from my walks, my impressions always left me feeling quite carefree and wonderfully calmed in my longings. When I felt the urge sometimes to attempt something special, to undertake something, it always seemed to me that everything has already been undertaken and done and achieved and now there is nothing left more to do other than to understand and enjoy what is here already, like a costly possession. Even if that is a fatal error, I have no intention now of making any effort to correct it. I have gone through enough, I should say; I have my share—and then some—of experiences and knowledge of people, can get by all right, and have my peace of mind. And now I also have the spring and this happy day full of sun and the fragrance of flowers. Pretty soon it will even be possible to sit outdoors. The coffee booths are already set up on the Graben. Everything else can be as it is. What does it really matter?

"Die Wiener Strasse." Original text in Felix Salten, *Das österreichische Antlitz: Essays* (Berlin: S. Fischer Verlag, 1910), 11–22.

1.   Hans Makart (1840–84), an immensely successful and popular Austrian painter of historical scenes.

PLEASURES OF THE NIGHT

Music. Young girls who dance. And champagne. This is how it has gradually developed in the last few years. But it was true even of the pious Brady:[1] "My dears, if you don't have any money, better stay at home . . ." The street singers bellow this simple philosophy right into the auditorium. Whoever heard it has been warned and shouldn't complain the next morning: You make the poor pay.

At first, Brady was alone. He was Viennese and simply didn't know better. He conducted a flourishing business in indigenousness, ran a folk-song bar. He regaled his customers with the humor that sprouts on the city pavement. And every evening he boiled the native zest for life to the point where, red hot, it dared take the world on. But he was, after all, alone, and because of it one could assume that we had no night life. Now we have one.

There are now in the Inner City some half dozen opportunities to squander away the night and give one's money "a good thrashing." The process, in the meantime, has become different. Young girls who dance. And champagne. Spanish fandango and Veuve Cliquot. Tunisian belly dances and American "drinks." Cakewalk and mineral water as well as Bordeaux. German fizz and the maxixe.[2] We have become international. The night pleasure spots almost all bear French names, and people amuse themselves behind the Kärntnerstrasse exactly the same way they do in Berlin, Paris, New York, or Copenhagen.

Despite that, local color is not entirely lacking. Often enough a glimmer of Viennese tint breaks through the French-Spanish-American motley. Even here one gets to hear the newest popular songs and freshest street ballads. Like the vegetable that grows just beyond the city, these little texts and melodies that grow out of the earth at city's edge are also brought in to the market at nighttime. And they, too, serve here only for trimming. The gentlemen of the band sing them. For it has become the fashion for the orchestra people not to limit themselves to their instruments but also to have acute attacks of joyousness. Attacks in which they can no longer subdue the bliss of existence they feel in their hearts. Their exultation arises so mightily that it can no longer be caught by a fiddle, can no longer be pounded into a piano. The musicians must then simply break out, must begin to sing in the very midst of their playing. They can't help themselves.

Most important, however, are the young girls who dance. People sit at small tables around an empty area in the center. And then come the young girls. Between one and four o'clock in the morning, it's really something very nice. They are just pretty little girls, some of them lovely, some of them merely pleasant. Some are talented, and some are without skill. Some are full of grace, and some are utterly helpless. Some are bashful, indeed ill at ease, and some, on the other hand, are very saucy. But all together have something gentle in their manner; all together are rather like children who seem to know nothing about real life. They are entirely guileless in their desires, in their pleasure seeking, in their small, transparent refinements.

All around at the tables sit the people who enter here from real life, from all kinds of seriousness and anxiety, from all kinds of work, hardship, and destiny. They sit here and are burdened with their thoughts, affairs, and obligations. Fettered and bound by things and people who live some-where outside; ensnared by all possible associations. And there in the middle, on the smooth stage, dance the young girls, and it is as if they existed in some special atmosphere, in a lighter one in which there are no thoughts and no cares. It is as if they danced because all associations dropped away from them and because as a result they have acquired so much suppleness. It is as if they had no destiny at all, only this smile. When morning dawns, they go to bed, and then the immense day's work of the city booms across their slumber. They don't hear it. They see only the many bright lights of the evening; they hear only the cheerful music. And they dance.

The orchestra brays, and a young girl hurls herself into the resound-ing foam of the fandango, hurls herself with an enthusiastic gesture into the flood of the high-spraying music, like a swimmer who cheerfully jumps from a diving board into the clear water. Her pretty face is all lit up with joy; her dark eyes shine and look off in the distance, seeing nobody; they appear as if surrounded only by a shimmering haze. The girl is filled wholly with herself. With her youth, with her beauty, with her dance, with the effect she produces. Dominated by the music, her delicate, slender body functions in all its muscles. This eighteen-year-old body fevers, burns, and rages. It senses its powers of gyration and yearns to let them loose in order to spend them, to surrender them to the exultation of the hour. In the same way, small, young larks hurl themselves into the air, dragonflies whir in the midday sun. The young girl, who really can't dance at all, who probably hasn't a shred of talent, is, nevertheless, something quite perfect at this moment. That is because she is dancing her youth, her eighteen years, her freshness and her spring. And she enjoys it all. Flying along with the music, she is entirely alone with herself, she imbibes the fiery drink of her existence and gets drunk on it. The people seated around at the tables observe her and somehow become swept along by her spell. They observe this unartistic, enthusiastic girl and become involuntarily refreshed, gentler, gayer. They gaze at her the way one gazes at a lovely insect dancing in the air, whose lightness and charm have a buoyant quality. It's as if they peeked over the edge of their own lives in the direction of this tireless, cheerful existence. And they smile. The music breaks off. The girl remains standing, as if frightened, silent, and then exits with a serious, awakened look on her face.

All these girls dance themselves, define themselves in dance, offer confessions, unconscious candor, forthwith bare their essence. Not just these girls here, but in general: dancing is self-betrayal. Here comes one who dances her silly vanity, blabs it out with every movement, shows with unbelievably false affectation and with terribly misplaced haughtiness how she imagines her stylishness and seductiveness. Another one is still almost a child, with blonde Gretchen hair, blue eyes, and a thin bourgeois face. But this face has only a single astonished, amused, frivolous, and bewildered expression, as if she had just learned the secret of love, as if just this second a girlfriend had whispered it to her in her ear. And it is this alone, just this that her dance expresses: I know it! The way she bends her shoulders, raises her arms, tosses back her head, suddenly blinks her eyes in an outburst of laughter, she just seems to be saying: I know it! Yet another dances her devil-may-care attitude, her utter mendacity and greediness, dances in her carelessly studied, faulty step her laziness and sloppiness. Still another always dances her intolerable attempts at connivance. Into every turn and twist, into every opening of her eyes, into every inclination of her head she'd like to put a cryptic meaning, she'd like to create the impression that she is here only incognito, only out of a playful whim, as if in the morning she could again resume her life as a member of the Order of Imperial Dames or a canoness. Another one, a neat little thing with simple expressions, good-natured gestures, and a provincial demeanor, dances her willingness to become at any moment a nursemaid or seamstress, dances the memory of a modest, poor outer-city dwelling, dances the innate fondness for dust wiping and window cleaning.

The more talented among these girls always have about them the landscape from which they come, the region to which they are native. The special coloring of their homeland is always discernible on them. Here is a little Parisienne, very thin, sharp-nosed and chalk-white. But with the huge, eloquent eyes of a girl from Montmartre and with her striking, witty gestures. And she recalls countless similar faces and similar figures which one sees in the evening darting past on the Place Pigalle or in the Rue Lepic. Here is a little Britisher, with the half-open, questioning rabbit's

mouth, with the cool, water-blue look, with the noncommittal coquetry
. . . Were you to encounter her at eleven at night in Piccadilly or in
Trafalgar Square, you couldn't tell her apart from the other girls running
around there. Here is a young Dane, and her clear brown eyes, her straight,
proud bearing bring to mind the pretty girls of Copenhagen, who all have
the clear, steady eyes of young falcons, and who all walk along so upright,
free, and healthy. The others, however, don't remind one of anything else
at all. Only nightclubs. Their expressions, their glances, their gestures, are
covered with the haze and smoke of the air of these places as with a patina.
Their smile is only the smile of paid evenings. They polished it on the night
frenzy of many cities. They are used to answering the shrill music with this
shrill smile, and the music froze this smile on their features, made it
impersonal.

A tall mulatto executes the virtuoso tap dancing of the hornpipe. The
ecstasy of the ankle joint, which causes the whole body to shake from below.
Basque girls writhe beneath the throbbing rhythm of the melody in the
amorous caresses of the maxixe. Then the cakewalk with the bold lewdness
of the wriggling, contorting Negroes. Impossible to say what this dance
expresses, the way it unmasks the "up-to-date gentleman," so to speak, as
a mating monkey in a tailcoat.[3] When the musicians again begin bellowing:
"Menschen, Menschen san m'r alle . . ." [We're all people, all of us], you're
suddenly back in Vienna again. It's only the street ballads that remind you,
you weren't in a nightclub in Paris, Athens, or Port Said. We have become
international.

And all around at the small tables sit the public. Staring at this blend
of entertainment from all the four corners of the earth. Being roused by
the incessant blaring music, by Spanish, French, English, Russian, American, and Viennese melodies. Being roused by Spanish, English, and
Viennese girls. They'd like to be rid of their own weight, their own middle-
class stolidity at least for one night, but they lack any talent for enjoyment
and have no real ideas about it. They sit there and doubt, and reflect, and
make suspicious faces, uneasy glances, as if they were afraid that their
dignity, their social position might be stolen when they weren't looking,
or as if their self-respect might suddenly get mislaid. They are unsure, both
of themselves and of the pleasures here. At once uncertain and lascivious,
and at the same time prepared to lie to themselves about anything, to come
up with all kinds of excuses. Women sit here with their husbands and look
curious and are dying of desire to cast a glance into the "sinkhole of sin"
in order to come face to face with "vice." And then, if they catch sight
somewhere of some charming gesture, some too obvious fondness, they
have such a shameless kindness in their smile, such a tactless, self-pleasing

indulgence, that you think that they have come here to show off a bit, to feel superior at the expense of the girls here. But if one of the dancers should ever happen to come up to such a woman and say to her: "I won't let you take advantage of me . . . ," one has to understand it.

There was one woman there whose behavior was touching. She was no legitimate spouse but obviously had been with the man sitting next to her for years. A woman, say, between thirty and forty. Perhaps earlier a chorus singer, but now used to a quiet life in comfortable circumstances. Still fashionably attired, with that care employed by a woman who is dependent and constantly has to please her friend. The man at her side was about fifty, elegant, well groomed, in a dinner jacket. And she saw how he devoured all the dancers with his gaze. One after the other. She saw how he eyed, scrutinized, and craved these young dancing girls. A few times she delicately laid her hand on his. He took no notice of it; he seemed to have forgotten her completely. A weak, humiliated smile quivered on her lips. She looked about to see if anybody had observed her. From then on she watched as the man next to her deceived her, as his desires became disloyal to her, before her very eyes. She keenly beheld these young, scintillating girls, naked in all their freshness, and her attractive, faded face became despondent. She averted her gaze. She no longer saw anything else. And she sat there as if bereaved, abandoned and utterly disarmed.

All around at the small tables sit the public, and there are invisible barriers between them, between their world and this dancing world here. But once in a while one of the serious men gets carried away for a moment, leaps over the barrier, and pulls a girl to himself in order to dance with her. It is usually an old man and he usually signals through some kind of tug that he gives himself, through an unspeakably melancholic look, that he has now made up his mind to be merry. There are always two types of men. One, who does it simply out of sensuality, who is no longer satisfied with just looking. He is always the most serious of all. He raises his eyebrows, frowns, shuts his mouth tight. Then, the girl in his arms, he begins to dance. Almost angrily, he turns her in a circle, squeezes her to him, whirls her about, and seems all in a rage. It is no longer a dance but a symbolic act that he executes, a kind of temporary possession. Then, when it's over, he returns to his place with lowered head, sits down, and looks around with an embittered look on his face.

The other type is vain, remembers all of a sudden that he can dance nicely, that when he was a young man he was complimented on his light six-step. And now off he dances with one of the girls, but not as if he wanted to show her his pleasure so much as his approval. Written on his face is the hope that people will admire him. He throws his chest out, turns to the left, executes gracefully measured little steps, delicately places the points of his feet outwards, swings his calves in affected circles, changes the gait, the tempo, carries out all kinds of little stunts, then suddenly stops because he begins to feel dizzy. Chalk-white, he takes his seat again, drinks in small gulps so that nobody should notice that he is panting and is out of breath.

Pleasures of the night. Outside in the sleeping, still streets, all of this vanishes without a trace in the cold winter air. For a little while yet the music rings in the ear before the last echo of it wafts away. For a little while yet a woman's smile glimmers before becoming extinguished.

But this is in no way an observation to which a concluding moral ought to be attached.

"Nachtvergnügen." Original text in Felix Salten, *Das österreichische Antlitz: Essays* (Berlin: S. Fischer Verlag, 1910), 85–96.

1.   Owner of a popular Vienna night spot.

2.   The maxixe (pronounced "mashish") is a ballroom dance of Brazilian origin similar to the two-step. It was popular in the early twentieth century before the First World War.

3.   "Gentlemen" and "up to date" appear in English in the original text.

Handwriting and Work

The kind invitation to provide information on my handwriting and the appearance of my manuscripts puts me in a somewhat embarrassing position. On the basis of the little I can say here, people will certainly not find any neat, prepared explanations. Indeed, I am not at all convinced that I can offer any information in general. I am of course interested in myself and it is against my nature to deny it. However, this obvious interest applies mainly to the phenomena that present themselves to my eyes, and to the images that a lively imagination forms or tries to form from whatever it has seen. In the subconscious, if you wish. In a consciousness befogged by the impetuous rush of the external as well as the internal world, I do indeed sense how my personality plays a role in these things. But up to now I have thought just as little about myself as I observe myself at work.

If today, in response to the invitation, I think about my work and about what others perhaps call my method of work, I discover, not without surprise, that I have really been a writer since the age of eleven. And at the same time, that until now I have not stopped being a pupil and quite seriously continue to regard myself as a beginner. Finally, that a fatally irresistible inclination to laziness has hindered me for as long as I can remember and still hinders me.

I do not dream of making myself better than I am, of putting rouge on my cheeks and coloring the "sweet mouth of song" more beautifully, more intensively with lipstick. I have no desire to paint myself to be an intellectual paragon. Certainly not. Yet nobody can claim that I make myself out to be worse. That is what is lamented by my antagonists, enviers, those indifferent to me, the critics who half understand me or not at all, or the people whose rhythm is too very different from my own to permit some connection to one another. When I speak now about my handwriting, about the appearance of my manuscripts, hence about my working habits, and, at the same time, unavoidably, about myself, I do it as I have already indicated, as an absolute novice. I hope that I can express myself in a way that honorable people write their memoirs. In cautious sincerity. As cautious as possible, but also as sincere as possible. This must be permitted me.

It seems to me that my handwriting is the image of different qualities. Graphologists can discuss them more precisely. And if they truly possess the gift of prophecy so as to discern a person's essence in handwriting traits, I shall have full confidence in their judgment. I am also convinced of the fact that not only handwriting provides insight into character, development, and possible destiny. A person is as openly and meaningfully readable as a book not just through the study of calligraphy but from many other external and bodily signs. His nose, his eyes and ears, his mouth, his brow, even more his laugh, each and very detail exposes him to his very depths. His neckline, his back, his walk betray him to anybody who intuitively evaluates these things. Only the superficial can maintain that the exterior is a secondary consideration. It is always the mind that shapes the body. And everything else related to it. Handwriting included. When one has to say something about his own handwriting, he remains, as we know, dependent just on suppositions. Moreover, such suppositions are often handicapped the more they collide with experience and the more a person is inclined to be strict with himself. That is because a person does not really know himself inside out. And such suppositions are also handicapped by the fact that a person is disinclined to surrender the last bit of knowledge about himself in case he has actually attained it.

My handwriting, which has remained the same for decades with slight variations, undoubtedly arose from a combination of pedantry and carelessness, concentration and laziness, from the halos around the musicality of speech, from the absolute necessity of representing in a plastic way what has been seen as well as what has been invented, from the impulse to communicate as well as from the equally strong effort to remain silent. There also has to be considered the discipline which my journalistic work taught me. And a drop of superstition, not too small a one, should also be taken into consideration. That I am as superstitious as a lottery player may well be a consequence of my very hard childhood years, a consequence, moreover, of my long-lasting cares and later of my constant anxiety concerning the well-being of my family. When I was still quite young, barely eighteen, necessity compelled me to take work as a journalist. I regret none of the difficulties I had to experience. It became clear to me a long time ago that a writer should have journalistic experience and that there is a bit of a writer in every important journalist. When I come across the word "feuilletonistic" in a judgmental sense, I smile out of pity for the person who in this way tries to make light of a great and rare quality. Voltaire, Lichtenberg, Carlyle, and an impressive number of immortals were just so feuilletonistically regarded.

The absolute precision demanded by journalistic writing made me realize that there must be no external or internal disruptions. It is to this understanding that I owe my insensitivity to noise of any kind when I work. However much the smallest noise irritates me otherwise, I am deaf during work. People can be in the room chattering loudly, carpets can be beat outdoors or guns fired, I hear nothing. One afternoon, for example, I wrote a short novella in the Markusplatz. And only when I was through with it did I notice that the arc-lamps were burning, that a band was concertizing, and that a crowd was swarming all around me. I have often written for days on end in the middle of a beach in our cabana while other members of my family were enjoying themselves with friends who dropped by. In the same way I learned not to wait for inspiration and not to pay attention to the absence of inspiration, to turn off private sorrow and to surrender myself totally, but really totally, to the necessary work of the moment. Nor have I ever begun a manuscript, whether a play, a novel, or indeed even the smallest feuilleton, without first having the conclusion firmly in mind. That is why my manuscripts are nearly entirely free of corrections. I write very slowly, and it can almost be said that I sketch one letter after another on the paper. And while I am engaged in this process, many, many details and ideas come crowding in, but they never change anything in the construction of the whole. I cross nothing out, since I put nothing down without forethought. As I write I always hear a voice speaking clearly to me that I do not believe is my own. I hear it in my ears. Sometimes it improves what I have written. It sounds irresolute and hesitant when it has not made up its mind about something and it gives the impression of nearly masterful determination when it seems to know what it wants to say. The figures in my plays and novels talk, and I follow their dictation. But I always have to wait until these people begin to speak. I must not begin any earlier with the material at hand. A few times, nevertheless, I did try this. Absolutely nothing came of it, or when I forced it, it failed terribly. Sometimes it takes a long time for a story to be ready enough for its characters to open their mouths. I dragged several of my books around inside me for ten or, in the case of one, twenty years before I reached the point where I was ready to write it down. Once again other plans simply melted away from me. Nevertheless, I will never in all my life exhaust all my ideas, designs, and characters. There is one thing I cannot possibly fathom: the writer who waits from one work to the next for a subject to strike him.

Alongside my carelessness, my laziness, and my surely exaggerated great joy in life, a laughable pedantry also developed, and in fact rather early. How, why, and where, I am unable to explain. For thirty years this pedantry has compelled me to use the same size paper and the same pencil (Koh-i-Noor), the same, really one and the same, writing pad made of an already worn board cover, the same little antique bronze hand that holds the paper firm, and the same sharpener. These objects accompanied me wherever I traveled. And when I confess that here, too, there is no small amount of superstition and habit, it must surely be the result of pure pedantry that in the course of time my handwriting has drawn ever closer to the printed copy. It has become an absolute necessity for me to have the approximate type-area in my manuscript before me. I of course know that in its diminutiveness and tightness my handwriting is a lot more copious than any book page. I also know that a single sheet of manuscript contains three to four pages of a book. How it happens that in the course of my work my handwriting gets smaller and smaller, narrower and narrower, and that besides I myself can read it only with a magnifying glass, I can offer no explanation. But I do believe that from everything that I have set forth here, an explanation will perhaps emerge.

In no way did I resolve to disclose this information on my own initiative. And now that the end is at hand, I must emphasize the reluctance that I occasionally felt. This is also really the very first time that I have so readily spoken about myself. Although I am a gregarious person and by all means capable of an equally fast-formed and lifelong friendship, I have far more often been the recipient of the intimate disclosures of my many friends than I troubled others with my own affairs. By the same token, I have not been able to compose my own experiences in a straightforward and recognizable fashion. Something holds me back from it that is stronger than everything else. Only three or four of my books have an autobiographical content. But I am quite sure that nobody would guess it.

"Handschrift und Arbeit," 1931. Felix Salten, "Handschrift und Arbeit," *Jahrbuch Deutscher Bibliophilen und Literaturfreunde,* ed. Hans Feigl (Zurich: Amalthea-Verlag, 1931), 90–94.

EGON FRIEDELL
1878–1938

EGON FRIEDELL[1] WAS A BORN ENTERTAINER, AND LIKE ALL TRUE ENTERTAINERS, DREW SUSTENANCE FROM AN AUDIENCE, WHETHER IN A COFFEEHOUSE, CABARET, OR ON THE STAGE OF A THEATER. A big, robust, cigar-chomping life of the party, he was a landmark of the Vienna coffeehouse scene and an intimate of Peter Altenberg. Storytelling came easily to him. His sparkling good-natured wit earned him a large following, and when cabaret culture became part of Viennese nightlife in the early years of the twentieth century, Friedell found a new environment as felicitous to his talents as the coffeehouse. When the short-lived Cabaret Nachtlicht opened in January 1906, Friedell

was one of its original performers. Once the Cabaret Fledermaus established itself as the most durable and renowned of the Nachtlicht's succes-
sors, Friedell threw himself into it with his characteristic gusto. Performing
solo as a storyteller, he regaled audiences above all with his Altenberg
anecdotes. Since Altenberg was already a Vienna legend and yet too shy
himself to mount the stage of a cabaret, he good-naturedly submitted to
serving as the butt of humorous stories about him manufactured and
delivered by Friedell. Despite his playing the straight man to Altenberg's
buffoon, Friedell's attachment to his friend was lifelong. Not by coincidence it was to Friedell that Altenberg's principal publisher, S. Fischer of
Berlin, turned for a book about him. The work appeared in 1912 under
the title *Ecce homo* (Latin for "Behold the Man"). To many it was a disappointment—not so much for what was said but for what was not said.
Friedell had taken his subject very seriously, omitted the anecdotes and
details of personal life that many people expected to find in a book about
Altenberg by someone who knew him as well as Friedell, and in any event
shifted the focus from the man to a more abstract consideration of art and
the artist. Once he got a sense of the book from reviews, Altenberg be-
moaned the effort and never could bring himself to read the copy Friedell
had sent him. After Altenberg's death in 1919, Friedell edited his own
anthology of his friend's writings, which appeared in 1922 as *Das
Altenbergbuch* (*The Altenberg Book*).

Alfred Polgar was another close, if not lifelong, friend of Friedell's.
With the Cabaret Fledermaus in full swing, he and Friedell teamed up to
write dramatic sketches for it. These proved immensely successful, and one
of them—the one for which they are most remembered, *Goethe* (premiered
1 January 1908)—became a genuine classic of the German-language cabaret. It has been performed a good few thousand times throughout Austria
and Germany and has never been equaled in popularity as a theatrical
work written expressly for a cabaret.

Friedell's penchant for performing led him naturally to a multifac-
eted involvement with the stage. In February 1907 he was asked to serve
as artistic director of the Cabaret Fledermaus. But when the cabaret
changed hands in 1909, he quit the post, thereafter appearing in it only
as a guest. Friedell remained an active cabaret performer until 1919. It
was through his performances on cabaret stages that Friedell first came
to the attention of the famed director Max Reinhardt. In November 1913
he made a guest appearance in Berlin's Linden-Kabarett in a play directed
by Reinhardt. Other roles in Reinhardt productions followed. Friedell
played the emperor in a version of George Bernard Shaw's *Androcles and*

the Lion that Friedell himself had prepared for the stage and that Reinhardt produced at his Deutsches Theater in Berlin. In 1923 Friedell had a major role in a renowned production of Molière's *Imaginary Invalid* in Reinhardt's Schloss Leopoldskron in Salzburg. The next year, 1924, he appeared in Reinhardt's theaters in both Vienna (Theater in der Josefstadt) and in Berlin. He remained active on the stage, particularly in Berlin, until 1932.

Friedell's work on the stage was paralleled by his writing about the stage. In fact, it was as a newspaper drama critic that he began his literary career in 1902. By 1905 he was contributing pieces to Karl Kraus's *Die Fackel* and in 1906 began a collaboration with the *Schaubühne*, later to become the *Weltbühne* and with which he cooperated until 1932. Drama reviews make up a fair portion of Friedell's essayistic writing. Apart from such Vienna papers as *Die Stunde, Wiener Allgemeine Zeitung, Die Schaubühne, Der Merkur,* and the *Neues Wiener Journal,* Friedell also contributed to Berlin newspapers, among them the *Weltbühne, Berliner Zeitung am Mittag,* and the *Freie Deutsche Bühne.* His newspaper experience stood him in good stead when, between 1921 and 1924, he and Polgar again combined talents to produce a *Böses Buben-Journal* (*Bad Boys-Journal*), which parodied leading Vienna papers of the time.

The talent for playwriting demonstrated in cabaret pieces such as *Goethe* and the only somewhat less popular *Soldatenleben im Frieden* (*Military Life in Peacetime,* 1910) tempted Friedell to essay dramatic works of a more serious nature. The principal fruit of this effort was a play on a biblical subject entitled *Die Judastragödie* (*The Tragedy of Judas*). It was finished in 1916, published in book form in 1920, and finally given its premiere on 3 March 1923 in the Vienna Burgtheater. Despite Friedell's high hopes for it, the play did badly. Critics were unkind, and the work was performed only eight times.

If Friedell is best known in the German-speaking world as a stellar cabaret performer and writer, actor in Max Reinhardt productions, drama critic, and theater administrator, his reputation abroad rests on entirely different premises. It is, in fact, based on a single work, a three-volume history of modern culture published between 1927 and 1931 under the original title *Kulturgeschichte der Neuzeit* (*A Cultural History of the Modern Age*). An ambitious undertaking by an amateur philosopher and historian of world culture and obviously superficial, it can still be read fitfully with interest. It was followed by two other similarly ambitious undertakings, a cultural history of Egypt and the ancient Orient (*Kulturgeschichte Ägyptens und des alten Orients,* published in Switzerland in 1936 after publishers in then Nazi Germany refused to accept anything from Friedell) and a cultural history of Greece, which Friedell did not live to finish and which was published posthumously in 1938 under the title *Kulturgeschichte Griechenlands*).

Friedell's scholarly pursuits could hardly have been forecast by his background and public reputation as a clown. He was born in Vienna in 1878 to a Jewish family named Friedmann. Childhood was marred by the breakup of his family and dislocation. A year and a half after his birth, his mother abandoned the family. His parents were formally divorced in 1887. Following the death of his father two years later, the three children were separated, with Egon being taken in by an aunt in Frankfurt. The trauma of these early years clearly seemed to have had an impact on his schooling. After being expelled from a secondary school in Frankfurt, he was enrolled in a boarding school in Baden near Vienna but was disqualified from the final examination, or *Abitur,* without which he was ineligible for a diploma. The *Abitur* in fact remained elusive until 1899 (and then only on the fourth try) at the end of an educational trail that led through a succession of schools of one sort or another in Germany and Austria. Armed finally with his diploma, Friedell began university studies in Vienna, completing them (on the second try) in 1904. His dissertation on the German writer Novalis as a philosopher was published that year. It was Friedell's first major publication and the first to bear the pseudonym Friedell, which he eventually legalized. Its subject evidenced an interest in philosophy traceable at least to Friedell's studies with a private tutor in Heidelberg in 1896. Although his formal study ended in 1904, Friedell had by now developed an appetite for scholarly pursuits that remained with him the rest of his life. These pursuits bore fruit not only in his cultural histories of the modern age, ancient Egypt, and classical Greece but also in a series of translations he edited of works by Emerson (1906), the English historian Carlyle (1914), and Macauley (1924). He also published a collection of largely philosophical aphorisms (*Steinbruch* [*Quarry,* 1922]), a condensation of which was published in 1930 under the title *Kleine Philosophie* (*A Small Philosophy*); and a study of Jesus (*Das Jesusproblem* [*The Problem of Jesus*], written in 1919 and published two years later). Friedell's interest in Christianity stemmed in part from his conversion to Lutheranism on 12 July 1897.

Although fun-loving and clownish in public, a real denizen of coffeehouse and cabaret, Friedell's private life tended toward the solitary. He never married, and there were those who found it easy to believe that he was either homosexual or impotent. Little, in fact, is known of his relations with women. His greatest romantic interest was the actress Lina Vetter, who was married to the architect Adolf Loos and is best known under the name of Lina Loos. The genuine feelings and duration of the relationship not-withstanding, there is nothing to suggest that it was any less platonic than that between Lina Loos and another of her great admirers, Peter Altenberg. No other woman ever appeared as important in Friedell's life.

From 1900 until his death in 1938, Friedell had the same residence in the Gentzgasse. In a curious link with his childhood, his housekeeper happened to have been his former nursemaid. When she died in 1917, her successor was a servant, Hermine Schiman, who had been in his employ since 1904. She eventually brought to live with her a fourteen-year-old daughter, Herma, who had been raised somewhere in the country and who many swore bore a resemblance to Friedell. When Herma herself married a carpenter named Franz Kotab at the age of twenty, Friedell magnanimously allowed the newlyweds to take up residence in a small room in his apartment, thereby providing more grist for the rumor mills. Within a few years, the Kotabs had become the parents of two children, further swelling the population of the once-bachelor apartment. If Friedell felt any discomfort in the arrangement, he never expressed himself on the matter, never did anything to alter it, and remained steadfast in his loyalty to Hermine Schiman and the Kotabs to his death.

As if to further test Friedell's endurance, his mother, who had been absent from his life virtually from the time of his birth, reappeared in 1928. Her timing was doubtless no coincidence, coming not long after the first volume of his *Cultural History of the Modern Age* had been published to rave reviews and substantial royalties had begun pouring in. She demanded support from him and instituted a suit against him when he refused. He finally complied with a court order requiring him to provide her with some financial assistance, but to protect himself against any greater claims on her part, he named Hermine Schiman as his sole heir. His mother died in 1933.

Friedell's engagements as an actor in Berlin kept him in the German capital for long stretches of time from 1929 until Hitler came to power in 1933. From then on, further stage appearances by him as well as publications of his works were out of the question. Hardly unaware of the possible precariousness of his situation despite his earlier conversion to Lutheranism, Friedell maintained a reasonably normal routine. This was brutally interrupted by the German annexation of Austria on 15 March 1938. The very next day, at about ten in the evening, two young SA-men came ringing the doorbell at Friedell's third-floor apartment on the Gentzgasse. Although it has been suggested that they had come errone-ously in search of someone else, the greater likelihood is that they were indeed after Friedell, especially since they are believed to have demanded the whereabouts of "the Jew Friedell." While his housekeeper was trying to stall them in the entrance hall, Friedell surmised the situation from his room, opened a window, and after shouting a warning to possible passersby, leaped to his death on the pavement below. Barely a dozen people attended his funeral in Vienna's Central Cemetery. Differences of opinion concerning the actual danger facing Friedell when he committed suicide continue to the present. Had Friedell wanted to go into exile, the possibility existed for him as late as the day before the annexation. But he expressed no interest in flight, claiming that as an Austrian writer he belonged where he was and pointing to a huge collection of books that he could not bear to leave behind. His health was also poor, owing to worsening diabetes and his too-ingrained habits. The appearance of the uniformed Austrian Nazis at his door must obviously have thrown him into a panic. Fear of degradation, imprisonment, torture or worse closed all other options; only suicide remained. That Friedell had already been flirting with the idea of taking his own life and just used his imminent arrest as the pretext for finally doing so is speculative at best.

Besides the works mentioned above, Friedell published in his lifetime a small biography of the German dramatist Friedrich Hebbel (1909); an edition of works by the eighteenth-century Jewish Freemason Georg Christoph Lichtenberg (1910); an edition of Hans Christian Andersen's satires (1914); a book entitled *Von Dante zu D'Annunzio* (*From Dante to D'Annunzio*, 1915); and an edition of the sayings of the nineteenth-century Austrian comic dramatist Johann Nestroy (1922). He also wrote the foreword to a cycle of erotic pictures by the Italian artist Mario Petrucci. Posthumous publication of his writings began within a few years of the end of the Second World War and has continued unabated to the present. Some fifteen collections of his works have appeared to date. These include: *Friedell-Brevier: Aus Schriften und Nachlass* (*Friedell-Breviary: From Writings and Literary Legacy*, 1947); *Das Altertum war nicht antik und andere Bemerkungen* (*Antiquity Wasn't Antique and Other Observations*, 1950); *Aphorismen zur Geschichte* (*Aphorisms on History*, 1955); *Kleine Porträtgalerie: Fünf Essays* (*Small Portrait Gallery: Five Essays*, 1953); *Briefe* (*Letters*, 1959); *Ist die Erde bewohnt?* (*Is the Earth Inhabited*, 1961); *Aphorismen und Briefe* (*Aphorisms and Letters*, 1961); *Wozu das Theater: Essays. Satiren. Humoresken* (*Whither the Theater? Essays, Satires, Humoresques*, 1969); a fantastic novella entitled *Die Rückkehr der Zeitmaschine* (*The Return of the Time Machine*, 1974); *Egon Friedells Konversationslexikon* (*Egon Friedell's Conversation Lexicon*, 1974); *Abschaffung des Genies: Essays bis 1918* (*Doing Away with Genius: Essays to 1918*, 1982); *Selbstanzeige: Essays ab 1918* (*Self-Advertisements: Essays since 1918*, 1983); *Meine Doppelseele: Taktlose Bemerkungen zum Theater* (*My Alter Ego: Tactless Observa-*

tions on the Theater, 1983); *Der verkleidete Dichter* (*The Poet with Make-up,* 1983); and *Das Friedell-Lesebuch* (*The Friedell Reader,* 1988). The work for which he is best known in English, the *Kulturgeschichte der Neuzeit* (*Cultural History of the Modern Age*), was published in its entirety as a single volume in 1960. The third volume, which in the original was published in Munich in 1931, was dedicated to George Bernard Shaw. When Shaw learned of it, he was told that Friedell was the "Austrian George Bernard Shaw." His reply was that he wanted to read the book to discover if he himself was indeed the "English Friedell."

1.   There are two monographs on Friedell in German and one in English. The German studies are a slight popular biography by Peter Haage entitled *Der Partylöwe, der nur Bücher frass: Egon Friedell und sein Kreis* (Hamburg and Düsseldorf: Claassen Verlag, 1971); and a more solid work by Raymond Wiseman, *Egon Friedell: Die Welt als Bühne* (Munich: Wilhelm Fink Verlag, 1987). The English study is an unpublished dissertation by Gordon M. Patterson, "The Misunderstood Clown: Egon Friedell and His Vienna," University of California at Los Angeles, 1979. There is also good material on Friedell in four collections of his works edited by Heribert Illig: *Abschaffung des Genies: Essays bis 1918* (Vienna-Munich: Löcker Verlag, 1982); *Selbstanzeige: Essays ab 1918* (Vienna-Munich: Löcker Verlag, 1983); *Goethe und die Journalisten: Satiren im Duett* (Vienna: Löcker Verlag, 1986); and *Das Friedell-Lesebuch* (Munich: Verlag C. H. Beck, 1988). For the only complete and accurate bibliography of Friedell's writings, see also Heribert Illig's *Schauspieler— Schausteller: Die künstlerischen Aktivitäten Egon Friedells* (Vienna: Löcker Verlag, 1987).

THE PANAMA HAT

Well, I bought myself a Panama hat. Everybody said I really had to have a Panama hat. It cost sixty crowns. I put it on and betook myself to the busiest street I could think of.

Right away, an acquaintance of mine saw me and said: "Ah, bravo, bravo! A Panama hat. Looks great on you. But watch out! *One* downpour and you're done for." I wanted to ask him for more information, but he was already gone.

A second one said: "*Very* chic. Really. But now you have to wear a decent tie and decent gloves. To say nothing of boots. In your *present* outfit, though, the nice-looking hat is just out of place."

Professor Müller said: "Eh, my young friend, what a splendid hat! But why not a good book instead? This hat costs at least eight crowns. For that kind of money you could have four issues of *Universe and Mankind*. Illustrated!"

Another just said: "For *that* you have money." He didn't know that even for the Panama hat I still owed money.

Finally, my friend Adolf Loos came along. In our town he's regarded as the leading connoisseur in matters of dress. He threw a scrutinizing glance at my hat and said: "What did it cost?"

"Sixty crowns," I answered proudly.

"Oh, I see!" said Loos. "In that case, it's all right. I was afraid you might have been taken in. For sixty crowns, of course, it *can't* be worth anything. A real Panama hat costs at least two hundred crowns. You have to understand—they're woven under water . . ."

But someone else came up and said: "Nonsense! Under water or over water—it's all the same. The main thing is it's pretty, and it *is*. That is, everything except the shape. *That* is, if you'll pardon my saying so, frightfully tasteless."

But then another one mixed in and said: "Don't let yourself be talked into anything. The shape is quite nice. The only trouble is, it doesn't go with your head." And he added, thoughtfully: "Maybe . . . you just don't happen to have a head for Panama hats . . ."

In the meantime, that creature also appeared for whose sake I had really bought the Panama hat in the first place. She said: "I don't know what you people want from him. I find the hat simply charming. The straw is good quality, the shape is attractive, and I think it suits him splendidly. Only . . . I do have one thing to complain about . . . but that's my own private affair. Anyway . . . God, it may be just a whim on my part . . . but the truth is, I can't stand Panama hats!"

As a result of all this, I gave my Panama hat as a present to a cab horse I befriended. He's now wearing it proudly as a sunshade. For myself, though, I bought a felt hat for two crowns fifty. No one can determine its shape and color. My experience has taught me that lovely and valuable things are troublesome and disturbing possessions, since they seem to provoke people's criticism. On the other hand, you can lead the calmest life in the world with poor cheap stuff.

"Der Panamahut," 1902. The sketch, originally a cabaret piece, was included in the collection of Friedell's early essays published by Löcker Verlag of Vienna in 1982 under the title *Abschaffung des Genies: Essays von 1905 bis 1918,* ed. Heribert Illig. The translation is based on the text as it appears in the identical Diogenes Verlag edition (Zurich, 1985), 18–20.

VIENNA THE "THEATER CITY"

"Look in thy heart and write," says Sidney. Hermann Bahr looked into his heart and wrote. What he recorded was a twenty-five-year rage at Vienna. It was a rage that doesn't rant and rave but instead keeps still and collects facts upon facts, makes files of them, and then looks for their meanings. It was a rage that became entirely systematic and scientific. Bahr relates the history of Vienna in the same way that the zoologist describes some involution of genesis. How the Celts came first, those sleek, crafty, adaptable people, who seemed to understand that by themselves they were nothing, but that they could be everything; how they then entered into very propitious crossbreeding with the South German tribe and found the appropriate rulers in the capable and worldly-wise Babenbergs. That was the great age of Vienna, the age of Walther von der Vogelweide.[1] But then came the Habsburgs, whose distinctive trait was that they had no sense of reality. The world was supposed to pattern itself on them, not they on the world. Therefore, they could only make use of creatures who had no will of their own, and so there arose the "Nation of Privy Councillors." Then came the Baroque with its double reversal of the idea of worldliness. It first rejected the world as mere dream. But since at the same time it affirmed dream as the only reality, it again returned to the world by a roundabout way. Thus it became the philosophy of the most worldly worldliness, since it rejected every accountability on the grounds that the world is just a dream. So arose that odd mixture of withdrawal from life and love of life, of submissiveness and pride, of incense and musk. And then there came the artificially created, hereditary Austrian liberalism, always trying to keep pace with life. And finally the immigration of reformed Jews with which the history of Vienna comes to a close.

Viewed purely from the literary perspective, Bahr's book is a cultural-psychological monograph of the first rank. To find works informed with a similar reliability and elegance of psychological vivisection, a similar sensitivity to the innermost and knottiest psychic complications, a similar precision and power of verbal expression, you have to reach quite high up, possibly to *The Genealogy of Morals* or Pascal's *Pensées*.

A well-known type is the "Gentleman from Germany," who is enthralled with Vienna. Nothing is more understandable but at the same time more gratuitous than this affection of the German for Vienna. He comes from his prosaic, efficient, industrious, honest native city and spends two weeks in "dear Vienna." In these two weeks he naturally experiences nothing but a certain feeling of relaxation and lightness. He sees people who don't work, play billiards all day long in the coffeehouse, or go strolling among lovely old buildings, besides taking well-prepared meals, riding in elegant carriages, and smoking Virginia tobacco. He can perceive none of the negative consequences of these forms of life during the short time of his stay and has just as little opportunity to acquaint himself with these people from some side other than that of their "easygoingness." Consequently, he believes that here is a city that has preserved something of that ancient beauty of existence for which so many people yearn, here still exists a little corner of that paradise from which Americanism has expelled us.

That Vienna has an antiquated public transportation system, awful paving, street lighting, and police, a laughable metropolitan railway, a wretched postal service, and so on is of no interest to our visitor. The entire two weeks he gets by without them. He contemplates the Votive Church instead. How should he know that among a hundred administrative officials there is hardly one who measures up to his responsibility, that the instruction in the schools is under the control of a heartless and narrow-minded bureaucracy, that Vienna expends more nervous energy on the purchase of a penknife than is expended elsewhere on the establishment of a factory? He had no penknife to buy in Vienna, no legal case to pursue, no children to send to school. He admired the Karl's Church. And since some waiters, coachmen, and porters were exquisitely polite toward the "newcomer," who is usually more easily taken in than the natives, he sums up his impressions in the sentence: "We are better business people, but the Viennese are more obliging and art-loving."

To be sure, when by "theater city" you have in mind a city in which everything to do with "theater" is nothing authentic and deep but all makeup and superficiality, a city in which comedy is played both day and night, then Vienna is the "theater city" par excellence. She is this also by virtue of the fact that nowhere else is the atavistic cult of the actor so much in the blood as in Vienna. And it is well known that it is only the actor who attracts the Viennese to the theater. And very often the theatergoer has no idea even who the author of the play is. That is why the plays that have had the greatest success in Vienna are those by writers who in their innermost being are themselves just actors. Think, for example, of Sardou,[2] Feuillét,[3] and all the Frenchmen with whom the renowned Burgtheater has for decades filled its repertoire. An excuse for gallantry, a "showpiece," a "rat race"—the theater has never been more to the Viennese. And their passion for the dramatic art stirs them only because this art can be kept at the greatest remove from life with impunity. Their ideal is the actor as fire-eater, as ham, as falsifier of life. Their instinct for the unreal is what draws the Viennese to the theater.

Since for the Viennese there is nothing real, the same can be said as well for this childish hero worship with which they cultivate actors. When they seem to adulate Kainz or Girardi,[4] it is themselves that they are really adulating. They want to make themselves important; nothing else matters to them.

How badly Beethoven, Grillparzer,[5] Kürnberger[6] fared in Vienna, Bahr showed at length in his book. It never went differently in Vienna for anybody who wanted or could do anything. The same for Bahr. For quite a few years he has been working in Vienna and on Vienna, passionately devoted to introducing the modern spirit, the spirit of the most refined impressionability, of intellectual discipline, of artistic objectivity. And all he has to show for his troubles is misunderstanding and ingratitude. "He writes interestingly," say his friends. "He's a poseur," say his enemies. By "He writes interestingly," what the Viennese really has in mind is to get rid of his teacher and to degrade anybody who has anything to say, who is filled with any kind of pathos, to the level of a prattler, juggler, or jester. If anybody makes the Viennese uncomfortable because of a love of truth, he is dismissed on suspicion of sensationalism and putting on airs, or even worse things. Whoever has any universality, depth, enthusiasm, objectivity, industriousness, and cleverness is hated, since all these qualities are regarded by the Viennese as hardly more than affronts to their own sense of self-esteem.

If the numbskulls who couldn't appreciate Bahr's critical activity as any more than an "interesting pen" could just once understand why, in fact, Bahr "writes interestingly," they would probably also try to stifle these remarks. For Bahr is an interesting critic for the simple reason that he recognizes what is good in artistic efforts. He grasps what is positive in the work of art, the plus in it, the thing or things that make it different. In his deficiencies and inadequacies, the artist is just like any other person; to talk about such things is completely uninteresting. Critics who concern themselves mainly with failings and shortcomings are boring. What somebody can't do we know ourselves without having to be told. When it comes to incompetence, we're the leading specialists. But we only stand to gain from a critic who makes us aware of hidden beauties and who possibly brings new ones to a work of art that weren't there before. It is this kind of critic who is interesting. And for the precise reason that he himself is an artist. After all, an artist is nothing other than a person who increases the wealth of the world's beauty.

Although such a critic is not "objective," he nevertheless understands a work of art better than other people. That is because the love he brings to art opens art to him. It is no different with art than with everything else in life. Coldness and hardness have no access to the secrets of the world. "Love is an eyewater," says Emerson.

The Viennese have no use for anything of the sort. They prefer critics who apply a correcting lens to everything, who strike out and cut, who like to "show influences," who draw embarrassing comparisons, who always have a cold shower ready at once for every enthusiastic endeavor. They like critics who turn the work of art into something ugly.

The Viennese are always prepared to see something phony behind every enthusiasm, a personal motive behind every ideal striving, and, when they have no other recourse, to see in every intellectual ambition at the very least a piece of nonsense. That is why the whole of Viennese life has a curiously grotesque character to it. Vienna is a lovely city with repulsive people. The poetry of Vienna lies in its stones and buildings. But the people who move among the stones and buildings suffer from a poisonous, disfiguring illness that ate its way into them in the course of decades. It is called lack of idealism. Vienna has slowly been going to ruin from this gravest of all epidemics. Nobody can localize it, since it is everywhere. Nobody can cure it, since it derives from the composition of Viennese blood. It is not as simple as with printed works.

"Die 'Theaterstadt' Wien." Original text in Egon Friedell, *Wozu das Theater? Essays. Satiren. Humoresken*, 168–72.

1.   Walther von der Vogelweide (c. 1170–c. 1230), the finest lyric poet of medieval Germany.

2.   Victorien Sardou (1831–1908), popular French writer principally of light comedies.

3.   Raoul Feuillét (c. 1660–c. 1710), a French ballet master.

4.   Josef Kainz (1858–1910), prominent Burgtheater actor. Alexander Girardi (1850–1918), a leading comic actor associated with the Vienna Burgtheater.

5.   Franz Grillparzer (1791–1872), outstanding Austrian dramatist.

6.   Ferdinand Kürnberger (1821–79), an Austrian critic, publicist, and feuilletonist who took part in the revolution of 1848.

THE AUSTRIAN SPIRIT

[Hans Sassmann, also Hanns Sassmann, 17.12.1882–8.5.1944]

1.
Dr. Egon *Friedell,*
Vienna

We would be delighted if you cared to participate in our Christmas poll, further information concerning which you will find in the enclosed. We are convinced that your contribution will be a pearl. You will certainly feel the need to express yourself on the matter in the most comprehensive and detailed manner. We would nevertheless ask you to condense your presentation out of consideration for the large number of other entries.

Yours respectfully,
The Editorial Staff of
the *Frankfurt Gazette*

2.
Most esteemed Herr Friedell!

We received a couplet—"The world gets torn asunder, but Austria never goes under"—from the pen of the salon humorist Eugen Fridel, to whom the postal service erroneously delivered our invitation. We are sending you herewith a copy of our letter and await your manuscript within eight weeks, that is before 15 December.

Frankfurt Gazette

3.
The writer Hans *Sassmann,*
Vienna

My dear friend,

It will surely please you to hear that the *Frankfurt Gazette* has requested a Christmas contribution of me. Rarely has a work interested me so much as this. At last we are reminded of the land of Walther von der Vogelweide! Foreign countries still need us! And Austria will show them what it is capable of. The contribution must be a pearl. You must understand, therefore, how important it is for you to undertake the work immediately. But please, not too short, or we'll be accused once again of writing only chit-chat. I await your manuscript within eight days at the latest.

Yours,
Egon Friedell

P.S. Make sure there's nothing there that can offend Bahr and Hofmannsthal. That is most important.

4.

Dear Friedell,

I am very pleased and flattered that you thought of me. I, too, have seldom been as interested in a piece of work as I am in this. But you cannot ask me to sacrifice my *most important convictions*. Why *not* slip some poison to *Bahr* and *Hofmannsthal*? In the treatment of such a serious situation, where the whole world is looking at us, no *personal considerations* should interfere. That would be *Austrian*.

You will receive the manuscript within three days. What is the subject of it supposed to be by the way?

Yours,
Hans Sassmann

5.

Dear Sassmann,

I knew the moment I began having any dealings with you I'd be in for trouble. Naturally, I didn't have any time to study the letter carefully, since I had to dash off to the theater in order to show it around there. Now I can't seem to find it anywhere. It's possible I left it behind on my table at the Café Prochaska. I know for sure I didn't have it in the Café Grillhuber. It can also be that somebody stole it from me at the City-Bar in order to show off with it. I authorize you to inquire of the *Frankfurt Gazette* what it's about.

Your Friedell

6.

Dear Friedell,

I am happy to do whatever is humanly possible, but you can't ask that of me. I can't simply write to a newspaper where I don't know a single member of the editorial staff personally. I also don't know how you address such a German editor's office. The least you can do is compose a draft of the letter.

Your Sassmann

They were all broken up at the "Writers' Club" yesterday because you approached me and none of them.

7.

Dear Sassmann,

Since you undertook the matter with enthusiasm, I'll do everything I can for you now. *To make big speeches* and then *do nothing:* that is *typically Austrian.*

Your Friedell

8.

Dear Sassmann,

Just learned from the waiter at the Café Demimonde that it has to do with an article about Austria. Now you don't have any more excuses.

Your Friedell

9.

Dear Friedell,

It's hard to write about Austria. What will people abroad say?

Sassmann

10.

Highly honored Master!
Much esteemed Herr Sassmann!

I learned in my restaurant that you are the chief collaborator of the *Frankfurt Gazette.* It has long been my wish also to be able to collaborate with this outstanding organ. I am sure it will be no trouble for you because of your connections to arrange this. I have, to be sure, not attempted anything literary up to now, but I am a longtime acquaintance of Franz Werfel. If you should wish to communicate with me personally, you can find me every day at the Café Pyramid from 10 to 1 and from 3 to 6.

In sincere admiration,
Franz Zehntbauer,
Municipal Trade Commissioner

11.
Esteemed Herr Friedell,

We are missing your contribution. We were so certain of your prompt transmittal of the manuscript that we cannot possibly find a replacement for you now so soon before Christmas.

Respectfully,
Frankfurt Gazette

12.
Dear Sassmann,

Christmas is around the corner, and you still haven't procured me the English soap for Lina. *Typically Austrian!*

Your Friedell

13.
Urgent telegram for
Egon Friedell.

Rasute blifta settmil hapta hapta 1/2.

Trankfurt Gazelle

14.
Dear Sassmann,

To my dismay, I've discovered in the Café Eden that you absolutely forgot about the contribution for the *Frankfurt Gazette*. You've caused me no end of trouble. That could have become for me the beginning of a lasting partnership. Not only that, but with the next poll they'll avoid me like the plague. To say nothing of *prestige abroad*. I have you to thank for all that!

Friedell

15.

Dear Friedell,

I don't know what more you want. Just a few weeks ago, I happened to be in three societies where they never heard the slightest thing about you before, but when they heard I know you, you couldn't get their hands off me. Everywhere I'm introduced as "the friend of the famous Friedell who left the *Frankfurt Gazette* in the lurch." You're the most popular person in Vienna. And you have me to thank for that. You see, I'm not really so "unreliable" as you always maintain.

Sassmann

16.

Dear Sassmann,

In Austria, you become a great man when you *don't* do anything *conspicuously*. With the greatest fanfare, Emperor Joseph accomplished no reforms whatsoever. With the whole world watching him, Laudon did not defeat Frederick the Great,[1] and Mayor Lueger,[2] with huge crowds around him wherever we went, did nothing for Vienna. There are many people who haven't written for the *Frankfurt Gazette,* but none of them has ever become the center of attraction in Vienna because of it. That's because none of the others had any talent. At least, no Austrian talent.

Friedell

17.

From the Tax Authority for
the 18th and 19th districts,
Vienna, Lower Austria.

Dr. Egon Friedell,
Editor-in-Chief of the *Frankfurt Gazette.*

On the basis of official inquiry, by reason of your wage benefits or continuing emoluments from your activity as sole author of the periodical publication *Frankfurt Gazette* for the years 1926 to 1929, you are classified in Group Ia of the general profit and income tax or in Ib of the temporary income tax. The amount of additional tax to be paid is assessed on the income level for the second term of the land-registry apportionment directly applied to the intermediate year as second installment on the level of accretion of the preceding third half-quarter. This is in addition to the mandatory municipal income tax surcharge for those not subject to exemption from the direct income surplus tax according to the tax supplementary law of 3 January 1921, which remains in effect until at the latest the set date of 1 December 1926. Previously paid sums on owed additional tax rates for the last three half-quarters of the preceding taxation period are excluded from the tax surcharge so long as the taxpayer falls within the stated period.

"Die österreichische Seele," 1926. Original text in *Das Friedell-Lesebuch*, 92–98.
    1.   Gideon Ernst Frhr. von Laudon (1717–90), an Austrian field marshal who in 1760 defeated Frederick the Great of Prussia at Landeshut.
    2.   Karl Lueger (1844–1910), the founder of the Christian Social party in 1893 and mayor of Vienna from 1897 to 1910. Exceptionally popular, particularly among the lower middle classes, and a vigorous promoter of Vienna's expansion and modernization, he was also notorious for his anti-Semitism.

THE CABARET

Every now and then people ask me what I think of today's cabaret and if I believe it has a future. But were I to tell the truth or, more cautiously stated, what I regard as the truth, I would answer this question only by means of a platitude. The truth is always, to be sure, a paradox or a platitude, and whether you regard it as one or the other depends entirely on the number of people who believe it. If only a very few people believe it, truth appears to all others as madness or at best some half-baked attempt at originality. But if everybody has gradually become convinced of its rightness, then the truth is called a dreary truism. Every truth, from the biggest to the smallest, is destined, therefore, to travel a line of evolution from "absurd" to "trivial." But when it has become trivial, it remains no less true and one must have the courage in such a case to say something commonplace. . . .

After explaining myself sufficiently, I now offer my own platitude: I believe that the institution of the cabaret has the right to exist only so long as it bears the character of dilettantism and improvisation. I say, the *character* of. This does not mean that only those people ought to appear in a cabaret who never learned anything artistic or that everything has to be ad-libbed. But it must always appear that there are only dilettantes there, and everything has to emerge as if it had arisen on the spot. The audience, which generally understands a lot more than the so-called professional artists would imagine, has a very keen feeling for this law of style and reacts in an instinctively critical way toward everything different in the cabaret no matter how inherently skillful or valuable it might be.

In other words, the spectators must feel that every single performer is still an amateur, in the original meaning of the word: a person who tremendously likes doing what he does, a person to whom it affords a genuine pleasure to entertain, and who steps before the public out of enthusiasm, out of caprice, out of a need to communicate and not because of a penalty for nonfulfillment of a contractual obligation hanging over him. (Naturally this doesn't mean that such a person shouldn't be paid for his efforts.) This, then, is what I understand by the *character* of dilettantism. The atmosphere of an amateur stage must always envelop everything. However successful the performances, however well trained the ensemble, the spectator must always have the vague sensation that here are people who are having a good old time for themselves and I happen to be observing them.

Furthermore, the program must not lapse into individual performances. "Program," in fact, is a word that really doesn't fit the concept of cabaret. On the contrary, people must feel that each individual performance proceeds from a sense of the whole and that each performer is complete only when he connects with all the others. People must feel that this person who is standing here on the stage couldn't bring off the same things nearly as well in just any hall, ensemble, or environment. Those artists who can, by the way, are nothing more than expensive phonograph records. Among protozoa, there are certain species that merge into large cell colonies or "cenobia." These creatures are really autonomous individual organisms, and each, therefore, possesses his individual soul. But besides that, the entire cell community also has its own inner life, a kind of super-soul, referred to as the "cenobia soul." By the same token, every proper cabaret also has to have such a cenobia soul. This is what I mean by the character of improvisation, which by no means excludes careful preparation.

Since a cabaret is also a discrete existential entity, an organism, it must also develop organically like a natural growth. All true cabarets have had just such an origin, and in the German-speaking world there have only been four of these, as far as I know: Wolzogen's Überbrettl [Superstage],[1] the Munich Elf Scharfrichter [Eleven Executioners],[2] the Vienna Nachtlicht [Nightlight][3] and Fledermaus [Bat] in the beginning.

With regard to the first of these, a clever and affable German writer [Ernst von Wolzogen] hit upon the idea of transposing an episode in Otto Julius Bierbaum's novel *Stilpe* into reality.[4] The experiment worked and enjoyed considerable success but only as long as it was nothing other than a bizarre literary joke that a gentleman of taste shared with the audience. But as soon as it became a commercial undertaking, the public immediately began deserting it. Then came the Elf Scharfrichter, whose composition at the time represented a real union of uninhibited and unprejudiced bohemians. The soul of the enterprise was the Frenchman Marc Henry, a last offshoot of the Provençal vagabond singers; Frank Wedekind was also among them. The Nachtlicht was something on the order of a Viennese colony of the Elf Scharfrichter. And later in the Fledermaus, a group of good-humored and sardonic people got together in the brightly tiled bar. They kidded each other incessantly and every so often reconciled and directed their joint fire at the rest of the world. And then along came the immense American energy of Fritz Wärndorfer and with one powerful surge of ten thousand volts turned these bar conversations into an evening of cabaret. In the long run, however, it was impossible to hold these mischievous and peevish rascals together. After two years risking his nerves, his money, and his reputation for sociability, Fritz Wärndorfer got tired of the whole thing and sold the Fledermaus to an even-tempered and pedestrian businessman under whom things didn't get worse but actually better for a while. But the place was no longer a cabaret.

Nowadays, all German cabarets, whether in Berlin, Vienna, Cologne, Hamburg, or wherever, have gone the way of the Fledermaus. They are properly run little variety theaters. No two are exactly alike, of course; the poorest of them come dangerously close to the café chantant,[5] while the most elegant offer one really original number among eight or nine boring, silly, or tasteless ones. A single good performer can certainly attract an audience, but he can't make a cabaret—unlike a satirical paper, which often needs no more than just a single person so long as he has a lot of humor and imagination. All good satirical papers arose in much the same way as the cabarets, as, for example, *Simplicissimus*.[6] A number of Munich artists and writers sat around a beer table once and made merry over everything under the sun. And then an American energy in the figure of Albert Langen also came along and welded these elements together into a newspaper.

Nowadays, when a cabaret is set up, the people behind it are either what we call marauders, that is, people who are too untalented or too unreliable for a regular theater, or competent, solid artists. These last figure: "My number begins at 11:20, then I'll work for fifteen minutes, nineteen with an encore." They come a half hour earlier, change their clothes, put their makeup on, and when they're all through, they remove their makeup, pick up their winter coat or boa, and head for home. On the first and the sixteenth of the month, they collect their salary, minus ten percent for their agents, and the only problems they have are when they call up their managers to find out if he still hasn't arranged a deal for them for April.

Nevertheless, such informal institutions as satirical papers and cabarets are a necessity, since there will always be original and lively spirits who do not fit into prevailing artistic forms, which are both too broad and too narrow for them. But the cabaret form is no longer useful for that purpose, if only for the reason that every artistic institution that is built on a specific exquisite idea always has a limited longevity. The same can be said as well for the satirical papers. As hard as it may be for us to imagine today, the "Flying Papers"[7] were once highly feared and detested for being both frivolous and revolutionary by reputation—even when jokes about professors, mothers-in-law, and lieutenants were still new. And today, by contrast, the *Simplicissimus* seems downright philistine and itself ripe for parody. And the same for the cabarets, the spoken and performed satirical papers. In sum: one has to find a new swindle.

"Das Kabarett," 1914. Original text in *Das Friedell Lesebuch,* 53–57.

1.   The Überbrettl cabaret founded by Baron Ernst von Wolzogen in Berlin in 1901. It was the first cabaret in the German-speaking world.

2.   The first cabaret to be established in Munich, also in 1901, and the most important in the pre–World War I history of the German cabaret.

3.   Founded in 1906 mostly by former members of the Munich Elf Scharfrichter after that cabaret closed its doors in 1903.

4.   The novel deals in part with the vain attempt of a bohemian artist named Willibald Stilpe to establish a kind of artists' café or cabaret on the model of the Parisian Momus. Stilpe hoped that the cabaret would serve as the catalyst for a transformation of the stodgy world of contemporary German art.

5.   The "café chantant," of Parisian origin, was an eating and drinking establishment that featured primarily a singer or singers and was open to the general public. They lacked any of the artistic pretensions of the more famous turn-of-the-century cabarets.

6.   The most famous German political and satirical magazine. It was founded as a weekly in Munich in 1896 by Albert Langen (1869–1909) and Thomas Theodor Heine (1867–1948).

7.   Most likely a reference to *Fliegende Blätter,* an illustrated humor magazine published by Braun & Schneider in Munich from 1844 to 1944. "Flying Papers" has also been used in German since Lessing's time as a synonym for rather crude one- or two-page, frequently illustrated, newspapers consisting for the most part of everyday, gossipy, crime, and sensationalist stories. They also on occasion contained popular songs. During the First World War, they were extensively used as vehicles of propaganda.

THE STORY OF THE FLEDERMAUS

In 1907, Fritz Wärndorfer, a clever gentleman with a great deal of money and taste—two things which, as we know, almost never coexist—had the idea of getting the Vienna Applied Arts Workshops [Wiener Werkstätte] to design a cabaret to be named Die Fledermaus [The Bat].[1] Both the brightly tiled bar and the auditorium done entirely in black and white were an extravagance of intimacy and noblesse. As a result, all Vienna was beside itself, since people were then still accustomed to getting red plush and gilded plaster for their money. The later proprietor had the misfortune, at least in part, to make up for it by having the doors done over in pink and a pair of stylish fawns painted on the walls. The original place setting also caused much distress, especially the spoon and knife, since with the first it was so hard to eat sauce, and with the second it was so easy to cut yourself.

The opening night proved a monstrous scandal. That is because the artists who were associated with the undertaking—Klimt, Hoffmann, Wimmer, Moser—had the monstrous audacity to do with greater clever- ness, intimacy, and sophistication everything the Blaue Vogel [Blue Bird] put on fifteen years later amidst a bone-crushing throng of people.[2] But they were ahead of their time. It's all a matter of luck.

Fritz Wärndorfer ran the place splendidly. There was never a more colorful, more animated, more unpredictable and original cabaret than the Fledermaus. And nowhere could you get any better wine than what was served in its bar. But Vienna was scandalized. Fritz Wärndorfer was taken terribly to task for being a wealthy man, a gentleman from good society, who degraded himself by becoming the director of a nightclub and for writing texts for fools like Peter Altenberg and good-for-nothings like Alfred Polgar. Had he had no money, he would have been forgiven for it, and he would have become the Reinhardt of the cabaret. It's all a matter of luck.

Nobody seemed to mind my own appearances in the Fledermaus, even though, I admit, I had money. They actually found it quite nice that, even though I "didn't have to," I put on a little show for people every evening. Later on, of course, I lost all my wealth, just like everybody else including Fritz Wärndorfer. After he went bankrupt, the Fledermaus was taken over by a specialist who staged flimsy little operettas such as "Putzi, Don't Be So Dull" and saucy little skits such as "The Secrets of a Bidet." But even this first-class authority went bankrupt, and the Fledermaus became a revue theater in which slim-legged girls appeared whom you could ask to your table. I have no objections to this phase of artistic development. If only the wine hadn't gotten so bad.

"Geschichte der 'Fledermaus,'" 1928. Original text in *Das Friedell-Lesebuch*, 32–33.

1.   Theater und Kabarett Fledermaus was the most outstanding cabaret of turn-of- the-century Vienna. It was established on 19 October 1907.

2.   Gustav Klimt (1862–1918), outstanding painter and leader of the Vienna Secession, which broke with the official painters' association in order to pursue modernist trends. E. J. Wimmer-Wisgrill (1882–1961), a Viennese fashion designer who became an important costume designer for the Fledermaus in its second season. Koloman (Kolo) Moser (1868–1918), a prominent graphic artist closely affiliated with the Wiener Werk- stätte. The Blue Bird was a well-known émigré Russian cabaret in the 1920s.

CABARET FLEDERMAUS

The reporters said: "The prettiest thing about it is the friendly bar with the original colored tiles and the absolutely faultless drinks." They also said: "Hopefully, the program will in time reach the artistic level of this interior." That is perfidy. The program has already reached this level, and Die Fledermaus is without doubt the best German cabaret that has been seen to date.

First comes our pianist, an utterly incomprehensible musician, of whom you have to ask yourself, astonished: Where does this artist come by his wealth of ideas, since it is assumed that every possible melody has already been composed by some prominent musician? Our lead dancer is a creature who succeeds in uniting grace and naturalness, while the other renowned dancers more or less possess a grace pulled by a wire. (Looking at them, you always have the impression: "Superbly constructed! Now how is it going to be set in motion? Presumably by means of the main pressure tank. No, that would be too costly, so it would have to be done by parallel connection.") And then we have a diseuse [a skilled, usually female monologuist] who is also distinguished most favorably from the majority of her colleagues by virtue of her understanding of the art of hinting and concealment. She assumes that the spectator is no utter idiot but a person with imagination, with a controlled imagination which he has only to set free it so that it can become spontaneous. The "Masks" are something utterly novel. Three pretty young women in gorgeous, fantastic garments utter some complicated lapidary aphorisms by Peter Altenberg to the accompaniment of an oddly provocative music. The three arts blend into one another to such an extent that you no longer know what actually produces the strong impression. The whole thing exerts a completely mysterious effect that is quite unique. It is entirely possible that the choruses of Greek tragedies seemed very similar: weirdly stylized female forms with evil eyes who delivered gnomic utterances to very bewildering music.

After these short reports, I suppose I don't have to mention that the whole thing just flopped in Vienna. People complained above all that it lacked humor. But for buffoonery we have the Burgtheater, after all, and besides, the Fledermaus does have a humorous number of the first rank, namely the big intermission in which the Vienna public delivers its opinions . . .

Only a minister of state who happened to be present was charitable, but perhaps only for the reason that he belonged to the Liberal Party. He said: "Well, I could also understand that people might find these things very pretty and good. It is ultimately a matter of taste."

No, Excellency. It is not a matter of taste, but matter for taste and therefore no matter for Vienna.

"Kabarett Fledermaus," 1907. Original text in Egon Friedell, *Wozu das Theater? Essays. Satiren. Humoresken*, 166–67.

HARESU

Friedell once mentioned the name of the Norwegian writer Knut Hamsun (1859–1952) in a review of the play *Unterwegs* (*On the Way*) by the dramatist Tadeusz Rittner (1873–1921), a Pole who wrote extensively in German and is often regarded as an Austrian writer. A printer's error transformed "Hamsun" into "Haresu." As inquiries mounted concerning a writer no one had heard of before, Friedell concocted a short "biography" and "appreciation" of the "classical Japanese author, Rennosuke Haresu." This is the subject of "Haresu." In "How I Came to Haresu," he takes up his "discovery" of him.

In a recent review, I wrote about the character of the Secretary in Rittner's *On the Way:* "He is Leporello,[1] but by all means a more spiritualized, more refined, intellectually superior Leporello who has Stendahl and Haresu in his blood." Since then, I have been asked many times by acquaintances who have heard the name Haresu just in passing, or in fact not at all, to provide more information on him. I must say I never believed that Haresu would today belong to the intellectual baggage of the educated German philistine (and I would not at all wish such a fate on this fine and far-distant genius, although it is most probably something that he would not have been spared). I must say I did think that one or another "connoisseur" had already brought him to the attention of a wider public. However, this appears not to be the case, and so I take pleasure in the opportunity to say what I know about him. To be sure, it is little enough, and even this little is difficult to put into words.

The difficulty begins, in fact, with the attempt to fit Haresu into some specific group. Among us, after all, everybody has to have a group designation, a label and nomenclature, otherwise he is not taken seriously. We Westerners wouldn't hesitate a moment to call Haresu a poet, but I believe that he himself wouldn't have really approved of this classification. He once wrote of himself: "I never regarded anything in life as valuable except for the devout and unconscious contemplation of the universe and its beauty, how this beauty continually manifests itself in each and every thing in a thousand ways, be it in a flower, a woman's face, the surface of a body of water, or a great mind. And I regard anybody as shamefully deceived who attributes some value to any other task or activity here below." And in another place: "What we can say no longer means anything to us. Our deepest and truest feelings have an aversion to being congealed into words." He obviously did not esteem literary activity very highly, since in the Orient generally the individual forms a more intimate unity with the poet than we do. He wanted not to write, but to live. He viewed his books merely as accidental by-products.

In spite of that, or perhaps just because of it, he found enthusiastic admirers both in his own country and elsewhere. Oscar Wilde said about him: "I love Haresu. Of other writers, I can say that I admire them, that I enjoy them, that I aspire to imitate them. But when I want to express the feeling that I have toward Haresu, nothing else comes to mind than the very ordinary and trite and yet for every one of us most deeply significant phrase, 'I love him like a friend, like a brother, or father, to whom I feel myself bound not just in a literary or artistic way, but wholly personally.'"

I have Hermann Bahr to thank for my acquaintance with Haresu. Today perhaps in the entire German-speaking world, but certainly in German Austria, his is the only mind of truly cosmopolitan form and style. He alone has a living feeling for what Goethe called "world literature," and his strong yet sensitive appreciation of the value of mankind did not stop at the Yellow Sea. Haresu, by the way, is a stranger only in Central Europe. He is fairly well known in England and France, and even in Russia. J. C. Collins, the biographer of Swinburne, wrote a critical essay about him, and Cornish F. Warre splendidly translated some of his works into English. The two luxurious yellow leatherbound volumes with the brilliant Japanese color woodcuts show up in beach chairs as well as in the boudoir of many a daydreaming lady. Georg Müller, who learned about Haresu while he was in London, planned a German edition of his works based, in fact, on the Japanese originals. But the outbreak of the World War prevented the project from being carried through.

Rennosuke Haresu was born at the beginning of the '30s of the preceding century; the exact date is unknown. He attended school in Hiroshima and the university in Semnon Gekko and then devoted his energies to enamel painting. Only in his more mature years did he discover his calling as a writer. He began with fairy tales and poems. Some of these fairy tales appear in George Holiday's collection *Storytellers of the East*. They are written in a light and graceful style, with subtle and worldly-wise characterization, and pleasantly animated by means of a variety of half melancholic and half ironic shadings. The tale of the "wicked cherry blossoms" in particular is full of humor and poetry. When you think of the great aptitude that almost all Asiatic peoples have for this genre, you will not find that Haresu accomplished anything unusual in this respect. Some twenty years ago, a selection of his lyrics in French translation was published, but I still haven't been able to find a copy of this *Anthologie de Haresu*.

You can assume, without fear of erring, that Haresu's principal talent lay in the fields of philosophy and drama. He wrote a large number of small pieces for the stage. Genuine miniature dramas, we would perhaps call them one-acters. Colorful and at the same time highly intellectual dialogues, they remind you of Plato, of Gobineau's Renaissance pieces, but above all of Maeterlinck's short plays. They are for the most part rather loosely composed, but they always present the reader with a dramatic situation in the most plastic and striking way. Haresu also comes close to Maeterlinck in his indebtedness to earlier dramatic forms. Just as Maeterlinck gave new life to the old Flemish puppet plays, so did Haresu hark back to the "Noh" tradition. "Noh" was a type of artistic performance that can be compared somewhat with our opera. The text was sung by actors, while the chorus played an important role. The action was not very complicated, but finely delineated. In its totality, "Noh" bore a resemblance to ancient Greek drama. The form was very popular in Japan during the Middle Ages and was also performed with much pomp and ceremony at the court of the Shogun.

What Haresu sought, as he himself says, was "Noh without music." "What need is there of the external melody," he declares, "when all deep things bear an inner music? Poetry is musical thought. The poet is a person who thinks in this way. See deeply enough and you see musically; the heart of nature is always music." This principle manifests itself in the entire architectonics with which Haresu constructs his works. They are always somehow symphonically structured. Take, for example, his dramatic cycle called *The Black Knight*, which presents a kind of "comédie humaine": loose pictures from the history of mankind. Unfortunately, the English edition contains just the first play. This takes us among the first people, into a kind of paradise, where original man, unaware of illness, death, and all earthly afflictions, lives with his many children. These include the brothers Ashikaga and Jyeyasu. Ashikaga was sinister and brooding and tormented by a lust for power. Jyeyasu, on the other hand, had a sunny disposition; he was happy and loved by all. We might think of them as Cain and Abel, and in fact the East Asian myth has distinct similarities to the Bible.

Both brothers loved their sister, Sada, but she tended to favor Jyeyasu. The motif of sibling love is here very ingenuously transformed. Ashikaga, who has long hated his brother out of envy of his independence, innocence, and confidence, and because everything seemed to come easy to him (here one is again tempted to think of Hakon and Jarl Skule[2]), resolves to get rid of him. He lures him into the labyrinthine "Forest of Serpents," but with uncanny sureness Jyeyasu again finds the way back to his native paradise. New conflict flares up between the brothers, and their father, who comes rushing in and learns that Sada is the cause of it, pronounces a curse on her, since "everything unholy comes from women." In his anger, his strength fails him and he falls, uttering the words: "I almost cannot see any more . . . everything is dark around me . . . as if I were blind. But now I begin to see as if from within." Suddenly in great terror and astonishment: "Ha . . . oh . . . what must I see?" He falls back, his limbs extended.

Sada: He sleeps in a strange way. . . like an animal.

Jyeyasu (constantly trembling, moving his lips, trying to say something, but unable to express it).

Sada: What does it . . . tell me, what does it all mean?

Jyeyasu (in a flash of recognition):   He will never awaken! (He is dumbstruck and terrified at his own words.)

Sada (not understanding):   Never awaken?

Ashikaga (muttering to himself occasionally):   Never awaken . . . (Stands close behind Jyeyasu. His hand gropes for the hammer. It grows very dark. Only the sparkle of his eyes is visible.)

This is the conclusion of the first play, which doubtless appears somewhat strange to us. The thought that the first awareness of human mortality immediately gives rise to the plan to kill is rooted in a monstrous, radical, and thoroughly un-European pessimism and immorality. And the entire dramatic cycle is equally pessimistic. It tells the tale of the "black knight," a God-hating demon, a kind of Lucifer, who as punishment for his rebellion has to dream of the world. Everything that takes place on earth is nothing but the terrible nightmare of a fallen angel. At the end of the cycle, which comes down to the present, the spirit casts off his harrowing dream in a powerful burst of energy, for the apparitions oppressing him are too dreadful. But now, for a short time, he is allowed peace. His guilt is still not expiated, so he will soon again have to sink into sleep, in which even more terrifying visions await him. This is Haresu's view of the future of man.

A second series is called *The Conqueror*. It is unified through the figure of Yoritomo, a powerful "Tenno" who has resolved to conquer the entire known world. How he actually succeeds in doing this is shown in a colorful picture-gallery. But the more he forges ahead, the more dissatisfied he becomes, without being able to understand the reason why. In the end, he reaches a distant land where Buddhism reigns supreme. There he holds a discussion with a Buddhist priest who tells him: "I want to relate a story to you. When Gotama was born, the astrologers foretold that if he chose to follow a secular life, he would become the ruler of the world, but if he renounced the world, he would become the Buddha.

> *Yoritomo:*   And what did Gatoma, or Glotama, or whatever his name, do?
>
> *The Priest:*   He naturally became the Buddha. Had he succumbed to the world, the earthly globe would have yielded to him and you would not be here now. But he became the Buddha; that was the harder choice. And it was also the best.
>
> *Yoritomo:*   Tell me, do you think that if I renounced the world, could I also become the Buddha?
>
> *The Priest:*   No.
>
> *Yoritomo:*   And why not?
>
> *The Priest:*   Had you been endowed with what it takes to be the Buddha, you could never have chosen the world. But now I will whisper something in your ear: You can always still become the Buddha. For yourself. Not for the world. But for yourself. Every person can become it (with a certain disdain), even you . . .

And now Yoritomo understood that you can indeed conquer the lands of the earth and their inhabitants, but you cannot possess them. And the same for the women you love and everything in the world, except for one thing—you yourself. But if you want to possess yourself, then you may not be a conqueror. And he had his physician give him a poison that put him in a state of suspended animation. And while everything dissolved into party conflicts and anarchy around his coffin, he secretly took refuge in solitude.

I regret that space does not permit me to go further into the matter of Haresu's philosophy. It is set forth essentially in a collection of aphorisms, parables, and small essays bearing the title *The Quarry* and the motto: "My purpose is not to be right, but to set thoughts in motion." The last sentence of the book reads: "The principal task of man is to be the helmsman of his own ship of fools." Haresu seems to have been something of a "decadent," at least in light of the aphorism in his book that reads: "When the heron grows new feathers, it is sick and ill-tempered. One should not expect the sage from whom new thoughts emerge to be healthy."

Haresu died in the year 1896, shortly after the Peace of Shimonoseki. He was no longer alive to witness the most recent ascent of his fatherland to world importance. But one may imagine that he, whose favorite saying was "The world is not outside," would not have attached too much importance to such events. His last words are believed to have been: "I am coming back." Whoever understands Buddhism knows that it replaces a triumphant belief in immortality with a resigned acknowledgment of imperfection. But those who read his works attentively will find that, despite some unfamiliar items upon which the European must first reflect, they are little gems and they will join Oscar Wilde in saying: "I love Haresu."

"Haresu," 1919. Original text in Egon Friedell, *Wozu das Theater? Essays. Satiren. Humoresken,* 164–70.

1. Don Giovanni's manservant in the Mozart opera.
2. Characters in Knut Hamsun's *The Growth of the Soil* (1917).

How I Came to Haresu

Not long ago, I wrote an essay for the *Neue Wiener Journal* about the Japanese philosopher and dramatist Rennosuke Haresu. Since then, I have often been asked how I actually came upon Haresu.

Indeed, this is a rather complicated story, that is to say, at the outset, it is quite simple, but later it becomes complicated.

Well, as I have already mentioned, a few months ago yet another new revue made its appearance in Vienna, this time for a change edited by a woman. Since it was her firm intention from the very beginning to make her publication cosmopolitan and distinguished, she had the equally obvious and fruitful idea of offering me the Burgtheater reviews . . .

Now it so happens that among other striking peculiarities, the journal in question is also disinclined to send its writers proofs. The result of this is that my critical endeavors reach the reader—I speak cautiously in the singular, since I have no positive information concerning any plural number of readers—in times substantially different form than were originally projected by me. I must interpolate at this point a brief observation concerning the psychology of the typesetter. He is not, as many laymen believe, slipshod or completely stupid. On the contrary, he is rather too careful and clever. He believes, for example, that it is his duty to improve the text. Should he happen to run across anything that seems strange to him, he changes it mercilessly. Let's say you happen to have concocted a new word, of which you are not a little proud. You can be sure that the typesetter will change it into something much better known and conventional. But every now and then, just the opposite occurs. Once, on the occasion of a Schiller celebration, I penned the not overly original sentence—as I must myself confess—that Schiller was a great idealist. But the typesetter turned it into the remark that Schiller was a great *Icarist.*[1] Naturally, I let the error stand and the next day received all kinds of compliments on this interesting enrichment of the German language.

But let us return to the thread of our narrative. I received, then, my review of [Tadeusz] Rittner's *On the Way* that had just been printed. At the very same time, it was circulating through the city like wildfire in countless copies. This time it had undergone exceptionally extensive meta-morphoses. I could not understand everything that was set forth in the review and had to first familiarize myself a bit with its enigmatic style before being able to follow it. But there was one sentence that gave me a par-ticularly hard time. I must point out that I made the assertion that the figure of the Secretary in the Rittner play is Leporello, but a more spiri-tualized, intellectually superior Leporello, with Stendahl and Haresu in his blood. I asked myself repeatedly, shaking my head, how did you come by this Haresu, where did you pick up the name? It is one of my little literary tricks occasionally to introduce—in a matter-of-fact way—a name that almost nobody knows. But it never happened before that I myself would then fail to recognize the name.

I must now make a comment about the psychology of the reading public. If you write something calculated to arouse admiration, nobody ever reads it. But if you happen to make a logical slip, a gross grammatical error, a blatant stupidity, or some other ridiculous thing, it is just these places that everybody studies diligently. And that is what happened this time. All of a sudden, the entire city consisted exclusively of readers of this sentence. Reactions differed according to individual temperaments. There were some who said to me: "What kind of baloney is it now with this Haresu business? It's absolutely ridiculous the way you try to shove any stray Czech or Jewish hack down everybody's throat." Others declared, winking: "It strikes me that you, too, don't know any more about Haresu than what you can find in small print in some literary history. You'd really be em-barrassed if you had to provide details about him." And one even said: "How you could put this Haresu on the same level with Stendahl is simply incomprehensible to me. I'd never have thought you capable of such a lack of judgment." In order, then, to take the edge off all these incrimi-nations, I sat down and wrote the essay on Haresu.

Do you believe perhaps that I did discover Haresu? But how can you think anything like that when I tell you explicitly that it was the typesetter who discovered him? I just call him Hamsun, and that name I'm sure you know.

I then went to Hermann Bahr and said to him: "I've almost made up my mind to leave things the way my typesetter has them. If he's right, then it's clear that only you could have discovered Haresu. Now it's a matter of a question that only *you* can answer: Where does Haresu live?" Bahr said, astonished: "How can he still be living if he wrote in the eleventh century?" I replied that that was more than doubtful, since Haresu was much too modern in his thinking for a medieval writer. Bahr again re-torted that the Japanese had a much longer development behind them and by Haresu's time had already reached as far as we are today. After lengthier discussions, we agreed on the compromise: dead, but present.

On the whole, I do not at all regret having written the essay about Haresu. First of all, this time I didn't receive a single solitary letter in which all kinds of crass misjudgments and basically wrong facts were pointed out to me, which surely would have been the case had I written an essay on Lessing or Jehovah. Furthermore, if people knew that I had, after all, strongly influenced Haresu's creative production, do you think there would have been a single person who'd have written me that one of Haresu's sayings (I will not quote it again) far surpasses everything the Occident has produced until now in the field of the aphorism, and that it was wrong of me to say that Haresu's dramatic pieces recall Maeterlinck, when in fact it is the far weaker Maeterlinck who most reminds you of them?

My relations with theater directors have also considerably strengthened since the appearance of my essay. One of them telegraphed me with prepaid reply: "Request earliest possible forwarding of works of Hamesle (this is already closer to Hamsun!) plus particulars re: lowest production terms. Advance no object." With this particular director, I always indeed knew that an advance was never an object. But anyway it was tempting. Another one asked about the possibility of doing an evening of Haresu together with *Goethe* and the *Muster-Operetta* [*Model Operetta*], two well-known masterpieces by Alfred Polgar and me. Well, you see, business is picking up. Director Bernau of the Vienna Deutsches Volkstheater came up to me beaming with joy and said: "This is really a tremendous discovery that you made! I will absolutely perform him, since he's even less known than Roswitha von Gandersheim.[2] Translate him as soon as possible; I'll audition the roles right afterwards." When I hesitated for understandable reasons, he misunderstood it and implied that he was no longer disinclined to tackle the staging of my *Tragedy of Judas* and that it would most probably be done this season.[3] (Until then, glue, a mountain peak, sheet metal, and the actor for the part of Pilate were lacking. Suddenly, everything was there.)

The only person who at once declared, My dear fellow, there is no Haresu! was my director, Hans Ziegler (Volksbühne, Vienna VII, Neubaugasse 36, the house to the left of the "Candy King"). But he is already so embittered with me after a two-year collaboration that he no longer believes me and most likely even regards Japan as a malicious invention of mine. I should take this opportunity to note at once that the other figure whom [Rittner's] Secretary had in his blood, namely Stendahl, was also concocted, but neither by the typesetter nor by me, but by Monsieur

Henri Beyle, who chose this name as his literary pseudonym. In a sense, there really was a Stendahl, and he even wrote a number of much-admired books. This is what Nietzsche has to say about him . . . but nobody will believe me any more, since the comment I quoted by Oscar Wilde about Haresu was also false.

So far everything has been fine and dandy, but now the matter is beginning to get somewhat more sinister and complicated. I am slowly coming to doubt, in fact, that there really was no Haresu. So many people believe in him that I don't know what to make of it. Every day when I open the newspaper I expect to read a notice to the effect: "The works of Haresu are now available in quantity at Heller's bookshop and cost, in elegant binding, 486.40 crowns." The other day, I even caught myself looking up Haresu in the big Meyer [encyclopedia]. But he wasn't under the *h*'s. This doesn't mean much, though, since Debussy, Altenberg, and Weininger also aren't in the newest edition of Meyer.

In sum: unless I am shown to the contrary—which would be very hard—I will continue to believe that Haresu is no simple fantasy but an inspired divination. The same thing happens to me often. Once I read on the poster of a charitable organization with which I had thought of collaborating: "Cäcilie Ingolstadt, Lieder for Lute." I couldn't get this suggestive name out of my mind. I kept asking myself constantly: Ingolstadt . . . Cäcilie Ingolstadt . . . how does she look? I came to the conclusion that she was forty-eight years old, with a parrot's beak for a nose, horn-rimmed glasses, buck teeth. I also had the feeling that flat feet couldn't absolutely be ruled out, either. When I entered the so-called Artists' Room on a recital evening, a young woman of about nineteen, with parted brown hair and soft blue eyes, was already sitting there. "My dear young lady," I said in a courteous but cold manner, "this is an entrance just for the performers, and you can hardly be one of them, since you are obviously under forty." "Excuse me," the woman replied timidly, "my name is Ingolstadt." "What," I shouted gruffly, "are *you* Ingolstadt? But she has buck teeth, horn-rimmed glasses, a parrot's beak, and flat feet!" "Pardon," said the young lady blushing, "you're thinking of my mother." So you see: there is always something to the things we imagine, whether they relate to Japan or to other cultural spheres.

"Wie ich zu Haresu kam," 1919. Original text in Egon Friedell, *Wozu das Theater? Essays. Satiren. Humoresken*, 171–76.

1.   The unsuspecting reader might have taken this to be a reference to followers of, or a cult of, Icarus, in Greek mythology the son of Daedalus.

2.   A reference to the medieval German nun whose writings were discovered long after her death. Friedell wrote a sketch about her under the title "Die Nonne Roswitha" ("Roswitha the Nun") and a verse "Prolog der Roswitha" ("Prologue of Roswitha"). Both were included in his collection *Selbstanzeige: Essays ab 1918*, 45–54 and 55–56, respectively.

3.   Friedell, in fact, wrote a *Judastragödie* (*Tragedy of Judas*) in 1916. The premiere of the play took place at the Vienna Burgtheater on 3 March 1923.

When I Was a Stage Director

I have often told how I became engaged by the administration of the Intimate Theater in Vienna to be its literary advisor. But since it happens that I don't care for literature, they changed me one day into a stage director. The idea was somehow to take advantage of my talent. I had no objections at all to this, since I imagined that by stage director one understood a person who has almost nothing more to do than be affable with the ladies and brusque with the gentlemen, and both are a distinct pleasure for me.

After I had practiced this profession for a few weeks, one of the two directors of the theater came to see me. There were two such directors, by the way, with separate purviews. One handled "artistic" matters, meaning the rejection of costumes, the other the "administrative," meaning the frustration of legal seizures. It was the "artistic" one who came and said: "You have to stage a play by Maeterlinck!" We then went through all of Maeterlinck's plays and considered which ones might be artistically suitable, meaning, which are "protected," and which not, and we agreed on *Intérieur* (*On the Inside*). Next, the scene painter was called in, a gruff person who, after some hesitation, declared himself ready to paint four pasteboard strips green in order to simulate for the audience a green forest. He was also going to cut a square in a cardboard sheet and this way create the impression in the spectator that he was seeing a house with windows.

After the scene painter, a lighting specialist was summoned, a shy man who, without further ado, declared himself ready to turn an incandescent lamp on and off with extraordinary speed, assuring us thereby that nobody in the audience would refuse in this optical phenomenon to recognize brilliant flashes of lightning. Next came the theater master, who brought with him a paper bag in which he blew, producing a sound not at all unlike a stormy wind; then the house manager, in whom I had no trouble recognizing the lighting specialist; and the prop man, who again in his external appearance resembled the theater master. All these people assured me, in that they kept calling me "Herr Oberregisseur" [Head Stage Director], that they would spare no pains in the deception and mystification of the audience.

Then came the rehearsals. Rehearsals for the most part consist of some people reading a bunch of speeches from notebooks with the understanding that these notebooks are just an aid "for today" and that "tomorrow" they would already be superfluous. This "tomorrow" obviously has only a marginal value, since it connotes the purely negative and re-strictive "not today."

From the scientific point of view, there wasn't the slightest thing to object to, since mathematics and mechanics, the exact sciences, in other words, have long operated with just such marginal values.

After several rehearsals, I had to admit that the whole business was excruciatingly boring. The actors' speech also wasn't comic enough even to be minimally entertaining. In the meantime, as I was conferring with the theater manager over the sounds of rain, I was struck by one of those lightning-like flashes of inspiration which were nothing rare in my life. He was trying to convince me of the illusionary power of dried peas on drums when the thought suddenly came to mind: how would it be if we added to the acoustical stimulation also the optical, in a word: if we actually had rain falling, really and truly, with real water? No sooner said than done, and already at the next rehearsal the interminable patter of falling rain could be heard. This was a splendid manifestation of nature which had the added virtue of completely drowning out the actors' speeches.

The time came for the dress rehearsal. A dress rehearsal differs from other rehearsals in very fundamental ways. In ordinary rehearsals, there's a lot of yapping, but at a dress rehearsal there's yapping and slapping. When I showed up at the dress rehearsal, the two directors, in fact, were having a go at one another with the result that the pince-nez of one were shattered and the other's right ear began bleeding. While all this was going on, the orchestra conductor appeared with four musicians intent on holding a music rehearsal, since some somber piece was supposed to be played as a prelude. However, he refused to hold the rehearsal unless he was paid an advance of ten crowns. Whereupon the two directors imme-diately reconciled their differences and both began drubbing the conduc-tor. Consequently, an actress fell into a hysterical crying jag. But she was helped on to the stage and, owing to the refreshing effect of the cool rain, calmed down.

Now the dress rehearsal could begin, since in the interim both di-rectors had made up with the conductor. I don't know whom they then drubbed together. By the way, I too came close to getting knocked around. At the close, I delivered an address to the performers in which I expressed my gratitude to them for holding forth so courageously onstage, despite the inclement weather, and I expressed the hope that everything would go splendidly in the evening. At that point, four people leaped at me from the stage and threatened me, since what I had said was a bad omen. As luck would have it, I got caught on a nail on the way out and tore my new coat, which was also a good omen.

And, as a matter of fact, things did turn out splendidly that evening. After the curtain came down, Peter Altenberg clapped his hands like somebody possessed. This in turn produced six curtain calls. Even the critics were on the whole quite pleased the next day. Most acknowledged that it was a well-staged water pantomime. A few others were clearly less friendly. One wrote, for example, that the very splendor of the production would not at all do, since such ostentatious décor was unartistic. One even went so far as to maintain that the naturalistic rain had destroyed the symbolistic Maeterlinckian mood.

You might imagine now that that marked the end of my directorial career. Oh, no. A little while later, a journalist came to me and said that the rain had been so natural, almost like the real thing, that he wanted to know how it was accomplished and that he'd like to write an article about it. I couldn't tell him that I had simply rinsed my mouth out through a strip of perforated sheet metal, so I replied: "Yes, the matter is rather complicated, but I'll divulge the secret to you. You know, don't you, that we have a transverse ground connection? So when the current enters the upper relay, it doesn't go right into the switch the way it usually does, but is first conducted along a primary coil. This causes a loop in the current. The whole thing is a connection with a longitudinal support made of neutral copper and works, therefore, like a receiver. The moment the transmitter makes contact with the receiver wire, a synchronous polarizing current is activated in the circuit closing, the collector intermits, and it rains. Did you understand everything?" "Oh yes," said the journalist and disappeared.

It appears that he really did not understand everything, for he wrote in only a very general way that in the Intimate Theater an electric rain is generated by means of some complicated apparatus.

"Als ich Regisseur war," 1908. Original text in Egon Friedell, *Wozu das Theater? Essays. Satiren. Humoresken,* 23–26.

WHAT IS A THEATRICAL TOUR?

One day, the door to my office was ripped open and in stormed the impresario Herr Fritz Schieber, whom I knew only fleetingly. Instead of any further greeting, he shouted: "Do you want to make four million marks?"

"Sure," I replied, quick on the uptake as usual.

"Splendid!" shouted Schieber. "Then the tour is all set."

"What tour?" I asked.

"You know, the tour! The tour of your cabaret! The Fledermaus cabaret tour! The gold is lying in the street! I'm telling you, you're going to make a bushel! A bushel! First we do Germany: Munich, Augsburg, Ulm, Nuremberg, Stuttgart, Frankfurt, Wiesbaden, Limburg (Limburg doesn't have any cabaret at all. That's where we'll rake it in!). Then: Cologne, Düsseldorf, Dortmund, Münster, Hannover, Bremen, Hamburg, Dover, Liverpool, Southampton, Chicago, Uruguay . . ."

"That won't do," I said.

"What do you mean? Uruguay's out? Sure, crap! Crap of course won't do in Uruguay! But if you offer them something good in Uruguay, something really classical, nothing risqué at all—that doesn't draw in Uruguay—but something decent, artistic, high-class! How? What? Uruguay, you say, won't do? I tell you, Uruguay is the best place for cabaret!"

"Fine, but I couldn't take the trip over."

"Is that so? Well, in that case, we'll call a halt in Calais. But it's your loss! I tell you, it's your loss! By the way, what are your terms? Do you want a percentage or fixed wages?"

"I prefer fixed wages," I replied modestly.

"That's fine! But I can't give you more than four thousand a month, I'm telling you that straight off!"

"That will be all right," I answered.

"Then we're all set! I'll send you the contract today!" shouted Schieber, already at the door. "But I'm telling you this: You're an ass! You'll be pretty upset if all the others take a percentage and rake in four and five times as much!"

"Well," I said proudly, "my life is devoted to quiet meditation. I have no needs. Four thousand marks a month are enough. I . . ."

"All right, then! But it's economic suicide! Suicide, I tell you! We're at our best now! You can pull in ten, twenty, thirty thousand a month! But do as you like!

"You really think so?" I said, irritated.

"Then you'll take the percentage!" yelled Schieber and disappeared out the door.

From this time on, he never left my side. When, by way of exception, he wasn't physically present, he showered me with countless telegrams, pneumatic-tube postcards, express letters, and special deliveries, all with incomprehensible messages. However, one phrase recurred with the greatest regularity in all of Schieber's conversations and letters. That was: "The organization of the troupe." I understood what this meant, but if I didn't understand it, I would have been amply enlightened about it from the visits of countless people all maintaining that they "could do something." There were especially a lot of weight lifters and ventriloquists, for example.

Little by little, the troupe took shape. It consisted of a musical director, who lectured me daily on the theory and history of music. (This seemed necessary at the very outset of our relations, since I left myself wide open in this area.) Then there was a tenor who would impress anybody by his girth. And, if you allowed him, he emitted such a noise that you couldn't help but be convinced that he was no person but a boiler factory. He had previously been an opera singer and his lead role was Lohengrin. But as he grew bigger and bigger, nobody could believe anymore that a swan could carry him. The friendly press tried to come to his rescue by arguing that since *Lohengrin* was a fairy tale, violations of the law of nature were permissible. But it was all to no avail; the illusion was gone. A telegram was sent to Madame Cosima Wagner to ask if she would make an exception in this special case and consent to three swans being used. No use. The excellent singer then sank ever deeper because of the fault of others and finally became a cabaret performer.

Now all we lacked was a female. But it was actually difficult for us to scare up a feminine creature who in Schieber's view would fit into our strictly artistic limits. Each one had some defect or other: either she wanted just to sing some popular ditties, or she wanted to appear as naked sculpture, or she wanted fixed wages or otherwise something unartistic.

However, a stunning young woman who took a fancy to our merry artists' life entered our circle a while ago. She was introduced by Peter Altenberg, who claimed that she was the only "modern female organism truly worthy of distinction." She wore a Cleo-de-Mérode[1] hairdo with thick ringlets around the backs of her ears and a kind of Pallas-Athena helmet as a head covering. (Others maintained that it was the model of a ship.) She was for the most part quite attractive and besides well-to-do and from a good family, which she sought to conceal through a carelessly tossed out comment such as: "Prostitution is ultimately a social institution like any other one." She became our star. Her name was Mizi, which is why everyone called her Maja.

We were at last all set, and so it was unavoidable that one day I received the following telegram from Schieber: "Departure Munich this evening 8:50 West Station."

I told Schieber: "I simply can't travel at night. I suffer from sleeplessness on a train." "I know what you mean, I know what you mean," yelled Schieber, "but I overcome every difficulty! Come along with me!" We went to a bodega. Schieber at once ordered a bottle of whiskey and a car to take us to the station afterwards. We drank. Gradually, I became indifferent to everything, even the tour. The only thing I could hear any more was Schieber's clear organ as if muffled by distance. A few times I caught the words "rake in a bushel," "ninety thousand," and "box office assured."

And then suddenly a man in the uniform of a Bavarian conductor said: "In ten minutes we arrive in Munich."

Eight days were contemplated for Munich. We did everything possible to win over this old art center to us. But it wasn't our fault that things didn't quite work out that way.

After the first performance, Schieber said to me: "My dear Doctor, don't you know that the general public absolutely never attends premieres but sits biding its time? But in view of the unheard-of moral success that we had today, you'll see how they'll come pouring in tomorrow!"

After the second performance, Schieber said to me: "My dear Doctor, you are quite right. Quite right! But whose fault is it? The idiot from the poster office. This fool has the announcements pasted up just four hours before the performance! Everything lost before we even get to town! Are the people supposed to *sniff out* the fact that we're doing guest shows here? For them to come, they at least have to *know* that we're playing here! Yes or no? Well, in the final analysis it's no more than *one* lost day. What will it mean compared to the weeks and weeks that we'll be overbooked from tomorrow on!"

After the third performance, Schieber said to me: "Come, dear Doctor, what are you surprised at? You can't get anywhere without the *press;* that's something you yourself ought to be aware of as an intelligent man! But the critics will put in an appearance only tomorrow morning! Tomorrow we'll be sold out."

After the fourth performance, Schieber said to me: "Surely, my dear Doctor, you can't be so naive about theater that you don't know that Friday is the worst theater day of the week? But tomorrow is Saturday; then you'll see what's what!"

After the fifth performance, Schieber said to me: "I say, dear Doctor, are you going through life blind? Don't you know that there are premieres in two other theaters today? In its stupid curiosity, the public always dashes first to the premieres! But just wait; tomorrow, after these two concoctions fall through, they'll all come contritely to us. Just remember what I've said!"

After the sixth performance, Schieber said to me: "Well, Doctor, you're really something! Don't you know that on Sunday only shoemakers go to the theater? To a fine, noble thing such as ours, no Sunday public bothers coming at all! The day for the elegant public is tomorrow, Monday. Everybody connected with the stage knows that, but you, an academically educated man, don't know it?"

After the seventh performance, Schieber said to me: "Dear Doctor, I beg you, don't make yourself ridiculous! Things have to get around. It takes seven days for that. I'm an old theater hound, believe me, I know what I'm talking about! It's a law of the theater. *Seven days!* Instead of lecturing me, you ought to be *happy!* Now that the seven critical days are over, tomorrow begins the Great Migration!!"

After the eighth performance, Schieber said to me: "Well, dear Doctor, tell me, what did you really expect from these beer-bourgeois? Did you seriously believe that Munich was fertile ground for high-class cabaret? If people had listened to *me,* we would have been in Frankfurt long ago!"

Fourteen days were contemplated for Frankfurt. Before we pulled into the train station, Schieber pulled me aside and said: "My dear Doctor, I don't want to have any arguments with you after each performance the way we did in Munich. And that's why I'm telling you straightaway, we're going to celebrate an unheard-of success in Frankfurt. But on one condition, and that is, that it rains. In nice weather during the summer, nobody goes to the theater. However, for the next two weeks continuing heavy precipitation is forecast. Chin up then! You are about to cross the threshold of your triumph!"

Immediately following this, I betook myself to a prominent Frankfurt meteorologist, described our situation to him, and asked him for a prognosis. The professor, a friendly old gentleman, heard me out patiently and then said: "Yes, my dear young friend, unfortunately I see from what you say that you are one of the many victims of the misleading theory of Professor Larsen in Cologne. How much misfortune this man has already caused! And people believe him because he's in fashion now!" I said: "It's not so much the theory of Professor Larsen, which is totally unfamiliar to me, so much as our Munich experience that . . ." But the scholar interrupted me, all excited: "Shall I tell you what this Herr Larsen is? An academic swindler, a criminal dilettante! What? This summer's dryness due to equinoctial storms? Why not from the *trade winds* as well? I tell you it is quite simply the gulf currents and nothing else! Besides, his last article shows just how carelessly this so-called researcher works." He pulled out a page from a newspaper. "Here it is in black and white: 'The complete dryness of this summer, the likes of which we have not had since the year 1895, will last until September.' This is utterly false."

"Bravo," I cried, excited.

"You see," said the scholar with a triumphant air, "even you know it as a layman! Only Herr Larsen does not! Only Herr Larsen, the so-called specialist, does not know that the last completely dry summer was in the year 1719!"

I said: "Yes indeed. Nevertheless, the dryness . . ."

" . . . is, theoretically viewed, nonexistent. On the contrary. Every specialist must regard this summer as one of the dampest. The dryness is connected only with the atmospheric layer of the earth. The stratum, in the strict sense, on the other hand—the only one that the geologists take into consideration—is made up of such humidity that . . ." I asked if there was any chance that the atmospheric layer would also become moist. "Certainly," replied the professor, "in the scientific sense it *is* moist. As a matter of fact, dampness can occur at any moment, which any layman can also feel in his bones. For this to happen, the little gulf currents that are clustered around the equatorial zone must turn in a north-northeast direction."

The heat remained so oppressive that not a single representative of a newspaper showed up for the press evening. That is no doubt why the next day we had laudatory reviews in several papers.

From then on, we played with variable success. The third evening's patron, for example, was an average person of quite ordinary taste who laughed only at the coarse lines but showed no understanding of any subtle humor or the really serious numbers. By contrast, the patron on the fifth evening was a well-educated man who fully appreciated precisely the artistically valuable items on our program. The sixth evening's patron was a burglar.

On the ninth evening, our musical director suffered a heat stroke. As luck would have it, I happen to have attended secondary school in Frankfurt, so on the eleventh evening practically my entire class showed up in the theater. (Only two asked to be excused by their parents because of nosebleeds.) No matter how unbelievable it may sound, on this evening there were actually more people in the auditorium than on the stage.

On the twelfth evening, some high-society people drove up in two automobiles and purchased two orchestra circle boxes. It turned out, however, that the fine folk were under the mistaken impression that it was the operetta *Die Fledermaus* that was being performed.

In such circumstances, one member of the company after another quit the tour. Quartets dissolved into tercets, tercets into duets. Finally, the company consisted just of me and the fat tenor. But, because of the turn of events, the poor fellow gradually became so thin that he could resume playing Lohengrin and was forthwith hired away to Bayreuth.

I went, then, to Schieber and said: "I think it would be best if we just dissolved the whole troupe. I don't believe it's worth going on any more. How much does my share amount to now?" Schieber fetched a huge cash-book, added up some columns, and replied: "If we count this evening, 823 marks and 40 pfennigs."

"What?" I said, dumbstruck. "That's actually a lot more than I expected!"

"Yes," said Schieber, "I too didn't think it would come to so much. But I'll be glad to oblige you. You can pay it out in monthly installments."

In light of this information, I resolved to break off the guest tour of the Fledermaus Cabaret company. And so I had myself called away, got out of the whole thing, and took off.

On the return trip to Vienna, I was compelled to get off at Nuremberg in order to buy a warm cap with earmuffs because of a sudden change of weather. The little gulf currents clustered around the equatorial zone had shifted north-northwest.

"Was ist eine Tournee?" 1909. Original text in Egon Friedell, *Wozu das Theater? Essays. Satiren. Humoresken,* 27–34. The sketch was originally titled "Meine Sommertournee" ("My Summer Tour").

    1.   Cleo de Mérode (1875–1966), popular variety theater and cabaret dancer.

THE PRACTICAL ART OF LIVING

Since I cannot imagine that my private whims are sufficiently interesting to the public, I would like to share some *general rules for living.* These have served me well over the years, and I believe that they should not interfere with any others.

1. Draw up ahead of time a real *schedule,* for the whole week if possible, but in any case always for the next day, and stick to it. It makes absolutely no difference if you reserve an especially large number of hours for work unless you actually do work in the time you have designated for work. You can calmly note in your schedule: from 4 to 6 in the afternoon, smoking and staring into space. In general, you can enter everything imaginable if it seems agreeable and worthwhile to you. The main thing is that you observe it.

2. Permit no unannounced *visitors.* Somebody unexpected who remains ten minutes can upset you for the entire day. Somebody anticipated, on the other hand, to whom you have allotted two hours, fits effortlessly into your day's plan.

3. Visit a *coffeehouse* as rarely as possible. In a coffeehouse, you encounter only so-called overburdened people who rob you of your time without affording you in return any real recreation. If they spent their time in true relaxation (for example, dreaming of lying in the sun) or in reducing their backlog of work, they would be neither overtired nor overburdened.

4. *Sleep* at least eight hours a day. But there are also people who need ten hours. It is quite erroneous reasoning to believe that you gain time by getting up earlier. What you withhold from sleep will make work not only slower but also duller, therefore valueless in a double sense.

5. Emancipate yourself from *lunch.* It costs you at least two hours in the middle of the day and produces paralysis of the brain. Take instead

a few slices of white bread together with a bowl of beef broth or a cooked egg in a glass or a container of yogurt or a cup of very light coffee or a serving of cooked plums (but not everything at the same time). In the beginning, you will experience a slight sensation of hunger, but in two weeks you will get used to it.

6. Spend your life partly *moving* (as quickly as possible), partly *lying down*. Sit or stand only when you are compelled to by external circumstances. Sitting especially is an unhealthy and unnatural nuisance which we are not even aware of, since we are trained in it from youth. Sitting is one of the many infamous and inhuman inventions of the modern age. For thousands of years, the Orientals have passed their existence in a reclining position. The Greeks and Romans used to lie down, as everybody knows, even when eating. No animal sits by nature. Dogs and cats do it every now and then, since they have been living for so long in the corrupting society of human beings. Cows, horses, and lions do not do it, except in the circus. A reclining position induces in us gentleness, objectivity, equipoise, and deliberation. Sitting induces nervousness, greed, malice, and dissatisfaction.

7. Finally, as concerns *alcohol*, I believe that for all activities demanding exact, rigorous thinking it is an absolute evil. Accounting systems, sharp, logical operations, arrangement of analogues, reviews of long series of facts—these and the like are incompatible with the use of alcohol. However, when it comes to a lightning-like grasp of widely distant connections, for the sake of daring, even absurd associations, for the sake of novel combinations, alcohol can often be helpful. The conceptions that are inseparably linked in our prosaically ordered way of thinking suddenly break away from each other once the normal restraints of logic and sense of causality disappear, and new connections become possible. I also believe that mankind will continue to use alcohol so long as it is compelled to delude itself concerning its own insufficiency, which means, therefore, for a rather long time to come.

"Praktische Lebenskunst," 1927. A reply to a questionnaire by the *Frankfurter Zeitung* (5 June 1927). Original text in Egon Friedell, *Selbstanzeige: Essays ab 1918*, ed. Heribert Illig (Vienna-Munich: Löcker Verlag, 1983), 204–6.

ALFRED POLGAR[1] ENJOYS A FORMIDABLE REPUTATION AS A WRITER OF "SMALL FORMS," SO MUCH SO THAT HE IS USUALLY REFERRED TO AS THE "GERMAN MASTER OF THE SMALL FORM" (DER DEUTSCHE MEISTER DER KLEINEN FORM). This is, in fact, the title bestowed on him by Walter Benjamin.[2] The list of his admirers among twentieth-century German-language writers is impressive. It includes, to mention just the best-known names, Thomas and Heinrich Mann, Robert Musil, Joseph Roth, Hermann Broch, Bertolt Brecht, Alfred Döblin, Karl Kraus, Stefan Zweig, Franz Werfel, and, of course, Walter Benjamin. The other side of the ledger is meagerly represented mostly by Arthur Schnitzler, who immortalized Polgar unflatteringly under the name of Gleissner in his novel *Der Weg ins Freie* (*The Way to Freedom*) and with whom Polgar carried on a lengthy feud.

Polgar was the consummate all-around master of "small forms." He wrote sketches; feuilletons; glosses; literary essays; portraits; aphorisms; theater, book, and film reviews; and short comic and parodic plays mostly for the cabaret. Additionally, he adapted several plays and novels by other writers for stage and film production. Some thirty-nine volumes of his short works have been published, including nine volumes of his critical writings, mostly on theater. Polgar's serious interest in the stage is reflected not only in his voluminous theater criticism but also in two more specialized books. One is a collection of essays on Otto Brahm's Ibsen productions in Berlin in the early years of the century; the other is on the German comic actor Max Pallenberg, with whom Polgar was close. Another theatrical crony was Egon Friedell, with whom Polgar coauthored three comic plays, which were published separately, as well as five parodic newspapers, each of which was also published independently. After Peter Altenberg's death, it was Polgar who assumed responsibility in 1921 for the editing and publication of his literary estate (Nachlass).

Polgar's reputation rests not just on his huge and varied output but also on the diversity of his literary world and his acknowledged mastery of language. His social and political views were liberal, which set him in the mainstream of the literary community of his time, and he was a deeply moral thinker without, however, the self-righteousness and stridency of Karl Kraus.

Like many other Austrian writers of his age, Polgar was a Jew. The original family name was Polak, which he never wrote under. After a few other pseudonyms, he settled on Polgar and legalized the name in 1914. He was born in the largely Jewish district of Leopoldstadt to a family of Hungarian-Slovak Jews. Because of the family's precarious financial health, he was educated only through the lower grade of the gymnasium. However, because of an aptitude for the piano (his father Josef taught piano), music lessons were kept up for a time.

By the age of nineteen, Polgar's career in journalism seems already to have been decided. It was at this age that he began writing for *Die Zukunft* (*The Future*), which was under the direction of Stefan Grossman (later the publisher of the *Tage-Buch* (with which Anton Kuh was affiliated) and functioned as the organ of the Vienna left-wing independent socialists. Polgar's first feuilleton, on the Norwegian writer Knut Hamsun's novel *Hunger*, appeared here. In 1895, three years later, Polgar signed on with the liberal *Wiener Allgemeine Zeitung*, for which he reported on judiciary and parliamentary matters. Felix Salten was also affiliated with the paper at this time and, while responsible for the theater review column, occasionally allowed Polgar to write for it in view of his interest in the stage.

Polgar's entry into the Vienna coffeehouse world coincided with the initiation of his literary career. He took to it like a duck to water and became well known for the hours he put in daily in the coffeehouse. The Central and then the Herrenhof became his principal stamping grounds, and he soon joined the circle around Peter Altenberg. Yet no matter how integral a part of Polgar's existence the coffeehouse became, it was typical of him that he could observe the phenomenon from a distance and dissect it dispassionately, as he does in his "Theorie des Café Central" ("Theory of the Café Central").

It was the Central, and the Altenberg circle, into which some time in 1897 Polgar ushered in one of the striking literary "groupies" of the time, the newly divorced Emma ("Ea") Rudolf, eventually best known as Ea von Allesch (after her second and ultimately unsuccessful marriage in 1916 to the psychologist Johannes von Allesch).[3] It was Ea whom Robert Musil, one of her admirers, had in mind when he coined the phrase "the lady friend of well-known men" (Freundin bedeutender Männer). For a while she was Polgar's great love. They shared an old villa in the suburb of Döbling from 1903 to 1906, but the relationship was flexible enough to permit the cohabitation of a third party in the form of an English pianist named Henry James Skeene. After the relationship ended and Ea resumed residence in Vienna following an interval in Berlin, she became the "grande dame" of the Café Central. Her circle of admirers was most impressive, including as it did Robert Musil, Karl Kraus, Franz Blei, Arthur Schnitzler, Rainer Maria Rilke, Oskar Kokoschka, the composer Eugen d'Albert, and the Vienna publisher Paul Zsolnay. The tall, thin, green-gray-eyed woman whose reddish blond hair hung loosely around her shoulders was also immortalized on canvas by Egon Schiele. Probably the greatest love of her life after Polgar was the writer Hermann Broch, to whom Polgar introduced her in 1918. Although that relationship, too, was destined to fail, Broch had a room in her apartment where he stayed whenever he was in Vienna and lived there full-time between 1925 and 1930.

Polgar's range of literary activity expanded considerably in the period 1902–5. In 1902 he began writing for the renowned Munich satirical magazine *Simplicissimus* and that same year also assumed regular reporting on the Burgtheater for the liberal *Wiener Sonn- und Montagszeitung* (*Vienna Sunday and Monday Paper*). In 1905 he began collaboration with Siegfried Jacobsohn's newly founded *Die Schaubühne*, which in 1918 became the very well known *Die Weltbühne*. When the first cabaret of distinction, Die

Fledermaus, opened in Vienna in 1907, Polgar became both a habitué and a contributor to its programs. He and Egon Friedell teamed up and together wrote three comic plays for the cabaret: the one-scene *Goethe* (1908), which became a sensation throughout the German-speaking world and was staged hundreds of times; *Der Petroleumkönig oder Donauzauber* (*The Petroleum King or The Magic of the Danube,* 1908), a "model operetta"; and *Soldatenleben im Frieden* (*Military Life in Peace-Time,* 1910).

By 1909 Polgar had written enough to warrant publication of two collections of his works. *Der Quell des Übels* (*The Source of Evil*) appeared in 1908, followed the next year by *Bewegung ist alles* (*Movement Is Everything*). The year 1910 brought publication of *Brahms Ibsen,* a collection of critical essays about Otto Brahm's productions of Ibsen's plays at the Freie Bühne in Berlin. Polgar's enthusiasm for the stage was reflected not just in his newspaper reviews and the collaborative efforts with Egon Friedell. In 1911 he staged a new version of the farce *Kampl* by the prolific and popular nineteenth-century Austrian dramatist Nestroy for the Berlin Freie Bühne. The next year he and Armin Friedmann jointly wrote a play called *Talmas Tod* (*Talma's Death*), which was staged with much success in Altona. Polgar's German version of the Hungarian Ferenc Molnár's best-known play, *Liliom,* was staged at the Lessingtheater in Berlin and began that play's successful international career. Before 1912 drew to a close, a collection of Polgar's novellas was published under the title *Hiob* (*Job*).

By the time the First World War broke out, Polgar was already established in his literary career and comfortably ensconced in far more elegant quarters in central Vienna than he ever knew in the Leopoldstadt as a boy. When war came, it was as much a hardship for him as it was for other writers who performed their service in the secure confines of the War Archives. One really could not have asked for better company. Hofmannsthal was there, Felix Salten, Rilke, the popular writer Franz Theodor Csokor, and others. All in all, a select club. Polgar was torn away from it for a few months in 1917 and dispatched to the front, but his previous status as a journalist assigned to cover the Parliament assured a timely return to the War Archives.

However limited his actual contact with war, Polgar returned to civilian life a dedicated pacifist. Before long he was writing pieces of a decidedly antiwar character especially for Benno Karpeles's weekly *Der Friede,* to which Anton Kuh and Joseph Roth, among others, also contributed. Most of these were collected in the volume *Kleine Welt* (*Small World*), which was published in 1919. When Stefan Grossman founded *Das Tage-Buch* in 1920, Polgar became a regular contributor to it. But whatever earnings he realized from this association as well as from his collaboration with other newspapers in Vienna, Berlin, and Prague, Polgar found it impossible to make ends meet in the economic hardship of postwar Austria. One of the people who helped him through the difficult times was the actor Max Pallenberg, to whom Polgar expressed his gratitude in one way by writing a book about him, which was published in 1921. It was also in this period that Polgar and Friedell teamed up together again, this time to put out a "bad boys" (böse Buben) satirical and parodic paper. Five issues appeared between 1922 and 1925: *Böses Buben Journal* (1921), *Böse Buben Presse* (1922), *Böse Buben Reichpost* (*The Bad Boys' Imperial Mail*, 1924), *Die Böse Buben Stunde* (*The Bad Boys' Hour*, 1924), and *Die aufrichtige Zeitung der bösen Buben* (*The Bad Boys' Candid Paper*, 1925).

Polgar's financial situation improved when, in 1922, he accepted the post of theater critic of the daily *Der Tag* (the successor to the defunct *Der Neue Tag*). Franz Blei, Robert Musil, and Joseph Roth were other contributors at the time. The same year Polgar joined *Der Tag*, he published a volume of his prose pieces under the title *Gestern und heute* (*Yesterday and Today*). The collection was notable particularly for the author's greater willingness to deal critically with various social phenomena. Besides drama reviews for *Der Tag* during this period, Polgar maintained a certain visibility for his own theater work. His coauthored play *Talma's Death* had its premiere in the Berlin Kammerspiel in 1922, and in 1923 Polgar adapted Karl Vollmoeller's *Turandot* for the Salzburg Festspiel, which was then under the direction of Max Reinhardt.

Polgar's relocation to Berlin in 1925 and his residence there until 1933 may have been motivated by his desire to strengthen his career through his contacts there. For several years, he had been actively collaborating with the *Berliner Tagblatt*, most of his books had been published by German publishers (Albert Langen, Erich Reiss, Fritz Gurlitt, Rudolf Kaemmerer), he was well known in Berlin theatrical circles, and he enjoyed a good relationship with Siegfried Jacobsohn, the publisher of *Die Schaubühne* (subsequently *Die Weltbühne*). Polgar was also respected in German literary circles. Since he was a bit vain on the matter of age and liked to pretend that he was two years younger, Polgar permitted his Berlin friends to celebrate his "fiftieth" birthday in 1925, the year he relocated there. One of the more incisive tributes that appeared in the press on that occasion was written by the Austrian novelist Joseph Roth for the *Frankfurter Zeitung*. Roth, who had worked under Polgar at *Der Friede* and *Der Neue Tag*, was an admirer of Polgar's writing and was consciously influenced by it. Attempting to define the essence of Polgar's literary style, Roth summed it up in these words: "Polgar writes little stories without plots and observations without summaries. He needs no real 'contents,' since each of his superbly crafted words is full of content. No occasion is trifling for him. On the contrary, it is with the most trifling that he shows his mastery. He polishes the ordinary until it becomes extraordinary."[4]

While in Berlin, Polgar developed a fruitful collaboration with the major German publishing house Ernst Rowohlt Verlag. Between 1926 and 1933, Rowohlt put out seven more collections of Polgar's writings—*An den Rand geschrieben* (*Written on the Margin*), *Orchester von oben* (*Looking Down on the Orchestra*), *Ich bin Zeuge* (*I Am a Witness*), *Schwarz auf Weiss* (*Black on White*), *Bei dieser Gelegenheit* (*On This Occasion*), *Auswahlband: Aus neun Bänden erzählender und kritischer Schriften* (*Selected Narrative and Critical Writings from Nine Volumes*), and *Ansichten* (*Views*), his last book to be published in Germany before the collapse of the Weimar regime; and four volumes of his critical essays on the theater—*Kritisches Lesebuch* (*A Critical Reader*), *Stücke und Spieler* (*Plays and Players*), *Noch allerlei Theater* (*More on Theater*), and *Stichproben* (*Spot Checks*)—which appeared under the collective title *Ja und Nein* (*Yes and No*).

Polgar also continued to adapt various types of literary works for stage and film. In 1930 he and Franz Theodor Csokor collaborated on the dramatization of the Soviet novelist and playwright Valentin Kataev's novel *The Embezzlers*. The play was staged for the first time at the Berlin Volksbühne the following year, when Rowohlt also published it in book form. Polgar and the German film director Fritz Kortner then did a film version of it under the title *Der brave Sünder* (*The Honest Sinner*). It was directed by Kortner and the lead roles were played by Max Pallenberg and Heinz Rühmann.

The disquieting political events in Germany and Austria in the late '20s and early '30s sharpened Polgar's pacifistic and socialistic attitudes. In order to strengthen the position of the Social Democratic Party in the elections of 24 April 1927, Polgar, along with Freud, Adler, Musil, Werfel, and others, signed a "Declaration of Intellectual Vienna," which was published in the socialist *Arbeiter-Zeitung* (*Workers' Paper*) on 20 April. His collection *Black on White*, which Rowohlt published in 1928, contains nine sketches of an antimilitaristic character grouped under the general title "Das Gedächtnis zu stärken" ("To Refresh the Memory"). The following year Rowohlt also brought out his markedly pacifistic volume *Hinterland* (*Back Country*), which included a number of sketches published previously in the *Little World* collection of 1919. When in 1931 the board of directors of the German Writers' Protective Association attempted to exclude a left-wing oppositional faction, Polgar joined Erich Kästner, Ernst Toller, Walter Mehring, George Grosz, Leonhard Frank, and other German literary figures in drafting a protest. In much the same spirit he registered his opposition to the politically motivated eighteen-month prison sentence handed down against Carl von Ossietzky, the manager of *Die Weltbühne*.

Polgar's democratic, antifascist, prosocialist writing and activism, compounded by his Jewishness, hardly escaped the attention of the Nazis. Polgar himself had no illusions as to what might befall him if Hitler came to power. The burning of the Reichstag in 1933 was the signal for him to leave. He packed his belongings and headed that same day to Prague together with his wife Elise (Loewy), whom he had married in Berlin in October 1929. After a brief stay in Prague, the Polgars went to Vienna, where they remained until the Anschluss of 1938.

The suppression of the Social Democratic Party in the wake of the February 1934 riots in Vienna considerably strengthened the right-wing elements in the Dollfuss regime and sharply curtailed the journalistic activity of socialist-oriented writers such as Polgar. In fact, the only publication outlets available to Polgar at this time were the Prague *Tagblatt* and Leopold Schwarzschild's Paris-based German émigré paper *Das neue Tage-Buch* (for which Polgar wrote under the pseudonym Archibald Douglas). As his financial situation worsened, Polgar was again able to count on the good offices of his friends to see him through. Besides older friends such as Rudolf Kommer and Max Pallenberg (who died in a plane crash in 1934), he was also helped by the Swiss writer Carl Seelig, whose acquaintance he had made on previous visits to Zurich.

From 1933, when he left Berlin, until 4 October 1940, when he and his wife sailed for New York from Lisbon after fleeing Paris, Polgar continued writing and publishing as best he could under the circumstances. He also became increasingly involved in film work. On the literary front, mostly thanks to Seelig's intervention, he began regular collaboration with the antifascist weekly *Die Nation,* which was published in Bern and where he had his own column called "Streiflichter" ("Side-Lights"). He also wrote for the Basel *Nationalzeitung,* which honored Polgar on his "sixtieth" birthday on 16 October 1935 by publishing felicitations by, among others, Thomas and Heinrich Mann and Joseph Roth. With Seelig's help Polgar managed to have a collection of sketches as well as political commentaries which had appeared in Swiss newspapers published by the Humanitas publishing house of Zurich under the title *Sekundenzeiger* (*Second Hand*). Two other volumes, one containing theater criticism and the other more sketches, were planned for the same publisher but never materialized. In 1938 another Zurich publisher, Oprecht Verlag, brought out his *Handbuch des Kritikers* (*Critic's Handbook*). Three years earlier, Polgar had initiated the pattern of opening contacts with publishers elsewhere in Europe due to the impossibility of publication in Austria or Germany. In 1935 the Dutch house of Allert de Lange, in Amsterdam, published a collection of his sketches under the title *In der Zwischenzeit* (*In the Meantime*).

Polgar's literary activity during this difficult period was supplemented by film work, which opened up contacts of inestimable value when the writer and his wife emigrated to the United States from war-ravaged Europe in 1940. In 1933 Polgar and Friedrich Kohner collaborated on the script for a film version of Knut Hamsun's novel *Victoria*. When the film was completed in 1935, the deterioration of the domestic political situation in Austria was reflected in the omission of their names from the credits. After the Hamsun project, Polgar was involved in a film about the romance between the illustrious nineteenth-century Viennese actor Alexander Girardi and Helene Odilon entitled *Es war einmal . . .* (*It Happened Once Upon a Time*). Preparation of the script took him to Paris for a while in March 1936.

When exactly Polgar met Marlene Dietrich is difficult to say. It seems likely that their paths crossed when Polgar was living in Berlin in the late '20s and early '30s. His later film work would also naturally have created possibilities of their meeting. At some point Polgar had the idea of writing a biography of the great star and in the fall of 1937 met her in Paris to discuss the matter. Dietrich agreed to cooperate and Polgar began serious work on the book. War, however, made the undertaking another casualty.

At the time of the German annexation of Austria, Polgar happened to be in Zurich. His wife joined him shortly thereafter. Although their plan was to remain there with the help of Carl Seelig, the Swiss authorities refused him a work permit, which was tantamount to a denial of the right of residence. The Polgars were hardly an exception. The number of Jewish refugees from Germany and Austria who sought a safe haven in Switzerland after 1933 was far larger than the Swiss cared to assimilate into their economy. Moreover, they had no desire to antagonize Nazi Germany by permitting significant immigration. The result was a rigorous exclusionary policy that made it impossible except for the select few to find refuge in the country.

Denied residence in Switzerland, Polgar went next to Paris, where he remained until the entry of German troops into France in June 1940. His means of support was severely limited, and he grasped whatever opportunity presented itself, including, among others, writing advertising copy for a Swiss tobacco manufacturer. He also became active in the Austrian émigré community in the French capital. He joined the Central Association of Austrian Emigrants, together with Joseph Roth founded the so-called League for Intellectual Austria, and published pieces predominantly political in nature in such émigré papers as the *Pariser Tageszeitung* and *La libre Autriche* (*Free Austria*). Like other refugees from Germany and

Austria, his German citizenship (by virtue of the annexation) was revoked in May 1939. Since this then necessitated regular visits to the French police, the precariousness of his position became obvious. When German troops began marching on Paris, the Polgars packed hastily, leaving behind a large number of books and manuscripts in their apartment in the Bois de Bologne, and took flight.

The route from Paris was familiar, one attempted by many: south from the capital to Montauban and then Marseilles to pick up a previously applied for French exit visa, illegal crossing of the border into Spain on foot when the visa was delayed or failed to materialize, travel from Spain to Portugal, and finally exodus to the Americas by boat from Lisbon. The lucky, like the Polgars, made it; others, like Walter Benjamin, were less fortunate. Their ordeal behind them, the Polgars set sail for New York from Lisbon on 4 October 1940, on the same Greek freighter (the *Nea Hellas*) bearing Heinrich and Golo Mann and the Werfels, Franz and Alma.

Polgar spent about a week in New York after his arrival on 15 October. He and his wife then went to Hollywood so that Polgar could begin working as a scriptwriter for MGM. While still in Paris in 1939, friends in the film industry as well as the American Committee for the Support of Emigre Artists helped secure him a one-year contract with the studio, which also facilitated his entry into the United States. The scriptwriting was obviously not taken very seriously, since it was primarily a way by which Hollywood could come to the rescue of German and Austrian émigré writers and artists. Because of it, a large colony of such emigres took shape in Hollywood in the late 1930s and the 1940s, so that when they arrived in California the Polgars could experience something of a homecoming. The Manns were there, the Werfels, Friedrich Torberg, Carl Zuckmayer, Walter Mehring, Alfred Döblin, and many others.

Life in Hollywood may have been pleasant for a while, but reality inevitably caught up. Having helped bring Polgar to the United States and guarantee him a salary for a year or so, MGM felt unconstrained to extend the relationship indefinitely. Indeed, few refugees actually succeeded in establishing careers in Hollywood. The most successful by far, of course, was Franz Werfel, whose novel *The Song of Bernadette* became an immensely popular movie and whose play *Jacobowsky and the Colonel* did as well as on film as it did on the stage. When Polgar was about to be set adrift by MGM, the personal intervention above all of Thomas Mann achieved an extension of his contract. But a heart attack in February 1941 and the eventual expiration of the MGM contract depressed Polgar emotionally and financially.

With the Hollywood experience behind him, Polgar reactivated his literary career, encouraged in part by the publication in 1942 by Oprecht

Verlag of Zurich of a collection of his sketches. The edition, for which Polgar's old friend Carl Seelig assumed responsibility, bore the title *Geschichten ohne Moral* (*Stories without a Moral*) and consisted in the main of (in some cases extensively revised) earlier sketches. In 1943 the Polgars left California for New York City, where publishing opportunities seemed better and where he could take a more active role in émigré Austrian cultural and political life. He became involved in a project to establish a newspaper for a liberated Austria to be called *Der Friede* (*Peace*), for which he had the promise of financial support from the Viennese industrialist Hans Heller and with which Bertolt Brecht also promised to cooperate; collaborated with the émigré *Austro-American Tribune;* and wrote for *Der Aufbau,* to which Anton Kuh was already contributing. Thanks to his friend Willi Schlamm, in 1944 he joined Friedrich Torberg, Leopold Schwarzschild, and other literary émigrés in the preparation of a German edition of *Time Magazine.* Unfortunately the project never reached fruition—the same fate as the plan to publish *Der Friede.*

Polgar became an American citizen in 1945. With the war over, he gave serious thought to returning to Europe, since his prospects in the United States were poor and homesickness began getting the best of him. His decision was also influenced by evidence of continued European interest in him as a writer. The Rowohlt Verlag in Berlin, which had published him before the war, came out in 1947 with a volume of his collected sketches under the title *Im Vorüberfahren* (*Passing By*). The next year the Amsterdam publishing house Querido published a book of articles by Polgar entitled *Anderseits* (*On the Other Hand*), which is interesting above all for the pieces dealing with the émigré's conflicting attitudes toward his newly liberated homeland.

Polgar finally returned to Europe in May 1949. After stops in Paris and Zurich, he and his wife visited Vienna for a while and then spent the greater part of the summer in Salzburg. In October, Polgar visited Munich, his first postwar trip to Germany. Polgar's account of his trip to Europe, "Notizbuch von einer Europa-Reise" ("Notebook of a European Journey"), was published by *Der Aufbau* in New York. Polgar returned to New York on 18 October 1950 and then the following spring was again in Europe. This second trip was a kind of personal triumph. The city of Vienna bestowed on him its first prize for journalism. Toward the end of October 1951 he was in Berlin for the publication of a new volume of sketches, *Begegnung in Zwielicht* (*Encounter at Twilight*), which Lothar Blanvalet brought out. His visit to the city where he had spent some of his most productive and happiest years was also the occasion for tributes to him by the press and others.

In 1952, Polgar and his wife took up a more or less regular residence in the Hotel Urban in Zurich. This served as a base for numerous trips throughout the German-speaking world where Polgar wrote on theatrical productions for such papers as *Die Süddeutsche Zeitung* (*The South German Gazette*), *Neue Zeitung* (*New Gazette*), and *Echo der Woche* (*The Week's Echo*). Two more volumes of his prose appeared in 1953 and 1954: *Standpunkte* (*Viewpoints*), published by Rowohlt, and *Im Lauf der Zeit* (*In the Course of Time*), also published by Rowohlt in the first paperback edition of a Polgar book.

On invitation from the film actress Lili Darvas, a family friend, Polgar made a trip back to New York in December 1952. It was his last time in the United States. He returned to Europe in January 1953, to the Hotel Urban in Zurich. The last two years of his life were spent traveling extensively in Germany, Austria, and Switzerland, covering theatrical premieres and writing drama reviews. The last book he worked on was a volume of theater criticism. In August 1954 Polgar was once again honored by his native city when he was named to the literary advisory board of the Theater in der Josefstadt. On 23 April 1955, he completed a piece called "Three Theater Evenings in Germany" for his old friend Friedrich Torberg's newly founded *Forum: Österreichische Monatsblätter für kulturelle Freiheit* (*Forum: Austrian Monthly Magazine for Cultural Freedom*). The next day he died of a heart attack in his hotel room in Zurich. He was eighty-two years old. Obituaries appeared in virtually every major newspaper in the German-speaking world as well as in *The New York Times*. Polgar's reputation has grown steadily since; he has been the subject of two biographies, several scholarly studies, and between 1982 and 1984 a new four-volume edition of his selected writings was published by, appropriately enough, Rowohlt.

Joseph Roth, who liked to refer to himself as Polgar's pupil, took the occasion of the "master's" "sixtieth" birthday on 17 October 1935 to express his indebtedness to him and to define his importance as a writer. "I have much to thank him for," recalled Roth:

> Among present German writers he is one of the most careful. I have learned this *verbal carefulness* from him. I confess that I tried to learn it by paying close attention to him, that I tried to detect the secrets of the German language, to hear and feel it, the way he among so very few can, thanks to his grace. I was grateful to him even *before* this time, then when one could still hope that the delicate and strong instrument of the German language might not be degraded into an imperial German loudspeaker. Today, now that it has become so, my gratitude to Alfred Polgar is even greater. His delicacy is victorious against

the loudspeakers. In these lamentable days in which barbarians and stammerers mistreat the German language, the work of Alfred Polgar is becoming more important than it may have seemed in those "calm times." I thank him from the bottom of my heart, for everything that he did for the German language, for everything that he taught me.[5]

In an incisive "Interview with Alfred Polgar" which was published in the Berlin *Die literarische Welt* on 5 March 1926, Robert Musil came closer than anyone to capturing the essence of Polgar's writing:

> Polgar . . . lets things go their own way. He just looks at them and describes them. But since [Wilhelm] Busch nobody has described their misery in so maliciously friendly a way. He apparently goes to the theater just because he is seeking out life where it is the most ridiculous.
>
> It would, therefore, be a mistake to apply to him him the notion that one today associates with the words "impression" and "impressionism," that of something faint, only the traces of something relinquished. His impressions conceal a system. He lets things go by, pounces on them from behind, and they completely fall apart like disassembled toys. That is his philosophy, and his technique of writing uses simultaneity, for example, for this purpose. He sets things quietly next to each other that are united in life but do not get along well together once the atmospheric gravy of habit is removed from them. Or if he wants to rebuke something, he guilelessly lets it stroll about in the midst of the praiseworthy impressions but secretly puts its verbal clothing on inside out. These rebellious little compositions are always grouped around a usually extremely comic wit, but I refuse to analyze this humor . . . [6]

1.   There is next to nothing on Polgar in English. The best book on him in German is Ulrich Weinzierl, *Alfred Polgar: Eine Biographie* (Vienna and Munich: Löcker Verlag, 1985). This book also has the best available bibliography of the literature on Polgar. Weinzierl's earlier work, *Er war Zeuge: Alfred Polgar—Ein Leben zwischen Publizistik und Literatur* (Vienna: Löcker & Wögenstein, 1977), is his published doctoral dissertation and represents basically an earlier version of the 1985 biography. Less biographical and more in the nature of a scholarly monograph than Weinzierl's work is Eva Philippoff, *Alfred Polgar: Ein moralischer Chronist seiner Zeit* (Munich: Minerva Publikation, 1980). The first volume of a four-volume edition of Polgar's short pieces also contains a list of Polgar's book publications and a handy chronology of his life. See Alfred Polgar, *Kleine Schriften*, ed. Marcel Reich-Ranicki and Ulrich Weinzierl (Reinbek bei Hamburg: Rowohlt Verlag, 1982), 1:507–19.

2.   In a review in 1928 of Polgar's book of sketches *Ich bin Zeuge*. See Walter Benjamin, *Gesammelte Schriften*, ed. Hella Tiedemann-Bartels (Frankfurt am Main: Suhrkamp Verlag, 1972), 3:107.

3.   There is a brief account of the Polgar-Emma Rudolf/Ea von Allesch relationship in Dietmar Grieser, *Eine Liebe in Wien* (St. Pölten-Vienna: Verlag Niederösterreichisches Pressehaus, 1989), 111–18 ("Hermann Broch und Ea von Allesch").

4.   Joseph Roth, "Einbruch der Journalisten in die Nachwelt," *Die Frankfurter Zeitung* (19 December 1925). Also quoted in David Bronsen, *Joseph Roth: Eine Biographie* (Cologne: Kiepenheuer & Witsch, 1974), 189–90.

5.   Joseph Roth, "Für Alfred Polgar. Zum 60. Geburtstag am 17. Oktober 1935," *Werke in drei Bänden* (Cologne, Berlin: Verlag Kiepenheuer &Witsch, 1956), 3:385. Also quoted in David Bronsen, *Joseph Roth,* 190.

6.   Robert Musil, *Gesammelte Werke* ("Prosa und Stücke. Kleine Prosa, Aphorismen. Autobiographisches. Essays und Reden. Kritik"), ed. Adolf Frisé (Reinbek bei Hamburg: Rowohlt, 1978), 2:1157–58.

The Viennese Feuilleton

You hear people complain that it's dead. The great masters of the Viennese feuilleton, who have already died or retired into their shells in unbreakable silence, have found pitiful imitators. And everywhere people say: "How sad!" instead of saying: "Thank God!" It is most encouraging that the talent for this flimsiest kind of literature is being lost. And that today, whoever wants to attract attention now has to have something to say and can no longer get by saying nothing in a sweetly curled way.

That, after all, is the essence of the Viennese feuilleton: vacuity, the wishy-washy visage, winsomely set off by stylishly frizzled little curls. Sweetness, gentleness, friendliness throughout, never an angry wrinkle, a deeper furrowing, a sharp grimace of determination by which the smooth surface of this countenance might be broken. Of the Viennese feuilleton, one can speak only in diminutives. It has neither hands nor feet, but tiny little hands and tiny little feet. It doesn't walk, it skips. It doesn't sing, it warbles. It doesn't laugh, it smiles. It isn't graceful, but gracile. It doesn't think, it muses. It doesn't talk, it chats.

The Viennese feuilleton is not noticeable. It evaporates at once from the brain onto which it is spilled. Once you have finished reading it, you feel nothing afterward. What stood in these six faultlessly pleated columns? A minute after you finish reading it, you have no answer. You know only that everything was affable and gracile. Not just life, but the Viennese feuilleton is an amusement-park slide. You're down and you can't say how you got there. Sliding down the six columns of such a feuilleton is one of the most unfatiguing of mental exercises. That is also why—especially on Sunday afternoons, after the black coffee, for digestion—the feuilleton-slide, with the help of the *Neue Freie Presse,* is one of the most popular Lower Austrian amusements.

Of course, it is only proper for the feuilleton to safeguard its character as a lighter art product, so long as it does not lose its calm breathing and fall into panting and sweating under the weight of excessive thought. But if it must also satisfy the interest of the reader for only fleeting moments and not remain for eternity, it should be weighted with a few stones of thought so as not to become simply sneezed away.

I miss these few weights in the Viennese feuilleton, which twines with partiality around the ideas of others, around books above all, and seeks its uniqueness only in the intricacy of entwinement. That is the formula of the Viennese feuilleton. First the language, and then the idea. The primary thing is the small talk, the chatter; the secondary, the "about what." You do not have the impression that an intellectual kernel is crystallizing verbally, that an idea has sweated out the words organic to it. You do not have the impression that kindred notions have clustered around one (or more) fixed, ideal central point, arbitrarily created by the writer's brain, that associations have linked with it in all gradations of intimacy. What you do have the impression of is that the still waters of language were first here and then through a variety of things thrown in (most, as I said before, not belonging to the author) were transformed into gentle undulatory movement.

The Viennese feuilleton exudes tenderness. It has a remarkably considerate intimacy toward all things with which it associates. Caressing is the most practical activity for its powerlessness. And so it caresses. The favorably inclined say that it has a lyrical personal touch. It caresses the Vienna Woods, scratches the neck of the Votive Church, lets the arabesques of its benevolent smile flutter around the tower of St. Stephen's Cathedral and swabs with gentle tears of melancholy the dead and dying Vienna—the "Vienna of Canaletto,"[1] Congress- and Baroque-Vienna,[2] and the receding Vienna of obscure, winding little alleyways.

The Viennese feuilleton is on intimate terms with its subject. Even if this subject is far from it, distanced perhaps by the haze of centuries. It addresses Madame Pompadour as "Dear Madame" and treats Louis XIV with the same intimate joviality as a country yokel. Nothing is ever too high, too big, too distant, too strong, too old, or too tragic not to be mashed in the Viennese feuilleton into porridge, into literary fare for the toothless.

The Viennese feuilleton is at its most intimate with landscape. Its feelings for the Vienna Woods and the Prater Park know no boundaries. It sings indefatigably of the nimbleness with which the wind runs down the slopes of the Vienna Woods and bustles about the city. It indefatigably ladles the magic that flows from the Kahlenberg into tender phrases. It indefatigably converts the silver strands of the Danube into exquisite cravats. And with its tender amorousness it importunes everything green that appears anywhere on the borders of the city, especially when, as in the western suburbs, it ventures a bit deeper into the housing complexes. When the Viennese feuilleton weaves graceful lines about the premieres of a Vienna theater in quiet pensiveness, the beech trees of the Prater waft in, the air turns silver, and the scent of Vienna at night crawls from the Vienna Woods straight into the membrane of the writer's nose. The Vienna landscape owes its singers such small reciprocity, even when they really sing about something entirely different.

Comparing life to a game is an old, good, and amiably exercised custom of the Viennese feuilleton, which likes to lapse into dream and in lapses dreams. When a Viennese feuilletonist needs some effective patch of color for the pallor of his stylish countenance, he calls on Life. It is defenseless. It can be compared with everything. Every offense draped on it is plausible; the same for every praise sung it. About Life, the Viennese feuilletonist always has something graceful-novel-exquisite-ironic to say, but when it comes to the diminutive part of life (a book, man, an event) that he subjects to discussion, he has absolutely nothing to say. And the women, the Viennese women! I might almost have forgotten them. But the Viennese feuilletonist never forgets them. Whether on their way from the Mariahilf to the Leopoldstadt or from the Leopoldstadt to the Mariahilf, the feuilletonist stands in St. Stephen's Square ready to intercept them. He bows before the women of Vienna, and does so as if he had a powdered wig atop his head and a gilded sword at his side. The beech trees waft, and the wind races from the slopes of the Vienna Woods, and besides: What is Life? A game. Ah!

A quite special characteristic of the Viennese feuilleton is the jocose mixture of the ultra-Jewish and the ultra-Aryan. Of the melancholy of the synagogue and the tipsy humor of Grinzing.[3] Is the sorrow over the thousand-year diaspora best drowned in Vienna's wine taverns? It seems so. Turning and twisting, that's my life—as sure as I live! The mixture manifests itself thoroughly in the construction and style of the Viennese feuilleton. It has a sensitive intellect and a remarkably intelligent emotional life. It practices logical mental games ornamented with feeling, and on the other hand always has a measure of emotion seated tenderly in the brain. The Viennese feuilleton makes up in resigned outlook for what it lacks in ideas, and in cerebral bustle for what it lacks in feeling.

The Viennese feuilleton dilutes seriousness into the fleeting humor of earnestness, and humor into mild jokes. Unfortunately, when it comes upon a subject with which its stylish grimaces prove to no avail, it oozes into it without leaving a trace, like a thin little brooklet into the ground. At the most, it makes the subject a bit moist. Voilà tout. It does not hurdle intellectual obstacles. nor does it overpower them with élan. It just crawls around them. It stops dead in its tracks at the first sign of trouble. It makes for the reader as little work as it did for the writer. In a word, it is purely a matter for the ladies. It is nothing for men. Sweet, coquettish, harmless, empty, flimsy, free of all toxins, smooth and inconsequential to the point of being detestable. Let us praise the time that no longer cares for it, the reader who no longer relishes it, the journalists who can no longer write it. Its gentle oiliness has become distastefully rancid. It stinks. All the beech trees around Vienna can't waft away this embarrassing odor; all the wind descending gracefully from the Kahlenberg can't blow it way. The Viennese feuilleton is dead. Peace be unto its ashes—so long as it doesn't call a lot of attention to itself by its efforts to give birth to a little clone.

"Das Wiener Feuilleton," 1906. Original text in Alfred Polgar, *Kleine Schriften,* 4:200–205.

    1.   Vienna as painted by the Venetian artist Canaletto (real name, Antonio Canal, 1697–1768).

    2.   "Congress-Vienna" refers to Vienna in the time of the Congress of Vienna (1815). "Baroque-Vienna" refers to seventeenth-century Vienna.

    3.   Grinzing is a nearby suburb of Vienna in the Vienna Woods famous for its wine taverns.

LEONHARD HAS AN EXPERIENCE

There was a ten-minute intermission after the second act. He used it to take a walk in the foyer, back and forth between the two huge mirrors that always lead you to believe that some strange man is coming toward you from the opposite direction. A small walking stick made out of rhinoceros hide danced between his fingers. It was a wooly light-yellow in color and looked like a pole of thickened honey.

He did not particularly care for the production that day. It was the next to the last of the season, and the people on stage seemed as though they were performing in their traveling clothes. Their minds only half on what they were doing, their spirits were already soaring about mountain peaks or stretching out in sand dunes.

As Leonhard paced to and fro during the break, he marveled at his good fortune in having a front-stall seat. If you saw the others who were coming out of the orchestra standing room with red faces and beads of perspiration on their brows and crumpled collars, and if you saw how they stretched their legs with sighs of relief, then you felt all the more the sheer delight of the front stalls. The people in standing room, or those hanging over gallery balustrades with contorted limbs, certainly have no time to be happy about the theater, so envious are they over all the free room the ones on stage have to move around in.

A bell summons the audience back to the auditorium. The foyer becomes empty. The doorman leans his gold-studded staff against the wall, brings out a glass from under his seat, takes a long drink, stops to catch his breath, and with two big, satisfying gestures brushes the residue of foam from his moustache. A girl is standing in a corner absorbed in the libretto.

Didn't she catch the ring? In any case, she belongs in the gallery. She is not attired in the style of the stalls.

Leonhard walks over to her. "Fräulein, you have to hurry; they've already rung once." She says: "Yes, yes." Just then the second bell rings, and Leonhard returns to his seat.

During the next intermission, he again encounters the girl.

"Fräulein, your seat is in the gallery, isn't it?"

"I am not in the gallery."

"May I ask where you're sitting then?"

"I'm not inside the theater at all."

"Oh, you're waiting for somebody?"

"No!"

"Forgive me if I seem to be interrogating you, but what are you doing here in the foyer if you're not waiting for somebody?"

"I'm listening."

"From outside?"

"Yes. The ticket collector knows me. He doesn't mind my standing at the doors and listening."

"Can you hear the music so clearly here?"

"I follow it along in the libretto and imagine all the places in the music I don't hear clearly."

He became ashamed of his front-stall smugness. "Well, are you satisfied with the performance?" he asked.

"Very!" she answered. "It's wonderful!"

A ring announced the beginning of the next act.

How they messed up the third act! This Elsa with the bloated arms! This King Heinrich who was just King Beer-Belly![1] These ludicrous men with their poorly glued-on beards! Leonhard closed his eyes and thought of the girl in the foyer. She says "wonderful" easily. She follows her perfect, flawless performance from the libretto, with a genuine Elsa and a genuine king and a genuine Lohengrin who comes from Montsalvatsch and not from Brno.[2] And why not? Shouldn't a person perhaps live his whole life this way? *From outside?* Immune from disappointments, in a transfiguring casualness of sensual perception? But people are fortunate to have a seat in the first row, and even here they still look through opera glasses.

When the opera ended, Leonhard went for supper. A few girls stood before the windows of the elegant restaurant. They were gazing enviously at the display, in the middle of which a dead pheasant smiled blissfully, as if immensely delighted that he would soon be eaten with cranberries. The girls turned about and crossed the street to a sausage stand.

"This 'outsider's logic' is always characteristic only of those who sit on the inside," thought Leonhard.

This touches him greatly. He wants to do something good. He gives the waiter his honey-yellow walking stick as a present.

And then as he eats and stares at the shiny tips of his patent leather shoes, he sees the young girl from the theater in his mind's eye, forty years later, as she tells her grandchildren in a dreamy voice: "Children . . . once upon a time . . . when I was young . . . there was this man who had the finest hands you could ever imagine . . . And he didn't say a word, just bowed silently . . . I never ever saw him again . . ."

"Leonhard hat ein Erlebnis," 1907. Original text in Alfred Polgar, *Kleine Schriften*, 2:3-6.

    1.   "König Gambrinus" (King Gambrinus) in the original, the legendary king whom German tradition credits with the discovery of beer.

    2.   Brünn, in German. The capital of Moravia in central Czechoslovakia. Here intended to suggest some backwater town.

SMALL WORLD

Before the beginning of the war, my barber was fifty-six years old. Now he's seventy, and then some.

He had an assistant, who was no assistant but a master. He lathered you up like he was caressing your chin and cheeks. He wielded the blade gently but firmly. He didn't scrape the beard so much as flatter it with tender determination from the skin down. He applied oil to the hair not like the others but dabbed the scalp with oiled fingertips, this way nurturing and at the same time massaging it. All told, it took him five minutes. He said to the customer only what was absolutely necessary. May his memory be honored. His number came up at [the battle of] Limanowa.

The next assistant fell in love with the cashier. This made his hand unsteady. The cashier had her eye on the boss's son, a reservist unfit for active duty, who helped out occasionally in the shop. The assistant and the son came to blows. The assistant was dismissed and the son married the cashier. Under the impress of historical events, he was suddenly called up for duty. His grave is at the Isonzo River.[1] The cashier had tear-stained eyes for weeks.

The new assistant was named Christian and taught her to smile all over again.

He served loyally for a certain period of time. Then, tired of the monotonous work and romance, he took the barber's golden watch and departed without saying a word. From then on, not a single assistant could please the boss and his ill-tempered daughter-in-law.

In the course of half a year, the little shop went through around thirty of them. Prices climbed higher, clients stayed away, the cashier swelled up, and in equal measure so too did the face of the little apprentice. And it was he who was made to bear the burden of all the enraged melancholy of the young widow and the master's powerless anger against a destiny that had turned the neat, elegant barber shop, to which so many prominent men came as regular customers, into a place of discord, poverty, and bad and unprofitable work.

The last assistant was an old, extremely slow person who muttered to himself while lathering up a customer and always had to make a slight pause when he bent over in order to overcome his lumbago. He stayed relatively long in the service of my barber. Ten days. On the tenth day, he absentmindedly drank from a bottle of imitation shampoo and was surprised by the cashier, who called him an old boozer. He replied with a low murmured "slut" and declared that in his life he had drunk better stuff than the stinking soap suds, to which the cashier answered that that was good enough for his pig-belly. At that point, his lumbago erupted from anger and he had an asthmatic attack. After socking one to the young apprentice, he grabbed his coat and left the place. The cashier cursed after him, began shaking the apprentice violently by the ears, and remained in this activity until the master appeared, said "Did the little shit cause any more trouble?" and boxed the apprentice a few times on the ear. Then they closed up the shop, since it was the lunch hour anyway.

From then on, the old man served customers himself. He reactivated himself after his well-earned retirement. But it didn't work out. From fatigue and shortness of breath he had to make still longer pauses in the midst of his work than the last assistant, and his efforts to help his lathered clients over the pauses by means of political conversation only earned him the greatest impatience on their part. Only one, a former baron, liked it. He complained about the Russians while his moustache was being colored black, and about the Americans while his bald pate was being rubbed with ointment.

One day, while the old man was working on the baron's lip bristles with the curling iron, a suppressed howl could be heard in the other room of the shop, and shortly thereafter out came the apprentice with bright red ears and cheeks and sobbing for all he was worth. The master dropped the curling iron, steadied himself for a moment, his hips groaning, and muttered: "You wait now, you little shit, I'll show you a thing or two." The baron examined his sallow visage lovingly in the mirror and said: "You have to keep these smart alecks in check or they'll become Bolsheviks."

I came to a noble if sentimental decision. I said to the red-faced apprentice: "Gustav, do you know how to shave yet?"

"Yes."

"Then shave me."

He shaved me.

As a result of this, the old barber let him loose on other clients as well and declared that he wouldn't take on any more assistants other than maybe a second apprentice at most.

And that, too, came to pass. A second little shrimp, a real tiny creature, was hired.

"Are you satisfied with Gustav now?" I asked the old man.

"He's doing all right . . ."

"You see, you've got to be kind to the youngsters, otherwise they'll be nervous and malicious . . ."

Yeah, the little Gustav sure does honor to the trust placed in his youth.

Whenever he has a free moment, he takes the still smaller apprentice by the ears, cuffs and pulls him, and says: "You wait now, you little shit, I'll show you a thing or two!"

In three years he'll become assistant. The cashier recently began wearing her hair waved.

Right now she's not in the shop. She's resting up at home. She just had a baby boy. His name is Christian.

"Kleine Welt," 1918. Original text in Alfred Polgar, *Kleine Schriften*, 2:39–42.

    1.   The river flows south into the Gulf of Trieste from northwest Yugoslavia and northeast Italy. It also known as the Soca in Serbo-Croatian.

POSTERS

If all the war-related posters with which the streets of Vienna were papered in the last four and a quarter years were put together, you'd have a splendid chronicle of the times.

Every eight weeks there were "military review proclamations," which were followed, as scarlet fever is followed by kidney inflammation, by "conscription announcements." With every fresh declaration of war, something invigorating "for my people" dripped from the street walls.

In nine flights, nine swarms of illustrated inducements to war bonds flew through the city. There were iron knights and defiant women and dragons' tails bristling with arrows and sowers with fatherly beards strewing gold into furrows and men in suits of armor leaning on huge swords.

The allegories were not entirely clear.

Consider the young woman who joined in the harangue for the ninth war loan by raising a chamberpot full of coins heavenwards with gestures worthy of the Duse.[1] A picture of woman's greed? Or a four-horse chariot galloping toward a many-headed Hydra. Was this aimed at the questionable guidance of the carriage of state or at the plight of the wage wagon?

Impressive aesthetically was the poster announcing general mobilization the end of July 1914. It rose up like a ghostly dam against the hot flood of patriotic music that gurgled through the streets for an entire week and was forced into all the restaurants, showering sparks under people's bottoms, so that late-evening diners and coffee drinkers had to keep on jumping up from their seats.

Song was now out. "O my Austria" lost its melodic thread, and in the presence of the still-memorable variant "it carried me away," the booming sentiment for the good comrades considerably subsided.

The creation of the Republic provided a powerful stimulus to the political poster. After November [1918], colorful banners sprang up profusely around buildings.

Of the new Republic's needs, the need for communication seems the most pressing. The pillars of the new regime are advertising pillars.

A frozen waterfall of political rhetoric, iridescent in the colors of the rainbow, hangs over all the walls. The sides of buildings and billboards cry out, exhort, arouse, demand, warn, inform, entreat. Waves of urgent printer's ink strike at pedestrians. "Citizens!" comes the call from the right, "Workers!" from the left, "Soldiers!" from above, "Unemployed!" from below, "Jews!" in between, "Wage Earners!" "Repatriates!" "Women!"

There are posters that are like pasted-up trumpet blasts: short, signaling. Others look like newspaper editorials. There is one, addressed "To Soldiers!" that is an entire book reduced to a single page. Nobody has finished reading it yet. Another poster addresses pillagers in Gothic letters. In a friendly way they are threatened with the death penalty. Announcements all speaking at the same time demand a great deal of the soldiers. They should be loyal and disloyal, they should do this and not that, they should go here and they should go there. The poor fellows are buffeted around by paper on all sides.

The Republic has transformed the street into a vertically spread newspaper. If a person happens to read the Herrengasse, let's say, on a daily basis, he might get his feet cold but at least he knows what's going on.

Wouldn't it be more important for him to know how to satisfy his daily requirement of calories?

But about such questions the posters remain silent, the big as well as the little, the white as well as the ochre, or the red.

Standing in front of them, people make wry faces. In the dull miens of the readers, troubled by hopeless curiosity, you can read hunger, apathy, melancholy, and despair.

They themselves are posters, those who stand before the posters.

They themselves are exhortation, warning, entreaty, death threat, the exhorted, the warned, the beseeched, the death threatened.

"Plakate," 1918. Original text in Alfred Polgar, *Kleine Schriften*, 1:56–58.

1.   A reference to the famous Italian actress of the time, Eleanora Duse.

Theater Evening 1915

It starts at seven-thirty. The yellowish lit clock on the town hall tower, across the street from the theater, seems to float freely in the air, so thickly does the watery haze envelop everything around in grayish colorlessness. The clock face stands high above like a sick moon.

The doorman on the outside staircase doffs his cap to the theatergoers. They pass by him with excessive haste, as if embarrassed at being there. The women wear jewelry—loot, you think to yourself—and in front of the mirror in the cloakroom straighten their hair, hastily daub some powder on their faces, and turn the upper part of their bodies in gentle spirals. They are very pleasant to behold, colorful, giddy, and tasteful, living dummies, graceful things. They can roll their eyes and smile and wag their heads and snuggle gently into narrow shoes and in general look as if they were carrying a splendid musical composition deep inside them. You can sense the workshop—smelling of good soap and mild oil and warm water and the sweet scent of tobacco, sparkling with glass and metallic little objects—from which they have come, the charming playthings. Where are their owners? Perhaps in a foxhole, stinking of sweat and filth, lice in their hair, rain splashing in their faces, their hearts aching with endless longing for what was before.

The orchestra circle sits properly arranged, the first rows of the balconies resemble lines of decapitated heads behind the velvet balustrade. The curtain hangs high in the air while an uncanny bustle unfolds on the stage. There is a cold and foul smell of dust, mustiness, and peeling paint. Everything is strange, ghostly, excessive, trifling, pallid, soundless. A cadaver, all gussied up as life in a mask-rental shop, crouched over for the sake of a friendly impression. The spectators sit tight together in the roomy shelter. They cower behind their interest in the performance as if seeking protection from some distant threatening evil. They stare intently at the stage, but it is as if this happens not on account of the stage, but because they do not want to look each other in the eye. A door onstage slams shut. It sounded like a shot, my dear neighbor! Something cheerful is said. A wave of laughter rolls through the auditorium, breaks against faces, and for a few moments causes them to stiffen in a twisted grimace. On some, the gums are exposed and the eyes become as small as pinholes on a rifle grenade.

An old actor sits in the box. Motionless, he gazes upon the stage with the intense hopelessness of the damned. In this same room there was a time when it was he who strode majestically up and down, his lips that formed these words, his hand that lay upon the back of this chair, against his legs that this sword clanged nobly, his laughter that shone throughout the auditorium. Another had now draped himself in the destiny that belonged to him as if in an abandoned coat. The old actor thinks that the warmth and very smell of his life must still cling to all the folds of this destiny. He stares motionless. A dead man who beholds his own earthly life from above.

A hundred billion miles from him is war.

A light in her right hand, the leading lady enters the dark stage. Carefully, she extends her hand. A soulful hand, rose hued from the candlelight. The delicate outline of the fingers seems traced by a pencil of blood. These hands would also have to be good for closing the eyelids of the dead.

"Comedy," says the playbill. The conversation on stage winds its way in sprightly turns around many things: marriage, love, timidity, money, career, feminine moods, travels, and happiness in life. All behave as if they knew without a doubt that they will still exist tomorrow and next year as well. The bonvivant, whose two squabbling girlfriends are now sitting down breathless, says cheerfully to a man entering: "A skirmish has just taken place here; the wounded are lying over there . . ." That is what he says.

How romantic it all is! And weird! As if the ground were pulled from under the feet of strollers and they continued walking in the air. From outside, the strokes of a tower clock, the clatter of the trolley, the sharp whistle of an ambulance are faintly audible. The people in the theater hear it quite softly and distantly. They sit beneath a globe of thick glass.

The end. The globe rises. On the street, haze and night are interwoven with dirty-yellow points and threads of light.

"M. was delicious!" says a tall, sharp-nosed doll, all wrapped up in brown fur.

"Don't talk now, my child; better hold your handkerchief over your nose. You can catch cold from the least little thing."

"Theaterabend 1915," 1915. Original text in Alfred Polgar, *Kleine Schriften*, 1:3–6. The work was originally titled "Theaterabend 1914."

VIENNA, DECEMBER 1918

A heavy cloud hangs over the city. Sulphurous light, tinged red around the edges, flickers in its grayness.

It is ending the way it had to end.

Or did anybody believe that the filth of the war heaped sky-high would again be carted off calmly and, with due observance of hygienic precautions, be emptied in the sinkhole of oblivion?

Decay and devastation are liquidating the great age. The cheerful wartime legend had it that the slaughtered millions would be overjoyed to be permitted to decay as fertilizer for a better future for those remaining.

But the dead are not so accommodating. The dead are taking revenge.

They are encircling us, besieging us, cutting off our supply of hope.

The living sense the rule of spirits, their guilt-laden hearts turn cold from anxiety and the dawning of a new day. They crouch close together, seek protection in the mutuality of their fear, and crawl beneath the leaky roof of a fatalism discovered in desperation.

This means that the Vienna coffeehouses are fuller than ever before. They were always the center of Viennese life. But now they are the center of the Viennese death agony.

In times like these, the perspiration of one's fellowmen is a nerve-strengthening fluid, and when two or more tremble together, they give off a calming sound.

The newspapers are very courageous. Illumined by the light of new freedom, the eye of public opinion looks bloodshot. The most servile shit-sheets, which for four and a quarter years brought the war to the imperial court and the generals, snap republican-style at their previous masters.

At last, the rabble can deal rabblelike with those who rabbled them in the first place.

Events have even overtaken the equilibrium of the Vienna literati.

Some of them are helping set up red gardens.

Envious impotents say: It's only because they don't want a reputation for being soft that writers are plunging into the clamor of the street.

But Peter Altenberg is something else. Even while the world is going to pieces, he calmly writes his little pieces about ideal skin cream, hotel chambermaids, sleep, and laxatives.

Honest Peter! Wise Peter!

On all sides, the signs and symbols of monarchy and empire are disappearing from the city's picture. The purveyors to the court are pasting plain paper over their once-resplendent gold-lettered titles. And as if shot straight through the heart, bronze, wooden, and plaster [Habsburg] double eagles are falling to the pavement from the facades of buildings, and signboards are being concealed behind cloth hoods. What a mass dying off among the royal fowl, which hold in their claws the curled banners with the inscription "Indivisibiliter ac inseparabiliter" [Indivisibly and Inseparably]!

What counts today: No bird in the hand at all is better than a two-headed eagle on the roof.

In the initial panic that followed the outbreak of the war, all the French texts fell from Vienna's business establishments: the "maisons," "modes et robes," and the like. Then the English ones were scraped off: the "tailors and outfitters," "English spoken," and "English songs." The day also came when the Italian businesses transformed themselves with the utmost speed into "posadas españolas." And finally, a great disappearance of "American bars" and "American shoes" took place. The Stars and Stripes hid behind gray wrapping paper.

The final upshot now is that, wherever possible, the Austrian is being effaced, scraped off, or pasted over.

That is how we have become cosmopolitan on the road to negation.

In the first days of the new German-Austria,[1] there was expectedly a tremendous ballyhoo about cockades. Excited civilians demanded of soldiers and officers that they remove the cockades with the imperial initials from their caps.

The military obliged them. The higher-ups also. Even the highest. And this was certainly the most sensible thing for them to do.

But just recall how firmly and uncompromisingly these reasonable and conciliatory generals used to see to it that the others kept the unconditional oath "Loyal to the death," on land, on sea, and in the air, how conscientiously and generously they had jailed, hanged, and shot any wavering of that loyalty, how strongly and gallantly they made a point of the obligatory heroism of their subordinates.

No Austrian general suffered a hero's death on the Ringstrasse.

But, as people said: Down with the cockade!

> First he grabbed for his cockade,
> And then for his own head.

For the cockade, in order to take it off. For the head, in order to keep it on.

"Wien, Dezember 1918," 1919. Original text in Alfred Polgar, *Kleine Schriften*, 1:68–71.

1.   The official name of the new Austrian state that emerged after the dissolution of the Habsburg Empire.

In the Telephone Booth

A little old lady was lying on her back in the street. A completely shriveled prune from the tree of life. It seems as if she were laid there, not fallen. The street cleaner sweeping the dirt into the gutter pays no attention to her. We pick her up. "Wasted away from hunger!" she says. I give her half of what I have on me at the risk of being taken for a panderer.

She is surely a crook and this is a gimmick of hers: laying herself down on the pavement and startling passersby. The street cleaner obviously knows the gimmick, otherwise he wouldn't go about shoving the tenacious grime into the gutter so imperturbably. But I think whoever lies down in street filth in broad daylight just for the sake of a few groschen earned them. He accomplished something. Nobody lies down on dripping cold pavement out of a liking for it. The old woman, too, would prefer to write about fashions or dance Chopin.

But that she can't do. So she does what she can. Has an inspiration, carries it out. Lies down in the filthy street and gets paid for it.

The knitter Josefine Strasser had no inspiration. Only the miserable idea of saying "Thank y'kindly, m'lord," "Thank y'kindly, m'lady" to the philistines. That way she whined a few groschen together. However, she doesn't use them for the acquisition of a good book or for a subscription to some populist newspaper, but to buy booze. This way, her view of life becomes tipsy. Or, as stated in the police report: "She sank lower and lower until she reached homelessness."

The February night from Saturday to Sunday was very cold. Josefine Strasser kept on saying: "Thank y'kindly, m'lord," "Thank y'kindly, m'lady." But among the thoroughly democratic fellow citizens it availed nothing in the severe cold. Only one person, a nihilist, was flattered into giving her a twenty-groschen piece.

The woman took the money and entered a telephone booth. She deposited the coin in the mystical aperture, it came to a stop, and the apparatus, which was damaged, began to function.

Josefine Strasser wanted to be connected with the State, which could not conceivably allow a human being to freeze and starve in the city of culture.

The State was not to be found in the telephone book, nor did Information know of its existence. Instead, the Public Office answered, a wrong number as so often the case. Is it something important? The Patent Act? The Supplementary Tax Evasion Act? The accountability of officials? Or even the elections?

At this point the connection was broken.

Josefine Strasser was confused, since she had no more money for telephone calls. But is the telephone the essence of a telephone booth?

No. The essence is the four walls. The closeness. The peace in noise. The designated demarcation from darkness and cold. The illusion of a small room.

And lovingly embraced by this illusion, the old woman dozed off. She dreamed that she was seeking a telephone connection with life, which her beggar's gestures could no longer reach. A connection with kindliness, whose line was always busy. With reason, which was deaf. With wealth, which lay snoring in bed. With the company "All Men Are Brothers." But there the receiver was completely broken.

In the end, she made up her mind to call merciful God.

She got this connection.

Now, were I a poet, you would have "Josefine Strasser's Ascension" placed before you.

But all I can say is: On Sunday morning she was found frozen to death. A bill sticker of election posters discovered the small stiff heap of rubbish.

He covered it compassionately with the largest sheet of paper he had: "Vote civic-democratic!"

"In der Telephonzelle," 1919. Original text in Alfred Polgar, *Kleine Schriften*, 1:281–84.

BEETHOVEN MASKS

Beethoven is a popular wall decoration. Like porcelain plates, antlers, and hangings with embroidered sayings. He is an international requisite for brightening up a room and goes with any philosophy nailed to the wall. With Lueger and Marx, with the nutcracker face of the general, with the high forehead of the venerable Rabbi Moses ben Maimon, and with the mournful-militant Polish-style moustache of the transvaluation of all values.

He hangs best of all, of course, above the piano. But he also doesn't do badly at the head of the bed, and he even lends a spiritual quality to the space above the anteroom cupboard on which stands the samovar.

The wise housewife prefers a larger-format Beethoven to conceal damages to a wall. For example, the well-known painting that shows the master seated at the piano surrounded by his enraptured audience. One of them in particular—arms folded about drawn-up legs, head resting on a knee—listens expressly with his soul. This picture is also popular: the head of Beethoven, in whose forest of hair a naked pair of lovers has nestled.

But more popular for purposes of wall decoration than all pictures— even the one where the democrat Beethoven keeps the courtier Goethe just standing in Karlsbad, or the one where he's dashing about Döbling with flying coattails while the *Eroica* quite plainly comes to mind—is the Beethoven mask, the plaster copy of the countenance as it was modeled in the year 1812 by the sculptor Franz Klein. (People speak erroneously of a death mask.)

Above how many hundreds of thousands of pianos from one end of the globe to another broods this mask, abandoned to the *Sonate Pathétique* (don't be sloppy, Melanie!) and the four-handed onslaught that makes symphonies groan and overtures tremble. The most extraordinary countenance that God's pencil ever drew—surrendered to housewives and popularity!

There isn't a dramatist whose scenario fails to demand the Beethoven mask over the piano. The fearful face menaces on the coats of arms of concert agencies, as an emblem of musical instrument dealers, stamped on leather music-cases, cut into wooden music-stands, on the bookplates of operetta texts, as the trademark for rosin, piano candlesticks, ear trumpets, bird whistles, and player pianos.

What about a Beethoven-mask-ball for the celebration of the hundred-and-fiftieth anniversary of the day on which the master first saw the darkness of the world?

Art is grave, life gay.

Gayer yet after death—immortality.

"Beethoven-Maske," 1921. Original text in Alfred Polgar, *Kleine Schriften*, 1:304–5.

LOOKING DOWN ON THE ORCHESTRA

A famous man is sitting on the conductor's stool. One day he will be dead and then the people who are seeing him conduct *Carmen* today will remember that they saw him conduct *Carmen*. I imagine the scene as if it were already fifty years later. The power of remembrance evokes this evening. I experience it in colors and sounds, as if I experienced it just now. Kill the moment and then recall it to life. Then, however it may be otherwise, it is marvellous at least through the marvel of resurrection. Dream your life!

I thus recall quite precisely that many years ago, in March 1926, I was listening to *Carmen* in one of the front boxes of the Opera. The waiter said, "Your servant," but he really didn't say it to me but to the box he was serving and to whose chance constituency I belonged that evening. He had snow-white hair and red, good-natured drinker's eyes. Today, I'm sure, daisies are blooming from them.

In the next box sat a beautiful, quite luminous woman. A silly enraptured expression on her face, she was eating plums with sugared nut kernels. Perhaps she's already dead, or has a paunch, or is grazing, sensibly reincarnated as a white she-ass.

I can still remember the orchestra quite clearly. I still see all of them, their faces and their movements, the reflexes perched on the brass instruments, the brown of the humming violin bodies, and the mammoth beetles called double basses. I see the spider step of the violinists' fingers, the unusual snatching gestures with which the harpist plucked tones from his instrument, and the fine whir of the bows. They were like long needles sewing music.

The first violinist had a thick moustache in a moon-shaped face. And just when he was coaxing something sweet from the instrument, he had to yawn. His soul was occupied in the wrist; the abandoned remainder was bored. It was offensive. Had the conductor's baton been just long enough to tickle his throat! A writing pad, if you please! I should note down that a person can create fervor and at the same time yawn.

Among the violinists there was one who wanted to tame a recalcitrant sheet of music with the neck of his violin without interrupting his playing. As often as he tried to hold it fast, the sheet jumped right up again. Finally, he had a pause and his hands free. But he disdained their help, and waged further combat against the unruly paper with the neck of the violin. This way or not at all! An obstinate character!

The trumpeters turned their trumpets over every time they took a breath in order for the spittle to flow out. By the second act it must have looked beneath their stands like the floor of the Café Central at midnight. Horn players secrete a lot of fluid.

The three older gentlemen who played the trombones—that that should be a hobby for angels!—were reading newspapers. In the meantime, their instruments hung silently on the side pegs of their stands. When the time came for them to play again—they felt with certainty the moment approaching—they fumbled for their trombones without taking their eyes from the newspapers. The first note on the sheet of music to be played again was grasped with the left eye while the right one was still fastened on the evening paper.

The horn slept whenever it had a break and always switched off beforehand the electric lightbulb over the music stand. A good, thrifty family man.

The double-bass players, at equal distance from each other, were at a loss as to what to do with their breaks. In motion, they presented an indescribably synchronized spectacle, as if somebody pulled on a little rope, whereupon eight elbows rode out at the same instant and eight left hands, one after the other, as if for the millionth time, glided downwards for long stretches. If one shut his ears for the sake of variety or out of sheer playfulness and observed them that way, they were the gang from Tartarus, chained to the wall, sentenced for some earthly wickedness to the punishment of sawing.

Viewed from above, the members of the orchestra gave the impression of mechanisms set in motion. They did what they were supposed to do, perhaps contrary to or at least without their will, but as if they indeed wanted to. They were a good replica of human activity. They inflated their cheeks and rested and sawed away and put a smile on the bad face of necessity and played movingly and were bored all the while and thought of the end and drummed with their fingers and slept and were soloists and yet dependent on one another and read the evening paper and served a higher will. Yesterday it was a different one than today and today a different one than tomorrow, but yesterday, today, and tomorrow with the same yawning fervor and the same partly externally, partly internally recompensed striving for perfection.

The flute sang a splendid passage. Then wiped its nose with a red-dotted handkerchief. I can't say why that was touching, but it was touching. I could have called down in the cadences of the newer drama: O Man! O Brothers!

My neighbor in the box shut his eyes. "I want the music," he said, "not the musicians."

He was a brute, a bourgeois, a cowardly epicure, a false signpost of life, a capitalist and box season-ticket holder. He narrowed his pupils when he wanted to believe and love.

By now I'm sure he's dead and the pasqueflower blossoms from his eyes.

"Orchester von oben," 1921. Original text in Alfred Polgar, *Kleine Schriften*, 2:90–93. The date 1926 in the sketch itself may warrant an explanation. The piece was originally published in the *Prager Tagblatt* in 1921, included in Polgar's collection *Gestern und heute* (1922), and subsequently in the collection *Orchester von oben* (1926). The text in *Kleine Schriften* is drawn from this last collection, in which the sketch carries the date 1926.

GOOD EATING

In wine there is truth, in good eating love. The besotted says what's in his heart; the besated suddenly has a heart he didn't have before. Forbearance, joy of understanding, the desire for fairness, overcome him. Bridges of feeling stretch near and far, a rose-colored haze shortens distances and conceals abysses, and man is good. His tongue transposes the ingested calories into chatter, unlike the tongue of the inebriated, which empties out the contents of the full shell of consciousness and brings to the surface what lay on the bottom.

The laws governing the spiritual effect of good eating, which go hand in hand (or better said: soul in stomach) with the physical, are enigmatic and inscrutable. Nevertheless, there are some recurrent basic types.

A schnitzel with cucumber salad, for example, promotes the development of a kind of personality adhesive that binds the table guests into a symbiotic unity. Each eater senses this unity so strongly that he experiences a need to rescue it from the fleeting dining hours. Such an individual is afflicted with love of mankind as soon as the soup is put before him. By the time the roast is served, he's already invited all those present to his table. By cheese time, the most inviolable arrangements for spending holidays together have been settled. And when black coffee is being drunk, the holidays have become the rest of life.

The opposite of this type is also familiar: the pessimistic glutton. His sullen and bitter disposition springs from moral overcompensation for physical well-being. This type senses that his pleasure in eating offends morality and by way of compensation generates distress. He is ashamed of his fondness for food and is inclined to make a point of disliking what he likes. If you ask him, "Do you prefer a compote or salad?" he replies biliously, "The matter is already resolved in the *Communist Manifesto,*" and takes both.

Quite noteworthy is another typical reaction to good eating. In this case, the eater, unexpectedly and without becoming nettled, takes a position with respect to the most varied questions toward which he indeed has no position. All of a sudden, without a train of association leading him there, he says something like: "Fräulein X has the loveliest soprano of all concert singers." It is not at all true that Fräulein X has the loveliest soprano, but it is also a matter of absolutely no consequence. The man might just as well have said: "She has the world's worst soprano" or "She has the finest bass." That is because he is less interested in expressing an opinion than in *mouthing something intellectual.* This way he produces the sounds of speech.

Originally, I regarded such pleasure in opinions without opinion, viewpoints without viewpoint, as a degeneration into the pantheistic of the heightened sense of self brought on by good eating, as a variant of "Be embraced, millions,"[1] as a consequence of an enhanced vitality wanting freely to expend its surplus. But then it dawned on me that the wonderful phenomenon has a basically simple psychophysiological explanation: a plain *belching of the brain.* The hodgepodge floating around inside is thrust upwards and outwards by blood pressure elevated by meat and sweets. At this moment, the speaker has obvious feelings of pleasure such as are afforded coarser natures, after good eating, through the usual heartburn, the familiar *singultus communis* in Latin.

"Das gute Essen," 1923. Original text in Alfred Polgar, *Kleine Schriften*, 2:166–68.

    1.   "Seid umschlungen Millionen!" The first line of the first chorus of Friedrich Schiller's famous poem "An die Freude" ("Ode to Joy," 1786). Beethoven incorporated it into his *Ninth Symphony* and composed the melody for it that has become universally known.

THEORY OF THE CAFÉ CENTRAL

The Café Central is indeed a coffeehouse unlike any other coffeehouse. It is instead a worldview and one, to be sure, whose innermost essence is not to observe the world at all. Then what do you see? About that, later. So much is experientially certain, that there is nobody in the Café Central who isn't a piece of the Central: that is to say, on whose ego-spectrum the Central color, a mixture of ash-gray and ultra-seasick-green, doesn't appear. Whether the place adapted to the individual, or the individual to the place, is a moot point. I would imagine a reciprocal action. "Thou art not in the place, the place is in thee," says the Angelic Pilgrim.[1]

If all the anecdotes related about this coffeehouse were ground up, put in a distillation chamber and gassified, a heavy, iridescent gas, faintly smelling of ammonia, would develop: the so-called air of the Café Central. This defines the spiritual climate of this space, a quite special climate in which unfitness for life, and only this one, thrives in full maintenance of its unfitness. Here weakness develops those powers unique to itself, the fruits of unfruitfulness ripen, and every non-ownership bears interest. Only a real Central-ist will grasp it entirely, one who, when his coffeehouse is shut, has the feeling that he's been thrown out into raw life, abandoned to the unpredictable circumstances, anomalies, and cruelties of the unknown.

The Café Central lies on the Viennese latitude at the meridian of loneliness. Its inhabitants are, for the most part, people whose hatred of their fellow human beings is as fierce as their longing for people, who want to be alone but need companionship for it. Their inner world requires a layer of the outer world as delimiting material; their quivering solo voices cannot do without the support of the chorus. They are unclear natures, rather lost without the certainties which the feeling gives that they are a little part of a whole (to whose tone and color they contribute).

The Central-ist is a person to whom family, profession, and political party do *not* give this feeling. Helpfully, the coffeehouse steps in as an ersatz totality, inviting immersion and dissolution. It is thus understandable that above all women, who can really never be alone and need at least one other person along with them, have a weakness for the Café Central. It is a place for people who know how to abandon and be abandoned for the sake of their fate, but who do not have the nerve to live up to this fate. It is a true asylum for people who have to kill time so as not to be killed by it. It is the beloved hearth of those to whom the beloved hearth is an abomination, the refuge of married couples and lovers from the fear of undisturbed togetherness, a first-aid station for the confused who, all their lives in search of themselves and all their lives in flight from themselves, conceal their fleeing ego behind a newspaper, dreary conversations, and card playing, and press the pursuer-ego into the role of kibitzer who has to keep his mouth shut.

The Café Central thus represents something of an organization of the disorganized.

In this hallowed space, each halfway indeterminate individual is credited with a personality. So long as he remains within the boundaries of the coffeehouse, he can cover all his moral expenses with this credit. And any one of them who shows disdain for others' money is granted the anti-bourgeois crown.

The Central-ist lives parasitically on the anecdote that circulates about him. That is the main thing, the essential thing. Everything else, the facts of his existence, is in small print, addenda and embellishments that can also be omitted.

The guests of the Café Central know, love, and disdain one another. Even those who are bound by no association regard this nonassociation as association. Mutual aversion itself has the power of association in the Café Central; it honors and practices a Freemason-like solidarity. Everybody knows about everybody else. The Café is a provincial nest in the womb of the metropolis, steaming of gossip, envy, and backbiting. I think the fish in the aquarium must live like the habitués of this coffeehouse, always in the narrowest circles around one another, always busy without purpose, using the slanting refraction of light of their environment for diverse amusement, always full of expectation, but also full of anxiety lest sometime something new, playing "Sea" with a stern look, fall into the glass tank, onto their artificial miniature sea-bottom. And if, God forbid, the aquarium should turn into a banking house, they would be utterly lost.

Naturally, the Central-fish, which share the same few cubic meters of breathing space for so many hours of their lives, no longer have any timidity or reticence. The proper Central-ist leads the private life of others and doesn't play the fence with his own. Supported by the customary inclination of the place to self-mockery and to calm surrender of one's own weaknesses, this creates a sphere of suspended sociability in which any kind of prudery withers and dies off. There are Central guests who go about psychically naked, without having to fear that their childlike-innocent nakedness be misinterpreted as shameless. Several years ago, the owner of the Café tried to accommodate this paradisiacal strain in the character of his regular guests by putting in a palm tree. But the young lady from the Orient did not endure the climate of the locale, despite its rather eastern character. She was hacked into small pieces, and her divided substance found use in the kitchen—either as fuel or as coffee beans—the researchers are not of one mind on the matter.

The only person who partakes of the most essential charm of this splendid coffeehouse is he who wants nothing there but to be there. Purposelessness sanctifies the stay. Perhaps the guest doesn't really like the place or the people who noisily populate it, but his nervous system imperiously demands the daily dose of Centralin. This can hardly be explained by habit alone. Nor by the fact that the Central-people are always attracted, like the murderer to the scene of the crime, to where they already killed so much time, wiped out entire years. Then what is the explanation? The atmosphere! I can only say: the atmosphere! There are writers, for example, who are unable to carry out their literary chores anywhere but at the Café Central. Only there, only at the tables of idleness, is the worktable laid for them, only there, enveloped by the air of indolence, will their inertia become fecundity. There are creative types to whom only in the Central does nothing come to mind, indeed elsewhere far less. There are poets and other industrialists to whom profitable thoughts come only in the Café Central; constipated people to whom only there does the door of relief open; those who long ago lost their appetite for the erotic who only there experience hunger; the silent who only in the Central find their own or somebody else's tongue; and the greedy whose money gland secretes only there.

This enigmatic coffeehouse soothes in the peaceless people who visit it something that I like to call cosmic uneasiness. In this place of loose relationships, the relationship to God and the stars also loosens. The creature escapes from its compulsory relations to the universe into an irresponsible, sensuous, chance relationship to nothingness. The intimidations of eternity do not penetrate the walls of the Café Central, and between them you enjoy the sweet unconcern of the moment.

On the love life of the Café Central, on the balance of social distinctions in it, on the literary and political currents by which its frayed shores are washed, on those buried alive in the Central-cavern longingly awaiting their excavation yet hoping that it will not occur, on the masked play of wit and foolishness that in those rooms turns every night into Mardi Gras, on these and other things there is still much to say. But whoever is interested in the Café Central knows all this anyway, and whoever isn't interested in the Café Central we have no interest in.

It is a coffeehouse, take it as it is! Never will you ever come upon such a place again. What Knut Hamsun says about the city of Christiania in the first sentence of his immortal *Hunger* applies to it as well: "No one leaves her whom she did not mark."

"Theorie des 'Café Central,'" 1926. Original text in Alfred Polgar, *Kleine Schriften*, 4:254–59.
    1.   A reference to the seventeenth-century German mystic writer Johann Schefler (1624–77), best known under his pseudonym, Angelus Silesius (the Angel of Silesia). His major work was *Das Cherubinische Wandersmann* (*The Angelic Pilgrim*), essentially a collection of moral apothegms.

Girls

"Girls" refers to groups of younger women who are prepared, quite undressed, to make precisely coordinated movements on a stage. The purpose of their appearance and activity is to arouse the spectators erotically and thereby console them for what otherwise transpires on the stage. Programs that are held together by such an elastic, flesh-colored ribbon, which should be as long as possible, are called revues and serve the additional purpose, herein supported by the performances of the theater, to wean people away from it.

"Girls" are a so-called "plurale tantum." That is, the concept occurs linguistically only in the plural. There is no such thing as *a* "girl" any more than there is, for example, *a* salt. At least with respect to the stage, one cannot speak of a "girl" (while, on the contrary, one can do that easily with respect to a director). "Girl" placed next to "girl" like entries in a ledger doesn't make "girls" by any stretch of the imagination. That can be accomplished only by the final addition, the amalgamation of the individuals into the collective. Several, let's say some twelve female beings, on two legs each, still don't yield "girls." Only when they have become *one* being with twenty-four legs can the name properly be applied to them.

The special appeal of "girls" lies in the fact that they constitute a collective. The womanly thus appears purified of the human, "refined" in the chemical sense of the term. Herein lies the wish fulfillment of the man who dreams of many women in one, at least in his mind's eye. Twenty-four legs (and everything that goes along with them), and yet just *one* being—that satisfies the erotic fantasy without overburdening perhaps the heart or brain involved.

A "girl"-less revue, hence a vegetarian revue, has absolutely no nutritional value. For the spectator as much as for the entrepreneur.

There is yet another attraction besides the erotic operative in the spectacle and performance of the "girls": the attraction of militarism. The thorough drilling, synchronization, rhythms, the clapping of exercises and movements, the obedience to an invisible but inescapable command, the pretty "training," the submerging of the individual in the multitude, the uniting of bodies into a single "body"—all this holds for the spectator the same appeal that makes military maneuvers so appealing to him, of course only as a spectator. Father Tiller, the head of the famous Tiller-Girls, also has a proper military organization for his troop. His companies or platoons do combat in all the larger revue theaters of operations. When there are retirements, he supplies his organization with manpower—that is to say, womanpower—from his large reserve cadre back home in America and assures for its replenishment the flower of the nation.

I really don't understand why women go to a revue theater. No ensemble of naked boys affords them stimulation the way the "girls" do us. In the revues, the primacy of the male remains unshaken. For the ladies, nothing at all happens.

"Girls" appear in many disguises. As bridge cards, gems, flowers, cigars, liquors, newspapers, butterflies, mailmen, soldiers, toys, folk songs, vegetables, and so on. One couldn't easily think of men as vegetables or gems. Clearly, the female of the species is better suited to represent *a thing* than the male. But the most important of all, even with respect to the liquors, butterflies, and cigars, are the legs, that truly vital organ of "girls," the many-limbed, delicate-jointed mobile transmitter that sends stimulating waves into the auditorium. All the more astonishing that "girls" think nothing of leaving it defenseless, without the dainty sheath of stockings.

The reason for this is that in the revue-religion nudity and sensuous appeal are closely related concepts. If I apply one, the other will be achieved, think the "girl"-industrialists. So nudity prevails—that's always taken for granted. The nudity of the pretty, young body. The more it strikes the eye as surprise, as apparent gift of chance, as booty, the stronger the sensuous appeal. And the appeal lessens the more it loses the character of a delicacy (understood in the double sense of the word) and comes to the table of the stage as the optical main dish, as a meat dish, in a manner of speaking. A good revue-cook won't make it too comfortable for the spectator in this regard.

Undress is certainly the point of all dress. The figure play of the curves, the cylindrical and conical sections of a well-formed feminine leg is an enchanting stereometric pleasure. Lovely nakedness is more aesthetic than the loveliest clothing. That is why people say, when wanting to compliment somebody's skin, that it is like silk, but nobody ever thought of praising silk by saying that it is like skin.

The ghostly thing about "girls" is that they also have faces. The human countenance as a bonus, as a truly senseless annex of breasts, belly, and legs . . . that's a bit weird. That's why clever "girls" also smile without letup in order to intimate, while soothing the sentimental spectator, that their physiognomies don't grieve over the minor part they have been assigned.

"Girls," 1926. Original text in Alfred Polgar, *Kleine Schriften*, 2:247–50. The terms "girls" and "girl" appear in English in the original and were used in the German of Polgar's time to refer to variety theater dancers and strippers. To avoid confusion, I set "girls" and "girl" in quotation marks throughout the translation.

RIGOLETTO

A provincial theater is performing *Rigoletto* with a guest artist from the big city.

In the stalls sit thirty people, in the gallery a fireman and a woman with a knitting sock, and in the boxes nobody. The vacantness has a positive effect on these people. They are similarly full of emptiness. Each box contains four little red seats and a mirror, which is already half blind, since so little is reflected in it. Above the boxes, in high relief, the busts of writers and composers have been mounted. They have black noses, since it is above all on them—as they protrude the farthest from the relief—that dust and dirt collect.

From the foyer alcove of the theater a wide square can be seen. Empty of people. A figure on a fountain, Cupid with bow, invites lovers to a tryst. Nobody is waiting near Cupid. Just evening, as it does every day, waiting for night.

The usher says that the city is so quiet only now, in these dubious late-fall days which cannot make up their mind between cold and warm, wet and dry, gray and blue. The usher talks about cramped rooms, beer, and local politics. He doesn't really dislike strangers, but he doesn't miss them, either, when they're absent. During the day he helps out in the dairy, and the woman in the gallery is his conjugal property.

Rigoletto calls with quivering voice: "The old man cursed me!" Then he betakes himself to his daughter, Gilda, in order to sing a trio with her and her nurse. But the latter has no real desire to, so it becomes just a duet. At C-sharp the two singers have a rendezvous with the orchestra, but in the darkness they head for C. Then masked courtiers appear who, rejecting the calls of the prompter with annoyed mezza voce, abduct the poor Gilda.

During the intermission the usher awakened his wife, she left, and then the gallery belonged to the fireman alone. But it didn't get him anywhere.

The third act shows Rigoletto rushing up to the pitiless courtiers. They elbow him aside and then, disclaiming the right belonging to them, to sing, hasten offstage. In the fourth act, Gilda peers through a window, as if beholding the Duke in flagranti. But he wasn't sitting in the room at all but rather up front next to the prompter's cage and was flirting with a voluptuous woman in peasant dress, Sparafuciles's sister. Then Gilda knocked on the door, but it didn't open although it was strongly shaken from within. So she sneaked secretly into the house. Donna è mobile.

The whole thing was ludicrous and yet oppressive. The muffled city, the empty theater, the gray autumn, the poor Rigoletto! How was he to find his child again? Dead, wrapped in a sack and thrown to the tiny orchestra, in the little city, in view of thirty visitors and one fireman. What lamented more woefully, his broken heart or his broken career? A blossoming daughter and a blossoming voice, respectively, were once his . . . but now both are gone. Gilda, oh Gilda! At one and the same time you die unto me before twenty-four first violins and eight double basses! Horrible Sparafucile, would that your murderer's knife instead struck *my* throat, since it's already having trouble with the middle notes. Ah, banished to the wretchedness of the province, to the province of wretchedness!

There was also a storm onstage while outside a light, sullen rain sprinkled lonely pavement, a real provincial rain for cities of under twenty thousand inhabitants. In the boxes, the emptiness was afraid of itself. How, my God, does this unfortunate theater manage? Rigoletto, poor fool, do you at least have your honorarium in a sack like your daughter, or do you have to fret about this as well?

He was sitting in the pleasant hotel parlor, a still-young man with old features, drinking Salvator beer, which is dark and frothy like a person's life, and was doing crossword puzzles in the newspaper. An old man at the next table was waiting for the paper and, since he wasn't getting it, left grumbling.

"The old man cursed me!" said Rigoletto sadly to the waiter.

"Rigoletto," 1926. Original text in Alfred Polgar, *Kleine Schriften*, 2:244–47.

INTERVIEW

The prominent Austrian novelist Robert Musil was asked by the journal *Die literarische Welt* (*The Literary World*) to write a piece on Polgar based on an interview. This "Interview mit Alfred Polgar" ("Interview with Alfred Polgar") appeared in the journal on 5 March 1926. The two writers were not close. Musil recalls his first fleeting meeting with Polgar, of whom he saw little thereafter until his interview, and then proceeds to discuss him as a writer. He makes a strong point of Polgar's "outsidedness" and his self-imposed alienation from the Viennese literary life of the time with its preoccupation with success and its narrow-mindedness. As to Polgar's attitude toward reality, Musil observed that he "lets things follow their own course; he just watches them and describes them." Polgar's kind of literary impressionism is nothing "weak, but rather an abandonment to impressions. There is a system to his impressions. He lets things pass him, then deals them a blow from behind so that they fall apart like disassembled toys."[1] Polgar's own "Interview" arose as a response of sorts to the Musil piece.

───────────────────

I have been interviewed, for the first time in my life, and in a startling way. The person whom the rare whim befell to look me over a little and to use me as a guide to myself is a higher intellectual power than I am. This complicates the matter.

I was made to appear like a fraudulent cashier whose accounts are being checked. "What are your true beliefs? Show us your philosophical cash balances! Let's see your Goethe-account current! Shouldn't there also be the interest from contact with important contemporaries? And the spiritual revenue from antiquity, what about that, eh?"

He posed very precise questions. And me surrounded by disorder, confusion, and absolute mess! I couldn't help blushing in his presence.

The psychic position in which such an interview puts a person is analogous to the physical one that occurs when somebody is artificially stimulated to vomit.

Ah, everybody is a stranger to himself! I discovered that, to my dismay, during the unexpected examination. It seems that I know absolutely nothing about myself, other than the little bit perhaps that reached my ears by way of gossip. But is that anything to set store by? Compelled to make a stroller the guide through my landscape, I realize, to my consternation, that I am totally at a loss, that I am unable to give the smallest clear piece of information about the location, origin, or history of the places I've been, I see just fog and nowhere a distinct outline before the fog. Everything rushes by and becomes blurred.

I lived peacefully and contentedly until the interviewer came along. His questions brought to light my dreadful innocence with respect to myself. And just as Meyrink's millipede couldn't move from the spot once he became conscious of the fact that he had a thousand feet,[2] so did I lose all inner balance when I became conscious of the thousand certainties that I do not have. Thrown into one's own abyss. Or: astray in oneself. Or: the terrible awakening of a daytime sleepwalker.

Perhaps things might have been different had I prepared myself in advance. But the interview came as suddenly as an earthquake, disclosing the looseness of the foundation, the shallow plaster, the casualness and fragility of my spiritual house. No wall to lean against, no piece of ground to provide some firm support!

"The principles on which your outlook on life is based, please." I had a vague sense that I might have had something of the sort at one time, but where was I to look for them now in such a hurry? (And generally such a dredged-up philosophy of life is as good as none at all.) "Frau Nowak, do you happen to know . . . ?" The straightforward housekeeper, who usually keeps my inventory in perfect order, could only whisk the duster helplessly.

If he had but wanted to ask me something to which I would have had sure answers drawn from long experience and probing reflection! For example, if I suffer from heartburn. Or from psychoanalysis. Or if I believe that people should be monogamous. But even if reluctant to poke into every nook and cranny, he still didn't address a single question to such issues about which I, the person best informed, have to be as clear as daylight. And I couldn't answer in the style of little Ploetz: "Present German drama I regard as distinct for the present, but man is not monogamous."[3]

Or: "The influence of reading matter on the individual depends on both of them, but unfortunately the writer has a pencil."

I am against interviews. They plunge the soul into a bottomless deficit, over which it had until then floated lightheartedly, and they rob it of all commercial impartiality. You feel as if you had been taken apart and are no longer capable of being put back together again, opened up, disposed of.

And you are so annoyed that you could spit right in the mirror.

"Interview," 1926. Original text in Alfred Polgar, *Kleine Schriften*, 3:367–69.

    1.   Robert Musil, "Interview mit Alfred Polgar," in Robert Musil, *Gesammelte Werke. Essays und Reden. Kritik*, ed. Adolf Frisé (Reinbek: Rowohlt, 1983), 2:1154–60.

    2.   Gustav Meyrink (1868–1932), a once popular Austrian writer best known in the English-speaking world for his novel *Der Golem* (*The Golem*, 1915; English translation, 1928). Meyrink also enjoyed a certain reputation for his fantastic tales and horror stories.

    3.   Although Polgar's text has "Ploetz" here, I believe that the reference is to the journalist and critic Eduard Pötzl (1851–1914), who was known as "Kleinpetz" (little sneak). Pötzl wrote principally for the *Neues Wiener Tagblatt*, where he also served as the feuilleton editor. From 1905 to 1908, he was vice president of the journalists' and writers' organization known as Concordia. A well-known and popular feuilletonist with a firm grasp of Vienna speech, he was also conservative in his views and hostile to the art of the Vienna Secession.

I Can't Read Novels

There are many people on the planet earth—may they all be well and live to a hundred! In China alone there are half a billion, while that cramped and crappy room in Vienna's 18th district where my shoemaker Potzner lives with his family houses six persons. The world is definitely too small. Although the broadminded writer says "The earth has room for all," just to prove the opposite, people quite recently fell upon each other angrily (don't you remember?), and around ten million of them emigrated forever beneath the earth, since there wasn't any more space for them on the surface. Are things easier now? *Au contraire.* In China, there's such terrible crowding people are stepping all over each other, and the shoemaker Potzner had another kid; now there are seven of them in that cramped apartment.

All these people, who together constitute a "frightful mass," want bread, air, and space. How you satisfy them is a problem that troubles the finest minds and makes them want to bang their heads against the wall. Communism purports to have a solution. But though its theory is quite irresistible and its practice no less seductive, I am very fearful of it. Not because it wants to take away my lands, my factories, and my palaces—it can have them all, along with my bank account, as earnest-money—but because it so mercilessly diminishes the possibilities of solitariness. It forces the individual into the mass; opened wide like Moloch's, the jaws of the collective beckon. I can't understand people's skin not crawling at the very idea of being together in heaps as living creatures, pursuing their work or their pleasures like so many clods, crawling on and over one another like lobsters in a cooking pot. The thought of being buried in a mass grave, in such too close contact with others, just has to be terrifying.

But this is leading away from the path and purpose of this meditation. What I really wanted to say is that a person—I myself, for example—though it's often not one's fault, knows a distressingly large number of people. While you're alive, acquaintanceship sets in like tartar in the teeth, and the drawers of your consciousness fill up with affairs of your fellowmen like those of your table with piles of letters. You ought to be able to clean out one just as easily as the other. But life keeps trickling along, and before you know it you're all bogged down in nays. You get caught up in a thousand destinies through curiosity, sentiment, and compulsion, a thousand winds huff and puff at your sails, ever more frightful becomes the inescapable vision of figures, faces, and voices that drives you offstage from the wings.

And a person should read novels?

In view of this overpopulation of consciousness, to admit more people who don't even exist and never did? To load to the breaking point the professed interest in life, in its figures and fates, with yet fictitious life, invented characters, contrived destinies? In view of this terrifying inflation of countenances that existence inevitably brings in its train, should I still introduce countenances from the fantasy-mint of the novel writer into my creative currency? Should I build up or cut down? Should I yet set in motion my sympathy, which falls in a faint before the apartment of the shoemaker Potzner, through the imagined sufferings of imagined earthlings whom a gentleman at a writing table sucked out of his inky finger? Should I add to the unsolvable problems already posed by the character of my housekeeper some others that the imagination of a novel writer has grafted onto the characters born of it? To be a novel reader means stuffing paper life into the hideously overstuffed real one, grafting the world of make-believe onto a real world already swollen to the bursting point, offering fake nourishment from the store of the falsifiers to an imagination already magnificently provided for by a god. Should I, who never makes any visits, let myself be dragged through huts and palaces, to gape at pots and beds and peer into brains just to see how things are simmering elsewhere when the steam of my own small life stupefies me, to whom cosmic mist appears boundless and impenetrable? Should I, who does not have sufficient tears to settle with my own dead—to say nothing of my own survivors—sob on graves that a pen has dug out of paper and in which nobody is lying? How can people read only novels? It's like carrying water to the sea, sand to the desert, tradition to the Burgtheater, more residents to Potzner's habitation, wind to Vienna, wit to Prague, owls to ruined castles, Greeks to Athens, boredom to literary magazines, goose breasts to Pomerania,[1] geniuses to Schwanneke's wine tavern.[2]

This is not to mention how time-consuming novels are, how full they are of tiresome description, of "in the next room" and "all around" and "meanwhile," of furnishings, landscape, clothing, implements, hairdos, plays of eyes and expressions, atmospheric conditions, and formalities; how they are laid out, how diffuse and viscous, in short: how epic.

What I like to read, on the other hand, are grammars. Of any language. There is something wonderfully fresh, firm, and durable about grammars. They relate to literature like a skeleton to the soft parts of the body. They whisk the soul away to the pure sphere of the liberated, their meaning entirely contained in their form. "Quoique nous ne nous en souvinssions pas" [Although we might not remember it] . . . "Quoique vous ne vous en souvinssiez pas" [Although you might not remember it] . . . refreshes rather like spirits. Here, in grammar, lies disassembled the basic frame of all imaginable structures of thought, with grooves, clamps, cross beams, and bolts. Everything can develop from it. There is no more modern book than a grammar. It is all expression, full of mystery and yet transparent like the air on an early spring morning. It reaches down into the earth; everything for feeling, for saying is planted in it. And like life itself, it has laws that you can never learn completely. It is always new, at least when, like me, you don't study it but just read it. If I am behind, having just come to the changes in the *participium passivum* of reflexive verbs, I have long since forgotten the chapter on the subjunctive mood in relative clauses. I can always read each chapter over again. I am always astonished at the novelties that it has to communicate to me.

Try that with *The Magic Mountain*.

"Ich kann keine Romane lesen," 1926. Original text in Alfred Polgar, *Kleine Schriften,* 4:259–63.

1.   Pomerania was that region of pre–World War II Germany lying along the Baltic coast. The local cuisine was known for its goose breast. Pomerania is now mostly within the territory of Poland, where it is known as Pomorze.

2.   A favorite meeting place of the theatrical community, film people, and writers in Berlin in the 1920s. It was established in 1922 by Viktor Schwanneke (1880–1931), a German comic actor and director who in 1920 became regisseur as well as actor at the Kleines Schauspielhaus and other Berlin theaters. It may be remembered that Polgar himself was very active in Berlin literary and theatrical life in the 1920s and early 1930s.

THE SMALL FORM

(A Quasi-Preface)

My book, *An den Rand geschrieben* (*Written on the Margin*), small stories and studies, found very indulgent critics. But the title had not been felicitously chosen. From the unpretentiousness of its name, many were led to conclude that the contents of the book would be similarly unpretentious. Others were led to the neat idea that I write my works on the margin because that's just where they belong. Armed with the catchword given them by the title, the readers beat me with it, and with the entry also provided by it, they displaced me. There also came running up, attracted by the phrase "written on the margin," many offensive associations, such as: plain, incidental, irrelevant, notes, jottings, crumbs, hem trimmings, border squiggles. In short, people had a good time critically at my expense, comfortable with the margin in the mouth. And I learned bitterly to regret that I didn't take the advice of good friends and title my book "The Silver Bell" or "Clouds to the South-South-North" or simply "Silpelith Rows over the Alders."

Humbled but wise by experience, I am calling the present second volume *Orchester von oben* (*Looking Down on the Orchestra*). This time, nobody can do anything to me. Now the critics are compelled, if they get to it, to judge the work from its contents and not from its title, and if they want to jab, they can do it with their own point and not with mine.

More pernicious than the title was the *small form* in which the works brought together under the title were composed. My poor stories were made to feel that ten pages of printed paper, placed on a correct scale (equal weights and an equal volume of paper), definitely weighed less than a thousand. In evaluations of my book, its light weight shifted effortlessly from the material to the spiritual, from the unmetaphoric to the metaphoric. Reading matter that takes five minutes prompted the critical (so to say) notion: reading matter if you need something to do for five minutes. As hours, mostly called "short hours," for which my book may be of use, the following were specified: the hour after lunch, the hour after dinner, the hour before falling asleep, the hour in the trolley, the rained-out holiday hour. Identified as places where the book would be good to read were: the benches around the winter fireplace, summertime meadows, the settee, the ottoman, the hammock, the armchair, the chaise longue, the sofa. The position to be taken on reading: anything that was casual, comfortable, relaxed.

True enough, my persistent literary efforts to make ten lines out of a hundred, which involved much torment, reduced me to an author for postprandial and presomnolent hours. True enough, I spin bitter fantasies in my mind of what might have been had I tried instead to pound a hundred lines into a thousand, if I had let it go at that—sunk in the mire of recognition, pleasantly occupied all day long receiving royalties and giving autographs, in possession of a motorboat, a gold fountain pen, and two Scottish sheep dogs, to whom I might give the names of the heroes of my most celebrated novels, not overlooked by inquiries of magazines (What is your favorite dessert? What are you working on and above all why?), pictured in the illustrated gazettes, and swarms of lovely women covetously fluttering all around me . . . But by no means do I want to suggest that my books suffer injustice when people treat them as bagatelles. Those who do, know why they do it, and they have no trouble justifying their opinion, even the false (a chief pleasure and amusement of the critical métier).

I am well aware, moreover, that a story of modest volume may also not hold up and that the small form may well be a necessary effect of shortness of breath. But I should like, if I only commanded the appropriate pathos, to speak up for this small form in very big words. For I believe that it suits the tension and need of the time, that it is in any case more suitable, as a flat analogy imagines, than written skyscrapers. I regard episodic brevity as thoroughly appropriate to the role today demanded of writing. Beyond doubt, the wonder of the large work remains, as there remains the justification of a thousand printed pages for one vision whose content could not be accommodated in a more modest space. But among us who write, how few are they who might claim such an awesome portion of space? Who of our storytellers and onlookers has such great things to say that he couldn't possibly write any more briefly than he does? Where is the mind that revealed to the world at large, with which it is bound, such new and important things about its chemical composition to whom the most concise form and formulae were insufficient to capture such revelation? I mean, they must be thoughts rare to the age, worldviews of the greatest clarity and depth, a more than grandiose imagination for the accommodation of which the architecture rather of the novel should be applied. Something more modest in this high form would appear as ludicrous as a cozy nest in monumental style.

Life is too short for long literature, too transitory for lingering description and observation, too psychopathic for psychology, too fictitious for novels, the fermentation and decomposition too swift to be preserved in long expansive books lengthily and expansively. That writers find time to write extensively I can understand only as need. The demon eggs them on, abundance oppresses them, the powerful current digs its powerful bed. There's nothing to be done for it. But that people in this tempestuous epoch, agitated by calamities never experienced before, find calm and time, inner time, to read extensively, is a real miracle to me. A great shaking tosses around everything that is standing, sinks the solidly grounded, throws new soil high. How presumptuous it would be to build ponderously and massively on such a foundation! Eternalities seem temporal, the most durable gods false idols, all anchors are weighed, nobody knows where the journey is headed, but that it is headed somewhere and headed somewhere with dazzling speed we feel in our very dizziness. At such a time, who wants to be burdened with superfluous baggage? Ballast has to be discarded—and what doesn't turn out to be ballast? The shortest line from point to point is the rule of the fleeting hour.

Even the aesthetic. "Fine literature" with a swollen belly is a contradiction in terms.

"Die kleine Form," 1926. Original text in Alfred Polgar, *Kleine Schriften*, 3:369–72.

THE LOOS CASE

The architect Adolf Loos has been taken into custody in Vienna. The mothers of two children who had sat for him as models complained that Loos had fondled them sexually and had, moreover, compelled them to take a bath.

The police, usually circumspect and cautious on such occasions, immediately sent a communiqué about the case to the newspapers. There is much speculation as to why the police were in such a hurry to expose Loos, the fanatic friend of Peter Altenberg and other wicked people, to public misinformation.

When Vienna learned that Loos had been placed under arrest, an unusual roar coursed through the city. It was the sound of the mouths of the Viennese watering.

For a long time now they haven't been comfortable with Loos. He has a lot to answer for. He is a willful man who often found himself vehemently at odds with Viennese taste in matters of art and life. Moreover, not only did he express very different, indeed revolutionary, views about many things that everybody here thinks he knows backwards and forwards, but in the end his views proved right all down the line. He adored and preached about Peter Altenberg at a time when people dismissed the noblest original who ever flourished in Vienna, and in spite of it, as nothing more than a *meschuggene* blemish on the family.[1] He placed Kokoschka in his debt through his early praise of him as a genius. He fought for the validity of the most modern music when its right even to be regarded as music was being contested. His hardness of hearing, which lent his efforts greater support, also had another consequence. It is surely because of it that Loos expresses his opinions so loudly, figuratively speaking. He commands attention. The newer history of culture, whoever may see and judge it, will have to devote fair space to his indefatigable, passionate, disdained campaign against ornament, against the clutter of art and handicrafts. In matters of aesthetic beliefs, he is intolerant, down to the smallest details, orthoparadoxical, so to speak, a master of formulation, a polished stylist, as sharp and witty in attack as in parry. In short, he is a man of individuality, merit, and significance. And the only qualification that can be made about him is that he collaborated for a time with the *Neue Freie Presse*. But he might almost have forfeited the indulgence to which he has legitimate claim on this basis because of his slander of Viennese cooking. On this point he does indeed fire right at the target, but also over it. He fails to take into account that the atmospheric pressure, the elevation, the amount of precipitation, the dialect, the ancestor worship, the national character, and so on and so forth determine the customary diet, and when he claims, for example, that plum dumplings are to blame for the heavy, somewhat doughy spirit of the Viennese, one can only say: "Loos is wrong here." In fact the opposite is true. It is the spirit from which the plum dumpling (and through it, the body) arises.

Be that as it may . . . in any event the city was absolutely in a state of moral outrage when it learned of the Loos affair. "Nothing distasteful," says the wise La Rochefoucauld, by the way, "befalls our best friends that doesn't have a little of the tasteful in it for us."

Out of the newspaper forest the wolves burst forth with a terrible howling, fell on the fallen, and feasted on him. Later, after a few turns of the rotary printing press and after the first bloody hunger was appeased, they sat grief stricken, the spittle of melancholy dripping from their flews over the fact that they had to sink their teeth into the body of an admired companion.

There were then long discussions in the press. The aggressors declared, in brief, that when all was said and done, after what we already experienced, we wouldn't put it past him. His defenders argued as follows: In the first place, he really didn't do it; in the second place, he did it with a purely artistic purpose; in the third place, he was mentally ill when he did it. All chose as the point of departure for their deliberations the building on the Michaelerplatz. (The controversial building which Loos in his time threw smack in the city's face.)

The architect himself says that he is being wrongly accused. Whoever knows him understands that he is speaking only the truth.

In the meantime, he has been released from custody after posting a bond of 20,000 schillings in accordance with the well-known way of justice as interpreted by a popular Viennese song: "Who's got the dough can go home free . . . and he who ain't's in custody."

We hope that Loos sees the affair through with humor. And that he takes it for what it's worth—publicity.

"Fall Loos," 1928. Original text in Alfred Polgar, *Kleine Schriften*, 1:380–83.
    1.   *Meschuggene* is Yiddish for "crazy," "cracked."

IT DOESN'T PAY TO DIE

The writer Wilhelm Stücklen died at the age of forty-two. The newspapers took notice of this event. Berlin papers devoted on average five lines to the deceased. For a living writer, that would be little; for one cut down prematurely, that is ultimately enough. The press, I suppose, can be indifferent to the dead author . . . What advantage is it of the newspaper's to busy itself with somebody to whom their opinion doesn't mean a damn, whom their praise doesn't promote, their criticism doesn't improve, their attention doesn't please, their inattention doesn't grieve, their wit doesn't injure, their favor doesn't reward, their nod of approval doesn't make proud, their nod of disapproval doesn't trouble, and who on the whole, since he's become definitely absent, no longer plays any role?

I don't know if Stücklen was a first-rate writer. He wrote successful plays, and his last novel, *The Tulip Ship*, was praised for its many qualities. In any case, he was a writer who was published and performed and also spoken about and so to say appreciated. The worst play by him, performed in the worst theater in the worst possible way, would have attracted the journals much more than his death. They would have related the contents of the play at greater length than the contents of his life, of which the particular play had been but a small part.

Dying is for sure harder than writing a play. Nevertheless, this latter achievement appears to people far worthier of attention than the former, and the press both represents this and mirrors it. The awful supremacy of the trifling over the important: a whole bunch of lines for a little slice of life, five for an entire death!

"Es lohnt sich nicht, zu sterben," 1929. Original text in Alfred Polgar, *Kleine Schriften*, 4:300–301.

MEETING

A man stopped me on the street: "Excuse me, I'm looking for Dr. Fränkel."

"What Fränkel?"

"Dr. Fränkel, on account of my kidneys."

"Oh, well, I'm sorry, I have no idea where he lives."

The man made a gesture as if rejecting an unseemly demand: "Should I know? I'm from Memel."

A thin gray beard hangs from his chin. It slopes as if the wind had pushed it to a side. He is well dressed, wears a padded waistcoat with long sleeves, and has a little cap on his head. Glasses. His hands are white, the fingernails black. His pants have sharp creases and are frayed on the bottom. He seems fashionably unkempt.

We go to a coffeehouse in order to look up Dr. Fränkel's address in the telephone book. My new acquaintance introduces himself. He is an observant Lithuanian Jew, and has come to Berlin, expressly, as he says, not to do business. But on account of Dr. Fränkel. He gives me a calling card. It bears a name and beneath the name a longer line in a foreign language. The man from Memel translates it for me: "I exterminate mice, rats, bedbugs."

"Can you earn a good living with this in Lithuania?"

He opens his mouth, shows me a pair of gold teeth in the upper jaw: "I paid for these with it."

He has letters of recommendation from all sorts of high and mighty people. Among them, one from somebody from Imperial Russia, where he was a guest and exterminated the rats in Riga.

"Do you have any particular method of extermination?"

"I have my own."

"What is it?"

"That's a professional secret."

This lack of trust upsets me. So I say to him: "Excuse me, but you're a pious Jew, aren't you? How can you kill living things? That is forbidden by law."

The man from Memel doesn't seem perturbed. He smiles in a superior sort of way. "I've examined the Scriptures carefully as to what I can and cannot do. Listen to me! There are creatures who should exist and those who shouldn't. Some field mice, for example, there ought to be, since they loosen up arable land. But too many field mice shouldn't be because they eat up the seedlings. So the ones that are too many I have to kill."

"And what about rats?"

"Rats? What do you want from rats? Rats are big mice!"

"And how is it with bedbugs?"

He thinks about this a while. Then, while drawing a curve in the air carefully with a finger, as if indicating to logic a little detour that it has to make, he speaks in the intonation of wisdom: "Bedbugs have to be killed, since deserving people can earn a living that way."

Well said, man from Memel! Has he not captured the deeper sense of the ideology of all wars in a single concise sentence?

"How many people do you support with your bedbug extermination?"

"I'm the only one."

"Are you also, then, one of the righteous men for whose sake the world exists?"

He shrugs his shoulders and throws up his hands, expressing a modest resignation to the gentleman's will, then inclines his head toward the tabletop. "None of the thirty-six righteous men knows that he is one of the thirty-six."

That there are exactly thirty-six of them is new to me. I am surprised that there are so many; I would have bet fewer.

But the man from Memel maintains that it is so written. He seems sickly and has pains in the kidneys. There have to be pains in the kidneys for the sake of Dr. Fränkel, just as Dr. Fränkel has to be for the sake of pains in the kidneys.

It's all geared the right way in the mechanism of the world.

"Begegnung," 1930. Original text in Alfred Polgar, *Kleine Schriften*, 3:25–28.

IN A TIGHT SPOT

On the stage are two rooms next to each other connected by a door. A normal stage. Hence the rooms lack the fourth wall, which the actors, of course, accept as present and respect.

It so happened, in the heat of the performance, that the heroine of the drama, as she had to pass from one room to the other, pushed the door to the outside that actually had to be opened from the inside. The door—and this was its proper mechanical right—offered resistance. The woman sought to overcome it with strength, "by force," but the door remained unyielding. The actress pushed and pulled in vain. The audience vacillated between merriness, sympathy, and vicarious discomfort (embarrassment on stage causes embarrassment to the spectators). The break in the action became excruciatingly large. Finally, the door was forced open so wide that the actress could hazard the attempt to slip through. But it didn't work. The poor thing remained between door and hinge. Meta-phorically and in the true sense of the word, she was really in a tight spot.

How she was freed from it is a secondary matter. I would just like to suggest that at the very outset of her misfortune she could have helped herself in a ridiculously easy way. Instead of wanting to force her way past the door, she could quite simply have stepped out through the nonexistent fourth wall of the room she was in onto the open front stage, taken a step around the wall separating the two rooms, and then entered the other one through its nonexistent fourth wall. Not only would the spectators have forgiven her the improbable route, but even if they laughed, they would surely have still been a little touched by the incident. In a battle between man and object, the spectator is, in the final analysis, on the side of man. Moreover, there is something engaging when a person courageously leaps right into the middle of a situation in order to save it from becoming ridiculous.

But then why didn't the actress choose such a convenient way out? She would have had to take leave of the world of delusion for only a second in order to return to it immediately. Did she not see, perhaps, the broad, so easily passable way to salvation? Was she like the moth that lands in a room and keeps on flying against the pane of a closed window without noticing the open one alongside it? Did the poor woman find herself in the sought-after magic circle the theater draws about the performers, which they cannot escape from despite the fact that no material border bars their way?

It could have been like that. It's more likely, however, that the actress simply didn't dare, even in the great urgency of the moment, to disregard the fictions of the performance. That she had insurmountable inhibitions about abandoning the assumption that there was a fourth wall there. That she couldn't for a moment disavow this imaginary thing although it exists only by virtue of the good-natured willingness not to see it of all concerned, performers and spectators alike.

The theater itself isn't so scrupulous about the truth of illusion. It often reveals before all the deceptions with which it operates. Out of casualness. Out of mischievousness. Also for the sake of the piquantness of playing with play. Its real effect proceeds, after all, from the mind, from the word, and everything else is only auxiliary lines that aren't worth the effort to obscure. The newer theater even lets them be visible, under-lining them perhaps in order to properly emphasize their subordinate significance.

And so, since the worthy actress preferred to botch the play rather than exit through the fourth nonexistent wall, she was, more than she may be usually, a performer of ordinary people. Can't one see, as far as the nearsighted eye reaches, that people do the same as she? Don't they make fools of themselves, aren't they miserable, don't they sweat it out in a tight spot out of desperate anxiety lest they betray a delusion prescribed by the scenario of their lives? They'd rather ruin themselves than transgress the law of illusion into which they have been straightjacketed: the illusion of profession, of talent, of honor, of immutable principles, of social success, and so on and so forth without end.

"In der Klemme," 1930. Original text in Alfred Polgar, *Kleine Schriften*, 3:7–10.

THE SUIT

The writer had two suits and one wife. He wore the suits by turns. The wife sewed on missing buttons and cleaned stains, which occurred frequently, with benzine.

His name was Maximilian. In warmer moments, his wife called him Milian, in colder ones Max, in company Maxim.

One day, the blue suit suffered a serious laceration. It also showed embarrassing traces of dilapidation. Maximilian wanted to give it away, but his wife cast one glance at the times, another at the empty clothes closet, yet another at Maximilian . . . and with the sigh she emitted blew the idea away.

Besides, the wife had a certain weakness for the blue one. Perhaps because it was so vulnerable, perhaps because it still bore a reflection of the days when the household was lit up with money and love, perhaps because the man in the blue suit, even if also not well off, nevertheless looked prosperous enough so that nobody might take him for a writer.

The tailor was a small, very small tailor. The show window of his shop beckoned with a fashion poster on which smooth-shaven gentlemen and some with fluffy pointed beards, stiff in exquisite attire, exchanged smiles. Inside the shop, the master and the brush maker from next door were playing cards. The back of the window poster served as a scorecard for their game results. When customers appeared, which didn't happen very often, they brought only modest patchwork on modest suits, thus the blue suit, which had to be repaired, cleaned, and pressed, and still appeared in worn-out condition, was respectfully received. The master was delighted with the item. He inspected it, inspected his clients, and nodded sadly, which could mean different things. Afterwards, he wheezed and coughed, since he suffered from asthma.

The wife, regarding the cougher suspiciously, laid her hand on the suit with protective gestures, the way the lioness lays her paw on her cub when danger threatens. But she had no cause for concern. When the master put the suit in the closet, he pushed the proletarian clothes hanging there decisively to the right and left sides, thereby creating special room for the special guest. Delivery date: Wednesday. Wednesday came, but the suit didn't. Thursday, after a restless night, husband and wife went to the tailor. The shop was closed, shutters rolled down. "Max, what does it mean . . . ?" "Maybe he went away somewhere, for winter sports." The wife did not enter into this forlorn humor but into the nearby brush store instead. She came back out onto the street, upset. "He had a stroke . . ." "Dead . . . ?" "Dead!" And not without an undertone of bitterness, she again said, but this time more to herself: "What does it mean?"

On the way home they spoke about death and at the same time thought of the suit. And thought how shameful it is that they were thinking about it now. How embarrassing, one moment to be reminded of eternity and the next moment to feel hurled into anxiety over a pair of trousers!

On another day, the shop was again open. In the place of the fashion poster, there now hung a handwritten obituary. And upon the seat in front of the store desk, which was intended for clients, the brother-in-law of the deceased sat freezing. The tailor died a quick and easy death, a newspaper in his hand, he reported, and every person could wish just such a death for himself. Maximilian and wife expressed their condolences before asking about the suit. The brother-in-law knew nothing about it. All three together looked for it in the clothes closet and throughout the workshop. Later on, the sister of the deceased also arrived and joined in the search. But the suit was gone and remained gone. The mourners, Maximilian and wife, kept nagging the survivors in ever-colder tones, the suit just had to be somewhere. But the brother-in-law dismissed such nagging with a shrug of his shoulders, and the sister, her gaze turned heavenward, said: "Yes, when one closes his eyes!" As if she wanted to say: Not only is death itself a riddle, but so, too, is everything having to do with it puzzling, and in its dark sphere the traceless disappearance of clothes is indeed a mystery, but for certain a comprehensible mystery.

Maximilian's wife refused to find comfort in this; the brother-in-law shouted, "We're honorable people!"; the sister began to weep; and the writer (was he really one?) consoled her, "Gone is gone!" It remained unclear whether he meant the tailor or the suit.

It never appeared. The wife held nobody responsible, but when she recalled the loving eyes with which the master regarded the suit, she felt somewhere in the vicinity of her heart the prick of a weird, disgraceful suspicion. It didn't reach the proportions of supernatural speculation that the tailor had taken the suit with him into the next world, and the same for the variant, that he died deliberately so as not to have to be separated from the lovely suit for the rest of his life. She spurned these notions (although inclined to unusual solutions and superficially familiar with the principles of psychoanalysis) . . . , but she remained convinced that connections existed between the demise of the man and the disappearance of the suit.

"You can think logically, Max, can't you? Where could the suit have disappeared, after all?"

"When I carefully consider all possibilities," answered Max, "of how to explain its disappearance, I come to the conclusion that we really should have given it away."

"Then at least we would have known where it is! Poor Milian, now you have only one suit left."

"And you, dearest!"

"Der Anzug," 1933. Original text in Alfred Polgar, *Kleine Schriften*, 3:100–103.

THE FEMALE TABLE COMPANION

The female table companion as a problem occurs only in more genteel homes. That is, where people are invited to dine and sup. Among everyday folk, where you eat plainly, the phenomenon of the female table companion also arises, but it appears in such an unpretentious form that it provides no incentive to research to address it.

In more elegant homes, the female table companion is a problem.

Above all, for the mistress of the house. A female table companion has to be correctly placed, and that is by no means as simple as the ordinary guest imagines. She may not sit next to her husband; that goes without saying. Why, after all, do the couple go out in company if not to forget that they are a couple? The lady should also not sit next to her male friend, since such an arrangement is apt to be regarded as intentional, as if announcing: You should know that we know. The place next to the man who would like to become a friend of the woman also doesn't enter the picture, lest that seem like tactless patronage, encouragement. Further care must be taken—at least in homes where a value is placed on perfect taste even in small matters—that the female table companion get a neighbor who accords with her hair color and political outlook as well as with her intellectual pretensions and yearly budget.

The problem of the female table companion is still harder for the guest who encounters her than it is for the mistress of the house. Since he naturally has two female companions at table, one to the right of him, the other to the left, it unnerves him to have to conduct two-sided sociable chitchat and expressive grimacing with the halves of two faces. But as for the actual table companion assigned him, she will always be a source of discomfort for the gentleman to her side. If she happens to be charming, she distracts from eating. If she's not, she affects the appetite. If she has a brain in her head, she forces her neighbor into the uncomfortable and ludicrous situation of having to act as if he, too, had one. When she talks, he has to listen as if really interested; when she remains silent, then he has to talk, otherwise embarrassing pauses result.

Especially dangerous is the female table companion a person never met before. How does the gentleman begin the conversation in such a case? The socially experienced male always has a few trustworthy phrases on hand with which to initiate the first contact with a female table companion. It might go something like this: "Is the company here as unbearable for you as it is for me?" or "I'd much rather be sitting with a beer now in some pub!" or "Not a single pretty woman here!" or "Always the same unpleasant faces!" or "If only the evening were already over!" But many female table companions provoke a suggestive conversation right then and there and so get the subject around to going to the movies together. It's simpler if the woman seizes the initiative and speaks first. That way she sets the tone and tempo of the conversation unequivocally. Once I had a female table companion whose first words, after I was introduced to her, were: "How funny! I was absolutely convinced you were already dead!" Right away, an amiable tone was struck and the conversation put in high gear.

The ideal female table companion is the one who makes you clearly understand that she exempts you from the duty of having to converse. But you immediately take such a strong liking to a woman of such good nature, taste, and sensitivity, to such a lighthearted, understanding creature, that you feel compelled to let her know it. So there goes your peace of mind all over again.

That is why Sophocles says the best thing is not to be invited at all!

"Tischnachbarin," 1935. Original text in Alfred Polgar, *Kleine Schriften*, 3:147–49.

Marionette Theater

It is reported from Naples that by administrative decree the Italian marionette theater is to be closed. The official explanation for the prohibition states that "in its tales and legends" the marionette theater "had clung to a deplorable past and had not found a connection with the new age. The marionettes were acting, therefore, like ghosts." What are these tales and legends in which the marionette theater clung to a deplorable past? They are, or were, plays in the spirit of the commedia dell'arte with Policinello, Arlecchino, Trufaldino, and other lovable figures whom the great Goldoni released onto higher literary levels. These marionette plays were, to be sure, not "modern." But the Italian people, especially the Neapolitans, loved them and preferred the silliest ideas of the marionettes to the cleverest ones of the equally amusing Marinetti,[1] the representative writer of the New Italy and advocate of war as the "spiritual hygiene of the world." Better the spirit of a deplorable past, say the friends of the marionettes, than the nonspirit of a bellowing present. But it was not because of the sympathy of the people for the little puppets on wires that the prohibition was to be obeyed. The decisive factor was the observation that the marionettes were "acting like ghosts." An observation doubtless based on accuracy. Where people are themselves marionettes and only as such have a right to life, real marionettes have to act like ghosts and, moreover, like mocking ghosts.

"Marionetten-Theater," 1936. Original text in Alfred Polgar, *Kleine Schriften,* 1:147.

1. Filippo Tommaso Marinetti (1876–1944), the founder of the Italian Futurist movement in literature.

HIGHER MATHEMATICS

The new German Reich legislation distinguishes between full-Jews, three-quarter-Jews, half-Jews, quarter-Jews, and one-eighth-Jews. For the time being, the mathematical distinction doesn't go any further. But it is already monstrously complicated, and the interbreeding of these fraction-Jews among themselves in particular makes the racial determination of their descendants exceedingly difficult. If, for example, a ¾-Jew marries a ⅛-Jewess, the child of such a marriage receives as a racial inheritance ½ plus ⅛, which gives it ⅞ Jewish, and ⅛ plus ⅞, hence 9/8 Aryan blood, which by balance, net cash, gives a clear profit of ¼ Aryan for the child, which he couldn't do much with in the Third Reich. He would still be a ¾-Jew. But if his ¾-Jewish father had married a full ½- or 2/4-Jewess, instead of the ⅛-Jewess, the blood balance of the child would be ¾ or 10/8 Jewish and 6/8 Aryan, leaving a surplus of 4/8, that is ½ Jewish. The child would be, therefore, a ½-Jew, certainly better than the one whose ¾-father had married a ⅛-Jewess. There could, of course, be a hitch to these figures. But you get so confused with this racial arithmetics that mistakes are hardly worth mentioning. Perhaps the whole thing would be easier if the fractionalizing were abandoned and the decimal point introduced instead in the calculation of Jews.

"Höhere Mathematik," 1937. Original text in Alfred Polgar, *Kleine Schriften,* 1:156.

A N T O N
K U H
1 8 9 0 – 1 9 4 1

ANTON KUH[1] MAY BE REMEMBERED MOST FOR HIS NO-HOLDS-BARRED ASSAULT ON KARL KRAUS IN THE FORM OF A PUBLIC LECTURE DELIVERED ON 25 OCTOBER 1925 IN THE AUDITORIUM OF THE VIENNA KONZERTHAUS. There were certainly many who thought Kraus had it coming to him—he had engaged in enough character assassination in his time—but few would have dared this kind of frontal attack in a public forum. Kuh could not have cared less. He was a monocle-wearing rebel who lived a bohemian coffeehouse life and obviously reveled in it. He had a great way with words, was as flamboyant in language as he was in his personal style, and never shunned a podium.

Taking unpopular positions, exploding myths, demasking pretense and posturing, Kuh delighted in ruffling feathers. The growing power of the Nazis in Germany and their threat to the rest of Europe, to say nothing of Austrian independence, gave him plenty of ammunition for his barbs of mockery and satire. He was consistently antimilitaristic and pacifistic. When the First World War engulfed the Habsburg Empire, Kuh shared none of the nationalistic chauvinism of some of the most outstanding of his literary colleagues (even the archetypical bohemian, Peter Altenberg, whom the war barely touched, still voiced his support of the German-Austrian cause). Rather than serve in the military or accept the kind of safe home-front War Archives jobs as did Hofmannsthal, Musil, Zweig, Salten, and other literati of the time, he feigned a nervous tic, managed thereby to avoid serving, but found himself unable to shake the tic afterward. It was an irony Kuh himself doubtless enjoyed, whatever the minor inconvenience.

Kuh's inclination toward an essentially journalistic career could easily have been determined by his background. His father, Emil, was for a time editor-in-chief of the *Neues Wiener Tagblatt* (*New Vienna Daily*). His paternal grandfather, David Kuh, founded a paper called *Tagesboten aus Böhmen* (*Bohemian Daily Messenger*), which was still being published after the First World War under the title *Montagsblatt an Böhmen* (*Monday Paper for Bohemia*).

As the names of Kuh's grandfather's papers suggest, the Kuh family came originally from Bohemia. They were part of the very old community of German-speaking Jews in Prague. The family settled in Vienna long before Anton Kuh came into the world; he was, in fact, nineteen when he first visited the Czech capital. But as time went on, he visited the city on many occasions, wrote for Prague papers, and made his way into the German-speaking literary community there. Before the dissolution of the Habsburg Empire, of which they had long been a part, and between the two world wars of the twentieth century, when Czechoslovakia existed as an independent state, the Czech lands accommodated, not always easily, two cultures, Czech and German. Before the creation of an autonomous Czechoslovak state after the First World War, secularized educated Bohemian Jews favored German culture. The Czech seemed abysmally parochial by comparison. German, on the other hand, opened the doors to one of Europe's greatest cultures. When Czechoslovakia became newly independent, and in a climate of increasing Czech nationalism that was not without its anti-Semitic dimension, a number of Jews threw their lot in with the Czechs. Others still clung to the German cultural tradition in the country. This was especially true of the Prague Jewish community.

Thus, when Kuh found his way into Prague's German-speaking literary world, he was indeed in good company. As much a regular guest in Prague's leading literary coffeehouses—the Arco and the Continental—as he was in Vienna's, he rubbed shoulders with the likes of Franz Kafka, Max Brod, Gustav Meyrink, Franz Werfel, Oskar Kokoschka, and the globe-trotting left-wing journalist Egon Erwin Kisch. Back in his native Vienna, Kuh was a regular member of the little circle around Peter Altenberg that clustered at the Café Central. With Altenberg's withdrawal from public life because of declining health and his eventual death in 1919, Kuh followed the migration of the coffeehouse's younger and more "progressive" habitués to the Café Herrenhof, which became his regular Vienna hangout until the German annexation of Austria in 1938.

Kuh earned whatever living he made by writing for newspapers and journals and by giving public lectures or acting as a cabaret *conférencier* (something like a master of ceremonies). He was well read, especially in German philosophy, but little is known of his formal education. As a speaker, he was animated, witty, and provocative.

In the early years of the post-Habsburg Austrian republic, Kuh gravitated to the political left, but without the enthusiasm for revolutionary activism of people such as Egon Erwin Kisch and Franz Werfel. True, he planned to put out a "revolutionary paper"—*Blätter zur Bekämpfung des Machtwillens* (*Pages in the Struggle against the Will to Power*)—along with Werfel and Otto Gross (1877–1920), a Viennese analyst and sexologist. But the announced "struggle" turned out to be more between Werfel and Gross with the result that the paper never got off the ground. If Kuh needed an outlet for his anticonservative, antimilitaristic, rather vague leftist sentiments, he found it in the pacifistic weekly *Der Friede* (*Peace*), then being put out by Benno Karpeles, who was a functionary of the Social Democratic Party and a previous collaborator in Victor Adler's *Wiener Arbeiter-Zeitung* (*Vienna Workers' Paper*). Karpeles had founded his unaffiliated democratic-republican paper in January 1918. It ran only until the middle of the following year, but its short life was distinguished by the collaboration of such writers, besides Kuh, as Robert Musil, Joseph Roth, Alfred Polgar, and the Czech Čapek brothers, Karel and Josef.

Kuh's willingness as a writer to tackle difficult and controversial subjects is evident in his *Juden und Deutsche: Ein Résumé* (*Jews and Germans: A Résumé*), a popularly oriented book calculated to upset traditional views on both sides and in which Karl Kraus is also taken to task. It was, for the most part, woven together out of lectures Kuh had given in Vienna, Prague, and other cities and was published separately in 1921. This was Kuh's first longer publication. It was followed by two others the next year. The first was a collection of aphorisms—a favorite genre of Kuh's as it had been of Altenberg's and Kraus's—published under the title *Von Goethe abwärts: Essays in Aussprüchen* (*From Goethe on Down: Essays in Aphorisms*). An expanded edition of the collection was published in 1931 as *Physiognomik* (*Physiognomics*). Kuh's second longer publication of 1922 was a collection of writings by the German-Jewish writer Ludwig Börne (1786–1837) preceded by an introduction by Kuh entitled "Börne, der Zeitgenosse" ("Börne the Contemporary"). Impressed by Börne as the embodiment of the liberal "engaged" man of letters, Kuh found parallels between his campaign against the authority-worshipping German philistinism of his own time and the need for contemporary German and Austrian writers to address the dangers posed by reactionary nationalism and a servile respect for authority. Kuh, a natural rebel, was also attracted to Börne's attacks on Goethe, who, to Börne, epitomized a smug elitist indifference to the plight of his fellowman. Writing of Kuh's essay in a Prague newspaper in February 1923, Alfred Döblin praised it as "exceptionally vehement and sparkling."[2]

From 1922 until he left Vienna for Berlin a few years later, Kuh wrote mostly for newspapers owned by the powerful but somewhat shady Hungarian press entrepreneur Imre Békessy. Békessy's papers included such well-known Viennese institutions as *Die Börse* (*The Bourse*), *Die Bühne* (*The Stage*), *Die Stunde* (*The Hour*), and *Die Sphinx* (*The Sphinx*). Before long, Békessy became the target of a particularly venomous denunciatory campaign by Karl Kraus.[3] It began, in fact, in January 1924 with the publication by Kraus of a pamphlet attacking Békessy entitled "Békessys Sendung" ("Békessy's Mission"). Since Kraus concentrated most of his withering satire on the contemporary Viennese press for its low moral and stylistic standards, its susceptibility to corruption, and its social and political power, Békessy and his empire sooner or later would have come into Kraus's cross hairs. But an unholy alliance between Békessy and the corrupt chief of police, Johann Schober, epitomized for Kraus everything that was rotten, in his opinion, with the Viennese press. He laced into the man he called the "Buda pest" (since Békessy was from the Hungarian capital) with unremitting ferocity. Not one to take things lying down, Békessy lost no opportunity to denigrate or belittle Kraus. Fearing too close an examination of his own activities, however, he refrained from taking Kraus to court. Matters reached a head when Kraus publicly denounced the Hungarian press baron in the Mittlerer Konzerthaus auditorium before an audience of nearly a thousand people and demanded that "the crook" (der Schuft) get out of Vienna. Eventually, evidence was collected against Békessy (who until then had the police under control), and a warrant was issued for his arrest. But Békessy quit Vienna in the summer of 1926 before he could be taken into custody and sought refuge first in Paris and then in his native Budapest. Even with Békessy out of Vienna, Kraus continued to demand that the Austrian authorities extradite him from Hungary, but the campaign was to no avail.

The Békessy-Kraus feud is the background against which Kuh's notorious "lecture" against Kraus in the Vienna Konzerthaus auditorium on 25 October 1925 has to be viewed. Kuh, as well as Felix Salten, wrote regularly for Békessy's papers, mostly *Die Stunde*. Whether both writers were actually asked or ordered by Békessy or his representatives to attack Kraus is difficult to prove. In a monograph on Karl Kraus, Harry Zohn, a well-known Kraus specialist, takes it for granted and writes: "To his [Kraus's] articles, several of which were read in public, *Die Stunde* . . . reacted by having Békessy's minions Anton Kuh and Felix Salten attack Kraus."[4] Salten's case is more clear-cut. He and Kraus had an enmity going back years before the Békessy affair, one which had, in fact, culminated in a physical attack by Salten on Kraus. Salten certainly would have needed little encouragement to abuse Kraus one way or another. Kuh, on the other hand, might well have been prevailed upon by *Die Stunde* to mount a public assault on Kraus. But Kuh was an anticonformist, antiauthoritarian bohemian with a mind of his own. Kraus's campaign against journalism—which is how Kuh earned his living, after all—obviously would have been an irritant. But Kraus's sense of moral uprightness and superiority, his denigration of Heine, his almost excessive fussiness over language, a kind of linguistic arrogance, if you will, and doubtless also Kraus's particular brand of Jewish anti-Jewishness seemed to have rubbed Kuh the wrong way. Kraus, moreover, represented to Kuh the very embodiment of a social phenomenon toward which he took a particular dislike, that of the "Bildungsphilister" (cultural philistine), a term he borrowed from his favorite philosopher, Nietzsche. So when in the heat of the Kraus-Békessy polemic Kuh had a chance to give Kraus a taste of his own medicine, and in public, and at the same time make himself look good in the eyes of an employer whom he seems to have liked personally, he could not let it pass. Hence the rambling, intemperate, largely impromptu assault on Kraus in the Vienna Konzerthaussaal on 25 October 1925 under the title "Der Affe Zarathustras (Karl Kraus)" ("Zarathustra's Ape [Karl Kraus]") and its subsequent publication. But that was hardly the end of it. Kraus sued Kuh for an insult to his honor. In January 1926 Kuh again ran afoul of Kraus by referring to him publicly on several occasions as "Vortrags-Affe" (lecture ape). Kraus sued again and this time had some measure of satisfaction. The court fined Kuh 40 schillings or 48 days in jail. Kuh paid the fine, but the matter never really ended there. Kuh continued to snipe at Kraus even when he was away from Vienna. However, the feud was played out on a low-key basis; there was nothing as sensational as the public appearances of June and October 1925. That is, until 1934. But more about that later.

With the rancor of the Kraus-Békessy affair behind him, at least for the time being, Kuh may have felt that a little breathing space and a change of scene were in order. He left Vienna and resettled in Berlin, where he remained until Hitler's acceptance of the chancellorship in 1933. His literary activity hardly abated in the German capital. He became an active contributor to such well-known journals as *Der Querschnitt* (*The Cross-Section*), *Die Weltbühne* (*The World Stage*), and *Das Tage-Buch* (*The Daybook*, or *The Journal*), which Stefan Grossman and Leopold Schwarzschild founded in 1920, and also published in such popular magazines as *Das Leben* (*Life*), *Die Clique* (*The Clique*), and *Die neue Revue* (*The New Review*). As usual, Kuh wrote on a variety of subjects. He also acted as a kind of roving cultural reporter covering literary, film, and theatrical events in Berlin, Vienna, and Prague and writing on them for publications in all three cities.

While in Berlin, Kuh witnessed the Nazi rise to power in an atmosphere of strident nationalism and intolerance. He reacted to it by turning his arsenal of wit and satire against it. By the time Hitler became chancellor, Kuh himself had begun to come under attack from Nazi quarters. Cognizant of the precariousness of his situation in Germany as a left-leaning bohemian antifascist writer, Kuh took stock of his options and decided the time had come to return to Vienna. It was not long after his return that the long-standing feud with Kraus ignited again in 1934.

The spark that set it off this time was the nonpublication of Kraus's anti-Nazi book *Die Dritte Walpurgisnacht* (*The Third Walpurgis Night*), the title referring to both parts of Goethe's *Faust* as well as to Hitler's Third Reich. The work was written in the spring and summer of 1933 and was supposed to appear in the fall issue of Kraus's *Die Fackel* (nos. 888–907). But it never did. Apparently fearing the consequences of its publication—for others—Kraus withheld it from *Die Fackel*. When no. 888 finally appeared in October 1933, not only was *The Third Walpurgis Night* not in it but the four-page issue contained just a funeral speech on the architect Adolf Loos and a last poem by Kraus himself in which he sought to "explain" his speechlessness with respect to the events then taking place in Nazi Germany. Kraus sought further to explain his seeming retreat in the face of Nazism in a lengthy article entitled "Warum *Die Fackel* nicht erscheint" ("Why *Die Fackel* Is Not Appearing"), which appeared in the July 1934 issue of the journal.

Kraus's failure to publish *The Third Walpurgis Night* as promised, as well as his attempts to rationalize his silence on the subject of the Nazis,

was enough to stir Kuh to ire. But what made further verbal assault on
Kraus virtually an imperative was Kraus's stance during what is often
referred to as the Austrian "civil war" of February 1934. The events of that
month were both a prelude to the German annexation of March 1938 and
the culmination of the struggle for power between the socialist Social
Democrats, who dominated Austrian and especially Viennese political life
from the creation of the Austrian republic in 1918, and the conservative,
clerically influenced Christian Democrats. Tensions were further exacer-
bated by the rapid rise of, and growing support for, Austrian right-wing
organizations, above all the *Heimwehr,* and the Nazis. The stage was set for
conflict, and it erupted on 12 February 1934. But despite much support
from workers, the Socialists' hopes for a general strike failed to materialize,
and this more than anything else contributed to their defeat. In the aftermath of the fighting, Socialist leaders were arrested or forced into exile,
and the Social Democratic Party as well as trade unions were outlawed.
Austrian democracy was at an end.

Kraus's "failure" to speak out against the Nazis was compounded by
his support of the Dollfuss regime against the Social Democrats (who lost
credibility with Kraus because of their internal squabbling and relative
inaction at a time when right-wing forces in the country were gathering
considerable strength). Whether unwilling or refusing to understand the
moral-philosophical reasons behind Kraus's reluctance to wage a battle of
words against the Nazis or the real fears motivating Kraus's support of the
Dollfuss regime during the February 1934 riots, Kuh joined the chorus of
Kraus's detractors. Apart from obvious temperamental differences between
them—Kuh was far more outspoken about the Nazis—the attacks on Kraus
have to be seen in the larger context of Kuh's long-standing feud with
Kraus going back to 1925.

Also distinguishing Kuh's reaction to the rapidly increasing fascist
threat from that of Kraus was Kuh's open collaboration with German and
German-Jewish émigré publications and organizations from the mid-1930s
to the outbreak of the Second World War. When the implementation of
the Nazis' anti-Jewish measures (the Nuremberg Laws) began to be undertaken after Hitler's assumption of the chancellorship, many German Jews
fled the country and took refuge in nearby Austria, Czechoslovakia, France,
and Switzerland. They established their own organizations and were soon
issuing publications. Before long, Kuh was an active contributor, often
writing on political topics, to such émigré weeklies as the satirical *Der
Simplicus* (founded in Prague in 1934), an imitation of the famous
Munich satirical journal *Simplicissimus; Die Neue Weltbühne,* which
Hermann Budzislawski began publishing in Prague, Zurich, and Paris in
1933; the *Pariser Tageblatt (Paris Daily),* a German-language émigré publication

established in 1933; and the Vienna-based *Jüdische Rundschau* (*Jewish Review*). The German-language *Prager Tagblatt* (*Prague Daily*), for which Kuh had begun writing before 1933, also served as another outlet for his antifascist writings. Music, on which Kuh frequently wrote, was no privileged sanctuary against his political satire and polemics. When the international music community was electrified by the open feud between Furtwängler and Toscanini in the summer of 1937, Kuh jumped into the fray by writing a piece for *Die Neue Weltbühne* in which he again warned against the political and ideological exploitation of music. The uses to which Bayreuth and the Wagner Festival were put by the Nazis were contrasted with the antithetical Baroque spirit prevailing at Salzburg and its annual festival. Because of his friendship with Max Reinhardt, Kuh had been close to the Salzburg Festival from its inception and remained one of its strongest supporters.

Kuh entertained a desperate belief in the possibility of the Austrian masses being roused to successful resistance to the German push for annexation. At one point, he tried to convince a high government official close to Chancellor Schuschnigg that the popular former mayor of Vienna, Karl Seitz, be allowed to issue a public appeal for support over the radio.[5] But even as Kuh was pressing his case, Hitler delivered his ultimatum. The game was lost. Harboring no further illusions, Kuh quit Vienna for Prague, where he knew many people, had many friends, and where at least for a while he could feel secure. But feelings of security were to be short-lived. When German troops began massing on the Czech border in May 1938, Kuh clearly read the handwriting on the wall and began planning his next move. Fortunately, the Emergency Rescue Committee came to his aid and secured his entry into the United States.

The early months in New York were anything but easy. But the substantial community of Jewish and non-Jewish refugees from Germany and Austria in New York just before the outbreak of the Second World War made available not only the companionship of people of similar background, to whom Kuh was already well known, but also outlets for his journalistic and literary skills. Financially supported by the Amalgamated Clothing Workers of America, the German Jewish Club, later to be known as The New World Club, did half-hour weekly broadcasts, which gave Kuh and other émigré artists and intellectuals a chance to be heard and to earn a little money.[6] Kuh's essay "Geschichte und Gedächtnis" ("History and Memory"), for example, was broadcast on 26 November 1938. Kuh also had at least one public appearance in New York. On the evening of 20 March 1940, he mounted the podium of the lecture hall of the 92nd Street (and Lexington Avenue) YMHA/YWHA and delivered a talk, before a largely Jewish audience, on the subject of "The Art of Surviving Hitler."

Kuh's essay "History and Memory" was subsequently printed in *Der Aufbau* (*The Buildup*), which was published by the German Jewish Club in New York, on 1 January 1939. It brought to an end an eighteen-month period in which Kuh published nothing and began a close relationship between him and *Der Aufbau,* which was—and still is—the best-known German-language publication in the United States. Before Kuh's death in January 1941, *Der Aufbau* published an additional fifteen pieces by him. Most of these appeared in a section of the paper entitled "The Sceptical Reader" and under the pseudonym Yorick.

Kuh's literary activity in the United States was not confined solely to the German-language *Aufbau.* Between 4 June and 18 June 1938, he published a three-part account, in English, of his escape from Vienna to Prague via Brno. It bore the title "Escape from the Mousetrap."[7] Among other things, it contains Kuh's account of how Alma Mahler-Werfel, the widow of Gustav Mahler and the wife of Franz Werfel, used her good offices to arrange for Kuh to meet a minister close to Chancellor Schuschnigg for the purpose of persuading Schuschnigg to allow the former Social Democrat mayor of Vienna, Karl Seitz, to broadcast an appeal to the Austrian workers to vote against Anschluss with Germany.

Kuh died in New York of a second cardiac arrest on 18 January 1941. His papers were collected in a carton and given to friends for safekeeping. They were stored in the basement of their house and promptly forgotten. Eventually, the house was torn down and the papers lost or scattered. The editors of the two existing collections of Kuh's writings, Ruth Greuner and Ulrike Lehner, have done a fine job of reprinting long-forgotten works by Anton Kuh and making more accessible than ever before one of the more colorful and talented Viennese artists of "small forms" of the twentieth century. So little has been published on Kuh that most of what is known of his life and career appears in Ruth Greuner's twenty-seven-page afterword to her 1981 Vienna edition of Kuh's works published under the title *Luftlinien* (*Air-Lines*).

1.   There is very little literature on Kuh. The best sources of information on him are the editors' afterwords to the 1981 (new edition 1987) and 1985 collections of his selected works. See: Anton Kuh, *Metaphysik und Würstel: Feuilletons, Essays und Publizistik,* ed. Ruth Greuner (Zurich: Diogenes Verlag, 1987), 499–525. The original edition of this same work was published by Löcker Verlag, Vienna, in 1981 under the title *Luftlinien.* I have preferred to use the newer edition. See also: Anton Kuh, *Zeitgeist im Literatur-Café: Feuilletons, Essays und Publizistik. Neue Sammlung,* ed. Ulrike Lehner (Vienna: Löcker Verlag, 1985), 257–60.

2.   Quoted in Anton Kuh, *Zeitgeist im Literatur-Café,* 258.

3.   On Kraus's polemic against Békessy, see especially Wilma Abeles Iggers, *Karl Kraus: A Viennese Critic of the Twentieth Century* (The Hague: Martinus Nijhoff, 1967), 110–13.

4.   Harry Zohn, *Karl Kraus* (New York: Frederick Ungar Publishing Co., 1971), 102.

5.   Anton Kuh, *Metaphysik und Würstel*, 522–23.

6.   Ibid., 524.

7.   The complete English text and a German translation appear in Anton Kuh, *Zeitgeist im Literatur-Café*, 227–46, and 263–80, respectively.

Spirit of the Age in the Literary Café

It seems impossible that there is still something to be said about the literary café according to the sentimental method, i.e., detailed-picturesque-ironic. Its earthly remains rest as clichés in the typesetter's letter case of the humor magazines. But just now, when it plainly follows its epitaphic wit into the grave, a ghost pantomime of its own essence, it is becoming almost socially effective, just like every startled human community. In its outer aspect it is uninteresting, unimportant, shadowy. But the rumpled traces of these shadows say to one movingly and sadly: These are people!

Today, the vegetation of the literary café appears chewed out and threadbare like the pelt of an old tomcat. Where earlier the steamy heat of established intellects hard by each other boiled, it is now cold from indulgence and forbearance. Where one couldn't hear his own voice over the din of vanities, clattering billiard balls and glasses, the garrulous silence and all the waiters' asides are audible, although they are sufficiently tactful to speak more slowly than usual in order to convince the poor customers therapeutically that nothing they have to say can be heard. Where earlier all sat there in the armor of their individual brand, they've now unbuttoned their vests and put their bellies on view. The belly, the dear belly—it's now the symbolic order of the day of their existence that reduces time to the deepest personal groan! The culinary spans the gap between apathy and higher meaning; in the menu, private interest and the world war meet in the most unaffected way. Here, where they can feel the most secure and superior, they are of one mind with the spirit of the age. Others rather miss the whipped cream in their coffee and they will become nothing. These don't miss it in the slightest, but this is the shortest way to it. They've covered themselves both on the world-historical and literary-sensitive sides when they speak in one breath of whipped cream and the bloody slaughter of human beings—and you don't know what sets the tone of it . . .

The statement "I see many who aren't here," is now becoming intuitive obtrusiveness in the literary café. There are distinct gaps in the type scale. The black-haired idea-of-development should be sitting here and ever nervously glancing up from his viewpoint-bible (it appears once a month) to see if anybody else has a soul. He's supplementing the Goethean totality probably in Russian Poland, but he's forgetting the fermenting half. Where are the painters and sculptors—all fit for military service? Their seemingly gregarious robustness in hacking and grabbing and the sure enterprise of their vitality could be counted on. One at least is here, outlining, of course, the essence of the platform, so some six kilos of naive creative power thus remain behind, rejected by the draft. The musicians seem to have drifted away with the second call-up; their sentimental tummies were no longer needed. Now they are composing on the buzzing loom of office service. Only a new-toner is lacking in the corner there; his face is being used before the enemy. I ought to be so pettily disrespectful in a calm way. He doesn't want it otherwise and in spirit belongs here as before. For he is numbered like all of them, the missing and the present, among the "in spite of it" contemporaries and writes to his friend from the trenches that he can't forget the marble tabletop which extended itself in a mystically animated way even over the child's outlook . . . All the aspiring, unknown, dynamic ones have gone. And as a result of it, the literary café lacks its heating, its foundation. The few men here, who represent something, after all, count for no more—when all is said and done—than cold pedestal figures in the niches. You could just as well paint them on the wall, and the establishment would make the same impression.

Today, the work of the young is incumbent upon you, the half-rotten fathers, the way the field wife undertakes the chores of the peasant who has been drafted. You have to see it through in their place and yourselves prepare the homework of the spirit of the age that has slipped away from the recruits. That's difficult when one sits comfortably in one's routine and then has to apply himself to a signature. And they've been doing this rather a long time, like substitute teachers. One doesn't have to be so precise about it, as long as the inclination exists . . . They have as little trouble with the date 1913 as with, say, . . . 1917. For the attitude toward heroic deeds and so forth they borrow bourgeois amazement, under letter *B;* for "pushing up prices" they bring along the appropriate adjectives. But one day, without dispensing with a certain reference to the general staff communiqué, will they be faulted for the fact that here in this chilly refuge they won't allow the aphorism of the day before yesterday to grow cold? The general staff communiqué, please note, is hung higher here every evening, although not so high that its readers can't still be higher. It allows them a short, detached glimpse—after which for eight hours long they act as if nothing referred to war or world history—through which they take leave of their social connection (for the departure into the secret politics of their souls) . . . They read the communiqué the way they do Gustav Meyrink, but better behaved.

The literary café is also waiting, with greater weariness, to be sure, than other institutions, since it knows at the least "nothing certain." In the meantime, it even receives a cosy "arbor"-thrust into the intimate. (Competition is going to be superseded by room warmth.) Goethe's botany, with which he saw himself through the Coalition Wars,[1] is replaced by card playing. There is indeed room for private life; the problems are still ashamed of their belletristic dialect. These relaxed, affected spree-happy energies, which make the visitor here yawn, these expressions of sorrow of the most ambiguous gulping, this photographic "Just Like Home" together pour out a drowsiness that the waiters are barely able to remove. They then become the jokesters who make their melancholic masters laugh. If it goes any further, they think, literature will come to an end, and then where do we look afterwards for such a pleasant occupation?

The literary café, which before was so orgiastically tired, has become drowsy. The previous tiredness was a smoking out of the crater, a resting of autobiographies . . . Today the torpor has no philosopher's mien and no self-composure. It is bourgeois and harmless. Indeed, the literary café has simply become a bourgeois café. That's the truth of the matter, and I've become forcibly complicated. Inside, its poor survivors are maintaining a historic hibernation. Before God and man they have the lofty duty when the combatants return of being seated exactly where they left them, in the same pose, at the same table, and of saying to them with tears in their eyes: "It's all right, we guarded your vocabulary while you fetched us new perspectives!"

"Zeitgeist im Literatur-Café," 1916. Original text in Anton Kuh, *Zeitgeist im Literatur-Café,* 9–12.

    1.   *Koalitionskriege* in German. A reference to the first phase (1792–97) of the campaign of the monarchies against the French revolutionary armies. The term itself derives from the Prussian-Austrian Pillnitzer Convention of 1791.

Melange = Milk + Coffee

The addition is correct. Melange means mixture, and when you mix milk with coffee you get the drink that's called "milk coffee" in France but "melange" by us.

But something must be wrong here!

A few days ago, I entered a coffeehouse after 2 in the afternoon and blindly ordered a melange. After all, who can keep in mind the intricate schedule for black, white, and mixed coffee? The waiter expressed regrets.

"After 2, I can't serve it."

"Why? Can't you get coffee here until 3?"

"Yes, black. But a melange only until 2."

"And in the morning?"

"Until 10 you can get a melange, from 10 to 1 only milk, since black is out of the question, from 1 to 2 black, milk, and melange, but from 2 to 3 . . ."

"Just black."

"No, you can also have milk. A cup of black and a little glass of milk. But both in the same cup, no. That would be a melange. Forbidden."

"But a person himself can make a melange from black coffee and milk, can't he?"

"That's not *our* affair. The authorities permit it only exceptionally."

"Is that so? Then bring me a melange!"

"I'm afraid I can't. Just a cup of black and a small container of milk. Or perhaps a cup of milk and a small container of black, as you wish."

"Then bring me a cup of black and a container of milk."

"Dearie! A melange for the gentleman at six!"

I got milk and coffee and made the appetizing mixture. It tastes better when you do it up yourself.

Hail the spirit of the law! It distinguishes between sum and summation, between melange and milk coffee. The respected customers are kindly requested themselves to figure up the detour. Then, thank God! Milk, coffee, and melange are still different things!

This miniature picture really belongs under a political rubric. Perhaps under "The Non-Convocation of Parliament . . ."

"Melange = Milch + Kaffee," 1917. Original text in Anton Kuh, *Zeitgeist im Literatur-Café*, 19–20.

VIENNA WITHOUT NEWSPAPERS

That is: Vienna without Vienna. Since the newspaper is Vienna, Vienna a newspaper. The city lives only when it reads itself in print. Everything that happens inclines to its reading pleasure. All reality has only the function of a mirror. What is the conquest of the moon without headlines? Or the war on page 5? Or a strike without a description? Phantoms, secondary matters. But the letter is the world. And this world shares its responsibility with the blessed poppy-seed roll; the better to wash down the morning coffee. Events are cushions, curtains, shawls, with which the background of the day is comfortably stuffed. Without newspapers, Vienna is time-less.[1] The clock that struck eight, twelve, three, and six stands still, for it is well known that Vienna's clocks are set according to the appearance of the morning, midday, evening, and late-evening papers. When the midday paper appears, the warder in St. Stephen's Cathedral pulls the bell rope.

For the first moment, the unaccustomed evokes a solemn, suspenseful mood. It is as if the withheld matter of information were secretly congealing into a ball in the streets, as if a wind had to blow in the news. A return to the fifteenth century. You wait, while the paperboard of the world is being torn away, for stronger elements. We become believers in rumors and miracles, inquire of all the people we know what's going on in this place or that,[2] and eavesdrop in every alley. When the eye is at rest, the ear is nervous. We are all, to be sure, Alpine vacationers,[3] two thousand meters above sea level, distant from every alarm. What reaches us unprinted and unwritten can disturb us little. We save only sensations, which in a week's time turn yellow.

You don't have to be present at everything, and this is true also for time. It is only our presence that makes it so tumultuous and constricting and ourselves no longer able to distinguish the ephemeral from the important. Balance of the first newspaper-less day: we take a rest. On leave from the front of contemporary history. People now see for the first time how much noise the printer's ink makes. The roaring sound in the ears again recalls the story of Niagara Falls gone dry.

In the morning, the coffeehouses present the picture of a day of fasting. The customers sit around paper-starved. An empty reader's stomach shows in their eyes. They stand at the newspaper racks and rummage around yawning. There is again a bull market for the *Wiener Zeitung,* whose Mistelbacher pigs' snout droppings and footrots from the Gmündner district seasoned perhaps only the time our beloved made us wait. It is the only paper one doesn't know from before. In the others, people read the advertisements or at the worst settle for the editorial.

Leisure sets rumors in motion. The waiter is again the center of interest. He got wind of something from the Brigittenau[4] and his brother is a metal worker. Very interesting. People sigh, check the time, and order *Über Land und Meer* (*Over Land and Sea*), then *Medizinische Wochenschrift* (*The Week in Medicine*), *Architekt,* and the *Kaffeesiederzeitung* (*Coffee Brewers News*). What are they waiting for? For the . . . but right, it doesn't come out anymore. A sad life, no matter how you look at it.

In the afternoon arrive the out-of-town papers. People tear them from your hands and stare venomously at the slow reader. Fresh printer's ink! Previously, it mirrored a reflected world—that of the last Vienna issue. Tomorrow it will be different. Vienna will again see itself in print and believe for the first time that it is without newspapers—since it will be in black and white.

Without newspapers? That isn't so. There's a paper lying on the table: *Mitteilungen an die Arbeiter* (*Information for Workers*), no. 1, volume 1, printed by the *Arbeiterzeitung* (*Workers' Paper*), just something more official, more strident, with appeals, blunt strike accounts, and yesterday's budget committee debate, three pages strong. A newspaper of an irregular number of pages may be unique, but that doesn't in the least signify the discovery that a sausage has one end and a paper just one page. The last page is plain empty. Big news fast. Strike and peace are the Lenten fare. The socialist dogma doesn't permit more. And if the general staff repudiates its propaganda, then the Rothberger reports can also be omitted.[5]

No paper is read more intensely than this one. Willy-nilly, all Vienna is becoming "comrade." But it's really too bad about the last page. Didn't the Nutil murder trial (torn apart mercilessly by the strike), a flowery item about the thaw, and the sequel of the novel *The Witch of Kreuzenstein* belong there? The standstill of the big rotary printing press, audible even in the smallest nook, brought time to a standstill among us. Today, Vienna no longer belongs to Europe. It is a small forsaken Alpine village to which a traveler will perhaps bring some news in a few days . . .

"Wien ohne Zeitung," 1918. Original text in Anton Kuh, *Zeitgeist im Literatur-Café*, 26–29.

1.   An untranslatable pun in the original German: Ohne Zeitung aber ist Wien zeitlos. The root of "Zeitung" (newspaper) is "Zeit" (time). Hence the pun "Zeitung" (newspaper; literally, "time-ing") and "zeitlos" (time-less).

2.   In the original: "am Neubau, in Favoriten, in Zwischenbrücken." These are well-known Vienna locations.

3.   In the original, Kuh specifically mentions Mt. Rax, a popular vacation destination just a few hours south of Vienna.

4.   Brigittenau is Vienna's twentieth municipal district (Bezirk).

5.   Conceivably a humorous allusion, in this period of great political unrest and stress, to the work of Karl Julius Rothberger (1871–1945), a distinguished Viennese cardiologist and pathologist.

THE AWFUL JOKESTERS

Why do people like to tell jokes? Out of friendship? In order to spice the sadness of existence with drops of refreshment? No, quite the contrary. Out of vanity. Deep in every person's bosom gnaws the longing for the podium, the wish to have the floor to oneself, to have an audience, to give a performance, to get applause. Where can this desire more easily be fulfilled than in the telling of a joke that demands almost nothing more than a good memory and a few minutes' endurance? I would now like to present some types of such insidious and indefatigable jokesters.

The Ones with Notebooks

With the help of their little notebooks they pursue two things: first the joke (and then it's like a botanist's case) and after that the listener (and then it's a lasso). Hardly do they begin talking when they pull out the book of horrors. People groan from curiosity. They open it up, wet their fingers, search further—and finally their face dissolves, they fall back into their seats, shake, laugh endlessly. You have to wait out their seizure with deathly composure in order to learn which new encounter with a punch line sends them into such spasms. But for the most part, it's already too late for the humor. They've laughed the best away from you. Furthermore, the seizure recurs right before the joke's end. You then have to have patience, look out at nearby roofs, and prepare the grimaces best suited to the expression of merriment.

The Ones with Genteel Jokes

. . . at which, please note, you can't laugh but just smile. But that's a greater insolence! Since I'm already condemned to listen to a joke, I'd like to laugh, too. Serving me lines just to smile at—that's all right for Voltaire, possibly Flers and Caillavet, elegant literature. But since my jokester is a gourmand and favors anecdotes from the Seven Years' War or puns of historical coinage, there isn't much I can buy with long-windedness. Usually, he constructs an apparatus that I would barely forgive in an introductory chapter of Dostoevsky's.

The Ones with Apparatuses

Apropos of apparatuses, many like them. The apparatus-joke has much in common with certain circus acts and looks, in imitation of this model, something like this: First the horse dung is cleared away, a carpet is ceremoniously spread out, after which a platform is brought in, and the ringmaster, clowns, and helpers are all set to go to work. The jokester begins with the craziest, most impossible assumptions. What strikes you as ominous is the ever more noticeable dependence of this entire word and phrase situation on an ordinariness suddenly plopped down from heaven. The carpet, the platform, the lighting effects are all of a sudden there just for the sake of a cheap salto mortale. Too bad, I could have found an easier way of being ordinary . . .

Tho Ones with an Occasion

When you tell jokes—since you don't want to annoy the listener or be caught napping—you need transitions and pretexts. Otherwise, it's all too obvious that you're not telling jokes ad hoc and not because you happen to be a gregarious type, fast at making connections, but because you're looking for a dump where you can unload them. There's a type who quite shamelessly and sparing no flattery chooses transitions and pretexts like: "Since you're talking about copper . . ." (I swear, no word like this passes me by) ". . . well, it happened once that . . ." (the joke follows). ". . . You're a real dreamer. So listen. A scholar comes . . . and so on." ". . . As I can see, you're the type who needs stimulating drinks . . . a head like yours . . . listen to me: An opium smoker says . . ." "Do you have a lot of success with women? I think so! . . . A young man who had a lot of success with women meets . . ." "You're so pale, I'll wager you write poetry . . . It so happened that a poet once . . ." What should one do with these false creatures? I don't write poetry, I have no success with women, I don't smoke opium, I'm no dreamer, but for the past two hours I've been lying chained to the cliff of joke-telling and instead of a face am wearing a smiling plaster mask.

The Only Salvation

On the whole, I don't like it when somebody elopes with my sweetheart, a request for a loan is rejected, a project falls through, or I am pulled by the sleeve by a deadly serious man who whispers to me: "Do you know what the opposite of a sales tax is?" No, I don't know, I don't want to know, I don't have to know! If you want to save yourself from these terrible people, there is a tried and proved method. Tell them, as soon as they start to open their mouths, with a parrying smile: "I've heard it, I've heard it!"

"Die furchtbaren Witzerzähler," 1925. Original text in Anton Kuh, *Zeitgeist im Literatur-Café,* 128–31.

ZARATHUSTRA'S APE

(Karl Kraus)

"Socrates stands accused of corrupting the youth."
—STEINER-SCHEINDLER,
*Latin Text and
Exercise Book for Lower Classes*

Foreword

"I have done what you only painted!" cries Fiesco, Prince of Lavagna, as he hurls the easel at the artist, who is frightened to death.

But don't imagine the contrary exultation, erupting more from shame than from pride: "I have only painted what you did"?

The publisher and author of the following talk is in the latter camp. The plan that arose in him by chance to draw the great pamphleteering sword against a bewitcher of youth who at the same time appeared symbolic of the bewitchery of an entire stratum of society—the plebeian intelligentsia—kept breaking down over the shameful consideration: how awful it would be to expend linguistic and intellectual efforts on such a work. How ungenerous—and indeed in the intention of this talk and its conclusion—how unworthy of Nietzsche it would appear, more an impulsive sacrifice of momentary energy to the demonstration of the worthlessness of a person, hence to a problem of overestimation, and not a "keeping silent about what you can't like." How it would taint one's own head to stick it in another's mess; how this typically local issue of contention would surely sound Chinese to the non-Austrian reader. And finally but essentially, that one who at least lives with the desire for the fragrances of intellectual existence and dwells on the summit of this wish burdens himself forever with malodors when he overarms himself and willfully takes the field against them.

So I drew forth the sword, using the lesser weapon of oratorical inspiration and the passion of the moment instead of a literary one. This is as much as the problem is worth, I believe. And if even here I can't escape wit- and word-spewing and anticipate, to use Börne's apt image, an "escorting through quotation marks," there remains the consolation that the work that it took brought me one good day and no bad night.

The speech itself, its coherence often torn by the shrapnel fragments of the rumpus, and hence the transcription made of it in the auditorium, in many cases vaguely, haphazardly, or scantily pasted together, touches on the personal, not just in the preface but in other places as well. Speech of this sort is sooner a recording than a work of style. But so much the better, perhaps, since it makes the illness—designated by me as "kike-itis"[1] —more audible than the oratorical unveiling of its essence and its causes.

In any case, I wanted to touch up only the most trifling things, restore, for example, sentences that were ruined in all the noise, complete inferred parentheses. Everything intentionally blunt and parodistically trivial—up to the rhetorical word order—I let stand just as bluntly. The same for the entire introductory discussion, which touches upon a press feud and presents an improvisation within an improvisation. [The actual speech begins on page 317.] So that this transcript might embrace the whole of Viennese public opinion down to the silliest outcry, I could not omit the notes "applause" and "laughter" (indispensable for a parliamentary stenographer). Alongside one or another phrase they may produce the impression of an instantly presented voucher.

Whether I undertook some basic corrections—except for a few more broadly defined views of Kraus's language—the auditors of my lecture may after all determine for themselves. But you can believe me that without the brawls and excesses which lasted for minutes and without the frequent police intervention, he might have received a formally more restrained aspect.

My polemical enthusiasm is herewith at an end. I have better things to do, and even if I didn't, it wouldn't make a difference.

Anton Kuh

(*Beginning of the lecture: 7:40 p.m. The speaker mounts the podium and is greeted by tumultuous applause. There are also lively shouts, repeated rhythmically, of "Long live Karl Kraus!" The applause for the speaker and the uproarious countercries continue for a longer time. Violent outbreaks occur in several places in the auditorium.*)

Anton Kuh:
Have the courage to hear me out! Cowards! (*Resounding cheers, applause, noisy interruptions.*) You'd have done better to have gone to your prophet's school in order to at least have respect for an intellectual effort. (*Resounding applause.*) Try hearing me out first, then you can have your turn! I know how to yell, too. (*The interruptions and outcries go on unabated.*)

I see, unfortunately: Hitler or Karl Kraus—it's all the same. (*Resounding approval. Renewed uproarious interruptions, loud booing and general noise.*)

I have a request to make of the troublemakers. There was a time—characteristically, in puberty—when I, too, might have been captivated by the man who exerts such a complex formative influence on the youth of this city. But I must tell you: I evidently hold him in somewhat greater esteem than these madmen. (*Lively applause.*) That is because I have not confused the man about whom I intend to speak here today with some provincial demagogue who drives you to smash a beer mug on the table. (*Renewed applause.*) I believe that when you take his early years into consideration, you may recall that one of his lasting accomplishments—at least holding good for his biography—was having taken a position against a world of terrorism and bickering. But if you now practice adherence to this man as if he were some political saint whom no word in principle ever touches, you dishonor his following. For he declared that what was necessary for *his* cause—I know that he deviates from this principle where another is concerned—was respect for the isolated intellectual achievement.

I ask you to bear in mind that I stand before you now as a man who is attempting, by the exercise of his brain, to explain to you psychologically, and I might just as well say philosophically, the madness of which you were recently either the witnesses or the instigators. (*Resounding approval. Continuous applause. More booing.*)

I could have wished for no better endorsement of what I am going to show you today than this crazed Jew-boydom. (*Lively laughter and agreement. Cries of: "Shame." Shout: "Whom do you mean?"*) Please accept this word in the spirit in which I used it; I've also allowed myself a new coinage. (*Laughter.*)

The subject of today's talk is not so much the man who, knowingly or unknowingly, guiltily or innocently, is the originator of the epidemic whose degeneration we have been a part of, but the epidemic itself, that epidemic for which I would like to propose the name "kike-itis" at some professional medical congress. (*Lively laughter and applause. Cries of: "Shame."*)

Before coming here, I became acquainted with the symptoms of this illness in a weaker, more urbane form. It was precisely for that reason that people came to me with the idea of talking me out of delivering this lecture by means of all manner of protestation. They also tried to make me understand, with the most exaggerated arguments, what a crime against the spirit, what a *crimen laesae majestatis,* what blasphemy it would be for me to step forward and present an aggressive lecture—as its title implies—against the man who sits here as their invisible leader.

Now something heretofore psychological will catch your attention. I am indulging myself completely in a kind of criticism that is neither intellectual nor aesthetic. I am also indulging myself, in the presence of the hostile people sitting here, in truth criticism. It will also strike you that I have used only circumlocutions, that I said: "the man this deals with," "the originator of the epidemic," "the invisible ringleader," and so on and so forth. Why have I not spoken his name? I'll tell you. I am ashamed, true to the warning of Friedrich Nietzsche, who was attacked by this man just as a thousand others, to put my superiority to the test where I can't keep an eye on it. I have kept his name silent until now from the sense of shame I experience at the effect this name triggers at a distance where people have a bird's-eye view, so to say, of all the microbelike insanities of this place and of the dazzling wretchedness that the affairs of this Jewish-Viennese mishmash, whether embattled or defended, signify to a foreign ear and for which there is no more comprehensive term than "kraus" [frizzy] with a small and large *k*. I am ashamed to use a word in a pathetic sense whose highly important utterance in the mouths of so many is one of the motives for this lecture. I am ashamed to mention in a loud voice the name of this man, which I shall now whisper to you: Karl Kraus. (*Laughter. Boos and unrest.*) You can of course upset me, too, but I believe that after the few introductory words you'll have less real pleasure from it. (*Laughter.*) People also came to me admonishingly to try to deter me from the lecture, and I intend to faithfully reproduce my conversation with these fretful headshakers in two typical instances . . . (*Shout: "Come to the point, if you please!"*)

That's the point! (*Continued booing and countershouts of "Calm! Calm!"*) I can't help it, my dear disturbers of the peace, if you apparently want to publish a spoken edition of *Die Fackel* here. (*Laughter.*) You might have read further in the books of your idol that to speak of the person means to speak of the thing.

A man came to me (*continuous disturbance*)—are you afraid of my objectivity?—and he said to me: "How can you do something like that? Lash out against Kraus?" Whereupon I replied to the man as follows: "I have absolutely no intention of engaging in any debate on the right or wrong of it, or, speaking in the private terminology of your master, whether one ought or oughtn't." (*Laughter.*) One thing, though, remains very characteristic: When an itinerant speaker says today that he is going to give a lecture on the person of Jesus Christ, and indeed as a heretic, an unbeliever, in the skeptical, historical-critical tone of Renan,[2] I do believe, and all of us here together are convinced of it, that not a single person would have anything against it. If, on the other hand, someone should come and say that he was going to give a lecture in the Eschenbach auditorium against Schopenhauer or Nietzsche, some people might possibly think that it was tasteless or ludicrous. But I don't think that some tightly organized Nietzsche-Party would suddenly appear against it and call attention to themselves by making a lot of noise and stamping their feet. However, should I like to talk on the latest European phenomenon—to go to the opposite extreme—you please supply the name for it, my dear ladies and gentlemen hecklers. (*Shout: "Kuh!"*) Thanks, that's just what I was expecting. (*Laughter, lively assent, and applause.*) So nobody will take it into his head to get excited about it in some hysterical, monomaniacal way.

Now how do you explain the fact—I'm on the subject dear to the hecklers of my impartiality—that it is precisely around the writer of whom I am today speaking that such a tumult can develop? Evidently because there is something not entirely in order in the normality-versus-hysteria functioning of this man. I, too, am a worshipper—however, not a worshipper of this man; I can also be an admirer, sometimes even an excessive admirer. But I can't imagine that from Jesus Christ to Buddha and down to Anton Kuh (*laughter*) there could be a person the public disparagement of whom or—that hasn't really yet happened—the public criticism of whom could bring such a howling down on me. There is evidently something wrong here. (*Shout: "But running down the Habsburgs is all right!" Applause.*) Here is what I replied, then, to this group no. 1, which was imploring me not to commit a sacrilege against the Karl Krausian person—to follow the possessive case usage of *Die Stunde.* (*Laughter.*) I could well imagine a theoretical case, I said, of people being outraged if some great artist— somebody of the genius of Michelangelo, or Beethoven—a man who creates works of value out of the building blocks of his imagination, was being disparaged—and moreover by somebody from the guild of those who make a career of nay-saying and who nurture their polemical passions on the enthusiasms and artistic passions of others. I could well imagine people full of disgust, contempt, and rage saying: "Hands off this great man who is piling up building blocks! Crawl into the badger hole of your negation!" But, my dearest ladies and gentlemen, when I recall or try to recall how this great holy man, this Buddha Karl Kraus, made his intellectual and artistic career, or when I ask myself what this man's building material consists of, then I have to say: The material of this inviolable one consists entirely of Anton Kuh lectures against Karl Kraus. (*Laughter.*) The work of this man is but a series of depreciations, uprootings, and polemical assaults. It is a quite separate and different question when you can dispute a person's right to do that and when not. I think your Professor Kraus will also have pounded into your heads that where right is concerned, only the form and outcome decide that there is no moral right involved! (*Shout: "Quite right!"*) Then how do you explain, ladies and gentlemen, that suddenly you deny me a moral right to polemicize against your idol and that you deny me it particularly with respect to a man whose entire life's work has been nothing other than an unbroken chain of polemics? Polemics against Harden, polemics against Heine, polemics against Nietzsche, polemics against Békessy! (*Approval and applause.*)

Another category of admonishers then approached me. This one was more interesting, and I must arise as an expression of my esteem. (*Again stands up while talking.*) The other category consisted of very very sensitive and fine people who were unsatisfied with the solemn intellectual argument. Wonderfully brought up on, brilliantly trained in, the Talmud-Torah-school of allusion, better known as *Die Fackel*, they came to me with the words: "I'll tell you something. I'm certainly not denying your right to do it. You already declared your position toward Karl Kraus before. You declared it so often that Kraus said you're bringing up the rear. (*Laughter.*) But tell me honestly—not as if I were entirely of this conviction, though it could be a matter for discussion—that in the Kraus vs. *Die Stunde* affair, you were a hireling."

Well, ladies and gentlemen! You see! It is precisely to this cowardly and insidious accusation bearing the unmistakable smell of this Augean stable of innuendo that I am reacting here by announcing to you the following: If one of the disciples of the Great Master should ask him, hand on heart, whom he has to thank for the three or four best jokes in the battle against *Die Stunde* newspaper, he would have to answer: "I am irritated by the fact that the fellow gives a lecture against me, but I must confess that the jokes were reported to me from him. Once I even quoted him directly."

Perhaps you regard this as a sign of a certain objectivity. I shall go further; it's not necessary to speak of it, but I do so willingly. If you ask me what role I played between these so to say parties, I would answer: "I rather doubt that the publisher of *Die Fackel* would offer me the possibility of expressing on its pages my opinion of Karl Kraus. (*Laughter.*) *Die Stunde* gives me the possibility. That is why, for me, the party question is settled. (*Resounding cheers and applause.*) I have more to say. I am now delivering a strong accusatory lecture. I really don't have to do it, but I can afford to, since I'm a spendthrift. I am doing it so that the accusation won't be spread about that I am a mercenary in the army of St. Canisius.[3] (*Laughter.*) I declare: Anton Kuh, step forward. I solemnly raise the accusation against you that for the purpose of venting your anger at Karl Kraus, under the cowardly protection of anonymity, you took advantage of that newspaper publisher who, as you know, as Kraus says, escaped from the Bakony Forest[4] and therefore has no idea what all this literary stink is about. Yes, I did it! I also did it with reason. If I had the choice today of being a thief, a libertine in the army of a Karl Moor—he's also called Moor Karol[5]—or a ministrant in the great hierarchy of kikeism, I'd sooner be a libertine in the robber army than a sexton in a temple. (*Loud laughter. Boos.*) Let me continue! If you behave nicely, I'll discuss things even with you. (*Resounding cheers and applause.*)

You will now perhaps reply: You yourself concede your cowardice. You placed yourself under the protection of the newspaper's impersonality in order to direct your vicious attacks against our revered master from this hiding place. I confess, I did it once before with open visor. At the time, I rather impetuously directed my attacks care of Karl Kraus's address, as they say in this jargon. The last of them remained unanswered, understandably in view of the "unheard-of lack of class" of my attack. I could afford the luxury of doing it then comfortably and anonymously. But I chose the anonymity even more for a reason that he will barely understand and you even less. Let me try to explain.

Let's assume that there is a person whose lifework does not consist of having some adventure or of thinking up an intellectual fact or a word. Let's assume instead that his calling is *to respond*. Then all other people whose calling consisted of something else—to wit, creating a world for themselves, opposing their mind to that of others, looking after their life's affairs—would come off badly. That is because these people are not response givers by profession; they lack the miserable, beastly vanity to insist on having the last word—in the sense of the last *word* and not in the sense of some deed, adventure, or discovery. Such people would naturally say to themselves: "For heaven's sake, I've got other things to do!" And if I had nothing else to do but have a good time with a pretty girl in a coffeehouse on the Ringstrasse, for the sake of getting amorous with her, the latter would be aesthetic, invigorating, politic, and from every point of view a thousand times more valuable than the insane Sisyphus efforts of a person whose goal in life is just to respond. Let's say, then, that there is a madman who has a mania for running back and forth between St. Stephen's Square and the Bridge of Mary continuously from morning till evening. Somebody else might think: "If I engage this man in conversation or if I pay any attention to him at all, then I'd be condemned because of it to spend years of my life running with him back and forth continuously between St. Stephen's Square and the Bridge of Mary. But that would be troublesome for me." What should this other person then do? He chose a method that spared him the danger of this running together—he gave up the prospect of a skirmish! You will also hear today why I view it as an honor and strive for the honor as well not to have the last word. For the last word is a piece of crap; the first word is everything. (*Boisterous, long-lasting cheers and applause. Shouts: "Bravo! Kuh!" Loud booing.*)

Through my efforts to be my own fireman here, I've become somewhat hoarser. Please calm down a little so I can speak more softly.

What I previously called the epidemic of Kraus-worship and the habit of wanting the last word are closely related. And after partly bringing to your attention the colossal hysteria beginning to stir right now around the name of Karl Kraus, and after its coming to your attention directly, and then my telling you what my last disinclination was, namely, to come forward here as a polemicist with such a subject, I am now at the point where you wanted me to be at the beginning, at the matter itself.

(*The speaker takes a swallow of cognac. A member of the audience shouts, "Cheers!" Laughter.*) Thank you! You know, every detail here really reminds me of the man and I'd like to deliberately lose myself in such marginalia. When I think that a demagogue like him, who sides with the banal and not the elect, enjoys himself over the fact that people of a more impulsive and excessive nature drink, I ask myself: What kind of a miserable pastry-shop- and whipped-cream-soul must he be, what kind of a dry sweet-talker, who doesn't know how necessary alcohol can be to the mental blood pressure? (*Cheers.*)

I repeat, then, that that epidemic as well as the habit of wanting the last word are the things whose connection provides me the basis for this talk. In what do they originate? I am now at the core of my subject. Years ago, I created a type, that is, I named an existing species of person. The name I gave this type is "plebeian intelligentsia." What is this plebeian intelligentsia? Just for the uneducated, I should mention beforehand that there is a difference between plebeian and proletarian (*"quite right!"*), and that there are plebeians who can perhaps also be found among the nobility, and proletarians who are aristocrats! (*Lively response and applause.*)

If only for the purpose of characterizing this plebeian intelligentsia, it is important for me to give this lecture. I forgot a bit earlier perhaps what I believe I can now make up for. I said at the outset that I am ashamed to pronounce the name of this man. That was no hypocrisy; I am truly ashamed. May I now tell you specifically why? As long as I live, I will always regard the specific and pathetic naming of this man as a symbol of what I have now remembered to present to you as intellectual plebeianism.

If some of you, for example, take a trip to Berlin, Hamburg, London, Zurich, or God knows where, and you happen to discuss the "Karl Kraus" matter with some intellectual person or other whose opinion you respect from the outset, you'll experience the same thing I experienced through the years—and then you'll understand my shame. The people you encounter—if you like, I'm happy to name names, and you'll be amazed how prominent these names are—will say to you: "You Viennese Austrians, Judaeo-Bavarians, must be absolutely cracked! Who is this Karl Kraus? He's the one with the red booklet, isn't he?"[6] To which the pathetic fellow will interject: "The one with the red booklet is our Jeremiah, our holy intellectual adornment!" I am less high-flown and would just reply: "Right, the one with the red booklet!" This is what a Dutchman who stopped off here on a trip once told me: "I read this red booklet; it's just a bunch of clever gossip." Then, too, a very famous Berlin writer—he hasn't yet been murdered by *Die Fackel*, but if I tell you his name he can count on it from today on—expressed the opinion: "I don't need the man, I don't need his brain, neither for my art nor for my life; I can live quite well without him!" And now, as loyal Haggadah readers[7] of *Die Fackel* (*laughter*), you'll say: "How is it that throughout the whole world, wherever ideas are exchanged, they write about him, in the *Weltbühne*, and the *Berliner Tageblatt* and the *Nouvelles Littéraires* in Paris?" I must tell you by way of a reply that many people do write about him—I'm thinking now of Paris—who used to go either by the name of "Schweizer" or if not directly Abeles then at least Monsieur Abèle. (*Laughter.*) I, who know Berlin and Prague and all these cities and could get to the bottom of a lot of things, have observed the following: In each city there is a corps of Viennese, Austrian, for the most part Jewish and, to a lesser extent, Aryan exiles. Whenever you see the name *Kraus* on any lecture-hall poster, then you can bet they'll all be there; his claque accompanies him throughout Europe.[8] (*Laughter.*) But if you ask people who don't belong to this good-for-nothing hierarchy[9] what they think of this whole Kraus phenomenon, they'll answer: "Oh, he must be a very talented man, but his tragedy seems to be that you don't have in Austria what you find, for example, in France, namely a really intellectual society." Moreover, the man who in Paris might be one of the most outstanding journalists, the equal let's say of Henri Rochefort and similar models, was compelled because of the vulgarization of intellectual society and intellectual culture in Austria to establish against journalism a little red "anti-journalism" corner-newsstand. As the most talented journalist of present-day Vienna, he became the great press-fighter, with all the right qualifications—articulate, witty, perceptive, and, above all, as all journalists attest, a superb editor whose sly fox's eye and scissors don't miss the smallest printing error. That would be the verdict more or less of the completely impartial, and in their presence I felt a European's shame. I suddenly had the unmistakable feeling that a provincial has when he comes into a metropolis all agog. I come all agog over Karl Kraus and the Europeans look at me and say: "Who is that? Leave him outside for the time being—or maybe we first ought to discuss it!" I certainly didn't have to make trips around the world in order to discover how geographically overrated the Karl Kraus phenomenon is and that it's absolutely a concern I won't say even of Austria's. Believe me, it is so.

After 1918, I also became convinced of something curious. The so-called succession states[10] have positive ties [to Austria] whereby they've still retained something of the old yellow-black [Habsburg] style. (*Cheers.*) For example: the slovenliness, the Baroque, the officialdom, the "Radetzky March." But besides these positive and external ties, there are also negative and internal Austrian ones. All the young students, for example, who were in Vienna before and are now scattered to such places as Agram, Prague, and Banja Luka, all the manufacturers who used to spend the greatest part of the year here and now reside exclusively in the capitals of the succession states, all the intellectual officers—I'm speaking of the reserve officers—who used to be in Vienna and mediated between Vienna and the provincial cities, all these people have retained one unifying tie, and that is Karl Kraus. (*Laughter.*) Karl Kraus, who now stands in antithetical relationship to the official ties, like night to day, or the opposition to the majority. Just as before the *Neue Freie Presse* officially embraced the present-day new states of the old Austria, so now does the inner tie of the *Neue Freie Presse* protest, which they had always found strong both politically and artistically, embrace all the peoples of these states. That is the basis of the Austrian veneration of Karl Kraus. To outsiders, non-Viennese, and those unfamiliar with the phenomenon of this insane cult, I feel obliged also to say: Yes, my dear friend, I must give you a lecture on the history of Austria and the *Neue Freie Presse!* I must explain to you the Austrian's overestimation of newspapers, which goes hand in hand with his exaggerated esteem of the theater, the deep-seated veneration of paper scenery. But these are matters which *sub specie aeternitatis et Europae* are not very important. Now, I believe, you will understand my shame. It is very unsophisticated to point out that somebody is unsophisticated. It is also very provincial to beat the drum loudly for things that one feels are fit just for some minor publication in order to show off before the public which insignificant little publication one has in mind.

I come back to the concept of the plebeian intelligentsia and ask: What is the plebeian intelligentsia? Pay close attention; I'll be speaking of the most important issue. You are already familiar with the political expression "The intellectual middle class." Well, I won't lose any sleep over its "intellectuality." It is the real loser of the war and in no way a sympathetic phenomenon. This intellectual middle class, which is to say the intellectual petty-bourgeoisie, is the soil from which the plant of the plebeian intelligentsia crawls out. (*Shout: "Right you are!"*) Now who exactly are these plebeian intelligentsia? (*Laughter.*) No, I'm not talking about you! (*Laughter.*)

If you try to incorporate it into a Linnaean plant system, how would you then characterize the derivative of this intellectual so-called petty-bourgeoisie and of that certain stratum composed of manufacturers, merchants, physicians, pharmacists, lawyers, and dentists—especially dentists? (*Laughter.*)

I cannot deny myself at this point a very brief psychoanalytical sketch. I know that Karl Kraus, who felt that psychoanalysis was also something evil and had something in store for him, killed it off immediately with four clever aphorisms, although it is still alive and well in Asia, Africa, and other places. This psychoanalysis is a very useful instrument of psychology. And I believe that if Friedrich Nietzsche had been able to take advantage of it, the significant things that were left unsaid would have been said.

Psychoanalytically viewed, the plebeian intellectual—whom I shall here define in his Viennese-Austrian and predominantly Mosaic version, although unfortunately Christians and Jews are in this respect identical—appears a being weighted down with unpleasant family complexes. He emerges from the haze of a small apartment not so much full of the noble love of the free man as of this false, stunted compassion of the person who has a daddy, a mamma, and six brothers, each smothered and devoured by the joint egoisms of the apartment. (*Lively laughter and agreement. Boos.*) That is the person who has been nailed to the cross of the "mischpoche."[11] His sense of smell becomes rebellious when he inhales the family vapors. He longs for an ideal world beyond these four walls. From earliest youth, he has been schooled in the so-called typical family devaluation psychology, in this societal game in the middle of which it becomes ascertained where Egon's problem lies and that Erwin is no brain and that Mathilde is a whore. (*Laughter. Shout: "Everything that's in* Die Stunde!*"*) Yes, it's in *Die Stunde,* too. That's the finest mission of this paper . . . The poor, unfortunate fellow who comes from this awful region is, to begin with, full of uncertainties. He abandons this residence as if it were a cage. He enters the world like that famous horse in Zola's *Germinal* that comes into the light for the first time and feels as if he were struck by a bolt of lightning or, better said, by a beam of light. He can't control himself, but would like to be steadfast. He senses his awkwardness and tries to compensate for it by means of an exceedingly intense and insistent intellectuality. But he perceives this also as a drawback, with the result that a false vitality emerges as a hysterical end product and, in a word, he spits at everything. (*Female voice from the audience: "Have you already come to the intellectual part?" Reply from elsewhere in the audience: "Yes, that's the intellectual part all right!"*) Dear lady! It's a pity, I'd have liked very much to describe for you the role of the poor women, since it is a quite special one. But women's Kraus-worship is really a matter now for the physicians; it no longer has a place before my tribunal. (*Lively agreement. Continuous interruptions.*) As for the lady's question, I shall soon come back to it more thoroughly.

The plebeian intellectual is, therefore, a fugitive from a cage, quite conscious psychologically of the wretchedness and inferiority of his origins and with the great need to make curtains for himself in order to prevent people from peering into his wretchedness. All his inferiority lies in the fact that on entering the outside world he has the feeling—and correctly—that his face, his gestures, his speech, his way of turning up his nose, zoologically reveal the signs of that cage of pity where people devour each other, of that psychological cage of depreciation.

This guilty conscience about his transparency, on account of which he forever hides his countenance beneath veils of mysteriousness and anonymity, together with the self-hate, family-hate, father-hate, and brother-hate from which he suffers, determines his character. Greedily-maliciously, he lies in wait for kindred accents around him in order to arrest them psychologically. Like a seashell, his ear retains the jibber-jabber of the subterranean environment.[12] Oh, if he could just show everybody their origins in the same shit-street in order to feel superior!

Sexually, the fate of this type works out more or less like this: Naturally, he feels somehow instinctively how beautiful the pleasure of complete and mutual desire and fulfillment is. But the only people in the world who experience this pleasure are those natural creatures who through some accident of birth or development became free, the cheerful, the chosen. (*Heckling.*) I implore you when heckling to exercise all possible intelligence. (*Laughter.*) It is characteristic that you interrupt my talk just at those points where you doubtless feel the greatest sense of guilt. (*Loud cheers and applause.*)

These people, if I may continue, naturally intuit that this selflessness offers the utmost possibility of happiness. But intellectually depraved as they are, muddled in their sense of certainty and the possibility for being charming, they have only one very shaky bridge to this great happiness, the bridge of intellectual persuasion.

These poor souls, who are wedged between a world that brings them more anxiety than pleasure and the cage-life at home, now entertain another thought occasioned by puberty: We have no other possibility for love than that of the persuader, the payer, or the violator in the most distressing sense of the word or from the woman's point of view; no other possibility for love than that of prostitution, the banalization of marriage, and delusion through persuasion. Such unhappiness and the most basic lack of experience have two great ramifications: either one heads straight for the bordello, or one goes after a good dowry. What other result can there be than that the young man who comes out of such a cage, with a background of such persuasion and intellectual drilling, will never be free of the feeling of his aesthetic inadequacy, of being doomed to gracelessness? Instead of enjoying a naive physical nearness to the beloved subject or object, he stares intently with the leopard's look of the cunning violator, and at the moment when the leopard leap of his brain has succeeded, he falls back into his isolated intellectual ego and says to himself: "God, how awful I feel!" (*Resounding laughter.*) And for these "God, how awful I feel!"-people who do not belong to the erotically chosen, that is, to the free, natural creatures of this world, there is no contradiction between intellect and love. That is because with such people mind and eros have merged into one, and their brains have no reason to be incessantly embarrassed in the face of desire. Such people already have a great philosophical bible, the great book of Otto Weininger, Karl Kraus's childhood friend, this Prometheus who, when chained to the cliffs of his Jewish boy's torment, did not cry out defiantly to the gods, "I hate you!" but wailed instead, "How awful I feel!"

The plebeian intelligentsia—unlucky in matters erotic, suffering from their fox's slyness and a gritty intellect that makes them isolated and all the more insecure, unhappy in love, hanging about with a feeling of transparentness, mendacious, eager to wear masks, irreverent—have several gods. And what is the principal attribute of these gods? That for this most profound, most wretched, most crestfallen unconsciousness or crap-consciousness of things, they provide them a lofty meaning, that is, they transform their depreciation of themselves and everything else into the pleasure of the "superior standpoint." This is always the attribute of their gods. They are shortcuts for them whereby they are allowed to see through things disdainfully without as yet ever having experienced them! You see: a pocket guide—without the effort and energy of field research! And along comes Otto Weininger, for whom these wretches have respect because he drew the heroic inspiration from his Karl Kraus-destiny to bump himself off at the age of twenty-three and thus not survive the brilliance of his puberty. So along comes Otto Weininger and says: You're absolutely right, poor Jew-boy, fearful of life, hungry for thought, you're absolutely right—a woman is as inferior as he must feel who pisses on her. (*Laughter.*) Forgive me, but I have to express myself that way. (*Shout: "Why?" Reply: "Because it's the truth!"*) The man is right, because it's the truth! (*Laughter.*)

I will not consider further the nature of these gods. Their mission must be to represent abstention from life as a plus, misfortune as an intellectual standard, and the agony of defilement as the destiny of Prometheus. And now you ask me and I ask myself: How did it happen that Karl Kraus was chosen to become a god of the plebeian intelligentsia, so that, when I see peeping out of a pocket behind a nervously obliging humpback's gait the little red mark that has taken the place of the yellow one from the ghetto period, I can immediately imagine what the man says about Nietzsche, the thoughts he has about Kaiser Wilhelm, what he says about the last Karl Kraus lecture. I could read even from his closed lips, when I talk to him, what he thinks about women. I can easily improvise it, theatrically exact, just from the little red mark. (*Resounding cheers and applause.*) What has Karl Kraus to do with God . . . (*Boos. Response: "Please let this flood of words calmly continue to the end!"*) (*To those who called out.*) Do you dare say that to my face? (*Shout: "Just give us the chance!" Boisterous shouts: "Shame! Shame!"*)

(*From here on, recurrent uproar lasting for minutes.*) May I please continue? (*Boisterous outcries and applause.*) Can we please have it quiet? I'm asking you, please! (*Continuous booing and commotion.*) Would everybody please be seated! (*Tumult in the rear of the auditorium and continued commotion.*) I ask you, would you please be so kind, I'm already completely hoarse. (*Great commotion. Scuffles in the rear of the auditorium. Police lead the troublemakers away.*) Would you be so kind, ladies and gentlemen, whether you are for or against me, to express your sentiments only after the close of the lecture. (*Noisy interruptions.*) Ladies and gentlemen, please, if you're interested in hearing my talk, then please calm down! (*Calls: "No!" Replies: "Yes! Yes!" Resounding cheers and applause.*) If you all take your seats, then we'll know who's causing the disturbance. Please, do me a favor and be calm! (*Calm gradually returns.*)

Hear me out to the end; it would be shame if you didn't. Up to now, I've set forth only the theses. You'll be interested, I'm sure, in how I shall now prove them.

Earlier, I gave you a rough character sketch of the type I call plebeian intelligentsia and at the end I raised the question: What is it that causes the phenomenon of Karl Kraus to be idolized by these people, just as the deceased philosopher Otto Weininger is and was an idol of theirs?

And I answered in the following way and begin, finally, with that which interests you so much, the special topic of Karl Kraus.

It was Karl Kraus himself who, by the title of his pamphlet *Heine and the Consequences,* articulated the principle—correct or not—of the responsibility of those who are followed and idolized for their followers and idolizers. If I now identify his following with him, including those who have made such a splendid exhibition of themselves here today—which he probably would not find very much to his liking—it is done only by way of application of the principle he himself advanced. But I have the right to do so not only from him. There is a deeper truth in the statement: By their fruit shall ye know them, even if it is altered to: By his fruitlets shall ye know him. (*Laughter.*)

Kraus, who himself in the case of Heine makes this poet responsible for the feuilletonists, can have nothing against my making Kraus responsible for the Krausians. My further right consists, however, in the following: Kraus has the peculiarity, which I shall later show you very precisely . . . (*Boos and interruption.*) Unfortunately, you lack the courage to listen to the last syllogisms. If I may go on. Kraus has the habit, when you use his followers as an argument against him, of answering with a gesture of disgust: What concern of mine are these disgusting individuals? (*Shouts: "That's a plain lie!"*) That is so true it might suit you better if it weren't true at all. (*Renewed booing and noise.*) Please, take notes, and I commit myself to answering each and every one of them, but please be civilized! I am one against nine hundred, so it just won't do! (*Boos.*)

If you say to Kraus personally, "My God, how these people look!" he'd reply: "I can't help them, what concern are they of mine?" (*Opposition from the audience.*) Not only did he say it, but if you were a faithful reader of his paper, you'd have found that he had in fact written it. (*Shouts: "When?"*) I seem to be a better reader of your savior than you! (*Applause.*) But I shall reply to this man as follows: If some not particularly sensitive person tells me that he couldn't care less from which quarter the applause comes, or what kind of noses his followers have, then he can do what he wants. But if some very sensitive and fastidious person does it, then you can reproach him for the obvious podium-jumping joy with which he accepts the applause of that very same following. Or does Karl Kraus think that when wild applause erupts during one of his lectures the applauders are just Goethes, Napoleons, and Jesus Christs? No! He knows well enough that the handclappers are for the most part identical to those of whom he disapproves in theory. And if not the flesh of his flesh, the blood of his blood, then it would be worse yet, for they would then be dissenters from Aryan districts, from the quarter of that other idealistic-Chamberlain unreality that gets along so well with the grammatical-Krausian, fellow delighters in Jewish self-hate for whom there is room on the same benches of Kraus-veneration. He gets over this fallacy with a small trick of dialectics. He can't renounce the worshippers, he's stuck with them, and it would be an absolute act of cowardice to shake them off and disassociate himself from them. He can't do it. Whoever saw the heaven of success dawn over him when he bowed before that youth from whom he was then distancing himself knows: He needs this following. That I can assert!

What makes him above all a god to these people? (*Boos.*) Now we're on the same track. We're approaching a part that you'll perhaps like somewhat better, the affirmations appropriate to the later and stronger action of negation.

It was about thirty years ago that Karl Kraus came to Vienna. He says it was forty-eight, and even if I'm mistaken, I'm right. (*Noisy interruptions and boos.*) When he arrived here, he still encountered the best Viennese culture symbolized by the efforts of the old Burgtheater. This man, coming from Bohemia, still saw here the most venerable, finest remnants of Viennese feudal brilliance. Now this was a circumstance, his very un-Vienneseness, which by all means qualified him to be the critic of the newer Viennese epoch. The native Viennese lacks that cold, unfriendly sharpness of mind, that eternal alienness of feeling which is necessary—despite the affirmation of everything elegant, beautiful, and noble in the Viennese cultural atmosphere—to experience a fervent opposition and aversion to the careless neglect and pollution of this atmosphere. This is due partly to the fault of the press—I am not here as a defender of the press, you see—partly to the fault of society itself, and partly to the fact that the Viennese has an almost passive destructibility, an extraordinary lack of resistance to attacks undertaken against him. (*Stormy assent and applause.*)

The sharpness of his alienness, that Prague dimension of him, so to speak, was what activated his talent. Had he been born here, had he been thus qualified by blood, it is quite likely that somehow he would have become a part of this great cordial clique-mechanism of art, literature, and society. His mischievous stranger's eyes—in the good sense of mischievous—his marvellous sense of smell of the person who is partly related to this atmosphere and at the same time partly opposed to it, qualified him to be the psychological plaintiff, the attacker with the flair for the theatrical and the knowledge of the assaulted object. I don't grant that lightly; it's an aesthetic-local gain. And so he came here, endowed with three qualities. First of all, his middle-class Jewishness. This quality, of which I previously spoke disdainfully, this quality of detection, of depreciation, of the urge to demask, which has its roots in the familial, can also assume great value for style and parody if directed against something different and distant. The detectivelike glance, which was honed by Karl Kraus within his own Jewish family milieu, was his first qualification for ferreting out the demaskable in the world around him so that it could be apprehended and taken into custody. Transposed into the flabby, gossip-giddy, hybrid Austrian atmosphere, it acquired X-ray power.

The second quality—and I am defining it more narrowly—was a talent for the theatrical, which came to naught for certain physical reasons[13] that also play an essentially psychological role in his life. Because of them, just as in the case of Alexander Strakosch, who as you know was small and deformed but was a marvellous reciter, it became impossible for him to become an actor, although the *mischpoche* doubtless must have told him: "Karl, you have a voice like the great actor Kainz's!" (*Laughter.*) Please understand, this really didn't do him any harm, since it was the suffering he experienced at the hands of his family that thrust him upward! That, then, is his second good and useful quality.

His third qualification was that he possessed a so to say legalistic mind. This also links him with a prominent political personality of this city who out of a kind of naive professional enthusiasm, which I never argue with, is on friendly terms with him. Especially among the Jews, as you can learn from the writings of Lassalle,[14] there are people who have an unusually legalistic mind. The ganglia of the brains of such people are practically curves of lawyerlike argumentation. I am convinced that even in his youth Kraus must have amazed his family with this legendary dialectical talent for being right, with these striking Dr. Viktor Rosenfeld-effusions of speech.[15]

These, therefore, are his three outstanding qualities: his physiological origin precisely from where his followers come; his talent for the theatrical; and the lawyerlike quality of his mind, this downright shysterishness, this obsession with the circumstances of a comma. Because of them he exploits the very same twists and turns and mischievous curves of language as all the clever Jewish lawyers whom we admire not because of the German melodiousness of their language but because it demonstrates its origins in the Jewish mind. All this was the natural material of this man, which partly made him and partly had to have made him an extraordinary oppositional, rebellious, and independent journalist.

I once spoke about the Karl Kraus problem with the dialect comedian [Heinrich] Eisenbach and said to him: You know, Kraus regards you highly, and has an important personal reason for doing so. The man is a lot more like you than you think. He possesses all these genial—Werfel robbed me of this word; no big deal, we'll share it (*laughter*)—as I was saying, all these genial talents for imitating animals' voices that you have, that wonderfully parodic and mischievous sense of hearing that imitates accents whether Jewish or Aryan. But, I continued, I value you more! And when he asked me why, I answered, more or less prepared for his opinion: More, because in art ingenuousness is preferable to complexity drawn from the deepest depths. Nature means more to me than self-analysis. Do you know what this Karl Kraus is in relation to you, out of what sense of kinship he admires you? You're one volume of an Eisenbach encyclopedia, and he's like the whole edition, applied to writing, with twenty-one supplemental volumes of self-explanation. About these twenty-one volumes—of which the Eisenbach edition has fewer—Eisenbach—I said so to him—is more of an original genius than Kraus, with his flair for the theatrical coupled with that extraordinary dialectical talent for being right. Given the greatness of this talent, I can even imagine that if you had a debate with the ten-year-old Kraus—Whose pen is it, yours or mine?—after two hours you'd have fainted dead away with the words "Yes, it's yours, yours!" on your lips. (*Laughter.*)

Now I ask you to bear this in mind. Physiologically, by blood, this man's parentage was the same as that of his band of disciples, this intellectually mediocre middle class clearly oversaturated with Jews. This he can the least dispute by swearing like mad and continuously bellowing: This trash is no concern of mine! But he was ever so much more talented. That is, he represents, so to say, a border case. In body and soul, he belongs to those who stand behind him and are of his blood: detectivelike, insecure, zealous about unmasking people, keen at every stalking ground to the Jewish babble in the cosmos, resembling, to a certain degree, Richard III of the house of Kraus, but by virtue of his higher talent scenting, with nose, eyes, and ears, everything that lies on the blissful opposite shore of better-naturedness. And so, as a border case physiologically, he somehow also remained artistically the best, most talented, most qualified journalist—in another city, in another cultural sphere, an esteemed Concordia-member, if you will.[16] (*Laughter.*) But besides journalism, he was already sniffing, hearing, tasting the big opposite shore of absolute art, of anti-journalistic, important, two-dimensional art that doesn't stick to paper. In both things, he is a border case. Such border people are the real leaders. For the person led by them has, on the one hand, the possibility of celebrating himself by virtue of recognizing in them all his own qualities; on the other hand, he cannot help but respect them, since he has to tell himself: Flesh of my flesh, blood of my blood, he is already halfway on the other shore, where I can hardly follow him and whence he brings back to me the new big discoveries and revelations! . . . I am a bit irritated now that only when I am about to develop a thought in come again the salvoes of a rumpus. Please appreciate my mental exhaustion.

That was the great, genuine quality of Karl Kraus, which might have made him into an important journalistic phenomenon in Vienna. Had Karl Kraus been rubricated as such a phenomenon, were he not otherwise, I would by all means acknowledge him, as I do here too in this setting, in this district, to this extent.

First of all, when I, as a living, seeing person, perceive a kind of epidemiclike hysterical overestimation—which is characteristic of the deeper problem—I reflect on it a moment and say to myself: Where in the personality of the person who is overestimated does the complex of qualities lie that make him an object of such hysterical overestimation? (*Shout: "In his integrity!"*) I remember you as clearly the most responsive auditor at the Karl-Kraus-School when he made the observation about the man "who lives from showing his clean hands." (*Applause and boos.*) Please listen to me further. If you like, I'll hold consultation hours afterwards.

The qualities of what sort of person are we talking about? Was it just the fact that every Jew-boy's heart had to burst out laughing when the master detected the latent Yiddish-German in the cosmos, as I just called it? (*Resounding laughter.*) Was it just the happiness of one weighted down with family complexes that somebody revealed to him the original sound of the family in the universe? (*Fresh hilarity.*) No! There were two, two closely related things. I'd like to explain them to you systematically. First of all:

I spoke earlier of the fact that plebeian intelligentsia of this type find themselves in a benumbed, constipated stage of puberty. I mentioned that Otto Weininger drew from this stage of puberty the splendid, heroic conclusion—if I may be allowed to so interpret—that it could not be survived. Karl Kraus survived it, Kraus, of whom I know, I am convinced, I swear, that he—today a breeder of distinguished students—was himself a distinguished student, that he delivered the most scintillating oratorical exercises, that German was his favorite subject, that he evidently combined in himself all those typical student complexes of self-ingratiation with the headmaster, of the Brutus mentality of the naughty boy, on the one hand, and of the head-of-the-class mentality of the ambitious boy, on the other. These, in turn, were coupled with the detective's suspicious look at his classmates, whom he even then foresaw as future Austrian ministers.

This pupil Kraus, undeveloped, admiring Otto Ernst, shy, undergoes the typical puberty experience in the psychoanalytic sense I described earlier. If you read his aphorisms you'll see that all his sexual comments are continuous variations on the theme of: anguish of life/pleasure of thought; pleasure/shame; before/after; genius/body; woman, I am compromised by you! Perhaps with a Wedekind-like "I am joyous sinking into you." Generally speaking, however, the typical dirty ideas of the sexual adolescent, who did not develop any further because of immutable physiological laws and for whom the whole of life is nothing but the tragedy of the so-called betrayal of the mind, a concept that derives just from puberty, that is from the time a person is not yet ready to love, to discover the liberating bliss of mutual desire, to rid himself of the loathsome isolation of his oppressive dreams, to be confident as a free person and to do something other than violate, persuade, or give it to people, in short, to finally crawl out of the genius-nest of vanity into freedom. But he stopped short. I can imagine that psychoanalysis is unpleasant to him. If this point were carried further, the external phenomena would be reached faster than any other way.

And then the following occurred: A sign of puberty is the appearance alongside a type of underdeveloped eros of an equally underdeveloped tendency toward self-assertion, the self-assertion, to be exact, of the word. This dialectics that is the weapon of the superior standpoint, of unmasking and revelation, and at the same time the best defense against painful self-awareness.

I will explain it to you quickly. The living, loving person who has become humble, who looks reality and the world straight in the eye, will renounce intellectual self-assertion. He will then attain superiority, greatness, and art. The puberty person—insofar as he does not, unlike an offspring of the Christian-Germanic mentality, take refuge in another unreality, to wit, the realm of picture-book heroism—thinks, sees, and speaks only intellectually. His only worry is that he might have to sacrifice the so-called superior standpoint. He lives with words poised on his tongue and in his ear. He doesn't think; he can't be persuaded. In his state of life-blindness, he regards rightness as seeing. When somebody says to him that the world is different, all he can hear is his puberty-ego, or Otto Weininger's fate is on his mind! In youth, it is often just a matter of this either/or: self-destruction or self-assertion. Thus the puberty person asserts himself in the word; nothing penetrates the word-wadding he has in his ears. It is a readiness to leap into airless space, the fervor of the unreal. That, too, became the fate of Kraus when he was, say, in his early twenties. He cultivated this virtuoso style, a bit reminiscent of Daniel Spitzer,[17] of Eisenbach's affected play-acting and a shyster's adroitness combined, and astride Shakespeare's steed. He crawled into this style, still a boy but rearing boys. (*Shout: "Hating boys!"*) Hating boys. (*Laughter.*) If so few clever interruptions are going to be made, I can't make much progress.

Well, I'm getting closer now to speaking of Krausian dialectics—though you will probably say: Sir! What about language? Or "lan-gew-age,"[18] as the master's favorite word is usually snarled by his pathos-vertigo-suffering followers. And now you will hear and come to know wherefrom your real following derives, apart from the embarrassing and unpleasant, indeed offensive sounding things related to such and such street, such and such district, and such and such complexes. And if you give me your attention now and are a little bit inwardly inclined to hear me out, then perhaps you will have a less harsh opinion of me, my subject, and my way of discussing it. (*Shout: "Will there be a discussion afterwards?"*) Only on condition that it is intelligently conducted. I am not averse to it, although I am rather exhausted at this point. But of course without unkind epithets and similar unproductive things.

I told you earlier, in an abstract way, that there is a kind of puberty that conceals itself in dialectics, entrenches itself there, and engorges itself on words while at the same time insulating the word from everything. What are the special properties of Kraus's dialectics? I will not now summon up my old newspaper wit, good as it was (*laughter*); I will not summon up my famous ability to turn a phrase—"A time that has no time for time even were it time" . . . none of that sort of thing.[19] I have no intention of burlesquing this kind of lawyer's pseudo-German the way they do in cabarets. Nor do I intend to prove to you that it is not the antithesis as such—which we know well enough from pleading on behalf of tenants' rights—but its application to the "metaphysics of the comma" that so fascinates you. No, none of that. I am businesslike, I am courting your goodwill. (*Laughter.*) I am telling you psychologically what the nature of this dialectics is. The undialectical person, the person, that is, who does not live on words, dwell in words, protect himself against words, such a person, as I was saying, is always ready to hear something that disturbs him, that's new to him, that he has to now regard in a new way. The dialectical person, on the other hand, always has the feeling that everything that's said—he suffers from so-called association mania—must be deprecatory, an allusion to his sense of inferiority, an attack on his seeing through people and unmasking them, and, at the same time, a demonstration of the superiority of the speaker.

The anticipations and objections "When he's right, he's right!" and "He's a Jew, after all!" spin about Kraus consistently and like leitmotifs. The dialectical, hence afflicted, person cannot hear plainly, nor can he stand to lend an ear to Nietzsche or me. With either one of us, instead of perking up and asking, "What are you telling me?" he says to himself instead: "How much time did you do? When did I offend you? What claim are you making?" (*Laughter.*) Or: "Who induced you to tell me . . . ? How can I pay attention if I first have to ask myself what I can answer?" Or: "How can I expect my audience . . ." (*Boos. To those booing:*) I know that you're madly clever, but let me speak. You see how I'm trying to keep my concentration. If I may continue. The undialectical person is resigned to the fact that the intellectual end of the world, which anything and anybody can bring about, can happen at any moment. The dialectical person, on the other hand, has only one thing on his mind: What kind of a retort can I give him? The very first word ignites these thoughts, since all speech and counterspeech are nothing more than a dispute in the arena before the public for the sake of discharging intellect, command of language, and superiority, and not for the purpose of proving any truth or value.

The language blossoms that bloom from this heat of unreality, from this inability to see and to hear, appear splendid. When weighed in the hand, however, they disintegrate into dust and paper. When once, by way of example, I was describing the phenomenon of Jewish self-flight, the fear of one's own racial voice, father- and family-hatred—which together represent the preconditions for Karl Kraus's style and work—what did the respondent reply? He said: "This . . . that . . . which . . ." My satirical personal description continued: "He projects his own shortcomings onto others." Fabulous! The reverence gang could have licked each word from the floor: "projects," "shortcomings"—splendidly Kraused-up! But what does the sentence mean when you really look at it and transpose it into common understanding? Nothing more than the words we know so well from kids-

and playground-quarrels: "It's all your fault!" Another time, a writer described in a *roman à clef* the greedy, unappealing way the great ethicist takes his meals. Kraus immediately retorted with twenty-five aphorisms under the title "At Night." One of them goes like this: "I eat greedily out of greed for non-eating." Brilliant! He might also have said: "I am consumed by abnegation!"

I would like to interpolate something, since it suits me here, and that is the following, which is characteristic of Kraus's monomania. I once wrote a book of 120 pages, of which three columns are devoted to Kraus. He was introduced as an example of self-anti-Semitism. The book is called "Anton Kuh's Kraus Book."[20] But I must first make an incidental remark. Kraus often engages people in polemics who are guilty of the madness, when they've been taken to task by him, of crawling into the barbed wire of his twenty-years-long-prepared dialectics. They allow themselves to be dragged into this badger's hole of salutations, anticipations, and twisted melodies, whereby they naturally chafe their bellies (*laughter*), and those are the people with the "Kraus-complex." Anybody who is so assailed and shows any resistance in this outpouring of words, anybody who ever wrote him fan letters and then feuded with him; anybody, that is, who, in the obvious school terminology of headmaster Kraus, inscribed the class-register, has his "complex." What happens, then, when one of his admirers or fan-letter writers or somebody who has been attacked by him tells him his opinion candidly and bluntly? Although I happen to have a very exposed face that nobody will disavow, not even anybody who calls me "rascal," what if somebody like me, without the "complex," without devotion, without ever having received a bad grade from him, were to do the same? I have to tell you this, I have to say it, even though it puts me in a bad light. This, to wit, is what he says: "Herr Kuh comes from the rear!" roguishly adding: "He knows his way around there!" What it means is to come from the front, not to be offended, not to be assailed, but to say: "Here is my word!" But this madman—who really does feel himself unpleasantly surprised, but by the sincerely, not the hysterically, motivated word—calls it coming from the rear! The same man who led the campaign against Harden,[21] since Harden, in order to overthrow the imperial German cabinet (which, at any rate, was a historical thing), had determined which people around Kaiser Wilhelm were inclined to perversions; the same man who on this basis labeled Harden as scum, rotter, and pest, on account of a small, purely Jewish, messy literary feud in his Talmud of insinuations known as *Die Fackel*, from which the boys peck out for themselves suggestive parentheses, will say for cognoscenti and non-cognoscenti alike: "Herr Kuh comes from the rear," and it will dawn on his disciples: "Ah, that must mean something special! Maybe there's something for the courts here! Certainly a pearl of wisdom! Grab it, if you can! He didn't mean anything by it; he just happened to say it!" For there are plenty such grateful snotnoses. I understand it. In youth, people need mental training; they exercise the brain on figures of speech. Getting around in this thicket of language, finding their way in this catechism of allusion, knowing to whom the Grand Inquisitor is pointing with his crooked index finger in this or that sentence, for whom this or that is intended—whether it's impudence or not, it's all the same to him—all that makes the disciple intoxicated on cheek-reddening cleverness and gives him the feeling that he's looking down from the top of the Eiffel Tower. And should his god of allusions then exclaim with unheard-of pathos, "A writer who is not ashamed of alluding to private sexual matters!" "Bravo!" will be shouted. And not a single follower will notice how one and the same dialectic can be used to reconcile two opposites. (*Laughter. Lively approval and applause.*)

Do you understand now why the guilt-ridden word "material"—used to get the jump on and parody not-yet-emergent accusers—also looms large in this man's vocabulary? He indeed does have material! He has his research team, which supplies him the necessary raw material from Nietzsche to Benedikt for parenthetic statements, word plays, and double entendres! And deep in his heart he knows full well that, by the same token, he is mortally vulnerable if exact conversations with Altenberg, Werfel, or with the uncle from Nikolsburg are reproduced and, instead of sticking his head in that badger's hole, he just relates how the badger looks inside it.

In the book I mentioned earlier—I hope you're patient enough, I've really dragged the matter out—well, in this book I said that Karl Kraus's language is a so-called homeward-companion language.[22] I'll explain to you what that means. The person who is at home in the world meets prowess with prowess, experience with experience, says his piece, shakes hands with whomever he's been talking to, and goes his way. But the person who holds his own only by virtue of the word, who, wherever a hole appears in the wallpaper, covers it over with word-calk, depresses a trap-door, whereupon another opens up, into which he rushes, thereby depressing it and starting the whole business all over again, just as in Nestroy's comedy *The Torn and Tattered*.[23] Like a mentally exhausted monk doing the same thing over and over again for thirty years, he keeps on stuffing holes opened up by reality with words, a ludicrous clown's work. This kind of man must then cultivate a literary style that preventively anticipates what anybody might think up by way of opposition. (And he will never ever be through with it.) You know that conceited individuals can never take leave of company, since they always have the unpleasant feeling that as soon as their backs are turned people will start saying things like "Well, quite clever, but one must say . . ." Or they worry that they developed outrageous ideas and that the person who listened to them might say: "Yes, I listened to him just so as not to show him that I was piqued, but there certainly are objections to be raised." The undialectical person would think: "Go right ahead!" But to the dialectical person the possibility that some hole in the wallpaper might open up is a terrible fear. And he will write prose that anticipates whatever objections one might yet think up with the last vestige of one's brain.

It is, in fact, very clear. A person who is inwardly great, complete, and solid has but to present his ideas fearlessly. Nothing can happen to him if they are knocked down. But somebody from the "optical illusion" category, that is a pseudo-great person behind whose sparkling words cowers a little bespectacled face (and this face needs more and more breath in order to fill out the slack places and pass off verbal effect as individual worth), becomes nervous at the slightest tear and rushes words into the breach. Antiquity produced it—against antiquity! The present is causing it—against the present! But if posterity is responsible for it?

That is the sore spot. The weaver becomes twofold, no, a hundred-fold, a thousandfold more energetic.[24] Just as he hides his face from himself, he conceals it in his style. He embosses, ornaments, trims, loops, stitches until the smallest wrinkle of coarseness disappears and the total depletion of the account of language creates the impression of utter purity! Naturally, there are naive enthusiasts who regard this marvel of self-training as the highest degree of purity, followers out of supposed reverence but actual inaneness. But then alongside them appear the so-called genteel ones, a group of anguished and malodorous noblesse-oblige-people who in a lesser style misuse word and language toward the same illusion. When they write about him, it's like German homework: they cannot exceed the limits of his style and self-interpretation and often produce five hundred pages of the most awful, hairsplitting jibberish, this solemn foolishness of counter-balanced relative clauses, inversions, and conjunctions. And their god collects it and delights in it! Is it not, after all, the fruit of his own sweat-drenched craft: scribbling madly night in and night out, so that the private sound of his voice, the snarling bewilderment of his face, may become invisible behind a row of words whose dignity seems heaven made and whose creator ethereal and with whose unsightly limbs he can by innuendo distribute rewards and punishments! As little as it takes to reproach an offender for being tempted to pound the asthmatic affectation until the true countenance pops out, so little is the guilt born by many honorable and upright people, to whom language is the direct expression of a person, for regarding the mad monk of punctuation as God Himself!

Let's stay with the image of gap-filling. Puberty people, we can assume, have not at all protected themselves against the world through proper respect for it. They are still unable to develop any psychology for dealing with it, they have not yet had enough encounters with it, and indeed for such they lack greatness, courage, humility, everything. On the other hand, they have respect for a person whose self-righteousness is achieved through the medium of language. Theirs is an adolescent admiration already fascinated with itself through the word and through intellectually manipulated phrases. What happens to them, then, when the skilled dialectician, the genius at persuasion, brings it about that he accompanies them home with his language? He says to himself: "You go on up now. Perhaps something against me will occur to you in the hallway on the first floor. I'll go with you only as far as the first floor. You go into the room, but on the way to bed you might say, 'But there is a counterargument,' or 'You don't impress me as a really great man.' So I accompany you to bed, lie down next to you, put your nightshirt on you, button it up, and wait until you fall asleep. Then I make a point and write down: 'The pleasure of thought, the agony of life!' I have thus once again assembled one of my dialectical masterpieces, which are constructed in such a way that the reader has no more air for his own breath."

And now I pass from the general to the specific fascination of this dialectics. It consists in the fact that the youth—or if he is no longer a youth but a person who has clung to the enthusiasms and defects of puberty—when he reads it, is dialectically persuaded without knowing why. I am persuaded, he thinks, whither language has led me; I know of no other world. I did not notice that in the meantime the seducer had enticed me many steps lower, into the realm of unreality and cleverness-unto-itself! After being led along all those highways and byways, this young man feels exhausted and hangs on to the umbilical chord of his god. Once he has been talked out of everything, nothing else remains to him on the level to which he has been led—that is the optical illusion—but to exclaim, utterly dead-beat: "Splendid!" And he is completely sterilized. If he asked himself what he had left besides that assenting "Excellent!" or "Quite right!" and that swiftly and cheaply acquired look of contempt for the unknown things of the world, what he had by way of new values, he would become sad. That's what it's all about. Whether Kraus by chance became the god of people who were already sterile and hysterical, or whether he first sterilized them and turned them into hysterics, I prefer not to go into. There is usually a reciprocal action in this sort of thing. However, I do not believe that any person who succumbs to this hysteria would also die in the trenches of the mind. I do believe that each finds his way to the other. But the source of the reciprocity lies in the fact that Kraus is the respondent.

If you read the aphorisms of Christian Morgenstern today, each sentence, even without his virtuoso formulation, will affect you as if a world arose with it. Even a phrase like "The flies, these sparrows among insects," you'll tell yourself, is worth twenty-five times more than the most Krausian Kraus-poem and a hundred times more than [Kraus's] sayings and countersayings. That is because there is life in them, which is to say a living, divinely tender, seeing human being. If you leaf through all of Kraus's aphorisms with their unheard-of cerebral energy and meticulous virtuosity of formulation, you'll always have the feeling: clever, good, clever again, very appropriate, and you'll be as if obstructed, completely blocked off from everything. And then each and every one of you—and this is the misfortune of the Krausian disciple—will have lost his own voice and his own mind just like people who can no longer produce anything more original because they hang on to the umbilical chord of dialectics. That's what's so ominous and fearful and why, when you raise objections to a younger person, he always replies: But Kraus states expressly in volume 26, number X, page such and such, line 3, and an answer follows. And should you reply to this, he'll answer: But he states expressly in volume 11, pages 43 to 45 . . . (*Lively laughter.*) He can't think of anything else any more; he's encircled, en-Kraused, and out-Kraused.[25] (*Laughter.*) His brain can now function only in the spirals of the master's ganglia. For that is the demonic youth-devouring dialectics of a person who, like the motionless Buddha of his own puberty, leads the puberty of others by a thousand wires and threads, of the high-school student vis-à-vis the junior-high-school student who advances to full professor of morality in the eyes of the greedy classmate who hangs on these wires. That is the picture.

And now you will ask: And morality? And ethics? Well, for the most part I have already spoken of these in that I have discussed the persuasive power of his style. What clever person, after all, wouldn't want to give evidence of his lily-white Christianity in accordance with the economic laws of this cleverness? But I am going further by asking not just about morality and ethics but about the huge political, immediate effect, about the utilitarian effect.

I was sitting once with Peter Altenberg. I have a new piece of information to communicate to you. Peter Altenberg was not as enthusiastic about Karl Kraus as you think. Do you know that? I'd like to share with you the most charming, most clever, most malicious observations, but that wouldn't mean anything. In essence, much more in essence—come, I'm really going to talk more clearly—in short, therefore, one of the most marvellous remarks Altenberg ever came out with was, and he was being gentle: "You know, Kraus is a dung heaper, the dung heaper who carries away all the crap of the age. Quite necessary. Do you need a dung heaper like that? Neither do I! But the young, they need him!" Whoever knew Altenberg will at once hear that the tone in which he formulated it was— I can't put it any better—wholly unique to him. In Altenberg's apparent commonplaces lay the captivating profoundness: "You need him! Neither do I!" (*Shout: "He also said, 'We need* Die Fackel!' ") Yes, he said that as well. But what he said at the time covers the whole problem. And this is what it is: Every age has its special rot, whether latent or obvious, appropriate to it and represented by certain names. Every one. Let's consider Goethe's age. There was a veritable Hans Müller, there was an Otto Ernst. All these phenomena against which Kraus is today waging war and whose inferiority, noxiousness, and despicableness he claims have always existed. But there was never a Kraus against them. Did these people ever reach posterity because of it? Have the majority of you ever heard, for example, of Master Nicolai, that absolutely dreadful scribbler phenomenon from Goethe's time? (*Shouts of "No!" and "Yes!"*) All right, thank you. (*Laughter.*) This good-for-nothing,[26] this rot, has the capacity for chemical self-paralysis. He will not pass down to posterity. He makes noise, but he paralyzes himself. There's also nobody who'll oppose this garbage. Who should do it? The person who is inferior himself doesn't even see him; the noble person has better things to do. Somebody has to come along who himself combines crap and fire, a borderline person who still fits right in and yet can see the opposite shore. And now we've come to Kraus's mission. Bounced between the crap of the age, designated by all the names you know from *Die Fackel,* and his own chemical self-liquidation, he has arrested the crap in the name of the law. (*Resounding laughter and applause.*) And what have been the consequences? This army of the plebeian intelligentsia, the uninformed who looked upon all of this with sparkling eyes, since they themselves are a part of it, and for whom the *Neue Freie Presse* is the in-tellectual Kilimanjaro and Hans Müller Shakespeare, said: "Fabulous! That's Kraus for you!" It also happened in truth that the good-for-nothing became larger optically, even more significant, but looming bigger-than-life above all was the watchman who arrested him and who now talks it into people that were it not for him, they'd believe that Hans Müller was Shakespeare and the *Neue Freie Presse* the *Times,* and so on. (*Laughter and applause.*) That was one of the greatest utilitarian operations. The wet-behind-the-ears newly arrived youngster, who came in this morning on the

"North Line," doesn't have to know, for example, that there is such a thing as the Burgtheater in Vienna, never having heard of it. He cracks open *Die Fackel* and has deprecation along with information, so that at 3 P.M. he can already declare: "Listen to me; there's no more Mitterwunzer!" You ask: "Why Mitterwunzer?"[27] There was a printing error in *Die Fackel!*

If you ask again: But morality, the wounded soul, the Christ-man? I must say to you: That ethos or, as I once so correctly called it, ethospetetos, we'd be better off leaving completely out of the picture! It's a phonetic, sound-thrifty matter belonging principally to the satirical profession as Kraus practices it. I stated earlier that the dialectical action creates the impression that it is attained not through itself but out of the deep boiling craters of the world's woes, out of the conscience, out of humankind. More important for you for the time being than taking in a full breath of Shakespeare is to provide your case with a powerfully punitive, hotly rebellious base or to lapse immediately into the lyrically caressing opposite. That is, from the same malevolent self-righteousness that ascends to "It is the truth I say to you!" to break out into the affected tenderness: "There will be too many butterflies!" The playacting of the word necessarily transforms itself backwards into the playacting of the soul. But in the long run, whom will it deceive? Who will believe the slightest conciliatory gesture of that inhumanity which borrows the breath of enraged mankind, or assume that the written joy—written in front of a mirror—in the warbling of nightingales plays any other role than that of an argument!

I would like to explain this phenomenon to you in yet another way. There is a level of virtuosity where a person can rest. There is a level of linguistic virtuosity where he feels the virtuoso and thinks: "That is so superbly executed that on the one hand I now have the chance to catch my breath, while on the other hand, as a contrapuntal necessity for me, so to speak, the moment arises when somehow my possible ego also emerges opposite my nay-saying virtuosity: I have overexposed my mind; now I am exposing my heart!" I call this quite rightly the birth of ethos out of the spirit of the ace. (*Resounding laughter and applause.*) It is the moment when after the logic of the art of persuasion, when after the extreme, nothing else, nothing superfluous, nothing more is capable of being said; everything already said forms the background, as if it had been said out of affirmation, out of sorrow and pain. I am myself enough of a virtuoso of the word to be able to reveal the famous secret that when I think I can show everything, I then allow myself the luxury and say, dialectically again of course: "I reveal it not just to deprecate, but because I am sorry for the man!" You can permit yourself that on the summit of virtuosity. One who is standing his ground against all by means of the word finally reaches a point where he folds his hands, shrugs his shoulders, and says: "I do it out of a deep Christian *non aliud posse* [it can't be otherwise]! But the difference between the man of worth and the man of the word is the difference between the person who courageously brings the smallest fragment of experience into the arena and the person who scrambles all over it and shows how cleverly you can conquer it with answers. This difference between the great person and the person with the pseudo-greatness of a small bespectacled personality (released from the satanism of the ghetto into Christianity) who is so afraid the spell might vanish that he dispenses punishments like a Buddha-idol, gives grades, and cries all over: "Torture him! Hold him!" and so on—this contrast between the two opposite types— the great person who places no value on having the last word, since he has other things to do, and he who always waits until somebody builds his own little pile so that he can stir it up with his clever gift of gab—has made something clear to me. Karl Kraus polemically cut down any person who was not a contemporary of his as soon as he entered his circle of concentration . . . (*Shout: "Like the editor of* Der Abend, *Carl Cohn-Colbert!"*)

When somebody was dead long enough, he honored him. If he was his contemporary, he honored him less. He gave his approval to Lichtenberg, he honored Lichtenberg—not much more can happen to him. Heine—he didn't read much of him. I can't argue about how little he actually has read, he who first began to educate himself so to say *coram publico* [in the eyes of the public]. But he insensitively and ignorantly chides all who made his newest discoveries (Claudius, Shakespeare, and so on) already at the age of fifteen (which is why, naturally, his followers also have a stupendous lack of education). I also know that once, when somebody brought up the fact that some idea he wrote down came in fact from Schopenhauer, he cried out with impressionistic pride: "I have never read Schopenhauer!" (See *Die Fackel,* 1903.) The reciter Ludwig Hardt once described to me (by the way, this too would be a significant story to tell), how [Kraus] read a few little poems of Heine: "I know not what it means [Ich weiss nicht, was soll es bedeuten] . . ." and some such. He butchered this writer, since somehow he sensed a consanguinity of Jewish intellectual brilliance and said to himself: One of us has to be killed. Either I'm brilliant or you are! (*Resounding laughter.*) He honored Liliencron.[28] After all, why should a Viennese Jew not honor the titled Christian? (*Laughter.*)

But before you reproach me with committing a crime against the spirit, let me say that there are things that should be respected. Ten years ago, Herr Karl Kraus alluded to the fact—I am a memory-retentive reader of *Die Fackel*—that there was a philosopher who had dance and dancers on his conscience and he hadn't yet come to terms with him. I thought to myself: Now he's going against God himself, now he's going against Nietzsche, against him whose outward relationship to his successor I once characterized as "Karl Kraus, the brilliant sapphire—that is to say, Gottlieb Moritz Saphir—in Nietzsche's crown." But Kraus must have thought it over, his admirers must have said to him: Don't get involved with that one! Something must have got in the way, probably difficulties stemming from a greater familiarity with his works. There is a lot of Nietzsche to read; and mobilizing language against Nietzsche is difficult. It's easier to blame Heine for the emergence of the feuilletonists than to hold Nietzsche responsible for the fiery madcaps of language and to represent him as their creator. Through a misunderstanding of the Nietzsche-philologists, Nietzsche himself is regarded as a dancing Dionysian, while in reality he was an anarchist. But then came the twenty-fifth anniversary of Nietzsche's death. Many important things were written, among them an essay by me. Karl Kraus didn't read it. He read only the contributions in the *Neue Freie Presse* and on that basis deduced, clever as ever, what an upstart, what a Kraus Nietzsche must have been. (*Laughter.*) And then he said, rather bluntly: What did this great man really write? A small, pretty poem once upon a time, but no great, artistically significant things. Now you will say: This is one instance at least when Nietzsche-Kraus, whom Herr Kuh represents as the respondent, answered nothing. No, my dear ladies and gentlemen, wrong, dead wrong, *he did answer!*

One night, Friedrich Nietzsche had a vision. Kraus appeared to him. But not just as a person. Kraus with his *Fackel*-German! The spitting image of him! And now listen and try not to be shocked by what Nietzsche, foreseeing Kraus's attack on him, wrote about Kraus and Vienna. The great city that appears here is Vienna. Who Kraus is, you'll figure out. Now please pay attention. [At this point Kuh reads all but the last few paragraphs of the episode entitled "On Passing By" from the third part of *Thus Spoke Zarathustra.* The episode relates Zarathustra's encounter with the fool called "Zarathustra's ape" because of his imitation of Zarathustra's words and ideas. Before completing his reading of the episode, Kuh interrupts himself in order to point out the parallels between Vienna and the city envisioned by Nietzsche in the "On Passing By" episode.]

And now please observe how correctly Nietzsche sees also that other city, Vienna, in the light of *Die Fackel:*

> Thus spoke Zarathustra; and he looked at the great city, sighed, and long remained silent. At last he spoke thus: "I am nauseated by this great city too, and not only by this fool. Here as there, there is nothing to better, nothing to worsen. Woe unto this great city! And I wish I already saw the pillar of fire in which it will be burned. For such pillars of fire must precede the great noon. But this has its own time and its own destiny.

> "This wisdom, however, I give you, fool, as a parting present: where one can no longer love, there one should *pass by*."
>
> Thus spoke Zarathustra, and he passed by the fool and the great city.

O deepest logic! The satanic talent-offspring of the Jews, frothy good-for-nothing product of decadence, ambition-crazed, self-righteous, full of the jumping, squeaky-voiced exhibitionism that leaps about ritual wedding tables, but at the same time a monkish watchman over every sound that upholds him. So pedantically sparing is he of his life for these efforts at spiritualization that, like a parched saint, he guards his store of speech or ascends to the prophet's aerie on a silvery-slimy vocal cable. He must be Zarathustra's ape; that is how the frothy one must look!

What will he do now when he receives this Nietzsche-figure for a face? What will stir in him, foam-covered and putrid and frothing and screeching? His torrent of words will drag a cleverly nasty web of spittle around these splendid five pages, and the adolescents already full of fear will think: "Heavens, I will be torn from the umbilical cord!" But they will see that this umbilical chord will again be discussed by him in its entirety. He will also madly delight in the fact that the answerer vanquished the respondent. But I believe, ladies and gentlemen, that there ought to be a biblical saying for it, although unfortunately there is not. But were there, it would go something like: "Woe to him who has the last word . . ." I don't want to have the last word here and will not have it. I don't want to run a race with the frothy fool and will not. I herewith relinquish the field to him, the Master of Speech, the "Servant of the Word!" (*Resounding, long-lasting cheers and applause.*)

The sketch is subtitled "An Extemporaneous Talk Delivered at the Vienna Concert House Auditorium on 25 October 1925. Stenographic transcript: Adolf Irschig and Joseph Meier. With a Foreword to the printed edition by Anton Kuh" ("Der Affe Zarathustras [Karl Kraus]. Eine Stegreifrede, gehalten am 25. Oktober 1925 im Wiener Konzerthaussaal. Stenographisches Protokoll: Adolf Irschig und Joseph Meier. Mit einer Vorrede von Anton Kuh zur Druckausgabe"). Original text in Anton Kuh, *Metaphysik und Würstel*, 153–205.

    1.   "Itzig-Seuche" in the original. This means "Itzig-epidemic," with "Itzig" (from Isadore) representing a familiar Yiddish given name. The English equivalent of this would be "Izzy." My somewhat blunter translation does justice to Kuh's intention here, which is in no way ambiguous, and at the same time avoids the problem of interpretation.

    2.   Ernst Renan (1823–92), French philosopher, historian, and scholar of religion, known widely for his controversial *Vie de Jésus* (1863).

    3.   A reference to the street named after the saint, where the offices of *Die Stunde* were located.

    4.   In the Bakony Mountains in northwest central Hungary.

5. The typical Hungarian inversion of first and last names being an allusion to Békessy.

6. "Red booklet" is a reference to Kraus's *Die Fackel.*

7. The nonlegal part of the Jewish *Talmud,* consisting mostly of ancient Hebrew lore.

8. In the original, Kuh uses the Yiddish term "kille," meaning band, claque, society.

9. "Tinnef-Hierarchie" in the original, "tinnef" being a Yiddishism meaning something or somebody useless, good-for-nothing, loathsome.

10. That is, the new states (Czechoslovakia, Yugoslavia, in part Poland) created in east central Europe after the breakup of the Habsburg Empire following the First World War.

11. A Yiddish term of Hebrew derivation meaning "family."

12. I have translated as "jibber-jabber" Kuh's original "Gemauschel," a concoction of his based on the German verb "mauscheln," which means "to jabber" but can also mean "to talk Yiddish." In the context, it is obvious that Kuh is alluding to Kraus's Jewish origins and his keen ear for anything linguistic hinting at concealment of Jewishness on the part of others.

13. An allusion to Kraus's slight curvature of the spine, which made him look a bit hunchbacked.

14. Ferdinand Lassalle (1825–64), a leading German socialist and disciple of Karl Marx. He was one of the founders of the German labor movement.

15. Viktor Rosenfeld (1852–1919), a well-known Viennese trial lawyer.

16. Concordia was a prominent Austrian literary society of the time.

17. Daniel Spitzer (1835–93), outstanding Austrian writer of feuilletons.

18. "Schaparache" for "Sprache" (language) in the original German.

19. I have omitted some six lines of text here in which Kuh additionally demonstrates his skill at verbal wit-making. The German is really untranslatable, since it plays with the word-building potential of the root "trag-" (carry, bear, and so on), as in "Vortrag" (lecture), "tragen" (to bear), "Ertrag" (produce, yield), "Erträgnis" (virtually the same meaning as "Ertrag"), "Eintrag" (entry, damage), and "vertragen" (endure, stand).

20. I believe that Kuh is actually referring to his book *Juden und Deutsche: Ein Résumé,* which was published by the Erich Reiss Verlag of Berlin presumably in 1921. No date of publication appears in the book. It has never been reprinted to my knowledge.

21. The prominent German publicist Maximilian Harden (1861–1927), another object of Kraus's scorn. Harden was a great admirer of Bismarck and after Bismarck's death attacked the men around Kaiser Wilhelm II.

22. "Nachhausebegleitungssprache" in the German.

23. *Der Zerrissene* (1845), by Johann Nepomuk Nestroy (1802–62), a major Austrian comic dramatist and actor.

24. I have translated the German "Fädenspinner" as "weaver," since I believe this comes closest to Kuh's satirical intention here. But Kuh is obviously playing with meanings. "Fäden" means "threads," "fine lines" (as in a spider web). "Spinner," literally "spinner," is more suggestive. In colloquial German, "Spinner" can also mean "crackpot." The verb "spinnen" can mean "spin," but also "rant" or "rave." "Spinne," the word for "spider," can also be used to denote a spiteful or malicious person. And finally, "Spinnfade" means a "spider thread." Alluding to Kraus's paranoia, Kuh presents him as a half-crazed, malicious person whose insistence on seeing plots everywhere to discredit him likens him to a frenzied

weaver trying to sew together any hole torn in the fabric of his public image. The image of a web-spinning spider is also apt.

25. An untranslatable pun in the original: "eingekreist (encircled, from "einkreisen"), eingekraust, ausgekraust (plausible-looking verbs based on the name Kraus.)

26. "Good-for-nothing" is my translation of Kuh's German-Yiddish "Zeittinnef."

27. A reference to the very popular Viennese actor Friedrich Mitterwuzer.

28. The German poet Detlev von Liliencron (1844–1909), who was of aristocratic origins.

The Second on the Right

Dear, unknown Fräulein, who evening after evening as a member of the captivating nude-machinery-"Girls" is a treat for the eyes in the Vienna Bürgertheater, this is my way of making a declaration of love to you.

I have no desire to nor can I hereby "spoil" you. The essence of charm consists in the fact that not even a maharaja's look of homage can harm you. Were that, in fact, possible, your effect would be gone. But the sweetly tormenting, conscience-oppressing, hymn-inspiring nature of a charm such as yours flows from the certainty that there is no object, no price that can buy your rhythmic freedom, so to speak, nothing that would be desirable or costly enough—if thrown into the mouth of this monster "beauty"— for it to give up the smile of victory.

You stand one day in flimsy green dress and then with brushwood around bare hips on the right as number two and afterwards as the fourth on the left. That's all I know about you personally. You execute the prescribed movements not as smiling nonsense like most of the others—if one looks more closely, the collective rhythm consists just of pleasant individual items under the heading "Laziness"—but in a mysterious way you exert yourself. That is, you don't exert yourself so much as stretch yourself, since in all likelihood your body and face bring you joy only when tension exists within you. When you toss your head back baby-like,[1] it's not a "girl" pose but the high-spiritedness of charm. And when, at the close of your number, you roll in front of the prompter's box like a small child in bed, anybody can see that for you symmetry is no work but muscular joy.

I don't know why you are so good-humored. I only know that you will remain so right down to the three-hundredth performance—although the *Arbeiter-Zeitung* (*Worker's Daily*) finds that the artistic needs of the working class are not served this way. Perhaps it comes from the fact that you, yourself "working class," are just eighteen or nineteen years old, or perhaps because you want nothing more than to be yourself and never envy the lead performer, Rita Georg, or some chosen one of Croesus. But probably because all who delight in your lovely back can have a good tumble over it.

Unfortunately, as I, the undersigned, know as well. I've tried to catch your eye, my dear, thin, tall young lady with the bangs that wreathe your brow, the open doll's mouth, and the saucy, coyish agility. And I've made a bet here just with others to entice you away from the smooth young gigolo or business manager who doubtless has the solo pleasure of escorting you home every evening or awaiting you in a small café.

Will I win?

"Die zweite von rechts," 1926. Original text in Anton Kuh, *Zeitgeist im Literatur-Café*, 131–33.
    1.   "Baby-like" appears in English in the original.

THE BOHEMIAN

I am a bohemian, people say. They have a kindly look in their eyes and a tolerant twist at the corner of their mouth. Their attitude is patronizing as they behold me from a height of 1,500 meters above sea level. The bourgeois, like literati, are quite comfortable with the idea that bohemianism is a form of early absentmindedness, a freely chosen state of disorder, a genuinely romantic topsy-turvy.

Whoever believes this was never a bohemian. Bohemianism is in reality just the expression of a definite, undesirable economic condition. Put 10,000 English pounds on the table in front of me—a settlement bid to the editorial department—and I obligate myself henceforth to renounce the profession of a bohemian! For 12,000, I'll get up at cock-crow. For 15,000 . . . I'll retract this essay.

Those bohemians who refuse to be bought out of their life-style are phonies! Dilettantes, small-time philistines. They regard inaccuracy as art and pay homage to the unsteady measure of their lives as to some beautiful idea. The real bohemian, on the other hand, is characterized by the fact that he is not happy being one. The bohemian longs for order. The bohemian would like to sleep nights. He locks all the drawers. He remembers every bill. Keeps track of his cash on hand. Reviews his possibilities. Tolerates no toothpick between his teeth. And pays . . . (But this is the least known, since he chooses a time and manner other than the usual for the manifestation of this punctuality and correctness.)

Can a post-office clerk appear more punctually at his office than John Höxter in the Romanisches Café?[1] Or is there a pedant who checks his bills any more reliably than I throw them away? It is the bohemian who is the true pedant. Example: me. I get up like clockwork at five in the afternoon. At the stroke of six, I shirk my correspondence. At six-thirty, I undertake the avoidance of work. And exactly at six in the morning, I am back in bed again. Loans are accepted by me on a moment's notice; their restitution follows promptly upon execution. Appointments are scrupulously subject to chance. I recognize no deviation from this program. There is only the unconditional, direct line of the principle.

To whom do I owe thanks? The scoundrel who denies me credit and support while smilingly pointing out that as a bohemian I have no need of them? Nothing but this loyal confidence placed in the unpredictability of my bohemianism made me a bohemian. Who will buy out my bohemianism?

"Der Bohemien," 1928. Original text in Anton Kuh, *Zeitgeist im Literatur-Café*, 135–37.

1.   The Romanisches Café was a well-known Berlin coffeehouse at the time, popular with writers and bohemians.

THE ARREST OF ADOLF LOOS

Adolf Loos, the father of the Vienna Applied Arts Workshops [Wiener Werkstätte]—in godfatherly Vienna, where the most eminent people are also referred to by their official registration and trade license, he was called "Architect Loos"—was arrested on the charge of indecently assaulting two children. In Vienna, as one should add today, almost drawing a deep breath and feeling a bit reassured. It had unfortunately got around by this time that in the once so tolerant and humanitarian city, whose finest attribute from time immemorial had been a willingness to differentiate the behavior of its artistic fellow citizens, a very malevolent provincial wind is blowing under the new police regime, which is driving away the creative people one after the other.

Loos was also one of the expellees. After the revolution,[1] the air became too close for him who in the good old days fought many a duel with the parochialism and philistinism of the academic slouch-hat wearers and because of it earned the title "troublemaker." At the age of fifty he went to Paris and lived there in wretched circumstances, but without ever abandoning the charm of the man of the world, which was stamped on him from his fine-featured weary-eyed face down to his exemplary clothing. (I say exemplary because, like his dearly beloved friend Peter Altenberg, he was always an enraptured propagandist in behalf of the smallest particulars of life.) Like a strange prophet of trifles, he immediately gathered about him a chosen circle of disciples who, to be sure, had a hard time understanding the almost deaf and French-fracturing eccentric from Vienna, but who nevertheless followed his path with affectionate instinct.

Year after year the man who discovered the functional style and the beauty of unadorned furniture was seized by homesickness, that most unfunctional of feelings. To be sure, not a sentimental but rather an intellectual homesickness, the longing of the rebel for the habitual offensive front. But perhaps this time his side trip to Vienna had more prosaic grounds. On the invitation of a manufacturer he was supposed to build workers' homes in a small Czech town. It's quite possible that Vienna was just his last business stop. But one way or the other, for exiles the return home is always a foolhardy adventure, and Adolf Loos is now caught in the fox trap.

The last time he visited Vienna, he mounted the lecture podium as a culinary or rather anticulinary Abraham a Sancta Clara.[2] He launched the most fearless assault that anyone in Vienna had ever dared—in a decisive blow at the local genius—*a declaration of war against starchy Viennese food*. The cooks of both sexes foamed at the mouth, struck in the heart of "tradition" and "culture." Loos was hissed down in the hall. "Come on!" and "Shame!" resounded through the rows. He could have slandered Schönbrunn and the Prater, defamed the composer of the "Radetzky March" and the German masters, perhaps even been drawn into blasphemy against Grinzing and its wine restaurants. But an attack on Vienna's starchy diet, no, that was treason.

Once before, and on a more serious issue, he ignited his delight in provocation and got the good burghers of Vienna up in arms. That was when he was commissioned by the municipal construction office to erect a commercial edifice on the lovely, venerable Michaelerplatz, on the site of the old court theater. He used the occasion to indulge his hatred of the senseless architecture of the epigone age and intentionally, like a manifesto become stone, he put an unembellished, naked box (a kind of penal institution with marble columns) in the midst of the most precious Baroque. It was an excess of conviction, but it remained standing, itself today almost newly venerable, despite all the howling of the slouch-hat academics and the protest gatherings of all those who would like to reduce art and diet to a common formula.

In Vienna, the chronically unsympathetic usually become popular in time. It is the city of the popular show of opposition, of the dusted-off frondeurs.[3] Had the rule found its exception in Adolf Loos? Were such dagger thrusts against the spirit of the Viennese diet truly unpardonable? If you read the Vienna reports about his arrest, you could almost believe it. The too-hasty arrest when other measures against the nearly sixty-year-old deaf man might surely have safeguarded the due process of law, the vagueness of the incriminating proceedings (he is supposed to have "touched" children who posed for him), the overreactive promptness of the police communiqués two hours after the first interrogation, all this strikes the person familiar with the new Viennese police methods as suspect (the more so when the statements of an eight- or ten-year-old child are presented as the basis of the official action). Adolf Loos is no ordinary citizen; his style was always, to put it the Viennese way, a bit "närrisch" [foolish]. But it is precisely for the "foolish" that the city has for ages had an affectionate soft spot. The originals, eccentrics, and barefooted of the spirit stood in her high esteem even when the style of their raptures—as for instance in the case of Adolf Loos's crony, the noble fool and enthusiastic friend of children Peter Altenberg—provoked the moralists. Old Vienna was truly a natural preserve for originals. They had here, as it were, a traditional, court-guaranteed right of asylum. The new Vienna—arrests them. And then straightaway beats the drums—it's caught another one!

No legal right of exemption, of course, is claimed for artists and cranks. But especially in Vienna, the city of tact, proceedings against the few individual exceptions used to tread softly even in the face of definite proof of guilt. And yet it seems appropriate that of all places the tragic misfortune had to befall him who was so well traveled and oft uprooted in Vienna . . . the city he so often and abundantly nettled.

"Die Verhaftung Adolf Loos," 1928. Original text in Anton Kuh, *Zeitgeist im Literatur-Café*, 194–97.

1.   Kuh is referring to the upheaval that ushered in the Austrian republic in 1918.

2.   Abraham a Sancta Clara (1646–1709) was undoubtedly the most renowned Austrian preacher of the Baroque. He was well known for a down-to-earth folksy style and frequently addressed himself in his sermons to matters of food.

3.   French seventeenth-century rebels who were called "frondeurs" (slingers, from the French word "fronde," meaning a slingshot) by their detractors, who compared them to schoolboys firing slingshots when their teachers were absent or their attention diverted.

CENTRAL AND HERRENHOF

In 1918, at the gates of the Estates House of Lower Austria in Vienna's narrow but stately Herrengasse, the thousand-year-empire of the Habsburgs was taken over by a few groups shouting "hurrah" and "down with" and under the name of "German-Austria" at once demonstrating a new capacity for history making. At precisely the same time, a secession occurred in Vienna's intellectual life that accidentally turned the same street into a showplace.

Until then, there existed far and wide just a single literary coffee-house. That was the Central.

Bibiana Amon, The Radiant, discovered as Gretchen by Peter Altenberg, but now blossomed out into Helena, stood on the highest of the three entrance steps, glanced at the throng around the Estates House, saw her beloved in the midst of it, and shouted: "Be careful, Anton! The revolution!" The mummies hidden behind her, who had crawled out of the card- and billiard-rooms out of curiosity, scattered back. But then her glance must have ventured too wide, to the new building right on the corner to the left, and she caught sight of the newly opened Café Herrenhof.

Short and sweet: two days later everything that was politically and erotically revolutionary-minded sat over there in the new coffeehouse. The mummies remained in the old one.

The divorce was logical.

The Café Central had its roots in the '90s, in early impressionism, in Hermann Bahr's reform Austria. It was here that the renegade journalism, the revolutionary enthusiasm of young theater and music critics, found shelter. That is because it was lodged in the building of the former produce exchange, solemnly embedded between the arcades and col-umned courtyards of the old liberalism.

The holiest of holies, the sanctum sanctorum, lay to the rear and was called the dome hall. Not just because of its shape, but because the smoke and noise of this square attained a height in this immense space where a cupola was hardly visible any more. But this chapel loftiness, this roofless smog, created the uniqueness of the chamber.

In the other areas sat socialism, pan-Slavism, and imperial-and-royal high treason; Dr. Kramarsch and Masaryk,[1] Slovenian students, Polish and Ukrainian parliamentarians, learned labor leaders—the fanatical editorial column. The coffee had a wonderful aroma and newspapers in every language of the realm were stacked on the large round table.

It was there in back that the feuilleton resided.

It dragged itself in around the turn of the century as Peter Altenberg's rattail. He was the first and most authentic coffeehouse writer. Although he lived nearby in the walk-up Hotel London, amidst impromptu romantic relationships, he listed his address with the furrier as "Vienna, First District, Café Central."

Above the table at which he sat there hangs today a miserable, overly refined pencil sketch of him. The headwaiter who passes on to an assistant an order from here orients him by means of the shout: "A black to Altenberg's!"

The conscripts acted like they owned the place. With the master out of the house, his monomaniacal voice, sometimes clacking in monologue, sometimes suddenly angered, no longer cleaved the air. An unnatural, elegantly rustling silence took its place; a pensioner's ghost who walked on the softest, most sensitive soles; Hamsun-ism sunk in a game of cards.

Only one thing was, by nature, excessive. The apostles assumed a quieter composure, at the same time bearing the Viennese Schopenhauer-bitterness that the young Otto Weininger had bequeathed them with painfully senile expression. Bank officials with ethical backgrounds. Their gesture: suicide forestalled by accident. Their achievement: the review.

There was always a moldy, grave-cool smell here. The chapel was now an asylum of resignation, inhabited by hermits who took pleasure in recognizing the former great Charles V by face.

Polgar Alfred[2]—today a classic—gentleness wrapt in such provocative thought that this piano of his being made the cups jingle, played tarok. But it was not the tarok game of a bourgeois; it was Buddha's flight into tarok. Looking at him sitting that way for hours at a time, you could barely help thinking: "My God, what the man could be if he didn't sit here for hours playing tarok!"

And so he sat and played.

It was the same with all of them. Their pursuits here, incidental and resigned in spirit, seemed like gestures of anonymity of their station. The impartial visitor indeed could have rightly sworn that he saw nothing in front of him but newspaper-reading and card-playing philistines. The falseness of this impression was known only to the deeply initiated. He could distinguish the delicate shading between appearance and reality, this daily embellishment of the evening newspaper (collected by Ernst Rowohlt, Berlin[3]).

So they applied mold to a vigorous complexion. Otto Weininger's star glimmered on their flabby faces, weatherworn from half-titillating, snivelling compliance with incestuous demands. Their philosopher was the little, nearsighted Grüner, with the bullet wound scar on the temple.[4] In spring, a side entrance to the street was opened so that the premises could be aired out. Grüner commented: "When the door to the Herrengasse is opened, then spring is here."[5]

Was it not a pleasure when Bibiana, unfairly taken advantage of in her illiteracy and notwithstanding the hisses of the decorous, appeared in the gallery of the arcades courtyard to recite a chapter of Dostoevsky?

Or, when all of a sudden a ruckus blew in from the rear chess-room, accompanied by curses, because the teenage girl who was playing chess for a gulden a game with the oldest used-clothes peddlers of the monarchy had put too great a financial strain on the table? Trotsky, who as we know spent many years here, head on elbow, contemplating his moves, shuddered with the rest of them.

Or, when the impoverished writer Ottfried Krzyzanowsky,[6] slovenly, bony, ugly, but educated and aristocratic and with two eyes that burned extortingly into every part of his fellowmen—which a Frenchman calls "Le manque de coeur" [the absence of a heart]—planted himself in front of somebody sunk in play like death itself and sentenced him with sharply extended forefinger: "Pay me a shot of wine!"

Oh, what joy it was to see in a moment's glance the agonizing dilemma of the faces, the deeply divided, captious self-torment over the battle between giving and not-wanting-to (or really: between wanting-to and not-giving)!

Since Krzyzanowsky was starving at the time—he did it out of conscience-incriminating malice—many feuilletons by givers and non-givers appeared. The givers had often teased him and now mourned the original; the non-givers, on the other hand, fled the teasers!

A bohemian dying of hunger? How could that happen in the city of charity, in the protective, tippling-safe atmosphere of the literary coffeehouse?

It was a tragedy: "Disloyalty in the hangout!" The concept of "regular guest," so innocuous and cozy, for the first time became a motif out of Aeschylus. This is what I mean:

Until the establishment of the coffeehouse on the opposite side of the street, the beggar-writer spent his days and nights in the Central. If he missed a single hour in the period between three in the afternoon and two in the morning, the question emerged from the mouth of one or another of his friends: "What's happened to Krzyzanowsky?"

But once the Herrenhof was opened, the writer, whose patrons now began to split into two camps, performed a pendulum action. If you didn't see him for a while in one place, you knew: "Aha, he's over there!"

Thus it happened that as time went on the clients of the two coffeehouses paid less and less attention to Krzyzanowsky's absence.

One day, somebody again asked about Krzyzanowsky. "He's over there" was what he got by way of an answer. "No, I've just come from there and he's not there, either." People who were in the habit of frequenting both places now asserted that they hadn't run across Krzyzanowsky for several days already.

The decision was made to head out to the suburb where Krzyzanowsky lives.

The little Czech journeyman-cobbler, at whose place he has his den, opens the door to the well-dressed gentlemen, agape. "Come in, come in," he says, his hand on the knob, and as he closes the door behind him: ". . . you know, Herr Krzyzanowsky died yesterday."

You learn that the poor fellow, who had the flu, kept on trying during the last days to prevail upon the provider of his lodgings to go to the Central or Herrenhof, where "his best friends are." The journeyman-cobbler took it for feverish rambling. "Y'know," he says, full of embarrassment, "I couldn't believe such fine people would have anything to do with him."

The fine people withdrew from there in silence.

Around this time the Central also died.

The funeral sermon for poor Ottfried was delivered not by any survivor here, but by Dr. Franz Blei. Krzyzanowsky, by the way—without my intending to offend Franz Werfel with this assertion—hated nobody so much as the hero Ferdinand from [Werfel's] *Barbara*. In his address, Blei kept referring to him as "Othmar" instead of "Ottfried," which gave rise to kinsmanlike hisses at the most solemn moments in the speech. But he spoke righteously in the name of his betters, those more deserving of starvation—in the name of the Herrenhof.

Brother, that was really something else!

A spacious, light, sumptuous, impersonal, bourgeois family coffeehouse. Emancipation from the blasé smell of bohemia. The coffee brewer seemed much less benevolent than mistrustful.

Weininger was no longer the patron saint, but Dr. Freud; Altenberg yielded to Kierkegaard; in place of the newspaper the journal nested itself; instead of psychology, psychoanalysis; and instead of the refreshing gentle breeze of Vienna, the gust of Prague blew in.

For that reason the air was at first anti-Viennese, European. People once again debated (which due to tarok, chess, and poker had already gone out of fashion), but not with *bonmots* and pointillism but with scalpels and amidst the simultaneous seduction of somebody's girlfriend.

That was above all progress. At every table only the most important issues, the most relevant had priority, often accompanied by cocaine. And in place of the word "relation" the term "connection" was bandied about everywhere.

Activism drew in Werfel, Robert Müller, and Jakob Moreno-Levy.[7]

The latter's philosophical fancy that every person is his own godfather, he above all, once prompted me to sigh innocently, "Oh, for God's sake . . ." Hearing this, he came rushing up from the next table and asked: "Do you want something of me?"

People were young at the time and so was communism.

It was the age of heroes. The gifted Otto Gross, the champion of literary thievery, psychoanalyst atop the barricades (career: son of a criminologist, university lecturer, anarchist, ship doctor, marriage, legal incapacitation, suspicion of murder by poison, insane asylum, writer, sanatorium, death), sprang up every two minutes and dragged some woman or man along on his peripatetic gambols about the establishment. He was unable to develop the last conclusion of a thought any other way.

The upright Melcher, the Danton of the Ottakring, as tall as a lamp-post, strong, handsome, made declarations of love in Marxist German.[8] Ernst Polak, from Prague, the obstetrician who brought Werfel, Kornfeld, and Franz Kafka into the world, dispersed the smoke with his razor-sharp nose and speech; by orienting yourself along both you could find your way back to whomever you were with. Once (the spring of '19), a young boy sat next to him; I thought: "The left-winger Kurt Wolff."[9]

The novice whispered to me in Swabian dialect: "What do you say about the hostage murder?"[10]

I learned that it was an apprentice butcher who escaped the Munich district attorney and that back home he was told: "The writers are all sitting around the Herrenhof—any one of them will be glad to put you up overnight on his sofa."

I wanted to say additionally that the women in the Herrenhof were much prettier than those in the Central. No wonder. They weren't neglected. They didn't just kibitz at games; they organized them. They were sought after from the moment they had established themselves here, cheerful with hope and change, awaiting appointments or relaxing from them, lively and passionate until there wasn't anything left of them. They often went astray unsuspectingly in these bear pits of the vanities and were beyond salvation.

Or they managed to save themselves, but then it was always a death blow for the coffeehouse.

For the forlorn survivors could not, either from the standpoint of the mind or the flesh, get around the judgment that—to remain with this comparison of the two coffeehouses—just as the Central was an asylum for masculine resignation, the Herrenhof was a coach house for waiting ladies. Hence, one was as much a coffeehouse for the bourgeois as the other.

"'Central' und 'Herrenhof,'" 1931. Original text in Anton Kuh, *Metaphysik und Würstel*, 20–26.

1.   Karel Kramár (1860–1937) was a Czech nationalist who served as prime minister of the new Czechoslovakia in 1918/1919. Tomás G. Masaryk (1850–1937) was president of the Czechoslovak Republic from 1918 to 1935.

2.   In Hungarian, of course, first and last names are reversed. Because of the strong Hungarian presence in such places as Vienna and Prague, the Austrians sometimes adopted this practice, often to express playfulness or intimacy.

3.   A leading German publisher then and now.

4.   A reference to the coffeehouse denizen Gustav Grüner, a member of Karl Kraus's circle and brother of the art historian and poet Franz Grüner (1877?–1917), whom Kraus held in high esteem. At one point, Grüner attempted suicide, hence the mention of the scar on his temple.

5.   Gustav Grüner was also well known for his observation: "A proper guest, on leaving the coffeehouse, puts his own chair on the table." This meant that the true guest would remain until closing time. On Gustav Grüner, see also the remarks in Friedrich Torberg's well-known essay, "Kaffeehaus ist überall," in *Die Tante Jolesch* (Munich: Deutscher Taschenbuchverlag, 1991), 138–40.

6.   Ottfried Krzyzanowsky (1891–1918), a bohemian poet known for his bouts of starvation (a *Hungerkünstler,* "hunger artist," in German).

7.   Robert Müller (1887–1924), Viennese journalist and novelist close to the Expressionist movement. For a time he was also head of the humor magazine *Muskete.* He lived in the United States from 1909 to 1911. J. L. Moreno or Jacob Levy Moreno (1892–1974) was a social psychologist and psychoanalyst well known for his work in psycho- and sociodrama.

8.   An obscure reference. Probably neither the German singer and actor Otto Melcher (1890–1938) nor the Austrian writer of fairy tales Karl Melcher (pseudonym Alarich, 1898–?).

9.   Kurt Wolff (1887–1963), a well-known German publisher who emigrated to the United States in 1941. The following year he founded Pantheon Books.

10.   An obscure reference.

THE DOG WHO BECAME A COFFEEHOUSE REGULAR

A person experiences every tragic event for whose understanding he is not yet mature twice in his lifetime. The first time as sheet lightning, the second time as a bolt of lightning.

So it is that this small excerpt from the biography of a dog properly belongs to a long woman's novel. I always see the dog who came to me as a stray as mysteriously as he became lost to me as a forerunner of the woman with whom the same thing happened to me later on.

The foundling's mystery hung about his small head. Where did he come from? Where was he going? Was I the ultimate destination or a stop on the way? The uncertainty lay like dark shadows over our relationship. First of all, let's look at it from his point of view (as with her). He howled pitifully whenever I left him alone for a moment, his whimper complaining: "Once again . . . back to nowhere!" I had to take him along on the smallest errands. Later, when he was out of my sight for only an hour, it was the other way around. Reproaches assailed my heart: Were you thought-ful enough? Didn't you take his anxiety too lightly? Did you ask him what he needed?

His head looked like that of an adorable wolf. That's why I named him Wolfie. Unimaginative, just the way I am with the fair sex. He was flattered and as a result immediately overestimated my understanding. Hence, one day, during the war, as I was passing an open supply truck in which soldiers were sitting, and one of them yelled down "Gretel! Gretel!" he took an impetuous leap in the direction of the truck, wanted to jump onto it, but reconsidered in light of the new domestic happiness he enjoyed at my side and ran back to me. So it's Grete, I thought. From then on he had the upper hand over me . . . The period of hysteria I experienced with him, the way friends avoided me on account of him, the way he toyed for days on end with the thought of abandoning me, and then, dripping wet, came home to me twice as loving, belongs to another story. There is, however, one incident of it which remains worth writing about.

One Sunday, as he disappeared through the open door of the an-teroom—for the first and last time I then inhabited several rooms—I placed an ad in all the newspapers I assumed would be read by concierges, people who really look through houses from top to bottom. It was just right for custodians' hearts:

> (Request of a lonely person.) A lonely gentleman, whose
> only friend on earth is his dog, turns herewith to all humanitar-
> ians to kindly help in finding the most dearly beloved animal. It
> . . . and so on . . .

The next day—my door always stood wide open—the shrill voice of a schoolgirl aroused me from a daydream: "Excuse me, is this where the lonely man lives?"

A moment later something wet lay on my chest, a tender apparition. The submissiveness of his tail quivered right up into my monocled eye. My nerves couldn't stand the foolhardy game any longer. I grew weaker and soon entered a Styrian sanatorium.[1] I gave the dog over to the woman who looked after my lodging. She had a sense of humor and the eyes of a murderess. The dog hated her, and she the dog. I promised her huge tips and urged her above all not to leave any doors open.

I must point out here that in communal living with me the animal had acquired a certain failing: a passionate predilection for the coffee-house visit. When I said to him "Central!" it had the same effect on him that the words "woods" or "meadows" have on other dogs.

One June night I returned to Vienna. It was half past midnight. "The Central is still open now," I thought, "take a little spin past it with the coach and see who's inside."

"Oh, here again, Herr Kuh?" said Jean when I entered. "Why, your dog was just here."

"Uh . . . who was here?"

"Well, that dog of yours!"

"My dog? With whom?"

"Alone."

"Alone? What do you mean?" (Six weeks' convalescence fell to chalk dust in my face.)

"But he shows up every evening alone. He's here 'roun' three, three-thirty, and he takes off again 'roun' twelve."

Three to twelve—my coffeehouse hours.

"And what does he do here?"

"Nothin' special, goes beggin' from people, sits down next to this one and that one. He's havin' a good time!"

My habits to a T!

I staggered back into the coach. "Fast—Löwengasse no. 8!"

It's not a short distance. He drives this way and that through the narrow streets of the inner city, then along the bustling quay, over the broad Aspernplatz . . . automobiles, trams, police all over the place . . . Oh heavens, what became of my dog?

In front of house no. 8., I ring. The concierge appears. I give her the obligatory twenty hellers.

"'Scuse me, sir, I get a gulden more . . ."

"A gulden? What for?"

"Y'think openin' up for the dog all the time's for nothin'?"

"The dog . . . ?"

"Oh yeah, every night he sits himself down in front of the gate to the house and cries and carries on like crazy till I open up for him, the mangy little beast . . . Just a little while ago I had to open up for him again!"

My dog had become a man of letters! He had made himself independent in my absence and for pieces of sugar, iced coffee, and bones offered samples of that convivial charm from which his master had for so long sought to cover his subsistence.

Four weeks later he ran off into the unknown.

"Der Hund als Stammgast," 1931. Original text in Anton Kuh, *Metaphysik und Würstel*, 48–51.

    1.   A region in central and southeastern Austria, the capital of which is Graz.

LENIN AND DEMEL

Bolshevism is standing at the gates of Vienna. Béla Kun[1] has unfurled his banner; between the Opera and the Grand Hotel beggars in soldiers' coats are putting their artificial limbs on display in the April sun; a cripple and a blind man negotiate an unreal walk together, their cry of woe reverberating through the streets: "Two poor disabled veterans . . . !"

The tatters of ersatz existence still cling to the city.

But the aristocrats? Harrach and Hardegg and Kinsky and Trautmannsdorf?

If they get sawdust to eat, they prefer to flee to their favorite refuge in the Kohlmarkt known as Konditorei Demel [Demel's sweets-shop] as if to a people's Arcadia of gluttony.

But they get ices and cream puffs and waffles. The most decorative dainties, scented observances of dietary rules.

The waitresses are always friendly, respectful, and dignified like sisters of a noble ladies' charitable association. They combine the allure of the Burgtheater-grandmother Wilbrandt-Baudius[2] and the quiet-hushing devotion of a theater-box doorkeeper. Their faces reflect distress over the new times that threaten to clear away princes, barons, bon-vivants, and single women. What is the world without the amenities of serving and thanking, without the pleasant foil of nobleness, without the good-humored gratuity from a titled mouth? The Demel-waitresses belong to a smaller and more intimate high class than Xandi Kinsky, Dolfi Starhemberg, and Playboy Auersperg. They wear on their black blouses invisible remembrance lockets of Old Austria. This beloved, unforgettable country finds here its last culinary resting place. When everything totters all around, Sister Thesa remains constant. Her kiss on the hand is the most spontaneous and lawful tribute to the old regime.

An extinct dialect resounds at Demel's: "crumpling," that well-known way of resignedly emitting sounds squeezed from the palate and nose without any concern as to whether they comply with the image of a sentence or not. As we know, lack of exertion is the first sign of nobility. The prince neither accentuates nor articulates, otherwise one might believe he wants something, if only privilege. Austria's aristocrats, therefore, have treated themselves to their own dialect: the negligé of intonation. The tongue indolently reclines as if in a club armchair, the vowels receive a small injection of the perfume "Boredom" from constricted nostrils, the r's are picked up from the dental plate like crumbs of a delicate pastry, the lips open to no more breath than one must absolutely take from the public domain—and this resonant store of speech is consumed in gulps and crumbled in a sauce of chuckles.

That was the speech of the upper hundred, who shared in the revenues of the "Austria" Company, Inc. That is the Demel-prose.

The count still wears his monocle and absent-mindedly gobbles his "goodies" as if plucking grapes. He asks: "Were the Boysheviks here already?"

The chorus of sisters: "Hihihi."

"No, Count."

"There's still time, Count."

"We can anticipate it, Count."

"Hihihi."

"I was 'fraid of that. I am so fearful, y'know. Please, an ice, Thesa. Greetings, Pauckerl, how is Aunt Klotüd?"

"She was at Hansi Palffy's."

"Nervous, is she, 'bout boyshevism?"

"You can imagine. Alexonder said she never leaves the house anymore—'count of boyshevism, says."

"Rather. We're the lot of us a bit anxious, eh?"

"Hihi."

The nightmare of Demel 1919: Between each serving of ice and the Gotha [almanac of European nobility] sits Lenin. They exorcize him with wit and mockery. But their flesh is crawling. They're singing in the dark forest of the time ahead of them . . .

And when death tugs them by the shoulder: "Come on, little brother!" they reply, a bit ill at ease: "Dégoutant!"

"Lenin und Demel," 1931. Original text in Anton Kuh, *Metaphysik und Würstel*, 92–94.

    1.   Béla Kun (1886–1939?), a Hungarian communist who attempted to establish a proletarian dictatorship in Hungary in 1919.

    2.   The actress Auguste Baudius, the wife of the German journalist, novelist, and dramatist Adolf Wilbrandt (1837–1911), who settled in Vienna in 1871 and became director of the Vienna Burgtheater in 1881. He held the position until 1887.

ADVENTURES OF A MONOCLE

I am a monocle wearer. But to its credit I must say that my monocle is a peace monocle. It came into the world in the year 1909 and has nothing in common with its false colleagues who after the war became common on the faces of people who either made money or lost their pants. Since then they have had to give many an intellectual face a thrust into the feudal past. My monocle is a unique, well-bred, utterly unhysterical monocle.

Consequently, there would be no reason to deal with it any further, if not for the fact that it shared with its owner a ruinous peculiarity—his bent to literary activity. But who'd want to deny that to a monocle, since "seeing" and "writing" are almost identical concepts? Not everything that my monocle records and whispers into my ear in the quiet hours is intended for publication. However, I cannot resist repeating some of it verbally as my monocle dictates it to me:

I was purchased on a sunny May morning. The purchaser wiped me with a small leather patch, took me between his thumb and forefinger and held me against the door of the shop. For the first time I beheld the building of the Vienna Court Opera, in infinite diminution.

Childhood impressions determine one's sympathies. Since then, I have loved this building.

Sad childhood of a monocle! To fear for its tender, fragile life at every moment!

But I shouldn't complain. A piece of good luck befell me the very first day. To begin with, I am a so-called shell glass. That is, I came into the world so stout and well-rounded that I do not touch the eyelashes of the person who wears me. In the second place, my master has thick tear ducts. Perhaps that brings harmony to his good looks. In any case, these bags under his eyes provided me timely support. When sometimes I happened to slide and my last moment seemed at hand, I grabbed hold firmly beneath me like a mountain-climbing tourist.

In a situation like that—dangling between eyebrow and cheekbone— I would not have cut a good figure at all.

But in those days at least I was still well liked. People smiled when they saw me, gave me a wink, and showed me affection.

Today things are different . . .

Lord above, why do I cause so much trouble?

I look at the world joyfully, enthusiastically, shiningly. Why does it stare back at me so bitterly and meanly? I would like to set laughter in the glass; why does the belligerent face of inferiority complexes inscribe itself on me?

Inferiority complex! Ugh, what kind of a foreign word is that? I am, after all, educated. I have minus 3.5 diopters (with a diameter of 42 mm.), and with such a concave polish one comes into the world already a learned man. The convex members of our race are much less educated and duller. Doubtless because they are used for reading and not for seeing. And as regards my doubles made out of window glass, I really would prefer to say nothing at all. They've become as extinct as the Guards lieutenants whose eyes they graced.

But it's precisely to these extinct beings, I believe, that we owe a part of our unpopularity. We are regarded as a symbol of class arrogance—how absurd! If people only knew how little money my master has! (Or do you hate me because you know?)

When, in the early days, an unfriendly glance got caught on me or a pair of lips broadened or when a bicycle splattered me, I had a strong desire to attach a note to myself that would make my needs plain to the inhabitants of the city the moment they saw me: "Poor, left-handed, nearsighted man requests kindly looks." Perhaps a little sign with the information concerning my diopter number might have sufficed. People are compassionate by nature.

I discovered this in a rather shameful way during the war. To be exact, the shamefulness was on the part of my master. He was put in an infantry regiment as a one-year conscript, a fearless defender of the home front. You can imagine how miserable he felt. His uniform, though worn out just from barracks duty, looked as if it had gone through the battles of Gorlice and Limanowa. It lacked, as the Horatian ode says, "curls under the sheers." In these circumstances, whether because he wanted to distinguish himself from the others by my help, or because he wanted to retain a valuable memento of his civilian existence, he suddenly had a burning desire for me. What to do? He turned to the head doctor of the company. "I have a nervous tick in an eye," he says, "and that makes a soldier look foolish to His Majesty. It can also lead to a weakening of the home front morale, for people would be sure to believe that I am a war casualty who despite shell shock still has to serve. For this reason, I am asking your permission to wear a monocle. The monocle, you see, will keep my eye from making any twitching motion, since it stretches the eyelids apart."

The doctor drew up the necessary papers. Austria was a gentle land.

But what then was the result? First of all, that, during every march through the streets, windows opened left and right and laughing faces called down to the man who in his crumpled, earth-colored uniform, but with a monocle in the eye, was marching along rank and file with his brave veteran reserve comrades. Then, in a tram or in public establishments many officers' faces—dumbfounded, perplexed, indeed dismayed at the sight of me—quivered and fixed me in their sights for a while until they made up their minds to ask the question: "Hey, draftee, what kind of monkey business do you call that?"

Ha, you should have seen my master then, how eagerly and triumphantly he showed the doctor's certificate! And what respect now followed his, or rather my trail!

And all the time my master, to tell the truth, has the tick in the other eye.

He is, on the whole, a strange person.

Often, toward morning, when I lie sleepless on the night-table, since he snores so loudly that the tailor's bills, love letters, and newspapers begin to flutter about me and cigarette ashes blow on my face like desert sand, I have to ask myself why the sleeper next to me bears me so steadfastly through life in spite of all the inconvenience. "I am a psychologist by profession," he once remarked to a friend while removing me from his eye and showing me off like some mysterious apparatus. "I mean that I collect faces the way another person collects flowers or butterflies or postage stamps. The monocle is my butterfly net, my botanist's case, my stamp album. You see, every face looks right in here with its dullest expression, with a sneering mouth twisted by a stroke, with a superior eye in which self-consciousness stands on its toes. For a psychologist, it's invaluable! They photograph themselves in my monocle, as if I had called out in advance: 'Please, no friendly faces!' The physiognomy of my contemporaries is thus preserved in my monocle. Yes, this monocle turned me into a misanthrope, but I am grateful to it for my knowledge of the world . . ."

My poor, much-tried master—I would feel guilty if I heard you talk so.

How hazardous and desolate his existence is because of me! How much unpopularity comes his way every day! Into how many affairs and lawsuits I dragged him!

Wherever I go with him, laughter greets us on all sides. But not good, happy laughing; no, the kind I can tell a skimpy lunch from—a laugh as green as cabbage and as yellow as margarine. When I ride with him in the subway, people opposite us nudge each other with their elbows in order to announce in all furtiveness: "Get a load o' monkey face!" When we cross a street together something clack-clacks in my ear, like clicking from a coachman's mouth or snappy-happy hubbub, but as soon as I turn around, it's as if it was blown away; just two troubled eyes stare at me, lingering and blameless.

The records of the local criminal court, Vienna I, contain my curriculum vitae, by the way.

Like the opening paragraphs in the holy suras [of the Koran], the sentence keeps recurring in them: ". . . the accused approached him with the words 'Why are you gaping at me like that?'"

Consequently, my master was convicted many times. For defamation, noncompliance, and creating a public scandal. (Public scandal? How can I help laughing! For this offence I should have been locked up, not the person wearing me.)

Once, too, for insulting the authorities. It happened on a bitter-cold night when my master, with just a thin topcoat on, stepped up to his house. A patrolman, who happened to be conversing at the time with a sausage vendor, couldn't keep from shouting as soon as he saw me: "Real bums go 'roun' dese days with monocles!"

Another time he was supposed to file a so-called affidavit of means, that is, on order of his creditors to take an oath, before two lighted candles, to the effect that besides me and his philosophy he owns nothing. But the moment he raised the two fingers of his right hand, the attorney for the other side—doubtless because my presence seemed to him too contradictory to the essence of the oath—ripped into him: "Take your monocle off before you swear!" That, too, ended in a fine . . .

I'm getting old. A person withdraws into himself and tries to see things from the other side.

It happens that more often than before I inquire into the grounds for my odiousness. "People don't like you," I say to myself, "because you place yourself like a window between the eye and the world, as if one shouldn't get too near the other, so as not to get smudged, as it were. You seem to them like a glass 'Keep your distance!' Not only that, but you make the eye so immobile that people think you're signaling indifference to their affairs. Isn't that arrogance, they think. Finally: you make the eye look bigger. Glass and pupil become one, and the simple people, short of the good things in life as it is, ask themselves: 'How does this man come off having a bigger eye than we do?'"

Solid grounds—sometimes, after all, I do look at the ground.

That is, when in a crowd in the street or from the table of a restaurant suddenly something insolent and inanimate glitters at me—a monocle.

"Erlebnisse eines Monokels," 1931. Original text in Anton Kuh, *Metaphysik und Würstel,* 7–12.

FROM *PHYSIOGNOMICS: OBSERVATIONS*

Res publica or The Citizen

Physiognomy of the age: The face of the leader has become identical to that of the led.

What is a collective? An accumulation of ciphers who have renounced individualism but attach importance to name dropping.

The entire struggle of mankind is played out between those who want to be something and those who want to be worth something.

The misfortune of the Germans: They believe that the word "Erotik" [erotic] comes from "erröten" [to blush].

Boys who underline the word "whore" in the Bible will become censorious public prosecutors.

Literatus in a Field Jacket

The so-called cosmicism of the Germans is an extension of their need for subordination into the other world.

Dirt and Rubbish

In front of the Innsbruck train station I once saw a man who was on his way home, supporting his alpenstock against his hips and aiming it at the people exiting the station. He wore a black frock coat over light-colored knee-high socks, a red knitted band around a stiff collar, a little Alpine hat with a feather in it tilted on his head, and with his pointy mouth and bird's eye winked mockingly at others, as if all of them were dressed like idiots. He was no man, but a design for a statue. The statue of constraint before the entry into Germany.

Among the middle class prejudice replaces judgment.

The bourgeois believes that idea relates to reality the way poetry does to prose. He doesn't know that together both are the poetic in life, while each by itself is the prosaic.

Austria

Austria: A Switzerland of comfortlessness.

The German is a regimental comrade. The Austrian, a schoolfellow.

He wears his privacy like a torn uniform.

France gave the world two great things: the revolution and the bidet. Her third task would now be to show that the two go together.

What is bureaucracy? An arrangement of individual incompetences for the purpose of general responsibility.

The Intellectual in Public Life

I'd be ashamed to argue about Expressionist dance and Negro sculpture on the first floor while on the ground floor below me people were being beaten.

Fascism: the militarism of civilians.

National slogan: With Kant against God for the Fatherland!

Decline of the West

The Germans are the undisputed masters in art. Out of an inability to establish a direct connection from the eye to the object they set up metaphysical trains of thought.

There is no greater contrast than between idealism and illusionism. One leads through prison to mountain peaks, the other across battlefields to the children's room.

Jews and Germans: the two tragic literalists of the universe.

There are printing errors of world history that obstinately regard themselves as reality.

Eros or The Beloved

Proper coquetry succeeds only when one has a superficial knowledge of oneself.

Irrefutable equation: obscenity = irrelevance.

Cheap Dialogue

"What do you want from me?"

"In view of the question, nothing."

Don Juan and Don Quixote—aren't they the same name?

Psychoanalysis gives its patient above all the comfort that his defects support a science.

Pangs of conscience are the first symptom of waning manliness.

Don Juan's advice: When a woman speaks, look her in the mouth, but don't listen to her!

Bookshelf or The Reader

The chief purpose of literature is to discredit genius.

Strindberg: Tantalus as a variety theater performer.

The literatus is a hermaphrodite from a would-be artist and a would-be bourgeois.

When an author disappoints you as a person, you've overestimated his work.

For the converted intellectual, Catholicism is a cloakroom where he checks his dread of the next world so that the goulash of this one can taste better.

There's nothing more painful than when a zealous stylist ceremoniously swings the hammer and doesn't hit the nail on the head.

I once saw a dada pamphlet. Everything was at sixes and sevens. The *i*'s were all crooked, the *u*'s upside down. Words dissolved, final syllables amalgamated. Only one thing remained the same, upright, and legible in all the disorder: that was the note beneath the title—"Price: fifty pfennigs."

The child genius was praised to death before he reached manhood.

What is the difference between the literatus and the poet? The literatus has more to say than he has experienced, the poet has experienced more than he can say.

Physiognomics or The Contemporary

His pearls of style are the pearls of sweat, now grown cold, that poured over his face while he wrote.

When the little Storm-and-Stress chansonnier fills up a whole page with his poems, he dries his hands with the blotting paper.

Regular patron in a literary café: He looks starved from inattention. God sent him back his face as unusable like the publisher his manuscript.

A Magyar gentleman: He looks like a cross between the chief of police of Budapest and somebody he's looking for.

The well-dressed literatus: A gigolo who can't dance.

New Generation

They don't know where God lives, but they've all interviewed Him.

They believe that not knowing German means having opinions.

On the subject of plagiarism: If writers steal, it's neither here nor there. But if pickpockets write!

The Satirist

That a person uses the night as a lonely stage for his thoughts doesn't say much for him. To big people, night also comes by day. But nights, which are the antitheses of day, only the antithesis is audible.

Encounter or The Plebeian

The bohemians these days look quite proper. Only they still have unwashed souls.

Dream of the snob: To be informal to the letter of the law.

There are reviewers who decline a ham sandwich so as not to have the reputation for corruptibility. That's how high they regard ham sandwiches.

Curiosity is the tense anxiety that there can be miracles.

To the plebeian the picture postcard is more important than the landscape.

On Aristocrats

The plebeian tells himself: "I'm a shit" or "I'm God." (Reverse sides of the same coin.) The aristocrat says: "I am I."

A "fine person"—what does that mean in 999 of 1,000 cases? An ordinary fellow who doesn't trust himself.

The Next Table

At the Creation, God distributed too many eyes for too few faces. The eight at the table over there, for example, should have only one together.

There are voices that one has to eavesdrop on in order to hear them and some that eavesdrop on one to find out if they have been overheard. Emperors, courtesans, and geniuses have the first kind; filmstars and feuilletonists the other.

My necktie makes him nervous. Not because it's carelessly knotted, but because despite that it has oomph. He'd like nothing better than to leap up, pull me by the neck, and say: "Kindly keep your political views to yourself!"

Friends of Nature

The spiritual man has an aired-out brain, the intellectual an unwashed one.

The Lantern

At eighteen, each of us is a genius; at twenty-eight, an editor.

Gluttons are melancholics who stuff the unfillable hole of their hearts with food.

What is melancholy? Homesickness for oneself.

One experiences the loveliest things in the present as remembrance.

The center of gravity of the actor's soul coincides with the vertex of both diagonals placed through the orchestra of a sold-out theater.

There is no better purgative than a chatterbox who clings to our buttons. The more insistently he wants to get inside us, the faster we get rid of him.

The Philologist

A bad conscience makes a bad complexion.

The dilettante is much closer to genius than to talent, just as the criminal is closer to God than the bourgeois is.

On the child prodigy: So young—and already so talentless.

Polemicist

When the moon breaks through the clouds, he turns his eyes indignantly upward: "Does he mean me?"

He who wants to be productive has to maintain a metaphysical diet.

Where it gets dark, there begins the occult.

The tiresome believe they are serious because they lack humor.

Faces of the Dead

About the lips of the dead there plays—now bitter, now blissful—a quiet: "Aha!"

All misfortune comes from terminology.

Sunday is as necessary as death.

Isn't it time to place European faces under nature conservation?

Unnoticed, we've acquired the countenance of the Middle Ages. The uniformed man, in field jacket and cap, doesn't look much different than the wry-mouthed, bulbous-nosed, slouch-capped boor in the old wood-carvings who feels himself prepared in the name of dogma to cut up the bodies of others and regards his own misdevelopment as morally licensed.

Occultism: metaphysics for servants.

The German writer sees God through an opera glass and the world through a keyhole.

Berlin

I'd like to know if the Christian deaf mute hears the accent when a Jewish one talks with his hands.

Physiognomik. Aussprüche, 1931. Original text in Anton Kuh, *Metaphysik und Würstel,* 255–309.

CABARET NONSENSE

Behind every minute of existence lurks the question, "What's the point?" One of the most essential tasks of art is to lure us away from it and in passing to hide the question mark from our view. But odd as it may seem, there is a branch of art whose uniqueness lies in its directing this question to itself, in its not venturing itself, so to speak, over the passage along which it wants to lead us, and consequently more urgently and sadly engraves on our souls the cry "What's the point? What's the point?"

When I reflect on the concept "cabaret," my cheeks immediately get numb. The invitation to put a good face on a bad situation in the hope that it would thereby become a good situation chloroforms the corners of my mouth. Stage eyes implore me, beseech me, crave for me, and at the same time demonstrate to me a smiling offhandedness, to join in and mimic them. The exertion of the person up there ropes me in and doesn't even release my own breath. His technique of signaling suggestive intentions by the voice transfers itself to me as a prescription for meaningful amusement. My laughter is the ordered cadence to his intonation. Indeed, I must go so far as to give him contractual loyalty against everything and everybody for the sake of a common good that I neither wanted or sought: for the mood. Am I enjoying myself? No. I am being questioned as to whether or not I am enjoying myself. Uncertainty keeps a watchful eye. It binds me fast here and lets me sweat and strain while it imposes on me that most troublesome of all labors known in the language of the entertainment world as "going along with."

Delicate and sensitive is the atmosphere of a place where such annoyances occur, sated with restrained tears of self-commiseration as with the mist of a storm. Public and podium relate to each other like the archduchess and the mayor in Werfel's poem who saw that they had to bring each other harm. Nowhere will "pst" or "quiet" be shouted; nowhere are the ears at once more tolerant and more nervous. They let themselves passively enjoy wordplay, gab, intimacy, and the esprit for words of an arrived newspaper reader but at the same time ungraciously repulse the slightest whisper, the most cautious knife-clattering form of the torment of this enjoyment. Where does this come from? From the fact that the productions are without absolute artistic value, hence they beg just for indulgence? In no way. It comes instead from forced auxiliary service of the guests and their belief that they have to play the part of co-conspirators in an intellectual association that has a common antiphilistine goal. Once, this belief was justified and the emergency service was thus voluntary. The cabarettist was then no professional and the cabaret itself no workplace.

The matter of "épater le bourgeois" [shocking the bourgeois] was his function at the time, not his union badge. Out of their excesses, rudiments of genius, talented imperfections and imperfect talents which already embodied the antithesis of the bourgeois world some people created a merry theater into which the spectator was invited as a forbearing and paying enemy. He put up with it, it was good; he frowned on it, it was even better.

From the performances and player-spectator cooperation a type of camaraderie could indeed arise true to the motto: caught together, hanged together! But when that bourgeois world had already sucked in the antidote as a new value and didn't have to cringe anymore, and all that was left was to finish it off, the end of the merry theater was also at hand. That's when it should have been closed down. But in the meantime a particular branch of industry had developed from it. In place of the inspired bohemian there now appeared the skilled cabarettist, the one-liner wag. This is the time now of the counter-jumper of negation, of the practitioner of improvised self-consciousness, the furnisher of presence of mind. And just when he was offering ready-made goods, not only did he become turned on by cheerful or hostile contacts, he wanted still more to create the impression that he was independent of the public and begged doubly for that "mood" which his predecessor had sought rather more against himself than for himself. Meanwhile—fortunately for him—the upper-middle-class- and society-people who fit in here and were educated had drifted away. Their seats were then occupied in a proper line of succession by petty-bourgeois, middle-class bon viveurs, and provincials who fancy themselves as thrill-seekers. Before such audiences, the cabarettist just has to tap the day's vocabulary a bit in order to give them the feeling that they are really oppositional, that they have been raised above the average, and that they stand in the same front line of cleverness as the cabarettist himself. They pick up every wink from him and feel themselves favored by the knowing smile of ignorance that hints at the abundance of culture. "We are political . . . ," We are nonpolitical . . . ," the cabaret says to them, and they agree. They believe that the use of newspaper words is called political and the abstention from them nonpolitical, and they don't know that neither the one nor the other is worth a damn intellectually. (Whereas the person originally opposed to the world of block letters can't help being political when he is really nonpolitical—and vice versa—and with the same breath can't help making convictions laughable and admitting to having convictions himself.) This new school of thought, therefore, is more concerned with their self-esteem than with their enjoyment. They really feel as one with the earnestness of that gentleman from the audience who is called onstage to check the magician, as if they shared a joint responsibility for the spirit of the performance, and they sit in the hall electrified by pretense and compassion (as allies of the one-liner and against its dislocation) as in a temple of quick repartee. So that it may even be learned by heart, prizes are awarded for tryouts of this repartee. If it applies to the intoxicated, champagne-guzzling troublemaker in the first row who rushed here out of a misguided sense of humor to interrupt the conférencier, the displeasure of the auxiliary service vents itself in gales of chatter.

People who in the enforcement of this exceptional sense of solidarity—which intensifies the dislike of followers, the impatience with amusement, and the suppressed crying-burst into a loud fit of laughter—demonstrate a certain dexterity and used to be called the life of the party. These people were cannons who at least were loaded with themselves, round as a ball and gay, yet more servile than impudent. They learned from the waiters how to serve guests whether the serving tray holds a cheap cut of meat or a good wine.

There is another type that follows close on the heels of the life of the party: the witty grape-shooter. I'm talking about the contemporary masters of ceremonies who as a result of our collusion got up on their own two self-conscious legs and with the loans extended them by groaning forbearance built a solid house of wit. They are distinguished by the possession of opinions, a mastery of newspaper material, and a far-reaching orientation in the interests of art and literature. Furthermore, they recite their part in the tone of that affable chattiness and casualness which from the days of the early cabaret is still regarded as a hallmark of improvisation. But they string their pearls of one-liners and anecdotes on the thread of a critical reflection on their age and then are concerned that people are getting smarter. Apart from the Viennese vulgarity of the Jewish-German jargon (which among them seems shifted from the realm of language into subject matter), they manifest all other signs of an unusual personality pleased as punch with itself. Nevertheless, every one of them reflects the original. One of them, for example, pulls the knot of his tie tighter when he approaches the punch line; another one blinks toward the ceiling as if the footlights bothered him; a third one narrows his eyes and lets the world shine in the sparkle of pupils, which couldn't give up staring at it deeply and wisely.

When the history of the cabaret is once written, its service in raising a superfluous métier to the summit of moral earnestness in a difficult and crisis-menaced time cannot be overlooked.

But as far as the social-revolutionary cabaret is concerned, I lack the competence to comment on it. A certain aversion toward bottled wines has until now denied the writer of these lines the possibility of drawing a picture of it. But I can swear to the fact that at least with regard to the famous line "Text by . . . Music by . . . ," it has not broken with the traditions of the bourgeois age.

"Unfug des Kabaretts," 1931. Original text in Anton Kuh, *Metaphysik und Würstel*, 240–45.

The World of the Variety Theater

Historical

The nineteenth century had three illustrious performance milieux: the gaming room, the racetrack, and the variety theater. (Casual observers also count battlefields.) It was here that a dying society experienced its most powerful tensions, reveled in the lure of its anonymity, played a theater unto itself. Three stages raised to immortality by the mastery of a Toulouse-Lautrec.

The nineteenth century would be unimaginable without the variety theater. The reason for this is that an artistic environment is distinguished not so much by its absolute entertainments as by the mixture of them. Moreover, it presupposes an audience that—just think of the old "Ronacher" in Vienna[1]—enjoys itself in foyers, exchanges greetings, consumes the evening meal at small tables with little red lights on them, and takes pleasure in the performances as an illuminated marginality of gymnastic, choreographical, musical, aesthetic, and humorous numbers (variety theater is called in German *Kunterbunt* [higgledy-piggledy]). You don't have to partake of every piece, but when you've had enough, you can skip from the requisite first one to the fourth to sixth in order to leave the establishment before the seventh. It was in such a way that Stendahl and Lord Byron enjoyed the beauties of the Italian opera in the box of the Abbé Breme of Milan.

The popular variety theater [Volksvarieté] is essentially as preposterous an idea as the popular opera.

Performance with a High Polish

The flawless optical linseed oil properly belongs to the variety theater. A brilliant world must open up before the spectator (as in the circus, but on a more sophisticated level), one whose dress alone expresses good fortune, wonderment, and buoyancy. The training that precedes success has pale, hectic morning cheeks. Success should also radiate in supernatural colors.

A special role devolves upon the tailcoat. In the variety theater it is the master over all garments, the purple in which the most difficult artistic work garbs itself. It is worn because it contradicts fatigue in the most striking way and hence underlines most impressively the apparent effortlessness.

The Music

With certain pieces of yesteryear that the health-resort band or the bar pianist plays, we snap our fingers and say: "That sounds like variety theater!" (Usually this relates to the ballet *Coppelia* by Delibes or the parade of the tin soldiers of Leon Jessel or the march of the gladiators. Sometimes also the mill in the Black Forest.)

What do these types of music have in common with each other? On one hand, they are as artistic and mechanical as the variety theater performance. On the other hand, they have something of the suspended and attenuated rhythm of bated breath to which we see grinning girls in tights jump up on a rod, steel balls whirling in the air, and jugglers throwing their top hats skyward. This music, too, is rich in contrast. For the ear, it should transform ten-kilo weights into light shuttlecocks.

And it is pantomime with sound. Accompaniment to the big, disquieting silence of the rascality that is the real, now-inaudible essence of the variety theater.

Have you ever imagined what variety theater would be like without music? And do you understand why the one sudden "Eh!" that the trapeze artist, clapping his hands, calls up to his partner on the high wire sounds so electrifying and musical?

Musical Clowns

(Previously: "knockabouts.") Their principal purpose (and their principal effect) is mischievously to disturb the above-described quiet. The tone with which they do it should be very carefully thought out. For twenty years Grock has been coming out with the two syllables "For what?" and Charlie Rivel[2] with the rapturous cry "Loovely!" Anybody who has studied harmonics his whole life can't devise any more effective, more concentrated sound. If somebody came along and pilfered it, the result would be unimaginable copyright and plagiarism lawsuits—more legitimate than those the literati and musicians are used to conducting against one another.

Next to this tone the most steadfastly adhered to, most jealously guarded specialty of the clowns is the mask. An artist often works for years at its creation. A thousand mirrors check its effectiveness. A tuft of hair over the forehead, the shape of the nasal protuberance, the dash of lipstick across the upper lip, all represent problems the audience can't even begin to imagine. The clown enters the stage as a trademark of himself. Imitation of his mask by somebody else is tantamount to the fall of his wages from a dizzying height.

By the way, musical clowns have lately been so much the subject of profound and serious essays that this species, too, will soon lose the liking for being funny.

The Juggler

People like us (the ungifted) dream of one thing: perfection. For our ambition, to dream of the greatest success seems a small thing, no more than a paper-thin hindrance—but this hindrance is insurmountable. We remain fragments, denied that favored freedom of being and movement through which the last rung of hardship is dismissed by a small, playful smile.

That is why we need heroes to whom this good fortune is given in our stead, heroes who breathe, sing, or play with balls the way we dream of doing it ourselves just before falling asleep. Their speech then redeems our tongues, their song our bosoms, their suppleness our body. Kainz, Caruso, Rastelli[3]—it's always the same. The juggler teaches us that the smile begins at the point where all effort is past.

L'art ne transpire pas

If this sentence applies to any form of artistic entertainment, it applies above all to the variety theater. For the idea of variety theater is this: the pretense of effortlessness through the absence of perspiration.

Sweat is the sign of a disproportion between the presence of mind of the body and of the will. You can also say: the consequence of the lack of unity with oneself. To be entirely whole of oneself (and it may be because of one's bodily makeup) rules out glistening brows and smoking lungs. If a person still has to contend with his own body and wrest from it what it does not voluntarily yield, his skin pants along with him.

That is why the audience doesn't like to see people with chubby builds or straining hearts on the trapeze. The heavy thunderstorm of raindrops that splashes from their brows onto the stage shatters the magic of the variety theater. And in such instances the spectators are as cruel as a Roman gladiator audience. If the performance before them is awkward, they will rarely applaud.

The Applause

There is a story about an acrobat who was only number two all his life and no matter where he appeared. Some performers were then asked what it means to be number two. It means that the public isn't yet fully with you. They look more at the beer vendors than at the stage. The interest in you isn't hot yet. People also tend to view the most sensational performances more or less indifferently. This hard-luck acrobat bore his fate with composure. When at the end of his number, with the music stopped and amid stirring drum rolls, he hung freely by his chin on the trapeze, not a single hand bestirred itself to applaud. He jumped down and nevertheless bowed as if he had been cheered.

One day the director of the provincial variety theater where he was demonstrating his art came up to him and said: "The sixth number is sick. You're going to take her place."

Tears came to the acrobat's eyes. He swung onto the platform more triumphantly than ever. The great moment again approached, the music broke off, drums were rolled, he hung by his chin on the floating trapeze, and then—the never before experienced, the eternally missed: the audience applauded wildly! And the acrobat, forgetting his position in his happiness, nodded back smilingly . . . He lies buried in the great cemetery of the martyrs whom applause threw down from the tightrope of life too early or too late.

Ambition

doesn't always have to be fatal, but in the variety theater it's also regarded more as a vice than as a virtue. The directors like best peak performances accompanied by an average degree of ambition. Too much ambition brings quarrels and can sometimes close a show.

Once there was a pair of brothers that nobody wanted to hire anymore. They performed in an exemplary manner, but whenever they exited the stage, the curtains resounded with swear words and slapping. The both of them always had a poor grip, a certain clumsiness, and an irritating habit of mutually reproaching each other then letting fly with their fists. They became unemployed.

After a hiatus of several years, a manager recently took them on again. He agreed in black and white that the director could fire them the moment there was any trouble with them.

They did their thing—quietly, peaceably, without any fights. No angry words were to be heard from them anymore. The director couldn't bring himself to accept this change of character. One day, after they had made their exit from the stage, he tailed them until they were inside their dressing room. For a while he eavesdropped at the door and then peeked through the keyhole.

A pantomime was in progress. The two young people were silently knocking each other about with shoves and pokes and after each blow placed a finger to the mouth entreatingly, as if saying "Calmly, not a word now!"

The Net

You experience an exceptionally tingling sensation when, as soon as you enter the auditorium, you see hanging above it a rolled-up net.

You take it as a sign that in the course of the evening something big is going to happen, that the arena of feats is going to expand into the infinite. Because of this you view all productions just as curtain raisers. And at the same time, in agreeable unease, you anticipate the moment when a body will be hanging ominously above the heads and beer glasses in the hall. From the outset, therefore, you become a supporting player.

Such a Damocles-wire is disadvantageous for the number by the Saxon humorist. While we await the marvel from the former, the latter strikes us as even more garrulous. But fortunately he almost always comes on right after the tightrope act.

La . . . ??

One type has died out in the variety theater: the fascinating big woman in crinoline or with bare feet, the queen of blue-bloodedness, the living toothpaste-commercial of beauty—La belle Otéro, La belle Saharet, the Cleos, Gabys, and also the Isadoras.[4]

This woman (who in her stunted version today is called "star" or "leading lady") used to be the focal point and soul of the variety theater. The fine folk who took their dinner in their box seats came only because of her. The mesmerizing step of her foot, the gathered-up petticoats, the way she grasps her neck as she shouts exultantly "Olé!"—between the ventriloquists and the plate throwers she was Eros itself, Tristan and Isolde plus Greta Garbo.

Does her dying out have something to do with the diminution of kingdoms in Europe? The lustre from the crowned heads fell for the most part on the queens of the stage. Republics appear as a rule utterly at a loss when it comes to such a reverse lustre (read here: loge and stage). Perhaps that is why today's variety theater lacks absolute monarchs.

The greater likelihood, however, is that the variety theater of the twentieth century doesn't know what to do anymore with beauty alone.

The Numbers Girls

are also not as numerous as they once were. With their tripping steps and their frozen smiles, they followed the queens into the realm of shadows.

In their place the variety theater borrows from the cabaret the master of ceremonies, the ironic, glib man who nowadays fires one-liners at a big house.

Such transplantations (the transfer of organs from a healthy body to the body of a sick branch of art) can often prove dangerous. The patient indeed recovers, but he changes into the other.

We would prefer not to think that of the variety theater. It is the last place where the down-to-earth still counts for something. The down-to-earth as opposed to what people call "spirit."

"Von der Welt des Varieté," 1933. Original text in Anton Kuh, *Metaphysik und Würstel*, 245–51.

1. After its reopening in 1930, Ronacher's, the best-known and most popular variety theater in turn-of-the-century Vienna, made a solid comeback under the leadership of Bernhard Labriola (1890–1960). It was Labriola who brought to Vienna such prominent entertainers of the time as Grock, Rivel, and Rastelli.

2. Grock (real name, Adrian Wettach, 1880–1959), a Swiss variety theater clown well known especially for his combination of music and acrobatics. Charlie Rivel was also another popular variety theater performer of the period.

3. Enrico Rastelli (1896–1931), a popular variety theater juggler.

4. La belle Otéro, or Caroline Otéro (real name, Caroline Carasson, 1868–1965) and Saharet (real name, Clarisse Campbell-Rosé, 1880–1942) were popular variety theater and cabaret dancers.

Diary of a Hotel Guest

I rent a room in a hotel by the year. My room (no. 173) is my apartment: anteroom, cloakroom, bedroom, bath, dining room, study, and parlor all in one. Now and then it really does resemble this combination. Manuscripts, toilet articles, breakfast dishes, and old pants lead a brotherly life in this twelve-by-six-inch space.

Once, the hotel keeper gave me a small sketch to read that he himself had written. He later looked me up in no. 173 and asked my opinion of the work. I was embarrassed. The landlord, who also happens to be a man of the world, said to me with a gesture of disparagement: "I'm sure you threw it into the wastepaper basket; no matter." My little Swedish girlfriend, who was present at the time, opined: "Did you make off with it, maybe?" And then she ransacked a pile of newspapers.

"Why do you live in a hotel?" somebody asked me.

I answered: "Out of mortal fear."

Nobody will understand this. Out of mortal fear you do indeed prefer furnished lodgings. As the idyllic saying goes, you build your nest. You create around you a circle of individual traits, you pad the atmosphere all around with pictures, display cases, and shelves. In short, you collect about you a plant life of velvet and furniture lumber. And in such a cosy shell you regard yourself as immortal.

A private dwelling place has just the opposite effect on me. The more individual and pleasant it is, the more I am reminded of the fact that sooner or later I have to give it up. The very attempt at feigning rescue and longevity disquiets me. All vegetation is just the symbol of transitoriness. I ask myself how soon before the pleasant dwelling place is put on the auction block.

The hotel room doesn't pull the wool over my eyes. It's a transit space for passersby and destinies. It's not going to seduce me into a sense of well-being, into the pleasure of possessions, into any lasting feelings. Here, where death is felt the pleasantest, life is no lie.

If only the pink-blue Gainsborough girl in the gold frame didn't gaze at me so seductively from the wall . . .

The symbol of the hotel is the push button. It is a huge, complete network of push buttons. The push button for the lift from the fourth floor; the push button to go back; the push buttons for the waiter, for the servants, for the maids; the push button for the bath and to leave the bathroom; the buttons on the telephone for the infinity of numbers, to Prague, Stockholm, Salzburg; the push buttons for eating, drinking, sleeping, loving . . .

For people like me, that is the agreeableness and charm of the hotel. The habitation is transformed into an automaton. We are spared, for the better, the exertion demanded by any individual arranging. Our life begins at the point at which other initiatives are exhausted by that exertion. In such blessed circumstances, you can easily be a monk transcribing the Bible in elaborate incunabulum script . . . or at least be able to write Rousseau's *Emile*.

But you don't get to enjoy pure comfort.

When I moved in, I was convinced that I was going to experience the end of the world in this place. Some electrical apparatus rattled under the floorboards. (When I came running to the night porter, white as a sheet, he told me it was a pump. The morning waiter thought it had to be the ventilator. My ears took it for a Niagara Falls of voltage current. Agreement on the issue will be reached only when I'm in a padded cell.)

I often get up at three in the morning from the rumbling of thunder. What's happened? The same thing that doubtless happens during a hot summer on the banks of the Niagara when the river bed dries up. The electrical apparatus (pump, ventilator) conked out—the waterfall stopped foaming, and to the ear used to noise the standstill is like an explosion.

Sometimes Thor strikes an anvil as big as a house beneath me. That's when the clock stops.

In my mind's eye I see down below here red-hot blacksmiths' faces on whose brows beads of sweat glisten in the night, while in the upper world, from the first to the fourth floors, financiers, loafers, and coquettes snore for all they're worth.

This world can't last long, I told myself in the beginning. One day it's all going to fall to pieces.

Today I'm used to the electric apparatus, Thor's hammer, the magnates' snoring. The hotel, I know, will remain forever.

While I'm on the subject of snoring:

Nothing dismays me so much on my nightly return home as a pair of pants hanging on a neighbor's door frame. I learned from experience that a mysterious connection exists between hanging pants out and snoring. But swinging suspenders from the pants besides, then I've had it! A sawmill must be out of control next door.

I tried to divide the snorers into groups on an ethnographic basis. The outcome: there are four predominant snoring nations—the Swiss, the Dutch, the Americans, and the Germans. Perhaps it has to do with nutrition, perhaps with landscape. In any case, I haven't yet run across a snoring Greek or Japanese.

There are people who fling the telephone book at the wall from which the snoring is coming and then remain as quiet as mice so as not to arouse the suspicion of the person awakened. Those are bunglers who for sure never lived in a hotel. They ought to realize, after all, that the snorer whose dream was interrupted by noise jumps up at first with a sudden suffocating sound, as if you stuck a finger in his throat, but immediately thereafter begins to blow off air and by means of a second and third puff of breath switches again to a new series of snores. I've discovered a new system for dealing with it. As soon as the telephone book lands on my neighbor's wall, I whistle a cheerful little song. I go la-la-la and await my murder. My neighbor stops his huffing and puffing, clears his throat, for a few moments remains undecided whether or not to call out names or fire back with something, and in the end settles on a more peaceable and melodic way of resolving the situation.

Folklore is the main thing you learn in a big hotel.

Since I've been living in number 173, I've divided nations into the loud and the low. Hungary marches invariably at the head of the loud. If a Hungarian checks into 172 or 174, my Gainsborough girl begins to wobble. She asks me, smiling, why my neighbor is making such a racket. I answer: Hungary is a large, pretty country with few people. They are used to being alone.

Germany is distinguished by its industriousness and morning-fresh vigor. People call up before the first cock crow. Usually you just hear variations on the (gutturally pronounced) words "construction project" and in between: general director, supervisory board, and walkout. The conversations are of a very mystical nature; they exhaust themselves in abstract formulae of industrial labor from which a person never learns the essence of the thing.

America chews words up in the nose and annoys its partner by bad breath. Conversations have to do for the most part with relatives' visits. You then experience conventions between impoverished Europe and bull-market America which are condensed in the sentence "Izzie, I am here with Mabel; will you meet us with Salo and Marjorie at Gorodetzky's?"[1]

The Viennese are easily recognized by their "ich pittsie" [Ich bitte Sie, "if you please"] and "Schauns" [schauen Sie, "look here"]. They have an all-consuming need to let the telephone operator know by means of a host of interpolated particles and phrases that they are: (1) strangers in this part of town; (2) of convivial manners; (3) not averse to advances, which means (4) they are real people and not passersby. Whereupon any time an interruption occurs the hopeless call pierces the wallpaper: "Hello, hello, what's going on? We're cut off . . ."

When I want to find out tomorrow's news, I go to the waiters' office. A map with small sliding paper plaques hangs over the table of the head-waiter (he's called chief). These are the room namecards. It's here that you can ascertain that Mr. Galsworthy is living in number 158, that the king of Denmark has Mme. Massary as a neighbor,[2] and who the woman was who got an urgent call from Paris at three in the morning.

Filled orange juice glasses stand in battalions on the sideboard.

The Americans and English have breakfast, as is known, in two stages. First, mouth and stomach are cleansed with orange juice; then comes the meal. The busboy has nothing else to do from six in the morning on except squeeze oranges.

In the meantime, here and there a red light flashes on the switchboard. It's fascinating to observe how differently the waiters react to this signal. They have a special technique, which is to take no notice at all, when the light comes on in the room of the baroness's maid. If it's the room number of Fräulein Lily Steinschneider of Vienna, they mumble: "Take it easy, m'dear . . ." But if somebody signals from the quarters of the king of Denmark, then they all race off at the same time to see who can get there first.

I would have preferred not to see that at all. From then on my imagination has painted depressing pictures whenever I press the button for the waiter and then have to wait several minutes. I ask myself at such times, what can they be saying about me? "Don't worry about it, Walter, he's staying here a while yet . . ."

You've guessed it. I've become used to my "ante-grave" (as the poet Altenberg called his hotel room) the way another person gets used to the warm nest he made himself. The death chamber became home to me. If ever I'm driven out into the cold of the night, it will be comfortably decorated. I cannot absolve my waiters (who turn their backs on the switchboard when 173 lights up) of shared guilt in their guest's perseverance. I often saw how, after a meal served in the general directors' rooms that made them sweat up a storm, they jointly divided up the leftovers (chicken salad, mayonnaise salad, cognac, fruit, ham in Madeira). The "chief" helped himself to cognac and ham; the apprentice got whatever pastry was left. My face betrayed envy without batting an eyelash. But one day, so as not to disturb my stream of work, I lived just on coffee and cigarette smoke. At seven in the evening there was a knock on the door. The food tray came rolling in: caviar, oysters, cold fowl, Armagnac cognac. "Let's not play games," I said to the busboy, "I didn't order that."

"Yeah, but the chief said we have to take it to you."

"Call the chief!"

"What's going on, chief, how come you're sending me this stuff?"

"Well y'know, the gentlemen from 102, German big shots, y'know, forked out a hell of a lot . . . yapped French like they didn't know no German. So I thought: why shouldn't our 173 pick up somethin' from the feast there, 'specially since he hasn't had anything to eat yet today?"

I am staying. I will most certainly not experience the end of the world in number 173.

"Tagebuch eines Hotelgastes," 1933. Original text in Anton Kuh, *Metaphysik und Würstel*, 51–57.

1.   In English in the original text. I have amended it ever so slightly. Kuh's English was less than perfect at the time and the sentence actually reads: "Ischu, I am here with Mabel, will you meet with Salo and Marjorie by Gorodetzky?"

2.   Fritzi Massary was a well-known German actress of the time.

Sanatorium Diary

1 July. Arrived in the evening. Everybody already in their rooms. A pretty housemaid brings the bedtime drink (Valerian tea). Her name is Nelly and she's from St. Polten. When she trudges out with her broad hips, the walls tremble.

3 July. Struck up an interesting acquaintance on the terrace. She's from Neutra. I didn't quite get her name right. Frau Doctor Gimmel or Kümmel. (I'm for Gimmel.) Blackhaired, Madonna's head. I showered her with clever sayings, displayed clairvoyant talents. A melancholic glimmer in her pupil could make the heart beat faster. There's something about her that goes with Chopin nocturnes and dim plush-cushioned dining rooms. On leavetaking, her warm, moist hand remained a while in your own.

4 July. I was introduced to Fräulein Irene in the bridge room. A cheerful creature with the aroma of the straightforward. One can get right down to business with her without the usual chit-chat. She's crazy, she says, about fat people. Since I'm on the slender side, I conceive of a duty—given the psychic advantage that fat people have over me—to stuff myself with her for a few weeks. Frau Doctor Kümmel (definitely with *K* and *ü*) told me about her husband. Don't I already know about it? No, I know nothing about it. Tomorrow she'll tell me everything. Now she has to go for her hot packs.

6 July. By the way, Fräulein Irene's companion isn't bad either. She has two prominent front teeth like a shrewmouse and every moment blushes for no reason at all. I have to get to the bottom of it!—Kümmel is divorced. For the symptoms, she gets a hip bath every morning at nine and hot packs in the afternoon. She asked me if all men are sadists or only the ones from Neutra. She further informed me that the physician has prescribed her a love affair to help her forget. I became embarrassed and said quite tactlessly and idiotically: "You don't say? With whom?" In

the evening, Fräulein Irene unpacked her handbag to show me photos. All of the same man, a good forty, who leaves me cold. The photos show him in a bathing suit, as a tennis player, on the base of a statue, thumbing his nose at somebody, then with two Scotch terriers, and finally as Rigoletto. About the dogs, she says: "They're ours . . ." About Rigoletto . . . she proceeds to her daily routine. I ask no questions.

9 JULY. My heavens, what a charming woman I met today! Very tall, English, with enamel complexion. Frau Brunner. Daisy. When she lowers her gaze, her eyelids cover the entire eyeball. She has a very interesting story: she ran away from her husband on their wedding night! Consequently . . . ? It will come out.—Fräulein Irene's companion is a countess. In a roundabout way I ask her why she blushes. She said: "You think it's psychic?" Whereupon she delivered a report about her imaginary stomach troubles, about how Wenkebach (Vienna) and Friedrich von Müller (Munich) assumed that they actually existed, while in Znaim, at a quite insignificant little doctor's, the truth came out, and so on. They steam her with heat compresses. "It's just repression."—Irene shows me fifty newly arrived photos. She didn't want to let go of one of them, but I was courteous enough to snatch it away from her and spotted the same fellow— this time as Hans Sachs.[1] Frau Kümmel has not yet found the prescribed substitute. She's going about it in a clumsy way. When I pointed this out to her—rather delicately—she called out, on parting, laughing: "Maybe I'm frichid??!"

14 JULY. A stroll with Daisy. Walking alongside long-legged women produces an exciting feeling of comradeship. I touched on the story of the wedding night. She smiled and said (with a Moravian accent): "Always er-r-rotic?" Then she pinched me on the arm. She'll be the one!

15 JULY. Played ping-pong with the countess. At every remark she turns red, even at the noun "racket." When we changed places and I brushed past her cheek, she cried out: "My stomach!" and ran off to the left.—I came across Dr. Kümmel in the reading room. Her eyes were red with tears and she waved me over. She had a letter in her hand. I sat down and she asked me: "Tell me, can you also be serious?" And when I assured her I could, she said: "Does sensuality play an important role in marriage?"—

Irene invites me to her room; she wants to show me records by the man in the photographs. I've known for some time that he's a baritone, but I played the fool. Doesn't do any good now.—New pictures have arrived.

17 JULY. She shouldn't have said that! (I'm talking about Daisy.) At the chapel in the woods—it rained and I breathed in the scent of damp linden blossoms as though it came from her and not from the trees—she

was leaning on me. I remained silent. Then she said abruptly: "I'm so inhibited . . ."

19 JULY. Irene tells me that her friend has had her stomach trouble from the time of the affair with the naval attaché. He told her one day: "I don't love you, you're too fat for me . . ." Irene adds: "Funny, isn't it—I prefer fat people!"—Kümmel is leaving today; she had a call from Neutra in the morning.—Met the attending nurse in the hallway as she was carrying three heat compresses to room 56 to the countess.—In the evening Canio's voice from *Pagliacci* comes rolling out of an open window. I see him in white silk with black buttons the way he's sitting on the steps of a statue thumbing his nose at me.

21 JULY. Three weeks are over. When Nelly (the housemaid) bent over my suitcase while I was packing, she struck me as prettier than ever before. She smiled at me from under a shoulder. I uttered her name a few times, with tremolo. When I patted her on the back, she said: "All the gentlemen come to me before they leave here—ain't there any other women here?"—I answered: "No."

"Tagebuch aus einem Sanatorium," 1934. Original text in Anton Kuh, *Zeitgeist im Literatur-Café*, 148–51.

1.   Hans Sachs (1494–1576), a leading poet of the Nuremberg school and the author of several popular Shrovetide plays. He appears as a principal character in Wagner's opera *Die Meistersinger von Nürnberg*.

EDMUND WENGRAF IS REPRESENTED HERE ONLY ON THE BASIS OF HIS SMALL PIECE
"KAFFEEHAUS UND LITERATUR" ("COFFEEHOUSE AND LITERATURE"), A CRITIQUE OF THE
VIENNA COFFEEHOUSE BECAUSE OF ITS HARMFUL EFFECT, IN WENGRAF'S VIEW, ON AUSTRIAN
LITERARY CULTURE. The piece was published in the *Wiener Literatur-Zeitung* on
15 May 1891. Wengraf himself was a well-known and respected Viennese
journalist in his day. He studied law and philosophy but soon turned to
a career in journalism. From 1889 to 1893 he wrote theater reviews and
social-political pieces for the *Wiener Allgemeine Zeitung*. In 1894, he and
Heinrich Osten became the editors of *Die neue Revue* (*Wiener Literatur-*

Zeitung), which had been founded by R. Bauer's publishing house. Five years later, he established his own paper, *Die Wage* (*The Venture*). He subsequently became a member of the editorial board of *Die Zeit*. He served as president of the Vienna literary union known as Concordia and was also on the board of directors of the short-lived Vienna Freie Bühne, which Friedrich Michael Fels founded, on the model of Otto Brahm's Berlin Freie Bühne, on 7 July 1891 as Freie Bühne, Verein für moderne Literatur (The Free Stage, A Society for Modern Literature). Besides his newspaper and journal writings, most of which address contemporary social issues, he was the author of the following books: *Die gebildete Welt* (*The World of Culture*, 1886); *Wie wir wirtschaften* (*How We Manage Our Affairs*, 1887); *Wie man ein Sozialist wird* (*How a Person Becomes a Socialist*, 1888); *Die Phrase: Zur Kritik der Gesellschaftslügen* (*The Phrase: On Society's Lies*, 1893); *Armer Leute Kinder* (*Children of Poor People*), which he edited in 1894; and *Bunter Abend: Fünfzig Gedichte und Lieder zum Vortrag in heiteren Kreisen* (*A Variety Evening: Fifty Poems and Songs for Performance in Merry Circles*, 1923).

COFFEEHOUSE AND LITERATURE

In French literary life the "salons" played an important role in the seventeenth and eighteenth centuries. In Germany in the first decades of our century "aesthetic teas" functioned in a similar, albeit more modest, way. In the Hotel Rambouillet and likeminded circles many tasteless follies were pursued by the "précieuses" ladies and their gallants, while in North Germany a lachrymose tea romanticism was cultivated by many overeducated females. In both places the penetration of social life by literary influences has had salutary consequences that can be felt down to our own time. This is especially true of France, whose rich literary flowering scarcely needed our preclassical forbears to seem more enviable, any more than today it needs their grandsons, the postclassical epigones.

In Vienna, which for so long was the capital of the largest civilized European state and today is still the capital of an empire of twenty million people, there was never anything resembling a "literary salon" or an "aesthetic tea." However, another establishment took root here that is unique in its own way and also puts a stamp of a special kind on social as well as literary life—the *coffeehouse*. It would be very superficial to see the Viennese coffeehouse just as an establishment for the provision of a popular stimulant, "black," "dark brown," or "light." Coffee is the most unessential of all the things that go with a proper coffeehouse. One can safely say that of a hundred visitors to this educational institution there are scarcely ten who are driven here for the indispensable little cup. The other ninety come here because . . . because . . . indeed, why?

Why?

Well, where else should one go then? Where should a person satisfy his "reading needs?" Where is a person supposed to learn "the most important" news? Where is a person supposed to meet his friends? Where is a person to play billiards or tarok? Where is a person supposed to kill time? And if he doesn't kill it, for heaven's sake, what is he to do with this burdensome excess of time?

In Vienna, people really do have an unbelievable amount of time. And that is the reason why our esteemed fellow citizens find time for nothing. You ask the average educated person here if he has already read this or that book that has caused the greatest stir everywhere and has already appeared in its twenty-third edition. He'll answer that unfortunately he doesn't have time for "such things." Ask him if he's already seen the painting exhibition. No, unfortunately he couldn't find any time for it. Ask him if he's already seen the art treasures of his native city, which every foreigner seeks out right after he arrives. Oh God, he's "ashamed" to admit that he "hasn't been there yet"—but (with a deep, heartfelt sigh) "what can you do when you don't have any time?" However, he is certainly not lacking time when it comes to spending two to three hours a day in a coffeehouse gaping, chatting, yawning, in short, behaving as if the day had a hundred hours more than the usual twenty-four.

The coffeehouse represents the ruination of Viennese society. The man who spends his leisure hours there grows out of the habit of ever having any serious exchange of views with his spouse or with women in general. Women who might be disposed at the earliest possible stage to take literature a bit seriously are left to their own devices and pursue the convenient path of shallow light reading. But the men completely give up bothering with "time-robbing" books and devote themselves exclusively to reading newspapers. The coffeehouse habitué reads only dailies and possibly—if he happens to be especially "educated"—also illustrated journals. But even this none too demanding reading matter soon becomes too much for him to handle thoroughly. Seriousness and thoroughness do not thrive in the atmosphere of the coffeehouse. This smoke-impregnated air, tainted by gas jets and polluted by the sitting together of many people, this whirring of people coming and going, of jabbering guests and bustling waiters, this tangle of shadowy apparitions and indeterminable sounds, makes any quiet reflection, any collected thoughts impossible. The nerves become overstrained, the power of recollection, attentiveness, and mental capacity grow weaker. The coffeehouse reader reaches the point where he finds every article, every feuilleton, everything that's more than a hundred lines long, unbearable.

"Kaffeehaus und Literatur," 1891. Original text in *Die Wiener Moderne: Literatur, Kunst und Musik zwischen 1890 und 1910*, ed. Gotthart Wunberg, with the cooperation of Johannes J. Braakenburg (Stuttgart: Philipp Reclam Jun., 1981), 638–42.

INDEX